STATE OF THE WORLD 1999

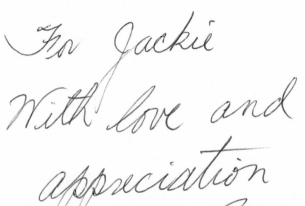

For Jackie

With love and appreciation

Ted Brurre

Other Norton/Worldwatch Books
Lester R. Brown et al.

State of the World 1984

State of the World 1985

State of the World 1986

State of the World 1987

State of the World 1988

State of the World 1989

State of the World 1990

State of the World 1991

State of the World 1992

State of the World 1993

State of the World 1994

State of the World 1995

State of the World 1996

State of the World 1997

State of the World 1998

Vital Signs 1992

Vital Signs 1993

Vital Signs 1994

Vital Signs 1995

Vital Signs 1996

Vital Signs 1997

Vital Signs 1998

ENVIRONMENTAL ALERT SERIES

Lester R. Brown et al.
Saving the Planet

Alan Thein During
How Much is Enough?

Sandra Postel
Last Oasis

Lester R. Brown
Hal Kane
Full House

Christopher Flavin
Nicholas Lenssen
Power Surge

Lester R. Brown
Who Will Feed China?

Lester R. Brown
Tough Choices

Michael Renner
Fighting for Survival

David Malin Roodman
The Natural Wealth of Nations

Chris Bright
Life Out of Bounds

STATE OF THE WORLD

1999

A Worldwatch Institute Report on Progress Toward a Sustainable Society

PROJECT DIRECTOR
Lester R. Brown

ASSOCIATE PROJECT
DIRECTORS
Christopher Flavin
Hilary F. French

EDITOR
Linda Starke

CONTRIBUTING RESEARCHERS
Janet N. Abramovitz
Lester R. Brown
Seth Dunn
Christopher Flavin
Gary Gardner
Ashley Tod Mattoon
Anne Platt McGinn
Molly O'Meara
Michael Renner
David Malin Roodman
Payal Sampat
John Tuxill

W·W·NORTON & COMPANY

NEW YORK   LONDON

The STATE OF THE WORLD and WORLDWATCH INSTITUTE trademarks are registered in the U.S. Patent and Trademark Office.

The views expressed are those of the authors and do not necessarily represent those of the Worldwatch Institute; of its directors, officers, or staff; or of its funders.

The text of this book is composed in ITC New Baskerville, with the display set in Caslon. Composition by Worldwatch Institute; manufacturing by the Haddon Craftsmen, Inc.

First Edition

ISBN 0-393-04713-X
ISBN 0-393-31815-X (pbk)

W. W. Norton & Company, Inc., 500 Fifth Avenue, New York, N.Y. 10110
http://www.wwnorton.com

W. W. Norton & Company Ltd., 10 Coptic Street, London WC1A IPU

1 2 3 4 5 6 7 8 9 0

This book is printed on recycled paper.

Acknowledgments

For this special millennial edition of *State of the World*, we would like to begin by thanking our many readers. You are the ultimate indicator of a world hungry for information about the environment. You have inspired us to produce this book for 16 years running. We thank you for the letters and e-mails with suggestions for enriching future editions.

Some of our readers have become quite involved in funding both our research and our outreach. Our recently formed Council of Sponsors includes those who support our work with personal contributions of $50,000 each year. Special thanks, then, to Sponsors Tom and Cathy Crain, Kazuhiko Nishi, Vicki and Roger Sant, Robert Wallace, and Eckart Wintzen.

We also rely on numerous foundations for support of our overall operations as well as research on specific topics. Our thanks to the Winslow Foundation for funding our research on food, and to the Curtis and Edith Munson Foundation for our research on oceans. We are particularly grateful to the following foundations for providing unrestricted grants: the Geraldine R. Dodge, Ford, William and Flora Hewlett, W. Alton Jones, John D. and Catherine T. MacArthur, Charles Stewart Mott, David and Lucile Packard, Rasmussen, Summit, Turner, Wallace Genetic, and Weeden Foundations; Rockefeller Financial Services; the U.N. Population Fund; and the Wallace Global Fund.

This year, we note with sadness the passing of long-time Board member Mahbub ul Haq, whose work inspired us all. Mahbub first made a mark at the international level while serving as advisor to World Bank president Robert McNamara nearly 30 years ago, when he challenged the "trickle down" theory of development. He argued that successful development efforts had to attack poverty directly. He was also the architect of the *Human Development Report* prepared annually by the U.N. Development Programme, which analyzes both economic and social trends. That his ideas, once deemed radical, are now mainstream is perhaps the best measure of his legacy.

Worldwatch is lucky indeed to have a particularly talented, dedicated staff. In addition to the authors of each chapter, we would like to acknowledge the hard work of staff researchers Lisa Mastny, who helped with Chapter 10, and Brian Halweil, who helped with Chapters 1 and 7. Seth Dunn, coauthor of Chapter 2, also helped with Chapter 1. Their data gathering and number crunching were aided by our 1998 interns: Sophie Chou (Chapter 5), Zoë Hartley (Chapters 4 and 5), Matt Howes (Chapters 2 and 3), Jennifer Myers (Chapters 3 and 10), and Daniel Schwartz (Chapter 9).

In addition, we are particularly indebted to Vice President for Research Hilary French, who took time away from working on a forthcoming Worldwatch book to review chapters and give extensive comments and advice to chapter authors, who asked us in particular to acknowledge her contribution. Her input on Chapter 10 was especially key. Senior Fellow Sandra Postel, who also directs the Global Water Policy Project in Amherst, Massachusetts, played an active role in the review process, supplying several helpful ideas for Chapter 1. Former staff member John Young, who reviewed several chapters, provided insights for Chapter 3.

In fact, we rely on many outside reviewers for research materials and often their reactions to our early drafts, as well as comments late in the production cycle. This year we would like to thank the following either for information they provided or for their candid and speedy reviews of various chapters: Frank Ackerman, Tundi Agardy, Charlotte Allen, Brad Allenby, Don Anderson, David Balton, Tara Bhattarai, Emmanuel Chidumayo, Anne Edminster, David Eisenberg, Haynes Goddard, Sidney Holt, Willem Hulscher, Tim Jackson, Auke Koopmans, Lars Kristoferson, David Luck, Amy Mathews-Amos, Grecia Matos, Alan McDonald, David McKeever, Peter Newman, Rutherford Platt, Donald Rogich, Friedrich Schmidt-Bleek, Kenneth Sherman, Vaclav Smil, Maureen Smith, Walter Stahel, Mary Evelyn Tucker, Julie Velasquez Runk, John Waugh, and Mike Weber. In addition, the research done by the Rural Advancement Foundation International was particularly useful in the preparation of Chapter 6.

Many chapter authors this year mention the various effects of the new information age. Overseeing our own involvement in the electronic age, as well as with good old-fashioned journals and books, is Research Librarian Lori Brown. Lori, who is also our Webmaster, prepares our Database Disk, which we are pleased to note is increasingly popular with readers. She has been ably assisted this year by Laura Malinowski and Anne Smith, who

also helps the Vice President for Special Activities.

At the other end of the life of *State of the World*, Worldwatch's publications staff makes sure the book is in your hands as soon as possible. Publications Sales Coordinator Millicent Johnson, Publications Assistant Joseph Gravely, and Receptionist Sharon Lapier face the daunting task of accepting and processing the thousands of orders that start bombarding the office as soon as our fall direct mail announcement goes out.

It falls to our Communications Department to work with the media and to use direct mail to let you know that the book is finally ready. Vice President for Communications Dick Bell oversees this monumental task, aided by Press Officer Mary Caron and Marketing and Production Manager Amy Warehime. We would also like to thank the *World Watch* magazine staff for keeping that publication excelling despite the pressures of chapter deadlines whirling all around them: Editor and Editorial Director Ed Ayres, Senior Editor Chris Bright, and Assistant Editor Curtis Runyan. Thanks, too, to independent editor Jane Peterson for handling Worldwatch Papers throughout the year.

The production side of *State of the World* is now firmly in our own hands, thanks to our in-house production and designer Elizabeth Doherty, who also produces our bimonthly magazine, the Worldwatch Papers, and all our promotion materials. The prose she lays out has been cut down (much to the authors' disappointment) and thoroughly massaged by independent editor Linda Starke, who edits all our Worldwatch books. And we'd like to thank Ritch Pope of Dexter, Oregon, for once again preparing a useful index.

The administrative part of our organization is what allows the rest of us to do our work worry-free. Reah Janise

Kauffman, Vice President for Special Activities, handles much of the work involved in our fundraising activities, as well as being Assistant to the President and Corporate Secretary. One of the many activities that she manages is our worldwide network of publishers in some 30 languages. We were joined this year by Vice President for Operations James Gillespie, who, among other things, manages our individual gifts program. Rounding out the administrative team are Assistant Treasurer Barbara Fallin and Administrative Assistant to the Vice Presidents for Research Suzanne Clift, who keep our lives running smoothly.

We have saved for last our acknowledgment of debt to our publisher, W.W. Norton & Company. We thank Amy Cherry, Andrew Marasia, and Nomi Victor for their unflagging help with the production and promotion of this book. But our superb 24-year relationship with Norton, which publishes all of our books in the United States, evolved over the last 15 years with Iva Ashner as our editor. Always a delight to work with, she was a dedicated professional and a personal friend to many of us here at Worldwatch. We were saddened by her death in March 1998 and continue to feel a strong sense of loss. In gratitude, we dedicate this special millennial edition of *State of the World* to Iva.

Lester R. Brown and Christopher Flavin

Contents

Worldwatch Database Disk

The data from all graphs and tables contained in this book, as well as from those in all other Worldwatch publications of the past two years, are available on floppy, 3 1/2-inch (high-density) disks for use with IBM-compatible or Macintosh computers. This includes data from the State of the World *and* Vital Signs *series of books, Worldwatch Papers,* World Watch *magazine, and the Environmental Alert series of books. The data (in spreadsheet format) are provided as Microsoft Excel 5.0/95 workbook (*.xls) files. Users must have spreadsheet software installed on their computer that can read Excel workbooks for Windows. Information on how to order the Worldwatch Database Disk can be found at the back of this book.*

Visit our Web site at www.worldwatch.org

List of Tables and Figures

LIST OF TABLES

LIST OF FIGURES

Foreword

As we began working on this, our millennial edition, we realized that the very concept of the millennium is arbitrary because it is based on the Christian calendar, which was not adopted for worldwide use until the late 1800s. If we were using the Jewish calendar, this year would be 5759, not close to a millennial year. The Hindu calendar says this is 5101, and according to the Muslim calendar it is only 1377.

The year 2000 on the Christian calendar is the first millennium on any calendar that will be widely noted. In the year 1000, there was no celebration even in the Christian world because, without printing presses, calendars were not generally available. Life was governed more by the change of the seasons than by the passage of years. Few people even knew it was the year 1000. This is the first time that the entire world will celebrate a millennium, sharing a review of the past and hopes for the future.

In planning this special edition, we decided that since we could not easily review the last 1,000 years, we would focus instead on developments over the last century, analyzing the vast changes since 1900 in order to frame the challenges of the next century. What becomes clear from our research is that the economic model that evolved in the industrial West and is spreading throughout the entire world is slowly undermining itself. As now structured, it will not take us very far into the next century. The question, then, is whether we can find another path that can be sustained. In Chapter 1, we describe what a sustainable economy would look like. In Chapter 10, we describe the policy measures needed to get from here to there. Fortunately, the need for a new economic model—one that is environmentally sustainable—is increasingly recognized both by governments and by corporations.

In focusing on the last century, we did not review the past year with the detail usually found in *State of the World*. Still, some developments cannot be ignored. Data that were available as we went to press showed that the first eight months of 1998 were the warmest of any comparable period on record. Furthermore, the increase over the previous record was itself a record. As we went to add 1998 to our long-term temperature graph, basing our annual estimate on the first eight months, the temperature literally went off the top of the chart, forcing us to recalibrate the vertical scale. The graph we have been using for years to show this key indicator is no longer adequate.

Higher temperatures mean there is more energy driving the Earth's climate system. This in turn means more evaporation, more destructive storms, and more flooding. When more moisture goes up, more comes down. Where it comes down is less predictable, but when it falls in deforested mountain and hill areas, the results are particularly devastating. We do know that 1998 saw some of the worst flooding on record. China was particularly hard hit, suffering an estimated $36 billion in losses due to the flooding of the Yangtze River. An estimated 2,500 Chinese drowned and another 56 million were displaced by the floods, the country's worst in 44 years.

Bangladesh was hit by an unusually long and severe monsoon season, which left two thirds of the country under water for more than a month and 21 million people homeless. This flooding, the worst on record, destroyed part of the rice crop and forced scores of textile factories in Dacca, the capital city, to close for several weeks, depriving the country of much-needed export earnings. All told, some 54 countries suffered from flooding in 1998.

Perhaps the most disturbing glimpse of what a warmer world may bring came just as we were going to press: Hurricane Mitch, a storm of near record power with winds of 270 kilometers (180 miles) per hour, hit Central America. With its movement blocked by a strong weather front to the north, the stalled storm dumped 2 meters (6 feet) of rain on parts of Central America within a week. The physical force of such a deluge collapsed homes, factories, and schools, and destroyed roads and bridges. These structures were simply not designed to withstand a force of this magnitude.

Honduras and Nicaragua were hit hardest. This was a storm of geological proportions. In Honduras, an estimated 70 percent of the crops were simply washed away, along with huge quantities of topsoil that had accumulated over the millennia. Huge mud slides altered the topography and obliterated dozens of villages,

entombing the entire population in some cases. Up to one third of the Honduran population was left homeless. Early estimates for the two countries indicate 11,000 deaths, with at least that many still missing. President Flores of Honduras observed that "Overall, what was destroyed over several days took us 50 years to build." His assessment was echoed by others, who estimated that it could take years for the Honduran and Nicaraguan economies to recover from this disaster.

A more unstable climate is also causing record-breaking heat waves. One hundred Texans died in a prolonged summer heat spell during which temperatures in Dallas rose above 35 degrees Celsius for weeks on end. And in India, an estimated 3,000 people died in the nation's most intense heat wave in 50 years.

In 1998, some 45 countries were stricken by severe droughts, many of which led to runaway wild fires. Tropical forests normally do not burn, but unusually harsh droughts contributed to a series of unprecedented fires in Southeast Asia starting in late 1997, as well as in the Amazon through most of 1998. During the spring, parts of southern Mexico were burning, leading to air quality alerts in Texas and smoke drifting as far north as Chicago. By early summer, fires were sweeping the subtropical forests of Florida, leading to the evacuation of an entire county.

In Russia, a combination of severe heat, drought, and economic mismanagement reduced the grain harvest to its lowest level in 40 years. By fall, Moscow was requesting massive food aid from the United States and the European Union.

Worldwide, economic losses from floods, storms, droughts, and other weather-related natural disasters totaled some $72 billion during the first seven months of 1998, a level that already exceeded the previous annual record of $60 billion set in 1996.

At mid-year, the World Health Organization released startling new data on HIV infection rates that showed the spread of the disease in sub-Saharan Africa reaching epidemic proportions. In several countries, including Zimbabwe, Botswana, and Zambia, HIV infection rates among the adult population have reached 20–26 percent. With the cost of drugs to treat the disease far beyond the reach of people in that region, these societies stand to lose one fifth to one fourth of their adult population within a decade from AIDS alone. To find a precedent for such a potentially devastating loss of life from infectious disease, we have to go back to the decimation of the New World Indian communities by the introduction of smallpox in the sixteenth century.

The epidemic is far from reaching its peak. Indeed, its spread in Asia, where more than half the world's people live, is gaining momentum. Spreading rapidly in India, it has now infected more than 4 million people. It is also beginning to spread in China, where the disease can be found in every province.

There is new evidence that water scarcity will be the world's leading resource issue as we enter the new century. The most dramatic numbers come from India, where withdrawals of underground water are now believed to be double the rate of recharge. With water tables falling almost everywhere, by from 1 to 3 meters per year, crippling water shortages may be inevitable. With massive aquifer depletion in prospect, some speculate that this could reduce India's grain harvest by as much as 25 percent. In a country that is adding 18 million people per year, this is not good news.

Such trends show clearly that from an environmental standpoint, we are not ending the century on a bright note. In *State of the World 1999*, we stress the need for a new economic model, one that is environmentally sustainable and that will permit economic progress to continue. Our work on this front is being rewarded as a small but growing group of corporate CEOs endorse the idea.

Meanwhile, our efforts to raise global understanding of the need for restructuring the global economy are gaining momentum. The Institute now has a record 160 publishing contracts in effect in some 30 languages for *State of the World*, *Vital Signs*, the various Environmental Alert books, the Worldwatch Papers, and *World Watch* magazine. Nearly all our publications now appear regularly in four of the world's major languages—English, Spanish, Chinese, and Japanese.

We are also expanding the marketing of publications through our Web site. In addition to selling hard copy editions of the English edition of our publications there, we are starting to market electronic versions as well. Anyone wishing to download a chapter from this volume, a trend from *Vital Signs*, a feature article from the magazine, or an entire Worldwatch Paper can do so for a modest fee. This further increases availability of the Worldwatch library and database for those who have access to a computer.

We hope you find this millennial edition of use. If you have any comments on this edition or suggestions for future editions of *State of the World*, please let us know by letter, fax (202-296-7365), or e-mail (worldwatch@worldwatch.org). We also hope you will visit our Web site to check on the latest releases.

Lester R. Brown
Christopher Flavin
Hilary French

Worldwatch Institute
1776 Massachusetts Ave., NW
Washington, DC 20036
www.worldwatch.org

December 1998

STATE OF THE
WORLD
1999

1

A New Economy for a New Century

Lester R. Brown and Christopher Flavin

In the 1890s, the American Press Association brought together the country's "best minds" to explore the shape of things to come in the twentieth century. Conditions at the time were in flux. Technological advances had recently made it possible to travel from coast to coast by rail, the first "skyscraper" had just been built, and electricity was becoming common in some urban neighborhoods. At the same time, the economy had recently been hit by a depression, cities were filling with growing numbers of poor people, and supplies of wood and iron ore that had always seemed unlimited were beginning to run short.[1]

As they looked forward to the century ahead, the country's "futurists" were almost universally optimistic, predicting that many problems would be solved, and that advancing technology and material growth would produce a near Utopia. Among the predictions that have held up well: widespread use of electricity and telephones, the opening of the entire world to trade, and the emancipation of women. Among the things they missed were the birth control pill and the Internet. Other forecasts proved to be naive, including the notion that people would live to be 150 and that air pollution would be eliminated. The dark sides of the twentieth century—two world wars, the development of chemical and nuclear weapons, the emergence of global threats to the stability of the natural world, and a billion people struggling just to survive—were predicted by no one.[2]

Today, at the dawn of the next century, faith in technology and human progress is almost as prevalent in the writings of leading economic commentators. Their easy optimism is bolstered by the extraordinary achievements of the twentieth century, including developments such as jet

The 1996 United Nations biennial population projections are used in this edition since the 1998 projections were published too late to be incorporated. The 1998 projections are modestly lower, but not enough to alter the analysis. Units of measure throughout this book are metric unless common usage dictates otherwise.

aircraft, personal computers, and genetic engineering, that go well beyond anything predicted by the most imaginative futurists of the 1890s. But like their predecessors, today's futurists look ahead from a narrow perspective—one that ignores some of the most important trends now shaping our world. And in their fascination with the information age that is increasingly prominent in the global economy, many observers seem to have forgotten that our modern civilization, like its forerunners, is totally dependent on its ecological foundations.

Since our emergence as a species, human populations have continually run up against local environmental limits: the inability to find sufficient game, grow enough food, or harvest enough wood has led to sudden collapses in human numbers and in some cases to the disappearance of entire civilizations. Although it may seem that advancing technology and the emergence of an integrated world economy have ended this age-old pattern, they may have simply transferred the problem to the global level.

The challenge facing us at the dawn of a new century begins with scale. Human numbers are four times the level of a century ago, and the world economy is 17 times as large. This growth has allowed advances in living standards that our ancestors could not have imagined, but it has also undermined natural systems in ways they could not have feared. Oceanic fisheries, for example, are being pushed to their limits and beyond, water tables are falling on every continent, rangelands are deteriorating from overgrazing, many remaining tropical forests are on the verge of being wiped out, and carbon dioxide (CO_2) concentrations in the atmosphere have reached the highest level in 160,000 years. If these trends continue, they could make the turning of the millennium seem trivial as a historic moment, for they may be triggering the largest extinction of life since a meteorite

wiped out the dinosaurs some 65 million years ago.[3]

As we look forward to the twenty-first century, it is clear that satisfying the projected needs of an ever larger world population with the economy we now have is simply not possible. The western economic model—the fossil-fuel-based, automobile-centered, throwaway economy—that so dramatically raised living standards for part of humanity during this century is in trouble. Indeed, the global economy cannot expand indefinitely if the ecosystems on which it depends continue to deteriorate. We are entering a new century, then, with an economy that cannot take us where we want to go. The challenge is to design and build a new one that can sustain human progress without destroying its support systems—and that offers a better life to all.

The shift to an environmentally sustainable economy may be as profound a transition as the Industrial Revolution that led to the current dilemma was. How successful we will be remains to be seen. Yet we have always stood out from other species in our ability to adapt to new environmental conditions and challenges. The next test is now under way.

THE ACCELERATION OF HISTORY

Although the specific turning point that will be observed on January 1, 2000, is a purely human creation, flowing from the calendar introduced by Julius Caesar in 45 B.C., the three zeros that will appear on that day are powerful reminders of the passage of time—and of how the pace of change has accelerated since the last such turning point, in the Middle Ages. Today's rapid changes tend to make us think of a century, not to mention a millennium, as a vast span of time. But the sweeping developments in the past century have all occurred in a period that represents just 1 percent of the time since humans first practiced agriculture.[4]

In a sense, the acceleration of human history began long before the first history book was ever written. Scientists note that the development of technology suddenly sped up some 40,000 years ago, marked by the proliferation of ever-more sophisticated tools used for hunting, cooking, and other essential tasks. With these tools, our ancestors grew in number to roughly 4 million, and spread out from their bases in Africa and Asia, gradually populating virtually the entire Earth—from the humid tropics to arid plains and frozen tundra.[5]

The second burst of accelerating change began roughly 10,000 years ago with the development of settled agriculture, first in the "Fertile Crescent" near the eastern Mediterranean, and soon thereafter in China and Central America. Although the early development of agriculture appears to have been spurred by growing populations and shortages of easily gathered food, the Agricultural Revolution soon transformed society, leading to more sophisticated tools and social structures, including the emergence of the first towns and cities. These advances increased the human carrying capacity of the planet: human numbers, which had been stalled at roughly 4 million for tens of thousands of years, jumped to an estimated 27 million in 2000 B.C., then to roughly 100 million at the start of the Christian Era, and to 350 million by the beginning of the current millennium.[6]

World population failed to grow much in the Middle Ages, as limited food supplies and devastating plagues swept Europe and China, and societies stagnated. The next acceleration of history began with the accumulation of human knowledge and the emergence of science in the middle centuries of the current millennium. These led to the early stages of the Industrial Revolution in the eighteenth century, as manufacturing grew, cities expanded, and trade increased. By 1825, our population reached the 1 billion mark for the first time. Even then, however, changes in communications, transportation, agriculture, and medicine were so slow as to be scarcely perceptible within a given generation. In the early nineteenth century, most people lived on farms, and travel was not much different than it had been 1,000 years earlier, limited to the speed of a horse: the trip from New York to Boston, for example, took six days. That this situation could change, and change profoundly, was to most people unimaginable.[7]

One hundred years later, the accelerating pace of change can be seen in virtually every field of human activity. The technological advances of this century, building on the scientific progress of earlier ones, can only be described as spectacular. Advances in mathematics, physics, and engineering have enabled us to explore other planets in our solar system and to visit Earth's moon. Astronauts routinely orbit the Earth in 90 minutes and can see it as never before. Prior to this century, economies were largely agricultural, and growth was generally limited to the rate of clearing of new land, since land productivity changed little over time. But as the century progressed, the modern industrial age unfolded and the western industrial development model began to spread. It was growth in the industrial sector that sharply accelerated overall economic growth during the early decades of this century.[8]

In many ways, the defining economic development of this century is the harnessing of the energy in fossil fuels. In 1900, only a few thousand barrels of oil were used daily. By 1997, that figure had reached 72 million barrels per day. (See Chapter 2.) We have also seen a vast increase in the use of materials, including growth in the use of metals from 20 million tons annually to 1.2 billion tons. (See Chapter 3.) The use of paper increased six times between 1950 and 1996, reaching 281 million tons. (See Chapter 4.) Production of plastics, largely unheard of in 1900, reached 131 million tons in 1995. The human economy now draws on all 92 naturally occurring elements in the periodic chart, compared with just 20 in 1900.[9]

Among the most obvious accelerating trends is the increase in human mobility, a development the forecasters in the 1890s did not anticipate. At the end of the nineteenth century, early steam-powered trains and the first motor cars with internal combustion engines were limited to speeds of about 25 miles per hour—and their high cost kept most people on foot. In 1900, there were only a few thousand automobiles in use worldwide. Today there are 501 million. During the first half of this century we went from the pioneering flight by the Wright brothers in 1903 at Kitty Hawk, North Carolina, to jet aircraft that could fly faster than sound. Today, jumbo jets routinely carry 400 passengers on transoceanic flights. Their wingspans of 200 feet exceed the 120 feet that Wilbur and Orville Wright traveled on their first flight. On modern aircraft, we travel faster than our biological clocks can adjust, leaving us jetlagged, our bodies out of sync with the local day/night cycle.[10]

Engineers built the first electronic computers in 1946; in 1949, *Popular Mechanics* magazine predicted that "computers in the future may have only 1,000 tubes and perhaps weigh only one and a half tons." Today, the average 5-pound laptop computer can process data faster than the largest mainframes available at mid-century. Tiny silicon chips can now perform 200 million calculations a second, up from 50 million just four years ago. Computers, software, and related products and services are fueling economic growth and doing it with a minimal use of physical resources. Just as mechanization raised blue collar and farm labor productivity,

computerization is doing the same for white-collar workers. In the United States, an important threshold was crossed recently when the market capitalization of Microsoft passed that of General Motors, signifying the dominance of a new generation of technology.[11]

One outgrowth of the information age is what *The Economist* editor Frances Cairncross describes as "the death of distance." The number of telephone lines leapt from 89 million in 1960 to 741 million in 1996, while cellular phone subscribers rose from 10 million in 1990 to 135 million in 1996. At the end of 1998, the world's first affordable satellite telephones went on the market, bringing the world's most remote regions into the ubiquitous information web. And the number of households with televisions went from 4 million in 1950 to just under 1 billion as the century closes, bringing the latest news and cultural trends to a global community. The explosive growth of the Internet, expanding from 376,000 host computers in 1990 to more than 30 million in 1998, has far surpassed the growth of heavy industry during its heyday.[12]

In biology, this century saw the emergence of antibiotics and a dramatic reduction in the toll of infectious diseases. Routine immunization of children has helped make infant and child deaths a rarity in many societies. Led by the United Nations, the world has eradicated smallpox, once a scourge for most of humanity. A more recent U.N. initiative has eliminated polio in two thirds of the world, and promises to do away with this frightening disease entirely. Organ transplants are now routine and the transfer of genetic material from one species to another is commonplace. At the same time, 29 new diseases have been identified in the last quarter of this century. Among them are Lyme disease, the Ebola virus, Legionnaires' disease, HIV, and the Hanta virus. HIV, now reaching epidemic proportions in Africa, is projected soon to eclipse traditional diseases such as malaria and tuberculosis as the leading cause of death from infectious disease.[13]

Aside from the growth of population itself, urbanization is the dominant demographic trend of the century now ending. (See Chapter 8.) In 1900, some 16 cities had a million people or more, and roughly 10 percent of humanity lived in cities. Today, 326 cities have at least that many people and there are 14 megacities, those with 10 million or more residents. If cities continue to grow as projected, more than half of us will be living in them by 2010, making the world more urban than rural for the first time in history. In effect, we will have become an urban species, far removed from our hunter-gatherer origins and more separated from our natural underpinnings than ever before.[14]

Our growing population has required ever greater quantities of food, and growing incomes have led many societies to diversify and enrich their diets. These burgeoning food demands have been met by a continuing proliferation of new technologies, including the development of more productive crop varieties, the expanded use of fertilizer and irrigation, and the mechanization of agriculture. Grain use has increased nearly fivefold since the century began, while water use has quadrupled. (See Chapter 7.)[15]

On the darker side, the twentieth century has also been the most violent in human history, thanks in part to technological "advances" such as the airplane and automatic weapons. Some 26 million people were killed in World War I, and 53 million in World War II; combined with other war deaths since the century began, the total surpasses the war casualty figure from the beginning of civilization until 1900. (See Chapter 9.)[16]

Another major change that distinguishes the twentieth century is globalization—the vast economic and information webs that now tie disparate parts of the world together. By 10,000 years ago, our ancestors migrating out of Africa had settled not only the vast Eurasian continent but the Americas, Australia, and other remote corners of the world as well. It took most of the time since then, until the European Age of Exploration in the 1500s, for the world's distant peoples to be brought into more immediate contact with one another. And it was not until late in the nineteenth century that the development of steam-powered ships dramatically increased international trade. A major depression, two world wars, and the cold war slowed the pace of globalization during the early stages of this century, but this has changed dramatically as the 1990s end. World trade has grown from $380 billion in 1950 to $5.86 trillion in 1997, a 15-fold increase.[17]

The market capitalization of Microsoft recently passed that of General Motors, signifying the dominance of a new generation of technology.

With the acceleration of history has come escalating pressures on the natural world—on which we remain utterly dependent, even in the information age. New forms of environmental disruption—stratospheric ozone depletion and greenhouse warming—have begun altering natural ecosystems in the past two decades, doing particular damage to coral reefs and suspected damage to species ranging from frogs to trees. In addition, the continuously growing global economy has collided with many of the Earth's natural limits. These collisions can be seen in such trends as the shrinkage of forests, the depletion of aquifers, and the collapse of fisheries.

Our ancestors survived, multiplied,

and advanced by continually adjusting their economic patterns and finding new balances with the natural world. The accelerating pace of change in the twentieth century has led us to new frontiers and wondrous changes that our ancestors could not have imagined. But the economy that has been created cannot be sustained for another century. It is worth noting that the Fertile Crescent, where the first humans settled and cities emerged, was turned into a virtual desert by ancient farmers and herders, and now supports only a small human population.

History will undoubtedly continue to accelerate, but if our descendants are to prosper, historical trends will have to move in a new direction early in the twenty-first century.

THE GROWTH CENTURY

Growth is a defining feature of the twentieth century, and has become the de facto organizing principle for societies around the world. Although growth rates have risen and fallen, the total scale of human activity has expanded continually, reaching levels that would have been unimaginable in earlier centuries.

This growth story starts with human numbers. It took all of human history for world population to reach 1.6 billion in 1900; the total did not reach 2 billion until 1930. (See Figure 1–1.) The third billion was added by 1960, the fourth by 1977, and the fifth in just 12 years, by 1989. World population will pass 6 billion in 1999. If population growth follows the U.N. mid-level projection, human numbers will grow by another 4.6 billion in the next century. There is a key difference, however. During the twentieth century, growth occurred in both industrial and developing countries; during the next century, in contrast, almost all the

increase will take place in the Third World—and mainly in cities. Indeed, the population of the industrial world is expected to decline slightly.[18]

The annual rate of population growth climbed from less than 1 percent in 1900 to its historical high of 2.2 percent in 1964. From there it has slowly declined, dropping to 1.4 percent in 1997. Despite this, the number of people added each year kept increasing—from 16 million in 1900 until a peak of 87 million in 1990. Since then the annual addition has also declined, falling to roughly 80 million in 1997, where it is projected to remain over the next two decades before starting downward again.[19]

Population is one area where detailed projections are not only available, they are revised biennially by the United Nations, giving us some sense of where the world is headed. According to the 1996 update, population projections for individual countries vary more than at any time in history. In some 32 countries, human numbers have stabilized, while in others they are projected to double or triple. With the exception of Japan, all the countries in the stable group are in Europe. The number of people in a

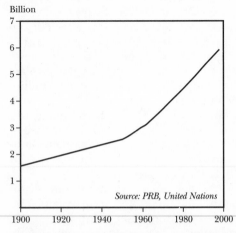

Billion

Source: PRB, United Nations

Figure 1–1. World Population, 1900–98

dozen or so countries, including Russia, Japan, and Germany, is actually projected to decline somewhat over the next half-century. (See Table 1–1.) In another 40 countries, which account for nearly 40 percent of the global total, fertility has dropped to at least replacement level—roughly two children per couple. Among the countries in this category are China and the United States, the world's first and third most populous nations.[20]

In contrast to this group, some developing countries are projected to triple their populations over the next half-century. For example, Ethiopia's current population of 59 million is due to reach 213 million in 2050, while Pakistan's 147 million are likely to become 357 million, surpassing the projected population of the United States before 2050. Nigeria,

meanwhile, is projected to go from 122 million today to 339 million—more people than in all of Africa in 1950. The largest absolute increase is anticipated for India, which is likely to add nearly 600 million by 2050, eclipsing China as the most populous country. Scores of smaller countries also face potentially overwhelming population growth.[21]

Some developing countries have followed China, dramatically lowering birth rates and moving toward population stability. But others are showing signs of demographic fatigue, a result of the effort to deal with the multiple stresses caused by high fertility. Governments struggling with the challenges of educating growing numbers of children, creating jobs for swelling ranks of young job seekers, and dealing with the environmental effects of

Table 1–1. The 20 Largest Countries Ranked According to Population Size, 1998, With Projections for 2050

Rank	1998		2050	
	Country	Population (million)	Country	Population (million)
1	China	1,255	India	1,533
2	India	976	China	1,517
3	United States	274	Pakistan	357
4	Indonesia	207	United States	348
5	Brazil	165	Nigeria	339
6	Russia	148	Indonesia	318
7	Pakistan	147	Brazil	243
8	Japan	126	Bangladesh	218
9	Bangladesh	124	Ethiopia	213
10	Nigeria	122	Iran	170
11	Mexico	96	The Congo	165
12	Germany	82	Mexico	154
13	Viet Nam	78	Philippines	131
14	Iran	73	Viet Nam	130
15	Philippines	72	Egypt	115
16	Egypt	66	Russia	114
17	Turkey	64	Japan	110
18	Thailand	62	Turkey	98
19	France	60	South Africa	91
20	Ethiopia	59	Tanzania	89

SOURCE: United Nations, *World Population Prospects: The 1996 Revision* (New York: 1996).

population growth are stretched to the limit. When a major new threat arises—such as AIDS or aquifer depletion—they often cannot cope.

As recent experience with AIDS in Africa shows, some countries with rapid population growth are simply overwhelmed. While industrial countries have held HIV infection rates among their adult populations under 1 percent, a 1998 World Health Organization survey reports that in Zimbabwe a staggering 26 percent of the adult population is HIV-positive. In Botswana the figure is 25 percent, and in Namibia, Swaziland, and Zambia, it is 18–20 percent. Barring a miracle, these societies will lose one fifth or more of their adult populations within the next decade from AIDS alone. These potential losses, which could bring population growth to a halt or even into decline, are the most demographically catastrophic human losses from an infectious disease since European smallpox decimated Indian populations in the New World in the sixteenth century or since bubonic plague from Central Asia devastated Europe in the fourteenth century. These high AIDS mortality trends in Africa are more reminiscent of the Dark Ages than the bright new millennium so many had hoped for.[22]

Although the notion that population growth can continue unaltered in the next century is now questioned by many, faith in the feasibility—and desirability—of unending economic growth remains strong. During this century, the global economy has expanded from an annual output of $2.3 trillion in 1900 to $39 trillion in 1998, a 17-fold increase. (See Figure 1–2.) Income per person, meanwhile, climbed from $1,500 to $6,600, a rise of just over fourfold, with most of this rise concentrated in the second half of the century.[23]

The growth in economic output in just three years—from 1995 to 1998—exceeded that during the 10,000 years from the

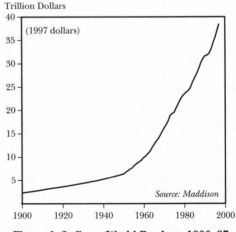

Figure 1–2. Gross World Product, 1900–97

beginning of agriculture until 1900. And growth of the global economy in 1997 alone easily exceeded that during the seventeenth century. Growth has become the goal of every society, North and South. Indeed, it has become a kind of religion or ideology that drives societies. From the posh penthouses of Manhattan to the thatched huts of Bangladesh, human beings strive to raise their standard of living by expanding their wealth. Aspiring politicians promise faster growth, and the performance of corporate CEOs is judged by how quickly their firms expand.[24]

Economic growth has allowed billions of people to live healthier, more productive lives and to enjoy a host of comforts that were unimaginable in 1900. It has helped raise life expectancy, perhaps the sentinel indicator of human well-being, from 35 years in 1900 to 66 years today. Children born in 1999 can expect to live almost twice as long as their great-grandparents who were born around the turn of the century.[25]

While one fifth of humanity lives better than the kings of yore, another one fifth still lives on the very margin of existence, struggling just to survive. An estimated 841 million people are undernourished and underweight, and 1.2 billion do not have access to safe water. The income gap between the more affluent and the more poverty-stricken societies in the world is widening each year. While growth has become the norm everywhere since mid-century, some countries have been more successful in achieving it than others, leading to unprecedented income disparities among societies.[26]

As the century comes to a close amidst financial crises from Indonesia to Russia, doubts about the basic soundness of the global economy have mounted. The needs of billions are inadequately met in the best of times, and as Indonesia's recent experience shows, even a brief reversal of economic growth can leave millions on the brink of starvation. More fundamentally, our current economic model is overwhelming the Earth's natural systems.[27]

OVERWHELMING THE EARTH

Easter Island was one of the last places on Earth to be settled by human beings. First reached by Polynesians 1,500 years ago, this small island 3,200 kilometers west of South America supported a sophisticated agricultural society by the sixteenth century. Easter Island has a semiarid climate, but it was ameliorated by a verdant forest that trapped and held water. Its 7,000 people raised crops and chickens, caught fish, and lived in small villages. The Easter Islanders' legacy can be seen in massive 8-meter-high obsidian statues that were hauled across the island using tree trunks as rollers.[28]

By the time European settlers reached Easter Island in the seventeenth century, these stone statues, known as *ahu*, were the only remnants of a once impressive civilization—one that had collapsed in just

a few decades. As reconstructed by archaeologists, the demise of this society was triggered by the decimation of its limited resource base. As the Easter Island human population expanded, more and more land was cleared for crops, while the remaining trees were harvested for fuel and to move the *ahu* into place. The lack of wood made it impossible to build fishing boats or houses, reducing an important source of protein and forcing the people to move into caves. The loss of forests also led to soil erosion, further diminishing food supplies. As pressures grew, armed conflicts broke out among villages, slavery became common, and some even resorted to cannibalism to survive.[29]

As an isolated territory that could not turn elsewhere for sustenance once its own resources ran out, Easter Island presents a particularly stark picture of what can happen when a human economy expands in the face of limited resources. With the final closing of the remaining frontiers and the creation of a fully interconnected global economy, the human race as a whole has reached the kind of turning point that the Easter Islanders reached in the sixteenth century.

For us, the key limits as we approach the twenty-first century are fresh water, forests, rangelands, oceanic fisheries, biological diversity, and the global atmosphere. Will we recognize the world's natural limits and adjust our economies accordingly, or will we proceed to expand our ecological footprint until it is too late to turn back? Are we headed for a world in which accelerating change outstrips our management capacity, overwhelms our political institutions, and leads to extensive breakdown of the ecological systems on which the economy depends?

Although our ancestors have struggled with water shortages from ancient Mesopotamia onward, the spreading scarcity of fresh water may be the most underestimated resource issue facing the world as it enters the new millennium.

(See also Chapter 7.) This can be seen both in falling water tables and in rivers that run dry, failing to make it to the sea. As world water use has tripled since mid-century, overpumping has led to falling water tables on every continent.[30]

China and India, the world's two most populous countries, depend on irrigated agriculture for half or more of their food supply. In China, water tables are falling almost everywhere that the land is flat. The northern half of the country is quite literally drying out. The water table under much of the north China Plain, a region that accounts for nearly 40 percent of China's grain harvest, is falling by roughly 1.5 meters (5 feet) a year. Projections by the Sandia National Laboratory in the United States show huge water deficits emerging in some key river basins in China as the new millennium begins.[31]

In India, the water situation may be deteriorating even faster. As India's population approaches the 1 billion mark, the country faces steep cutbacks in the supply of irrigation water. David Seckler, head of the International Water Management Institute in Colombo, the world's premier water research body, observes: "The extraction of water from aquifers in India exceeds recharge by a factor of 2 or more. Thus almost everywhere in India, freshwater aquifers are being pulled down by 1–3 meters per year." Seckler goes on to speculate that as aquifers are depleted, the resulting cutbacks in irrigation could reduce India's harvest by 25 percent—in a country where food supply and demand are already precariously balanced and where another 600 million people are expected over the next half-century.[32]

At present, 70 percent of all the water worldwide that is diverted from rivers or pumped from underground is used for irrigation, 20 percent is used for industry, and 10 percent goes to residences. The economics of water use do not favor farmers. A thousand tons of water can be used in agriculture to produce one ton of wheat worth $200, or it can be used to expand industrial output by $14,000—70 times as much. As the demand for water in each of these three sectors rises and as the competition for scarce water intensifies, agriculture almost always loses.[33]

As the history of Easter Island suggests, wood has been essential to dozens of human civilizations, and the inability to manage forests sustainably has undermined and destroyed several of them. Today, we have a global forest economy in which the demands of affluent Japanese or Europeans are felt thousands of kilometers away—in tropical Africa, Southeast Asia, and Canada. (See Chapter 4.) Since mid-century, the demand for lumber has doubled, that for fuelwood has nearly tripled, while paper use has gone up nearly six times. In addition, forestlands are being cleared for slash-and-burn farming by expanding populations and for commercial crop production and livestock grazing. As population pressures intensify in the tropics and subtropics, more and more forests are being cleared for agriculture.[34]

A combination of logging and clearing land for farming and ranching has weakened forests in many areas to the point where they are vulnerable to fire. A healthy rainforest will not burn. But large segments of the world's rainforests are no longer healthy. During the late summer and fall of 1997, forests burned out of control in Indonesia. For months, heavy smoke filled the air in the region, causing millions of people to become ill. Some 1,100 airline flights were canceled. Earnings from tourism dropped precipitously.[35]

Although the fires in Indonesia captured the news headlines, there was even more extensive burning in the Amazon, which received much less attention because it was more remote. And in the spring of 1998, forests began to burn out of control in southern Mexico. The nearby state of Texas had several dangerous air alerts as the smoke moved northward. At times, it drifted as far north as Chicago. In early summer 1998, fires also started burning out of control in Florida. Even with personnel and equipment from some 23 states brought in to help, efforts to tame the fires failed. One entire county was evacuated along with parts of several others—and this in a country that probably has the most sophisticated fire-fighting equipment in the world.[36]

No one could have anticipated the extent of the burning around the world during this 12-month span. But in retrospect, there was a human influence in each of these situations. A combination of forests weakened by the forces just cited, El Niño–related droughts, and in some cases, as in Florida, record high temperatures contributed to this wholesale burning.

Fisheries actually preceded agriculture as a source of food, but ours is the first generation to reach—and perhaps exceed—the sustainable yield of oceanic fisheries. In fact, in just the last half-century the oceanic fish catch increased nearly five times, doubling seafood availability per person for the world as a whole. Marine biologists doubt, however, that the oceans can sustain a catch much above the 95 million tons of the last few years. According to the U.N. Food and Agriculture Organization, 11 of the world's 15 most important fishing areas and 70 percent of the major fish species are either fully or overexploited. The welfare of more than 200 million people around the world who depend on fishing for their income and food security is threatened. (See Chapter 5.)[37]

If the biologists are right, then the decline in seafood catch per person, which started in 1989, will persist for as long as population growth continues. Those born shortly before 1950 have enjoyed a doubling in seafood availability per person, whereas those born in recent years can expect to see a halving of the catch per person during their lifetimes. The beginning of the new millennium marks the turning point in oceanic fisheries, a shift from abundance to one where preferred species become scarce, seafood prices rise, and the conflicts among countries for access to fisheries multiply.

A healthy rainforest will not burn, but large segments of the world's rainforests are no longer healthy.

Although the yield data are not as precise as those for oceanic fisheries, the world's rangelands cover roughly twice the area of croplands, supplying most of the beef and mutton eaten worldwide. Unfortunately, as with fisheries, overgrazing is now the rule, not the exception. Sustaining future yields of meat, and in some cases milk as well, and providing livelihoods for ever-growing pastoralist populations will put even more pressure on already deteriorating rangelands. Yet another of our basic support systems is being overwhelmed by continuously expanding human needs.[38]

Perhaps the best single indicator of the Earth's health is the declining number of species with which we share the planet. Throughout most of the evolutionary history of life, the number of plant and animal species has gradually increased, giving us the extraordinarily rich diversity of life today. Unfortunately, we are now in the early stages of the greatest decimation of plant and animal life in 65 million years.[39]

Of the 242,000 plant species surveyed by the World Conservation Union–IUCN in 1997, 14 percent or some 33,000 are threatened with extinction. (See Chapter 6.) Some 7,000 are in immediate danger of extinction and another 8,000 are vulnerable to extinction. The principal cause of plant extinction is habitat destruction, often in the form of land clearing for agriculture and ranching, for housing construction, or for the drainage of wetlands for agriculture and construction. Large-scale species migration—propelled by growing trade—is compounding that threat, as is climate change, which could eliminate whole ecosystems in the decades ahead.[40]

The status of animal species is equally worrisome. Of the 9,600 bird species that populate the Earth, two thirds are now in decline, while 11 percent are threatened with extinction. A combination of habitat alteration and destruction, overhunting, and the introduction of exotic species is primarily responsible. Of the Earth's 4,400 species of mammals, of which we are but one, 11 percent are in danger of extinction. Another 14 percent are vulnerable to extinction if recent trends continue. Of the 24,000 species of fish that occupy the oceans and freshwater lakes and rivers, one third are now threatened with extinction.[41]

The globalization of recent decades is also reducing the diversity of life on Earth. Mushrooming trade and travel have broken down ecological barriers that existed for millions of years, allowing thousands of species—plants, insects, and other creatures—to invade distant territories, often driving native species to extinction and disrupting essential ecological processes. Recent "bioinvasions" have forced the abandonment of more than 1 million hectares of cropland in South America and devastated the fisheries of East Africa's Lake Victoria.[42]

The presence of chemicals in the environment is affecting the prospects for some animal species as well. In 1962, biologist Rachel Carson warned in *Silent Spring* that the continuing use of DDT could threaten the survival of predatory birds, such as bald eagles and peregrine falcons, because of its effect on eggshell formation. More recently, there is grow-

ing concern that a family of synthetic chemicals associated with pesticides and plastics, so-called endocrine disrupters, could be affecting the reproductive process in some species of birds, fish, and amphibians.[43]

The global atmosphere also faces growing stress. As our fossil-fuel-based global economy has expanded, carbon emissions have overwhelmed the capacity of natural systems to fix carbon dioxide. The result is a buildup in CO_2 from roughly 280 parts per million at the beginning of the industrial era to 363 parts per million in 1998, the highest level ever experienced. This buildup of CO_2 and other greenhouse gases is responsible for rising temperatures over the last century, according to leading scientists. The 14 warmest years since recordkeeping began in 1866 have all occurred since 1980. The global temperature in 1998 is projected to be both the highest ever and the largest annual increase ever recorded. (See Figure 1–3.)[44]

If the world stays on the present fossil fuel path, atmospheric CO_2 concentrations are projected to reach twice preindustrial levels as soon as 2050—and to raise the Earth's average temperature

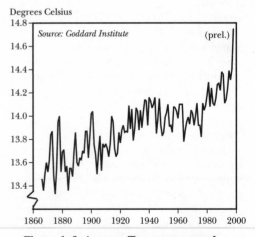

Figure 1–3. Average Temperature at the Earth's Surface, 1866–1998

1–3.5 degrees Celsius (2–6 degrees Fahrenheit) by 2100. This is expected to bring more extreme climate events, including more destructive storms and flooding, as well as melting ice caps and rising sea levels. A new computer simulation by Britain's Hadley Centre for Climate Change in late 1998 projected major reductions in food production in Africa and the United States as a result of climate change. The Hadley scientists also identify the potential for a "runaway" greenhouse effect after 2050 that could turn areas such as the Amazon and southern Europe into virtual deserts.[45]

The global climate is an essential foundation of natural ecosystems and the entire human economy. If we are entering a new period of climate instability, the consequences could be serious indeed, affecting virtually all of Earth's ecosystems, accelerating the pace of extinction, and leaving few areas of economic life untouched.

Even in a high-tech information age, human societies cannot continue to prosper while the natural world is progressively degraded. Our food crops and medicines are derived from wild plants, and even genetic engineering is based on rearranging the genes that nature has created. Moreover, our crops, industries, and cities require healthy ecosystems to store our water and to maintain a nurturing climate. Like the early residents of Easter Island, we are vulnerable. But unlike them, we can see the problem coming.

The Shape of a New Economy

As noted earlier, the western industrial development model that has evolved over the last two centuries has raised living standards to undreamed-of levels for one fifth of humanity. It has provided a remarkably diverse diet, unprecedented levels of material consumption, and physical mobility that our ancestors could not have imagined. But the fossil-fuel-based, automobile-centered, throwaway economy that developed in the West is not a viable system for the world, or even for the West over the long term, because it is destroying its environmental support systems.

If the western model were to become the global model, and if world population were to reach 10 billion during the next century, as the United Nations projects, the effect would be startling. If, for example, the world has one car for every two people in 2050, as in the United States today, there would be 5 billion cars. Given the congestion, pollution, and the fuel, material, and land requirements of the current global fleet of 501 million cars, a global fleet of 5 billion is difficult to imagine. If petroleum use per person were to reach the current U.S. level, the world would consume 360 million barrels per day, compared with current production of 67 million barrels.[46]

Or consider a world of 10 billion with everyone following an American diet, centered on the consumption of fat-rich livestock products. Ten billion people would require 9 billion tons of grain, the harvest of more than four planets at Earth's current output levels. With massive irrigation-water cutbacks in prospect as aquifers are depleted and with the dramatic slowdown in the rise in land productivity since 1990, achieving even relatively modest gains is becoming difficult.[47]

An economy is environmentally sustainable only if it satisfies the principles of sustainability—principles that are rooted in the science of ecology. In a sustainable economy, the fish catch does not exceed the sustainable yield of fisheries, the amount of water pumped from underground aquifers does not exceed aquifer recharge, soil erosion does not exceed the natural rate of new soil formation, tree cutting does not exceed tree planting, and carbon emissions do not exceed the capacity of nature to fix atmospheric CO_2. A sustainable economy does not destroy plant and animal species faster than new ones evolve.

Once it becomes clear that the existing industrial development model is not viable over the long term, the question becomes, What would an environmentally sustainable economy look like? Because we know the fundamental limits the world now faces and some of the technologies that are available, we can describe this new economy in broad outline, if not in detail. Its foundation is a new design principle—one that shifts from the one-time depletion of natural resources to one that is based on renewable energy and that continually reuses and recycles materials. It is a solar-powered, bicycle/rail centered, reuse/recycle economy, one that uses energy, water, land, and materials much more efficiently and wisely than we do today.

The challenge in energy is to replace the fossil fuel economy with an efficient solar economy (see Chapter 2), defining solar energy to include all the energy sources that derive from the sun directly or indirectly. Although solar energy in its various forms has been widely considered a fringe source, it is now moving toward center stage. Wind power, for example, now supplies 7 percent of electricity in Denmark and 23 percent in Spain's northern region of Navarre, including the capital, Pamplona. More important, however, is the potential. A survey of U.S. wind resources by the Department of Energy concluded that just three states—North Dakota, South Dakota, and Texas—had enough harnessable wind energy to satisfy national electricity needs. China has enough wind potential to easily double its current electricity generating capacity.[48]

The use of solar cells to supply electricity is also spreading rapidly. As of the end of 1998, some 500,000 homes, most of them in Third World villages not yet connected to an electrical grid, were getting their electricity from solar cells. Technologically, the most exciting advance comes from solar roofing material developed in the past few years. These solar tiles and shingles are made of photovoltaic cells that convert sunlight into electricity. They promise not only to create rooftops that become the power plants for buildings, but to revolutionize electricity generation worldwide.[49]

Widely disparate growth rates in energy use show that this new climate-stabilizing solar energy economy is beginning to take shape. (See Table 1–2.) While the use of coal during the 1990s has been expanding by 1.2 percent a year and that of oil by 1.4 percent, sales of solar cells have been climbing 17 percent annually and wind-generated electricity has increased 26 percent a year. Although the base from which these two new sources are developing is quite small, they are both projected to grow rapidly, with the potential to become cornerstones of the world energy economy over the next few decades. Thus far, most of the installed wind power, for example,

Table 1–2. Trends in Energy Use, by Source, 1990–97[1]

Energy Source	Average Annual Growth Rate (percent)
Wind power	25.7
Solar photovoltaics	16.8
Geothermal power[2]	3.0
Natural gas	2.1
Hydroelectric power[2]	1.6
Oil	1.4
Coal	1.2
Nuclear power	0.6

[1]Energy use measured in installed generating capacity for wind, geothermal, hydro, and nuclear power; million tons of oil equivalent for oil, natural gas, coal; and megawatts for shipments of solar cells. [2]1990–96 only.
SOURCE: See endnote 50.

is concentrated in Germany, the United States, Denmark, and India, but as more countries turn to wind, growth is likely to accelerate.[50]

In 1997, British Petroleum announced that it was taking the threat of global warming seriously and was putting $1 billion into solar and other renewable energy resources. Royal Dutch Shell followed shortly thereafter, announcing a commitment of $500 million to renewable energy resources, with additional funds likely to follow. For energy companies interested in growth, it is not likely to be in petroleum, since due to resource limits, oil production is projected to peak in the next 5 to 20 years, and then to begin declining.[51]

As the cost of electricity from wind and other solar sources falls, it will become economical to electrolyze water, producing hydrogen. Hydrogen thus becomes a way of both storing and transporting renewable energy. A device called a fuel cell efficiently turns hydrogen back into electricity in automobiles or small power plants located in homes or office buildings. Several major oil and gas companies, including Royal Dutch Shell and Gasunie in the Netherlands, have begun to take an interest in hydrogen, while Daimler-Benz, Ford, General Electric, and Toyota are all investing in fuel cells. By the middle of the next century, hydrogen produced from wind-generated electricity in the plains of Mongolia or solar electricity from the deserts of Arizona may be sent by pipeline to distant cities.[52]

The notion of transport systems centered on bicycles and railroads may seem primitive at first, but this is because governments everywhere have assumed that the auto-centered transportation system was the only one to consider seriously. The unfolding reality, however, is quite different. In 1969, the world produced 25 million bicycles and 23 million cars. And although car production was expected shortly to overtake that of bicycles, it actually fell further and further behind. In recent years, annual production of bicycles has averaged 105 million while that of automobiles has averaged 37 million. In contrast to the United States, where most bicycles sold are for recreational use, most of the 105 million bicycles sold each year worldwide are for basic transportation.[53]

In 1997, British Petroleum announced that it was putting $1 billion into solar and other renewable energy resources.

There are many reasons why bicycles have gained in popularity a century after the automobile was invented. One is that the number of people who can afford a bicycle is far greater than the number who can afford a car. Not only has this been true in recent decades, but it is also likely to be so for some decades to come. Cities are turning to them because they require little land, do not pollute, and reduce traffic congestion and noise. Even though some cities in Asia, notably in China and Indonesia, are discouraging the use of the bicycle instead of the car, a growing number of cities are favoring bikes.[54]

People everywhere are discovering the inherent incompatibility between the automobile and the city as traffic congestion, air pollution, and noise diminish the quality of life. Land scarcity, especially in severely populated countries, will limit the role of the automobile. In China, a group of prominent scientists has challenged the central government's decision to build an auto-centered transportation system, arguing that the country does not have enough land both to feed its people and to build the roads, highways, and parking lots needed for cars. The new economy will not exclude the automobile, because in many situations it is indispensable, but it is unlikely to be the center-piece of the transportation system as it is in many nations today.[55]

Bill Ford, Chairman of the Ford Motor Company, has predicted the demise of the internal combustion engine popularized by his great-grandfather.

Replacing a throwaway economy with a reduce/reuse/recycle economy is perhaps more easily understood than restructuring the transportation system because of the progress already made in recycling. Nonetheless, even with substantial recycling gains, the flow of garbage into land-fills is still increasing almost everywhere in the world. We still have a long way to go in increasing material efficiency. Some argue that it is possible to reduce materials use by a factor of four. Indeed, the Organisation for Economic Co-operation and Development is investigating ways to reduce the use of materials in modern industrial societies by 90 percent. (See Chapter 3.) The overall challenge in manufacturing is to follow a new design principle, with services rather than goods as the focus. Interface, for example—an Atlanta-based firm operating in 26 countries—sells carpeting services to its clients, systematically recycling the worn-out carpets, leaving nothing for the landfill. The key is to gradually reduce the material throughput of the economy, reducing energy use and pollution in the process.[56]

Companies around the world are now pursuing a concept known as "eco-efficiency," with the goal of maximizing production while minimizing or, in some cases, eliminating effluents. William McDonough and Michael Braungart argue that these principles can underpin a "new industrial revolution" in which material and energy flows are minimized and the water and air leaving a factory are in some cases cleaner than that going in.[57]

As water scarcity continues to spread, the need to make the global economy more water-efficient will become even more apparent. This includes both turning to more water-efficient sources of energy and dramatically increasing the efficiency of water use in agriculture. Fortunately, the energy sources that do not destabilize climate, such as solar cells and wind turbines, do not require large amounts of water for cooling, in contrast to nuclear energy and coal.

Early signs of the emerging new economy can be seen in recent decisions by corporations and governments. In addition to the oil companies that are now investing heavily in wind and solar resources, other firms are also moving in a sustainable direction. MacMillan Bloedel, for instance, the leading timber company in British Columbia, is abandoning clearcutting, replacing it with the selective cutting of trees.[58]

Bill Ford, who became Chairman of the Ford Motor Company in late 1998, declares himself a "passionate environmentalist" and has predicted the demise of the internal combustion engine popularized by his great-grandfather early in the century. "There is a rising tide of environmental awareness," says Ford. "Smart companies will get ahead of the wave. Those that don't will be wiped out." Thomas Casten, CEO of the fast-growing Trigen Energy Corporation, has embraced the threat of climate change as one of the greatest business opportunities of the twenty-first century. The small, extraordinarily efficient power plants his company provides can triple the energy efficiency of some older, less efficient plants. The issue, he says, is not how much it will cost to reduce carbon emissions, but who is going to harvest the enormous profits in doing so.[59]

At the government level, Costa Rica

plans to generate all its electricity from renewable sources by 2010, and the Danish government has banned the construction of coal-fired power plants. China has banned timber harvesting in the upper reaches of the Yangtze and Yellow river basins, noting that the water storage capacity of intact forests makes trees three times more valuable standing than cut for lumber. And most exciting of all, Germany, now governed by a coalition of Social Democrats and Greens, plans a massive tax restructuring, reducing income taxes and raising energy taxes.[60]

These are just a few of the early examples of companies and countries that are beginning to envisage, and work toward, a sustainable future. The century to come will be the environmental century—either because we use the basic principles of ecology to design a new economic system or because we fail to, and find that continuing deterioration of the economy's environmental support systems leads to economic decline. The issue is not growth versus no growth, but what kind of growth and where. Converting the economy of the twentieth century into one that is environmentally sustainable represents the greatest investment opportunity in history, one that dwarfs anything that has gone before.

RETHINKING PROGRESS

As we approach the twenty-first century, many respected thinkers seem to believe that we are in for a period of inevitable economic and technological progress. Even the recent economic crisis that has spread misery from Indonesia to Russia is seen as a brief pause in an unending upward climb for *Homo sapiens*. In a special double issue on the economy in the twenty-first century, *Business Week* ran a headline proclaiming, "You Ain't Seen Nothing Yet," forecasting even faster rates of economic progress in the century ahead. The magazine's editors expect the global economy to ride a wave of technology in the decades to come, solving all manner of social problems, as well as adding to the investment portfolios of its readers.[61]

This view of the future, fueled by heady advances in technology, is particularly prevalent in the information industry. It reflects a new conception of the human species, one in which human societies are seen as free of dependence on the natural world. Our information-based economy is thought capable of evolving independently of the Earth's ecosystem.

The complacency reflected in this view overlooks our continued dependence on the natural world and the profound vulnerabilities this represents. It concentrates on economic indicators while largely overlooking the environmental indicators that measure the Earth's physical deterioration. This view is dangerous because it threatens to discourage the restructuring of the economy needed if economic progress is to continue. If we are to build an environmentally sustainable economy, we have to go beyond traditional economic indicators of progress. If we put a computer in every home in the next century but also wipe out half of the world's plant and animal species, that would hardly be an economic success. And if we again quadruple the size of the global economy but many of us are hungrier than our hunter-gatherer ancestors, we will not be able to declare the twenty-first century a success.

One of the first steps in redefining progress is to recognize that our generation is the first whose actions can affect the habitability of the planet for future generations. We have acquired this capacity not by conscious design but as a consequence of a global economy that is outgrowing its environmental support systems. In effect, we have acquired the capacity to alter the Earth's natural systems but have refused to accept responsibility for doing so. We live in a world that has an obsessive preoccupation with the present. Focused on quarterly profit-and-loss statements, we are behaving as though we had no children. In short, we have lost our sense of responsibility to future generations.

We need a new moral compass to guide us into the twenty-first century—a compass grounded in the principles of meeting human needs sustainably.

Parents everywhere are concerned about their children. In their efforts to ensure a better life for them, they invest in education and medical care. But unless we now assume responsibility for the evolution of the global economy, our short-term investments in our children's future may not amount to much; our principal legacy to them would be a world that is deteriorating ecologically, declining economically, and disintegrating socially.

Building an environmentally sustainable global economy depends on a cooperative global effort. No country acting alone can stabilize its climate. No country acting alone can protect the diversity of life on Earth. No country acting alone can protect oceanic fisheries. These goals can be achieved only through global cooperation that recognizes the interdependence of countries. Unless the needs of the poorer nations for food, sanitation, cooking fuels, and other basic requirements are being met, the world's more affluent nations can hardly expect them to contribute to solving long-term global problems such as climate change. The challenge is to reverse the last decade's trends of rising international inequalities

and shrinking aid programs.

In short, we can no longer separate efforts to build an environmentally sustainable economy from efforts to meet the needs of the world's poor. According to various estimates, some 841 million people in the world are malnourished, 1.2 billion lack access to clean water, 1.6 billion are illiterate, and 2 billion do not have access to electricity.[62]

Forbes magazine estimates that the 225 richest people in the world now have a combined wealth of more than $1 trillion, a figure that approaches the combined annual incomes of the poorest one half of humanity. Indeed, the assets of the three richest individuals exceed the combined annual economic output (measured at the current exchange rate) of the 48 poorest countries. It is now becoming obvious that the widening gap between rich and poor is untenable in a world where resources are shared. In the absence of a concerted effort by the wealthy to address the problems of poverty and deprivation, building a sustainable future may not be possible.[63]

Efforts to restore a stable relationship between the economy and its environmental support systems depends on social cohesion within societies as well. As at the international level, this cohesion is also influenced by the distribution of wealth. As communications improve, and as severely deprived people everywhere come to understand better their relative economic position, they are likely to take action to achieve a more equitable share of the economic pie. In October 1998, the disenfranchised in the economically depressed southern part of Nigeria began taking over oil wells and pumping stations to protest their government's failure to use its vast flow of oil wealth to benefit people in the region. A villager noted that even though oil had flowed out of the area for 30 years, his village still had "no school, no clinic, no power, and little hope."[64]

The trends of recent years suggest that we need a new moral compass to guide us into the twenty-first century—a compass that is grounded in the principles of meeting human needs sustainably. Such an ethic of sustainability would be based on a concept of respect for future generations. The challenge may be greatest in the United States, where the per capita use of grain, energy, and materials is the highest in the world, and where in the 1990s half of all adults are overweight, where houses and cars have continued to get larger, and where driving has continued to increase, overwhelming two decades' worth of efficiency improvements. The world's ecosystems have largely survived 270 million people living like this in the twentieth century, but they will not survive 8 billion or more doing so in the twenty-first century.[65]

At issue is a change in understanding and values that will support a restructuring of the global economy so that economic progress can continue. Although such a transformation may seem far-fetched, the end-of-century perspective offers hope. The past 100 years have seen vast changes in ethics and standards. The concept of "human rights," for example, has flowered in the twentieth century. The basic principles of human rights have been around for several hundred years, but only in 1948—a mere half-century ago—did governments adopt a complex body of national and international laws that recognize these rights. Another example of changing attitudes and values,

one that has occurred even faster, is the growing understanding of the effects of cigarette smoking on health. This recognition has led to a sea change in public attitudes and policies toward smoking within a few decades.[66]

It is difficult to overstate the urgency of reversing the trends of environmental deterioration. Archeologists study the remains of civilizations that irreparably undermined their ecological support systems. These societies found themselves on a population or economic path that was environmentally unsustainable—and were not able to make the economic adjustments to avoid a collapse. Unfortunately, archeological records do not tell us whether these ancient civilizations did not understand the need for change, or whether they saw the problem but could not agree on the steps needed to stave off economic decline. Today, the adjustments we need to make are clear. The question is whether we can make them in time.

We know what we need to do. We have a vision of a restructured economy, one that will sustain economic and social progress. In Chapter 10 we describe the policies—including the key one of restructuring the tax system—that can be used to get us there. The challenge is to mobilize public support for that economic transformation. No challenge is greater, or more satisfying, than building an environmentally sustainable global economy, one where economic and social progress can continue not only in the twenty-first century but many centuries beyond.

2

Reinventing the Energy System

Christopher Flavin and Seth Dunn

When the American Press Association gathered the country's "best minds" on the eve of the 1893 Chicago World's Fair and asked them to peer a century into the future, the nation's streets were filled with horse-drawn carriages and illuminated at night by gas lights that were still considered a high-tech novelty. And coal—whose share of commercial energy use had risen from 9 percent in 1850 to more than 60 percent in 1890—was expected to remain dominant for a long time to come.[1]

The commentators who turned their crystal balls toward the nation's energy system foresaw some major changes—but missed others. They anticipated, for example, that "Electrical power will be universal....Steam and all other sorts of power will be displaced." But while some wrote of trains traveling 100 miles an hour and moving sidewalks, none predicted the ascent of oil, the proliferation of the automobile, or the spread of suburbs and shopping malls made possible by cars. Their predictions also missed the many

ways in which inexpensive energy would affect lives and livelihoods through the advent of air-conditioning, television, and continent- bridging jet aircraft. Nor did they foresee that oil and other fossil fuels would one day be used on such a scale as to raise sea levels, disrupt ecosystems, or increase the intensity of heat waves, droughts, and floods.[2]

To most of today's energy futurists, the current system might seem even more solid and immutable than the nineteenth-century system appeared 100 years ago. The internal combustion engine has dominated personal transportation in industrial countries for more than eight decades, and electricity is now so taken for granted that any interruption in its supply is considered an emergency. Today the price of energy is nearly as low—in terms of consumer purchasing power—as it has ever been, and finding new energy sources that are more convenient, reliable, and affordable than fossil fuels is beyond the imagination of many experts. Former Eastern Bloc countries seek economic salvation in oil booms, while China and other developing nations are rushing to join the oil era—pouring hundreds of billions of dollars into the construction of coal mines, oil refineries, power plants, automobile factories, and roads.[3]

Fossil fuels—coal, oil, and natural gas—that are dug or pumped from the ground, then burned in engines or furnaces, provide 90 percent or more of the energy in most industrial countries and 75 percent of energy worldwide. (See Table 2–1.) They are led by petroleum, the most convenient and ubiquitous among them—an energy source that has shaped the twentieth century, and that now seems irreplaceable. But as the Chicago World's Fair writings remind us, energy forecasts can overlook what later seems obvious. A close examination of technological, economic, social, and environmental trends suggests that we may already be in the early stages of a major global energy transition—one that is likely to accelerate early in the next century.[4]

To understand energy in world history is to expect the unexpected. And as we live in a particularly dynamic period, the least likely scenario may be that the energy picture 100 years from now will closely resemble that of today. Although the future remains, as always, far from crystal clear, the broad outlines of a new energy system may now be emerging, thanks in part to a series of revolutionary new technologies and approaches. These developments suggest that our future energy economy may be highly efficient and decentralized, using a range of sophisticated electronics. The primary energy resources for this system may be the most abundant ones on Earth: the sun, the wind, and other "renewable" sources of energy. And the main fuel for this twenty-first-century economy could be hydrogen, the lightest and most abundant element in the universe.[5]

This transition would in some sense be a return to our roots. *Homo sapiens* has relied for most of its existence on a virtually limitless flow of renewable energy resources—muscles, plants, sun, wind, and water—to meet its basic needs for shelter, heat, cooking, lighting, and movement. The relatively recent transition to coal that began in Europe in the seventeenth century marked a major shift to dependence on a finite stock of fossilized fuels whose remaining energy is now equivalent to less than 11 days of sunshine. From a millennial perspective, today's hydrocarbon-based civilization is but a brief interlude in human history.[6]

The next century may be as profoundly shaped by the move away from fossil fuels as this century was marked by the

Table 2–1. World Energy Use, 1900 and 1997

Energy Source	1900		1997	
	Total	Share	Total	Share
	(million tons of oil equivalent)	(percent)	(million tons of oil equivalent)	(percent)
Coal	501	55	2,122	22
Oil	18	2	2,940	30
Natural gas	9	1	2,173	23
Nuclear	0	0	579	6
Renewables[1]	383	42	1,833	19
Total	911	100	9,647	100

[1]Includes biomass, hydro, wind, geothermal, and solar energy.
SOURCE: See endnote 4.

move toward them. Although it may take several decades for another system to fully develop, the underlying markets could shift abruptly in the next few years, drying up sales of conventional power plants and cars in a matter of years and affecting the share prices of scores of companies. The economic health—and political power—of nations could be sharply boosted or diminished. And our industries, homes, and cities could be transformed in ways we can only begin to anticipate.

Through the ages, the evolution of human societies has both influenced and been influenced by changes in patterns of energy use. But the timing of this next transition will be especially crucial. Today's energy system completely bypasses roughly 2 billion people who lack modern fuels or electricity, and underserves another 2 billion who cannot afford most energy amenities, such as refrigeration or hot water. Moreover, by relying on the rapid depletion of nonrenewable resources and releasing billions of tons of combustion gases into the atmosphere, we have built the economy on trends that cannot possibly be sustained for another century. The efforts made today to lay the foundations for a new energy system will affect the lives of billions of people in the twenty-first century and beyond.[7]

PRIME MOVERS

Energy transitions do not occur in a vacuum. Past shifts have been propelled by technological change and a range of social, economic, and environmental forces. Understanding these developments is essential for mapping out the path that humanity may follow in the next 100 years. The emergence of an oil-based economy at the beginning of this century, for example, was influenced by rapid scientific advances, the growing needs of an industrial economy, mounting urban environmental problems in the form of smoke and manure, and the aspirations of millions for higher living standards and greater mobility.[8]

Resource limits are one force that could help push the world away from fossil fuels in the coming decades. Oil is the main energy source today, accounting for 30 percent of commercial use; natural gas has emerged as an environmentally preferred alternative for many uses, and has a 23-percent share; coal has maintained a key role in power generation, and holds a 22-percent share of total energy use. Natural gas and coal are both available in sufficient amounts to last until the end of the twenty-first century or beyond—but oil is not. Just as seventeenth-century Britain ran out of cheap wood, today we face the danger of running out of inexpensive petroleum.[9]

Although oil markets have been relatively stable for more than a decade, and real prices approached historical lows in 1998, estimates of the underlying resource base have increased very little. Most of the calm in the oil markets of the 1990s has been due to slower demand growth, not an increase in supply. Despite prodigious exploration efforts, known oil resources have expanded only marginally in the last quarter-century, though some nations have raised their official reserve figures in order to obtain larger OPEC production quotas. Approximately 80 percent of the oil produced today comes from fields discovered before 1973, most of which are in decline. Total world production has increased less than 10 percent in two decades.[10]

In a recent analysis of data on world oil resources, geologists Colin Campbell and Jean Laherrere estimate that roughly 1 trillion barrels of oil remain to be extracted. Since 800 billion barrels have already been used up, this suggests that the original exploitable resource base is nearly half gone. As extraction of a nonrenewable resource tends to follow a bell-shaped curve, these figures can be extrapolated to project that world production will peak by 2010, and then begin to decline. (See Figure 2–1.) Applying the more optimistic resource estimates of other oil experts would push back this production pinnacle by just a decade.[11]

A peak in world oil production early in the new century would reverberate through the energy system. The problem is not just the large amount of oil currently used—67 million barrels daily—but the intent of many developing countries, most lacking much oil of their own, to increase their use of automobiles and trucks. Meeting the growing needs of China, India, and the rest of the developing world in the way industrial countries' demands are met today would require a tripling of world oil production, even assuming no increases in industrial-country use. Yet production capacity in 2020 is unlikely to be much above current levels—and may well be declining.[12]

Long before we completely run out of fossil fuels, however, the environmental and health burdens of using them may force us toward a cleaner energy system. Fossil fuel burning is the main source of air pollution and a leading cause of water and land degradation. Combustion of coal and oil produces carbon monoxide and tiny particulates that have been implicated in lung cancer and other respiratory problems; nitrogen and sulfur oxides create urban smog, and bring acid rain that has damaged forests extensively. Oil spills, refinery operations, and coal mining release toxic materials that impair water quality. Increasingly, oil exploration disrupts fragile ecosystems and coal mining removes entire mountains. Although modern pollution controls have improved air quality in most industrial countries in recent decades, the deadly experiences of London and Pittsburgh are now being repeated in Mexico City, São Paulo, New Delhi, Bangkok, and many other cities in the developing world. Each year, coal burning is estimated to kill 178,000 people prematurely in China alone.[13]

Beyond these localized problems, it is the cumulative, global environmental effects that now are calling the fossil fuel economy into question. More than 200 years have passed since we began burning the sequestered sunlight of fossilized plants that took millions of years to accumulate, but only recently has it become evident that the carbon those fuels produce is disrupting the Earth's radiation balance, causing the planet to warm. Fossil fuel combustion has increased atmospheric concentrations of the heat-trapping gas carbon dioxide (CO_2) by 30 percent since preindustrial times. (See Figure 2–2.) CO_2 levels are now at their highest point in 160,000 years, and global temperatures at their highest since the Middle Ages. Experts believe human activities could be ending the period of relative climatic stability that has endured over the last 10,000 years, and that permitted the rise of agricultural and industrial society.[14]

In recent years scientists have extensively documented trends—receding glac-

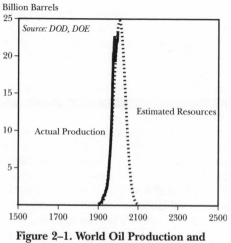

Figure 2–1. World Oil Production and Estimated Resources, 1500–2500

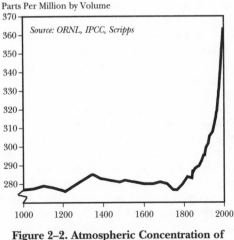

Parts Per Million by Volume

Source: ORNL, IPCC, Scripps

**Figure 2–2. Atmospheric Concentration of
Carbon Dioxide, 1000–1997**

iers, rising sea levels, dying coral reefs,
spreading infectious diseases, migrating
plants and animals—that are consistent
with the projected effects of a warmer
world. The extraordinary heat of 1998—
on pace to hit a new record—was related
to, but extended well beyond, an unusually strong El Niño phenomenon. This
contributed to a range of extreme weather events, including droughts and rare
fires in tropical and subtropical forests
from Indonesia to Mexico; historic floods
in China and Bangladesh; severe storms
and epidemics in Africa and North,
Central, and South America; and deadly
heat waves in the United States, southern
Europe, and India. The climate system is
nonlinear and has in the past switched
abruptly—even in the space of a few
decades—to another equilibrium after
crossing a temperature threshold. Such
shifts have the potential to greatly disrupt
both the natural world and human society. Indeed, previous changes have coincided with the collapse of several ancient
civilizations.[15]

Stabilizing atmospheric CO_2 concentrations at safe levels will require a 60–80
percent cut in carbon emissions from
current levels, according to the best esti-

mates of scientists. The Kyoto Protocol to
the U.N. Framework Convention on
Climate Change, agreed to in December
1997, is intended to be a small step on this
long journey—which would eventually
end the fossil-fuel-based economy as we
know it today.[16]

Energy transitions are also shaped by
the changing needs of societies. Historians
argue that coal won out over wood and
other renewable resources during the
eighteenth and nineteenth centuries in
part due to the requirements of the shift
from a rural, agrarian society to an urban,
industrial one. Abundant and concentrated forms of energy were required for the
new industries and booming cities of the
period. In this view, coal did not bring
about the transition but adapted to it more
quickly. Ironically, the success of water-
mills and windmills in promoting early
industrialization led to expanding energy
demands that could only be met by the
coal-fired steam engine.[17]

Today's fast-growth economic sectors
are not the production of food or automobiles, but software, telecommunications, and a broad array of services—from
finance and news to education and entertainment. The Information Revolution
will, like the Industrial Revolution, have
its own energy needs—and will place a
premium on reliability. Computer systems
freeze up if power is cut off for a fraction
of a second; heavy industries, such as
chemical and steel production, now
depend on semiconductor chips to operate. Yet the mechanical machines and
networks of above-ground wires and
pipelines that power current energy
systems are vulnerable. Today's systems
are also centralized, while much of the
service economy can be conducted from
far-flung locations that are connected
through the Internet, and may require
more localized, autonomous energy supplies than power grids or gas lines can
provide. As with the water wheel, so with
oil: the growing demands of the new

economy might not be met by the energy system that helped launch it.[18]

In the twenty-first century, the requirements of the developing world—where 80 percent or more of the new energy investment is expected to take place—are likely to be the leading driver of energy markets. Eighteenth-century Great Britain shifted to coal, and the twentieth-century United States to oil, in part to meet the demands of growing populations; similar changes might be expected as more than 5 billion people seek more convenient transportation, refrigeration, air-conditioning, and other amenities in the years ahead. Technologies that can meet the demands of developing nations at minimal cost may therefore assume prominent roles in the overall transition.[19]

SYSTEMIC CHANGE

The closing decades of the nineteenth century were a fertile period in the history of technology, as inventors applied novel scientific advances to a range of new devices. The incandescent light bulb, electric dynamo, and internal combustion engine were invented in the late 1800s but had relatively little effect on industry or daily life as the century ended. As they came into widespread use in later decades, however, it became clear in retrospect that the technological foundation for the transition was largely in place by 1900.[20]

Today a new energy system is gestating in the late-twentieth-century fields of electronics, synthetic materials, biotechnology, and software. The silicon semiconductor chip, promising increased processing power and miniaturization of electronic devices, allows energy use to be matched more closely to need. Wider use of these chips offers efficiency gains in appliances, buildings, industry, and transport, making it possible to control pre-

cisely nearly all energy-using devices. Electronic controls also enable a range of small-scale, modular technologies to challenge the large-scale energy devices of the twentieth century.[21]

Breakthroughs in chemistry and materials science are also playing key roles in energy, providing sophisticated, lightweight materials that operate without the wear and tear of moving parts. Modern wind turbines use the same carbon-fiber synthetic materials found in bullet-proof vests, "gore-tex" synthetic membranes line the latest fuel cells, and new "super-insulation" that reduces the energy needs of buildings relies on the same aluminum foil vacuum process that keeps coffee fresh. The latest electrochemical window coatings can be adjusted to reflect or absorb heat and light in response to weather conditions and the time of day.[22]

A particularly fertile area of advance is in lighting, where the search is on for successors to Thomas Edison's incandescent bulb. Improvements in small-scale electronic ballasts have given rise to the compact fluorescent lamp (CFL), which requires one quarter the electricity of incandescent bulbs and lasts 10 times as long. Manufacturers are now working on even more advanced models with tiny ballasts that work with any light socket, and that cost half as much as today's models. Yet the new light-emitting diode (LED), a solid-state semiconductor device that emits a very bright light when charged, is twice as efficient as CFLs and lasts 10 times as long. Today's LEDs produce red and yellow light, which limits their market to applications such as traffic signals and automobile taillights, but scientists believe that white-light versions will soon become practical.[23]

Late-twentieth-century technology has also revived an ancient source of energy: the wind. The first windmills for grinding grain appeared in Persia just over 1,000 years ago, and eventually spread to China, throughout the Mediterranean, and to northern Europe, where the Dutch developed the massive machines for which the country is still known. Wind power emerged as a serious option for generating electricity when Danish engineers began to apply advanced engineering and materials in the 1970s. The latest versions, which are also manufactured by companies based in Germany, India, Spain, and the United States, have variable-pitch fiberglass blades that are as long as 40 meters, electronic variable speed drives, and sophisticated microprocessor controls. Wind power is now economically competitive with fossil fuel generated electricity, and the market, valued at roughly $2 billion in 1998, is growing more than 25 percent annually. (See Figure 2–3.)[24]

Use of the sun as an energy source is also being renewed by modern technology. The solar photovoltaic cell, a semiconductor device that turns the sun's radiation directly into electric current, is widely used in off-grid applications as a power source for satellites and remote communications systems, as well as in consumer electronic devices such as pocket calculators and watches. Improvements in cell efficiency and materials have lowered

costs by 80 percent in the past two decades, and the cells are now being built into shingles, tiles, and window glass—allowing buildings to generate their own electricity. Markets are booming. (See Figure 2–4.) The cost of solar cells will need to fall by another 50–75 percent in order to be fully competitive with coal-fired electricity, but automated manufacturing, larger factories, and more- efficient cells promise further cost reductions in the near future. Semiconductor research is also nurturing the development of a close cousin of the solar cell, the "thermophotovoltaic" cell, which can produce electricity from industrial waste heat.[25]

The technology that could most transform the energy system, the fuel cell, was first discovered in 1829, five decades before the internal combustion engine. The fuel cell attracted considerable interest at the turn of the century but required efficiency improvements before its first modern application in the U.S. space program in the 1960s. Fuel cells use an electrochemical process that combines hydrogen and oxygen, producing water and electricity. Avoiding the inherent inefficiency of combustion, today's top fuel cells are roughly twice as efficient as

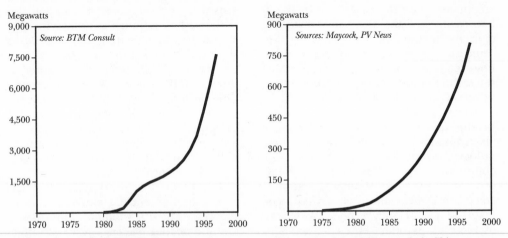

Figure 2–3. World Wind Energy Generating Capacity, 1970–97

Figure 2–4. World Photovoltaic Shipments, Cumulative, 1970–97

conventional engines, have no moving parts, require little maintenance, are nearly silent, and emit only water vapor. Unlike today's power plants, they are nearly as economical on a small scale as on a large one. Indeed, they could turn the very notion of a power plant into something more closely resembling a home appliance.[26]

Although the first fuel cells now run on natural gas—which can be separated into hydrogen and carbon dioxide—in the long term they may be fueled by pure hydrogen that is separated from water by using electricity, a process known as electrolysis. Researchers are also testing various catalysts that, when placed in water that is illuminated by sunlight, may one day produce inexpensive hydrogen. Chemists have recently developed a solar-powered "water splitter" that nearly doubles the efficiency of converting solar energy to hydrogen. Some scientists note that finding a cheap and efficient way to electrolyze water could make hydrogen as dominant an energy carrier in the twenty-first century as oil was in the twentieth.[27]

Many energy analysts argue that it will take a long time for such devices to become competitive with fossil fuels. But dwelling on the current cost gap ignores a principle that Henry Ford discovered earlier this century. Mass production allowed Ford to cut the cost of a Model T by 65 percent between 1909 and 1923. As with the Model T, the costs of the new, modular energy devices are expected to fall dramatically as their markets expand.[28]

Historically, energy innovations have first emerged in specialized "niches" where they were, for a variety of reasons, preferred to the conventional fuel. Petroleum's initial market was as a replacement for whale oil used in lighting kerosene lamps; what now seems a marginal use of oil was a powerful force in the late nineteenth century, sufficient to attract millions of dollars of investment.

Today's emerging energy technologies are exploiting similarly small but growing niches that are spurring investment and larger-scale manufacturing. Shipments of solar cells doubled between 1994 and 1997 as a result of burgeoning niche markets such as powering highway signals and water pumps, as well as a half-million homes not connected to a grid, where solar power is the most economical source of electricity. Fuel cells are first appearing in buses, hospitals, military bases, and wastewater treatment plants, and are being developed for cellular phones, laptop computers, and cabin lamps. One day, they could be found in most buildings and automobiles.[29]

As these examples suggest, downsizing and decentralization may become major features of the twenty-first century energy economy. While the twentieth century has seen a trend toward larger facilities and greater distances between energy source and use, the new technologies would place an affordable, reliable, and accessible power supply near where it is needed. This would retrace the computer industry's path from mainframe to desktop computers in the past two decades—and resurrect Thomas Edison's vision of decentralized, small-scale power generation. In contrast to today's monoculture of power generation, a distributed energy system would combine a range of new devices: small turbines in factories, fuel cells in basements, rooftop solar panels, wind turbines scattered across pastures, and power plants that can be carried in a briefcase.[30]

The information age—itself downsized and decentralized—could help ensure the reliability of a distributed power system through instantaneous telecommunications and sophisticated electronic controls that coordinate millions of individual generators, much as the Internet works today. Computer and telecommunication companies are developing "intelligent" power systems that send signals over phone lines, television cables, and electric lines. Micro-generators and even home appliances can be programmed to respond to electronically relayed price information, providing power to the grid and storing it—in the form of hydrogen, or the kinetic energy of a flywheel—as demand fluctuates. This fine-tuning of the balance between electricity supply and demand would increase the efficiency of the new system—reducing pollution and saving energy and money.[31]

The key to a reliable, diversified energy system will be the use of hydrogen as a major energy carrier and storage medium.

Buildings were energy self-sufficient for much of history, but in the last century they have become dependent on increasingly distant sources of supply. A distributed energy system would allow buildings to once again meet most of their own energy needs with rooftop solar systems, fuel cells, and flywheels—even becoming net energy generators that sell excess power back to the grid. Basement fuel cells could provide electricity and heat during the day, while automobiles and electric bicycles might be replenished with household-generated hydrogen or electricity at night. "Zero net energy" buildings can be tightly designed to rely on passive solar energy and on the body heat of occupants. Buildings themselves may be made of mass-produced components and modules that can be shipped to a site and then assembled.[32]

The automobile, too, is likely to be reshaped. Oil's automotive successors—be they batteries or turbines, flywheels or fuel cells—will likewise motivate engineers to make the rest of the vehicle as lightweight as possible, as demonstrated with the bulky

lead-acid battery and sleek exterior of the first modern commercial electric car, designed by General Motors (GM). The first commercially available "hybrid-electric" vehicle, Toyota's Prius, uses engine and battery in tandem and is twice as fuel-efficient as the average U.S. car. (More than 7,700 sold in the first eight months, leading the company to double production during its first year; Toyota plans to market the vehicle in North America and Europe by 2000.) In a combination of these two ideas, the first hybrid-electric fuel cell taxi has appeared on the streets of London. Trucks, locomotives, and other heavy vehicles may also soon shift—and adjust—to the new technologies.[33]

Running a modular energy system on renewable resources will require adapting the system to their intermittent nature. A temporary measure might be to build backup generators using efficient gas turbines, fuel cells, or pumped water storage; new technologies such as compressed air, plastic batteries, flywheels, and other energy storage devices also have parts to play. But the key to a reliable, diversified energy system based on renewable sources will be the use of hydrogen as a major energy carrier and storage medium.[34]

Developing a system for storing and transporting hydrogen will be a major undertaking. In the long run, materials that can store large amounts of hydrogen, such as metal hydrides or carbon nanotubes, are being developed for use in electric vehicles and other applications. And deriving hydrogen from natural gas for the initial generation of fuel cells would allow the early stages of a hydrogen economy to be based on the extensive natural gas pipelines and other equipment already in place. Small-scale reforming units that convert natural gas into hydrogen could be placed in homes, office buildings, and service stations. The carbon dioxide released from this conversion would be far less than from internal combustion engines, and could be turned into plastics or sequestered in underground or undersea reservoirs.[35]

The use of natural gas as a "bridge" to hydrogen might allow for a relatively seamless transition to a renewable-energy-based system. Hydrogen could be mixed with natural gas and carried in the same pipelines, then later transported through rebuilt pipelines and compressors that are designed to carry pure hydrogen. Large amounts of hydrogen might be produced in remote wind farms or solar stations, and then stored underground; homeowners could produce hydrogen from rooftop solar cells and store it in the basement. Liquid hydrogen could find a niche in air transport—replacing the kerosene that figured prominently in the rise of oil and that still fuels most commercial jets.[36]

Systemic change can begin slowly, but gather momentum quickly. The transition from gas to electric lighting proceeded quietly at first: in 1910, only 10 percent of U.S. houses had electricity. At the turn of the twentieth century, the gasoline-powered car was still competing with the horsedrawn carriage and the steam engine– and electric battery–powered car, while oil accounted for just 2.4 percent of U.S. energy use. Within a generation, however, the internal combustion engine had displaced the others; oil had surpassed coal by 1921; and by 1930, 80 percent of the country's houses had been electrified. The pace and direction of an energy transition, then, are determined not just by technological developments, but also by how industries, governments, and societies respond to them.[37]

AN INDUSTRY TRANSFORMED

The oil industry that formed in the rough hills of western Pennsylvania in the 1860s was fiercely competitive, prone to wild price fluctuations, and full of entrepreneurs who found niches supplying equipment, drilling wells, and running railroads, pipelines, and refineries. But the entrepreneurial phase of the industry lasted less than two decades. A young man by the name of John D. Rockefeller entered the oil refining business and began buying up his competitors—first going after other refiners, and then moving into the drilling and transportation business. Using tactics ranging from persuasion to coercion— some of which would be illegal today— Rockefeller built Standard Oil into a virtual empire that dominated the oil business, from the well to the retail markets, along the eastern U.S. seaboard. "It was forced upon us," Rockefeller explained later. "The oil business was in chaos and daily growing worse." Rockefeller tamed the competition, increased the scale and efficiency of the refining process, and created one of the world's first multinational corporations.[38]

Standard Oil's monopoly eventually became so egregious that it led to the government-mandated breakup of Rockefeller's empire, but it had already created a new industrial model that has been followed by the energy industry ever since. Although no longer a monopoly, the oil industry is dominated by a dozen large corporations, four of which— Amoco, Chevron, Exxon, and Mobil—are "Baby Standards," offspring of the breakup. After World War II, large oil discoveries were made in increasingly remote, inhospitable locations such as the deserts of the Middle East and Alaska's North Slope, all of which favored large multinational corporations equipped to mount decade-long, multibillion-dollar development projects. Then in the 1960s and 1970s, the nations that are home to the largest of those reserves—countries such as Mexico and Venezuela as well as the Persian Gulf kingdoms—threw out the multinationals and formed their own state oil monopolies.[39]

The trend to bigness in the energy

business moved quickly beyond oil. Prior to 1910, scores of small companies built an array of handmade cars, but the diversity ended in the next decade with Henry Ford's pioneering assembly lines, which lowered the cost of production and spurred a host of others to imitate. Soon auto companies were gobbling each other up, a trend seen most clearly in today's General Motors, which was assembled from a half-dozen early-century automakers.[40]

The energy business is once more opening up to a new generation of entrepreneurs selling revolutionary new devices.

The electric power business was also quickly consolidated, with giant firms controlling everything from the power plant to the electric meter. To this day, most U.S. companies are regulated by state governments as legal monopolies. In many other countries, national and state governments took over their electric utility systems, viewing them as strategic industries that are too important to be left to the vagaries of the marketplace. These huge, centrally planned entities seemed to reflect the economic visions of Lenin rather than Adam Smith, yet for decades these utilities succeeded in building large, reliable power systems while cutting prices.[41]

Like the energy sources and technologies to which they are tied, these economic structures have remained largely intact for much of the twentieth century. They have justified their gargantuan size as a means to the end of exploiting economies of scale. According to Rockefeller's logic, high-volume, low-cost production required large, sure markets, which led to vertical integration—and limited competition.[42]

The energy system that is now emerg-

ing follows a different economic logic, one closer to the precepts of the information age. Under this economic paradigm, new machines and methods are once again being invented, while companies are restructured. Numerous mainstream energy companies, including British Petroleum (BP, in solar energy), Enron (solar energy and wind power), and General Electric (fuel cells and micro turbines), are investing in these technologies. It remains to be seen whether these new devices will eventually be controlled by a dominant group of companies, or whether a more open, competitive economic model will prevail.[43]

Decades of public ownership in the energy sector have already been swept aside in many countries in the 1990s, fostering a period of unprecedented competition, innovation, and diversity in energy-related industries. Echoing the chaotic early days of the oil industry, the energy business is once more opening up to a new generation of entrepreneurs selling revolutionary new devices, such as fuel cells, and services, such as the efficient use of combined heat and power, or cogeneration. (See Table 2–2.) National oil companies are being "privatized"; fuel prices are being decontrolled; and the electric power industry, which has for most of the century been a government-owned or regulated monopoly nearly everywhere, is being radically restructured in dozens of countries.[44]

"Independent power producers," a new breed of largely unregulated power suppliers, are increasingly dominating the business in countries such as the United Kingdom and the United States, but they are also being welcomed by governments in developing countries where many electric utilities are bankrupt and unable to keep up with demand growth. There are now more than 300 independent power companies, and they are growing particularly rapidly in Asia and Latin America. Firms once limited to regions or countries

Table 2–2. Energy "Microsofts"

Company (Country)	Technology	Start-up Date	Capitalization (million dollars)
Ballard (Canada)	Fuel cells	1979	2,360
Vestas (Denmark)	Wind turbines	1987	204
Trigen Energy (United States)	Cogeneration	1986	182
Energy Conversion Devices (United States)	Solar PV cells Electric batteries	1960	74
Solectria (United States)	Electric vehicles	1989	n.a.

SOURCE: Discussions with company representatives, and annual reports at their respective Web sites.

are building power plants all over the world, with natural gas turbines the technology of choice. A more competitive power industry is also likely to diversify its generation base quickly, developing new decentralized generators that are located in customers' buildings. The businesses best positioned to compete in this market may turn out to be firms that already sell air-conditioning and energy control services to commercial building owners. Some energy service companies now sign contracts to provide customers with a full range of heat, refrigeration, and power—in part by upgrading windows, lighting, air-conditioning, and other systems.[45]

Changing market conditions have also spawned a new breed of "virtual utilities" that meet customers' energy needs without owning any of the assets involved. Such companies are essentially intermediaries—firms that bring together a range of assets to meet needs, free of having to protect an array of earlier investments. Energy consultant Karl Rábago, who helped pioneer the concept, describes the virtual utility as "nimble and fleet of foot, less encumbered with physical assets, exploiting its intelligence and capabilities, embracing change and delivering outstanding customer satisfaction."[46]

A variant of the virtual utility, the "green power" supplier, has emerged in the last few years. These companies—taking advantage of the opening of retail electricity markets and many consumers' disdain for electricity generated from coal or nuclear power—offer customers the option of purchasing power generated from wind, geothermal, or biomass energy. While some of the half-dozen companies that have entered the market in California are subsidiaries of utilities, others are new firms that own no actual power plants—and whose employees are often thousands of miles from the market. Instead, they are energy brokers, linking windfarm owners with electricity customers willing to pay a little more each month to help keep the air clean. Though the green power market is growing slowly at first, surveys suggest strong consumer interest in the concept—and businesses like Toyota have already signed up.[47]

Ever since the nineteenth century, energy trends have been dictated in part by a complicated dance between industries and governments, with the former seeking economic gain and convenience and the latter focusing on strategic, social, and environmental concerns that the market is prone to neglect. The U.S. government accelerated the rise of coal by subsidizing rail barons during the nineteenth century, for instance, and helped usher in the oil age with contracts to the automobile industry and massive investments in an interstate highway system after World War II.[48]

Although it is popular in some quarters

today to think that energy is rapidly becoming the pure province of the private sector, this seems unlikely. Much of the energy industry is still government-owned or regulated in many countries, and a host of unresolved social and environmental issues will require a guiding— though relatively light—governmental hand. As governments retreat from direct ownership of power companies, they will be in a better position to encourage greater reliance on cleaner energy sources by using both regulations and financial incentives. Just as financial regulators are required to have a functioning stock market, so is a degree of regulation essential if we are to have a sustainable energy market. Governments are responsible, for example, for setting the rules for grid interconnection of generators, supervising price-setting on monopoly power lines, and requiring adequate disclosure of the sources and emissions associated with power that is being sold.[49]

Another energy-related industry in which growing competition is being influenced by government policies is the automobile business. Decisions by the state government in California in 1992 to mandate zero-emission vehicles and by the U.S. government in 1993 to form a coalition with the Big Three automakers to pursue a new generation of technologies have spurred faster innovation in the industry than at any time since the Model T was introduced. Today, the dozen companies that dominate the global car business are being challenged by a host of venture-capital-fueled start-ups that are designing cars powered by batteries, flywheels, turbines, and fuel cells. Large auto companies have responded with multibillion-dollar efforts to develop the new technologies themselves—and have also begun to form strategic coalitions with some of the high-tech start-ups. One example is the $870-million fuel cell partnership forged between Ballard, a small Canadian company, and the German auto giant Daimler-Benz in 1997. Ballard will supply the new fuel cells, while Daimler will build them into new drive trains, and then assemble and market the cars.[50]

The energy industry of the next century is still in its formative years, and it is not yet clear what kinds of companies will be best able to provide the new technologies and services. Similar to the shift from the mainframe to the personal computer in the early 1980s, the move to a decentralized energy system may make the market dominance of big players like Exxon and GM a thing of the past, as smaller, more versatile players attract more business— just as IBM's control of the computer industry was loosened by Apple and Microsoft. One thing seems likely, however: those hoping to survive the upheaval may need to be, as was said of Rockefeller himself, "always ready to embrace change."[51]

GREAT POWERS, GEOPOLITICAL PRIZES

In his Pulitzer-Prize winning book *The Prize*, historian Daniel Yergin notes an important turning point in the ascendance of petroleum: Lord Winston Churchill's decision in 1911, after years of resistance, to switch Britain's war fleet from coal to oil. Many experts thought the move risky and expensive, but Churchill felt it strategically necessary, as it would provide the speed and power needed to defeat the German navy on the high seas. Within a few years, coal-fueled vessels had become a rarity, as freighters and passenger ships joined the stampede to petroleum.[52]

Energy and geopolitics have become closely intertwined during the past 200 years. The British Empire was buttressed by an Industrial Revolution, which was in turn powered by the heavy use of coal.

The twentieth century, called the American century by some historians, has also been dubbed the century of oil, with its industry and progeny—mass-produced automobiles, spreading suburbs, and ubiquitous plastics—all "made in the USA." Access to petroleum has underlain many of the twentieth century's international conflicts—including the Japanese attack on Pearl Harbor in 1941 and the Persian Gulf war in 1991—and become virtually synonymous with the power balances among western economies, the Middle East, and the developing world.[53]

Governments have taken a strategic interest in the energy industry during the past century for a variety of reasons: advancing national security, reducing oil import reliance, and promoting technological innovation as a means to economic development. In the next century, the climate change battle may assume the kind of strategic importance that wars—both hot and cold—have had during this one. In a call to arms in the journal *Nature* in October 1998, leading scientists argued that global climate change could soon become the environmental equivalent of the cold war. They pointed out that twentieth-century wartime and postwar research and development have produced such advances as commercial aviation, radar, computer chips, lasers, and the Internet. The large-scale deployment of carbon-free energy technologies over the next 50 years, they conclude, may require an international effort conducted with the urgency of the Apollo space program.[54]

Unlike the effort in the 1960s to put a man on the moon, the shift to a new energy system could be led by both public and private sectors. Indeed, there may be a private-sector parallel to Churchill in the unexpected decision of British Petroleum Chairman John Browne to announce, as climate negotiations gathered momentum shortly before the historic Kyoto conference in 1997, that his company now took climate change seri-

ously and would step up its investments in solar energy. Like Churchill, Browne was at first ridiculed by colleagues. But the months following the Kyoto agreement witnessed a string of industry announcements of new partnerships, investments, and breakthroughs in new energy technologies. John Smith, Chairman of General Motors, surprised observers at the 1998 Detroit Auto Show when he proclaimed that "no car company will be able to thrive in the twenty-first century if it relies solely on internal-combustion engines."[55]

In October 1998, leading scientists argued that global climate change could soon become the environmental equivalent of the cold war.

National governments are themselves beginning to formulate energy-related responses to the climate challenge, many of them eschewing highly prescriptive "command-and-control" regulation in favor of market incentives. Governments in Europe are setting standards for connecting small-scale power generators to the local electric system, and determining the appropriate price—based on economic as well as environmental costs—to be paid for the power. Other governments, including those in China and the United Kingdom, are improving the efficiency of energy markets by getting rid of tens of billions of dollars of subsidies to fossil fuels, while Denmark and Sweden are taxing carbon emissions as a way to "internalize" environmental costs, encouraging private energy users to make decisions based on the full costs of their actions.[56]

The end of the hydrocarbon century could redraw a set of international fault lines that have sharply defined the past few decades. Oil is unevenly distributed, yielding disproportionate power to those with access to these concentrated stocks—particularly the United States, Russia, and the Middle East. But as petroleum is seen less as a "prize" and more as a dangerous dependence, western economies may become less reliant on Middle Eastern oil, and less focused on political developments in the region. The possibility that the world economy could be thrown into another crisis—today, more than half the world's oil is traded internationally—might also be diminished.[57]

A solar-hydrogen economy would be based on resources that are more abundant and more evenly distributed. Some countries are better endowed than others: Mexico, India, and South Africa are particularly well positioned to deploy solar energy, while Canada, China, and Russia have especially large wind resources. But although some countries could export renewably generated electricity or hydrogen, few are likely to depend mainly on imports. The international energy balance might be more like the world food economy today, where some countries are net exporters and others importers, but the majority produce most of their own food. In other words, energy would become a more "normal" commodity, one not constantly on the verge of international crisis.[58]

Since renewable energy resources are relatively evenly spread, leadership in the new industries is less likely to go to countries with the most resources than to those with the know-how, skilled labor force, openness to innovation, efficient financial structures, and strategic foresight to position themselves for the new era. Today, it is the world's three leading technological powers—Germany, Japan, and the United States—that are ahead in the development of many of the key devices. But nations need not be large or powerful to find a strategic niche, as demonstrated by Denmark's preeminence in wind power today. More than half the global wind power market is now supplied by Danish firms or licensees—an achievement made possible by a two-decade-long strategic partnership between government and industry.[59]

The conditions for an energy transition are particularly ripe in developing countries, most of which are far better endowed with renewable energy sources than with fossil fuels. Most of these countries have embryonic energy systems and massively underserved populations, and therefore represent a potentially far larger market for innovative technologies. Developing nations are in position to bypass or "leapfrog" the twentieth-century systems that are quickly becoming outdated—and several of them, including Costa Rica, the Dominican Republic, and South Africa, have already plunged ahead with some of the new technologies. Given their large populations and surging energy demands, China and India are especially well positioned to become leading centers of the next energy system. This could mean a reversal in the flow of initiative and innovation between East and West—and could perhaps precipitate a broader shift in the world's economic and political center of gravity back to where it was a millennium ago: Asia. In the New World, Brazil, with its vast supplies of renewable resources, could also become a major player.[60]

The relatively diffuse nature of renewable energy sources, and the need to accelerate their use worldwide, might help diminish international conflict and stimulate cooperation. The evolution of the energy system may be determined less by OPEC cartels and struggles over oil leases than by the ongoing international negotiations to protect the climate, as "de-carbonizing" the world economy becomes a greater "geopolitical imperative," yielding its own prizes. One small country that has already made such a strategic move is Iceland. In 1997 the small nation's Prime Minister announced a plan to convert Iceland to a "hydrogen economy" within 15 to 20 years; the government is working with Daimler-Benz and Ballard Power Systems to shift its fishing fleet to hydrogen, and its motor vehicle fleet to methanol and hydrogen. Icelandic officials are also exploring the prospects for exporting hydrogen to other countries.[61]

ENERGY AND SOCIETY

In medieval Europe, feudal lords derived most of their wealth and privilege from their control over land, forests, and water courses. Peasant farmers were unable to grind their own grain, and so had no choice but to sell it unmilled to their landlords at a low price. But the lords did not own the wind, and when windmills were introduced in Europe in the twelfth century, a struggle ensued over whether the farmers would be able to build their own windmills and use this previously untapped and "free" energy source.[62]

The peasant farmers eventually won this test of wills, and their struggle is a reminder that energy has long been closely tied to questions of power, wealth, and equity. The energy system that has developed in industrial nations over the past century has led to a new generation of societal disparities as well as serious environmental problems. The question today is whether societies can use a new generation of revolutionary technologies and practices to overturn the existing order, just as windmills undermined the power of the aristocracy in the Middle Ages.[63]

One legacy of the fossil fuel economy is an unprecedented concentration of economic wealth. Four offshoots of Rockefeller's Standard Oil are among the world's 50 largest companies. And measured by 1997 revenues, the two giant automakers—General Motors and Ford—are the world's largest corporations, with Toyota among the top 10. (See Table 2–3.) GM's 1997 revenues of $178 billion exceeded the combined national economies of Bolivia, Chile, Ecuador, and Peru. In terms of sheer size, multinational suppliers of electrical equipment—ABB, General Electric, Mitsubishi, Siemens—are among the world's largest. In personal terms, five of the world's

Table 2–3. World's 12 Largest Corporations, 1997[1]

Company	1997 Revenues (billion dollars)	Industry
General Motors	*178*	*Automobile*
Ford Motor Company	*154*	*Automobile*
Mitsui & Co., Ltd.	143	Trading
Mitsubishi Corporation	*129*	*Trading (including automobile)*
Royal Dutch/Shell Group	*128*	*Energy*
Itochu Corporation	127	Trading
Exxon Corporation	*122*	*Energy*
Wal-Mart Stores, Inc.	119	General Merchandise
Marubeni Corporation	111	Trading
Sumitomo Corporation	102	Trading
Toyota Motor Corporation	*95*	*Automobile*
General Electric Company	*91*	*Electric power*

[1]Energy, automobile, and electric power companies are indicated by italics.
SOURCE: *Fortune Magazine*, "The Global 500 List," <http://www.pathfinder.com/fortune/global500/index.html>, viewed 26 August 1998.

wealthiest individuals are sheiks, sultans, or princes who have profited from the twentieth-century oil boom.[64]

Today's energy regime has also heavily concentrated political clout. Oil, coal, automobile, and electric utility trade associations are among the world's most heavily funded and influential lobbies. Through groups like the Global Climate Coalition, multinationals can—in near anonymity—finance misleading advertising campaigns, defend outdated subsidies, and fight international treaties. Like their lordly predecessors, German electric utilities campaign to repeal the government policy that has enabled wind turbines to spread across the country.[65]

Meeting the needs of the 2 billion people who do not have modern fuels or electricity might become a new social imperative.

But such "fronts" are slowly losing influence. Some prominent oil companies have broken off from their fossil fuel brethren who oppose the climate treaty, while others have joined progressive business groups that lobby for change. And in Bonn, German environmentalists organized a large protest in 1997 that succeeded in staving off opposition to government supports for renewable energy. Meanwhile, those with a possible stake in a new energy system—energy efficiency, renewable energy, and insurance companies—are beginning to mobilize and fight for changes in government policy.[66]

Over time, shifting to a decentralized energy system may help distribute revenues more equitably and devolve decisionmaking to the regional or local level. Danish wind power promotion is based on a decentralized, community-based

model in which the machines are built by local companies, financed by local bankers, and owned and installed by local farmers. Unlike traditional large energy projects carried out by corporations based halfway around the world, the Danish approach has raised incomes and created jobs within communities. With the current financial system biased toward large-scale, centralized projects, special efforts are required if communities are to obtain the financing needed to put a new system in place.[67]

In addition to concentrating wealth and power, today's fossil-fuel-based system has engendered large imbalances in energy use and social well-being. Its benefits have not been extended to roughly 2 billion of the world's poor—a third of global population—who still rely on biomass for cooking and lack access to electricity. Today, the richest fifth of humanity consumes 58 percent of the world's energy, while the poorest fifth uses less than 4 percent. The United States, with 5 percent of the world's population, uses nearly one quarter of global energy supplies; on a per capita basis, it consumes twice as much energy as Japan and 12 times as much as China.[68]

A more decentralized, renewable-resource-based energy system may have a better chance of spreading energy services more broadly. In fact, meeting the needs of the 2 billion people who do not have modern fuels or electricity and of another 2 billion who are badly underserved might become a new social imperative—akin to the push to electrify rural areas of the United States in the 1930s. Providing clean, advanced energy services would stimulate development in the poorer regions of the world, provide rural employment, and lessen the burden of daily wood gathering that now falls on hundreds of millions of women and children. The World Bank, which has devoted tens of billions of dollars to electrifying cities using central power plants over the past several decades, has recently undertaken a range of initiatives intended to provide decentralized, renewable power supplies to hundreds of millions of rural people.[69]

Even with a shift to more energy-efficient technologies that rely on renewable resources, societies will have to confront basic consumption patterns in order to make the energy economy sustainable. In the United States, the energy efficiency gains of the past quarter-century have been overwhelmed by escalating consumer demand for energy services. U.S. per capita energy use neared its previous 1973 peak in the late 1990s, with gasoline use per person already at record levels. Increased driving, sports utility vehicles, larger homes, and "killer kitchens" with all the latest energy-hungry appliances have created an insatiable appetite for fuel.[70]

The mass consumer culture of twentieth-century North America—and to a slightly lesser extent, Europe and Japan—has been predicated on a "high-energy society" that has viewed inexpensive, abundant energy as something of a constitutional right. But Americans' energy-intensive lifestyles, and the U.S.-led global energy consumption trend of the past century—a 10-fold increase, with a quadrupling since 1950—cannot possibly be a sustainable model for a population of more than 9 billion in the twenty-first century. (See Figure 2–5.)[71]

It will be far easier to meet the energy needs of the world in coming years if sufficiency replaces profligacy as the ethic of the next energy paradigm. This will require a breakthrough not so much in science or technology as in values and lifestyles. Modest changes, such as owning smaller cars and homes, or driving less and cycling more, would still leave us with lifestyles that are luxurious by historical standards but that are far more compatible with an energy system that can be sustained. Several studies show that societies that focus less on absolute consumption and more on improving human welfare

can meet development goals with much lower energy requirements. Russia, for example, has higher per capita energy use but far lower living standards than Japan, whose economic success of the 1970s and 1980s was greatly assisted by its "delinking" of energy use and development.[72]

The energetic challenge facing humanity is not unlike that confronting Russians a decade ago: creating a decentralized, demand-oriented system when a centrally planned, consumption-oriented economy has been the industrial norm for three generations. Like the Soviet system, the fossil-fuel-based model is losing authority as people become more aware of its negative social and environmental effects and the constrained choices that it offers. And like the reform movements that swept Central Europe in 1989, the new energy system must be built from the bottom up, by the actions of millions, through democratization of the energy decisionmaking process. Only through the efforts of a diverse cast of characters—activists protesting air pollution, consumers seeking lower energy bills, villagers demanding power, and industry captains pursuing profits—are societies likely to build a sustainable energy system.[73]

Trillion Tons of Oil Equivalent

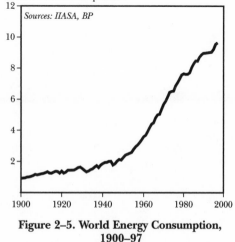

Figure 2–5. World Energy Consumption, 1900–97

Designing a new energy system suitable for the twenty-first century may help reestablish the positive but too often neglected connections between energy, human well-being, and the environment. Rather than treat energy as a commodity to be consumed without regard for its consequences, we might instead recover a much older notion of energy as something to be valued, saved, and used to meet our needs in ways that respect the realities of the natural world—thereby avoiding the kind of ecological catastrophe that has befallen civilizations that overdrew their environmental endowments. The sooner we can bring the fleeting hydrocarbon era to a close and accomplish the historic shift to a civilization based on the efficient use of renewable energy and hydrogen, the sooner we can stop drawing down the natural inheritance of future generations and begin investing in a livable planet.[74]

Utopian dreams, borne of societal mores, are hallmarks of energy futurism. In turn-of-the-century America, oil was described as "black gold," and automobiles were depicted as a cure for urban woes. At the 1893 Chicago World's Fair—itself a Utopian exposition—electricity had already become a symbol of the coming century, a marvel to be spread throughout the country as a near-religious crusade. Together with lightweight metals and high-speed trains, it was one of the three most-cited technological marvels in the 160 Utopian novels that blanketed the United States between 1888 and 1900. In the most famous of these, Edward Bellamy's *Looking Backward*, the main character travels to an America in the year 2000 where "electricity…takes the place of all fires and lighting."[75]

The pursuit of energy Utopia could soon be revived, as a host of innovations once again provide glimpses of a better future. But these wonders represent more than technological solutions. They also symbolize a broader vision—formed by old values and new choices—of creating an energy system that brings billions of people into the light, treats energy as a means to a social end, and heeds the requirements of the natural systems that make life on Earth possible. Such a vision might yet inspire us to make the next energy transition before it is too late—much as the quest for "black gold" drove our predecessors to accomplish the last great transformation.

3

Forging a Sustainable Materials Economy

including recycling...

Gary Gardner and Payal Sampat

Imagine a truck delivering to your house each morning all the materials you use in a day, excluding food and fuel. Piled at the front door are the wood in your newspaper, the chemicals in your shampoo, and the plastic in the bags that carry your groceries home. Metal in your appliances and your car—just that day's share of those items' total lives—are also included, as is your daily fraction of shared materials, such as the stone and gravel in your office walls and in the streets you stroll. At the base of the pile are materials you never see, including the nitrogen and potash used to grow your food, and the earth and rock under which your metals and minerals were once buried.

If you are an average American, this daily delivery is a burdensome load: at 101 kilos, it is roughly the weight of a large man. But your materials tally has only begun. Tomorrow, another 101 kilos arrives, and the next day, another. By

month's end, you have used 3 tons of material, and over the year, 37 tons. And your 270 million compatriots are doing the same thing, day in and day out. Together, you will devour almost 10 billion tons of material in a year's time.[1]

Americans, Europeans, and Japanese use far greater quantities of materials today than their ancestors did in the nineteenth century—and far more than people in developing countries do today. More metal, glass, wood, cement, and chemicals have been used since the turn of the century than in any previous era. Industrial nations are responsible for most of this: Americans alone use about a third of the materials that churn through the global economy. Such excessive consumption is not required to deliver the services people want, yet the material-intensive economic model is still used or pursued in most of the world. Indeed, the widespread human appetite for materials has defined this century in much the same way that stone, bronze, and iron did previous eras.[2]

An expanded version of this chapter appeared as Worldwatch Paper 144, *Mind Over Matter: Recasting the Role of Materials in Our Lives.*

Material use this century has been distinctive for two more reasons. Materials became increasingly complex: today's stock, for example, draws from all 92 naturally occurring elements in the periodic table, compared with just 20 or so at the turn of the century. This allowed materials scientists to move well beyond the classic material forms of wood, ceramics, and metals, but it also made recycling difficult and introduced unprecedented toxicity to human and natural habitats. In addition, waste was generated at far greater rates than in any previous era. Even late in this century, when interest in recycling has surged, most materials moving through industrial economies are used only once, and then thrown away.[3]

The features that made this century materially unique also brought unprecedented damage to human and environmental health. Mining has contaminated thousands of kilometers of rivers and streams in the United States alone, and logging threatens vital habitat, often of endangered species. Air and water pollution from manufacturing plants have sickened millions, often shortening lives. Some of the 100,000 synthetic chemicals introduced this century are a ticking time bomb, affecting the reproductive systems of animals and humans even a generation after initial exposure. And the effort to make waste disappear—by burying it, burning it, or dumping it in the ocean—has generated greenhouse gases, dioxin, toxic leakage, and other threats to environmental and human health.[4]

Given the record of this century, an extraterrestrial observer might conclude that conversion of raw materials to wastes—often toxic ones—is the real purpose of human economic activity. Fortunately, such archaic wastefulness offers ample room for radical reductions in materials use. Indeed, researchers and policymakers are exploring ways to reduce by 90 percent or more the materials that flow through industrial

economies, as well as the burden that these flows have imposed on the natural environment. This will require an imaginative rethinking of how to deliver the services that people want. But it also offers the potential to bring economies into harmony with the natural world that supports them.

CONSTRUCTING A MATERIAL CENTURY

The intensive use of materials this century has deep historical roots. Since the Industrial Revolution, advances in technology and changes in society and in business practices have fed on each other and built economies that could extract, process, consume, and dispose of tremendous quantities of materials. The roots of this evolution extend back centuries, but most of these trends have matured only in the last 100 years.[5]

Production of iron, the emblematic material of the Industrial Revolution, illustrates how technological advances fed materials use. In 1879, a British police clerk and his chemist cousin invented a process for making high-quality steel—a harder and more durable alloy of iron—from any grade of iron ore, eliminating the need for phosphorus-free ore. This process cut steelmaking costs by some 80–90 percent and drove demand skyward: between 1870 and 1913, iron ore production in Britain, Germany, and France multiplied 83-fold. Further innovations and robust demand led to a sixfold increase in world production between 1913 and 1995. Today, iron and steel account for 85 percent of world metals, and a tenth, by weight, of world materials production.[6]

Similarly, new extractive technologies made it possible to mine metal from relatively poor veins, a practice known as "low-grading." In 1900, for example, it was not feasible to extract copper from ore that contained less than 3 percent of the metal. But technological advances have lowered the extraction threshold to less than 0.5 percent, increasing the number of sites at which mining is viable. Low-grading is one reason that the copper industry was able to meet the 22-fold growth in demand for copper from the automobile, electrical, and other industries since 1900. Likewise, modern mining and logging equipment have made it easy to reduce tracts of forests into evenly chopped lumber in a matter of hours, or to shear off mountaintops to reach mineral deposits.[7]

Meanwhile, transportation and energy developments greased the wheels of the materials boom. Completion of the Canadian Pacific Railway in 1905, for instance, laid open the country's rich western provinces to mineral exploitation, while locomotives later helped empty Liberian mines of iron ore that was sent to Europe. And throughout the century, the cheap availability of oil—a better performing fuel than coal or wood—made materials production more economical than ever. Declining costs for energy and raw materials fueled expansion in industrial scale and kept the cycle of exploration and production in constant motion.[8]

Perhaps the most powerful stimulus to materials extraction throughout the century has been the economic incentives that governments offered to producers. An 1872 U.S. law, for example—which regrettably is still in effect—gives miners title to federal mining land for just $12 per hectare ($5 an acre), charging no fees for metals extracted from these holdings. The title also allows the miner to build homes, graze cattle, extract timber, and divert water on this land for no extra fee. This century, governments in all parts of the world—including Indonesia, Ghana, and Peru—have intro-

duced similar incentives, including tax breaks to attract mining and logging companies. These policies are typically uneconomical: the U.S. government still spends more in building logging roads than it earns from timber sales.[9]

An extraterrestrial observer might conclude that conversion of raw materials to wastes is the real purpose of human economic activity.

Subsidized access to materials and energy, combined with technological advances, increased the scale of industry and prompted new ways of organizing and managing production. Inspired by the use of standard, interchangeable parts to facilitate large-scale musket production in the early nineteenth century, Henry Ford adopted the concept of mass production in his automobile factories. Ford's moving assembly line and standardized components slashed production time per chassis from 12.5 hours in 1913 to 1.5 hours in 1914. Costs also fell: a Ford Model T cost $600 in 1912 but just $265 in 1923, bringing car ownership within reach of many more consumers. And Ford's total output jumped from 4 million cars in 1920 to 12 million in 1925, accounting for about half of all cars made in the world at the time. Soon these mass production principles were adopted by manufacturers of refrigerators, radios, and other consumer goods, with similar results.[10]

As the scale of production ballooned, demographic shifts and new business strategies created a market to match it. The U.S. and European labor force became increasingly urbanized, middle-class, and salaried in the first third of the century, characteristics that facilitated the creation of a consumer class. Business initiatives encouraged and capitalized on these trends, with Henry Ford once again a leader. In 1914 Ford introduced a daily wage of $5—more than twice the going rate—thereby augmenting his workers' spending power. He also reduced working hours, believing, in the words of one analyst, that "an increase in leisure time would support an increase in consumer spending, not least on automobiles and automobile travel." Other employers vociferously opposed shorter workdays, but conceded increases in pay for the same reason Ford did: to prompt consumer spending.[11]

Prospering workers and their families quickly became the targets of sophisticated marketing efforts. Department stores and mail-order catalogs funneled a wealth of goods to the consumer, and consumer credit made those goods affordable: by the end of the 1920s, 60 percent of cars, radios, and furniture were being purchased on credit. Clever strategies were also used to boost sales: in the 1920s General Motors introduced annual model changes for its cars, playing on consumers' desires for social status and novelty. Meanwhile, advertisers used insights from the new field of psychology to ensure that consumers were "never satisfied," in the words of a DuPont vice-president, linking the consumer's identity to products. The ability of advertising to influence purchasing decisions propelled global advertising spending over the century, reaching $435 billion in 1996. As people in developing countries have prospered in recent years, advertising spending has grown rapidly there too: by more than 1,000 percent in China between 1986 and 1996, 600 percent in Indonesia, and 300 percent in Malaysia and Thailand.[12]

Increasingly wealthy industrial nations invested heavily in materials research, prompting the development of new and versatile materials. Smelting of aluminum was subsidized for use in tanks, bombers, and fighter planes during World War II. Its use spread quickly to consumer products after the war, even for low-value household items like soda cans, boosting aluminum production 3,000-fold this century. Plastic, too, quickly became popular, growing sixfold worldwide since 1960 as a seemingly endless array of uses were found for it. And growth in the use of synthetic chemicals this century is nothing short of spectacular. More than 100,000 new chemical compounds have been developed since the 1930s, many of them for use during World War II, boosting synthetic chemicals production 1,000-fold in the last 60 years in the United States alone.[13]

These new materials often replaced traditional ones—plastic for metal, for example—leading to lighter products. But the materials savings from "lightweighting" were nearly always offset by increased consumption, especially as military suppliers turned their energies to consumer goods after World War II. The share of Japanese households with refrigerators grew from 5 to 93 percent in the 1960s, for instance. And global ownership of cars grew 10-fold between 1950 and today. Cars are an especially materials-intensive product, claiming a full one third of U.S. iron and steel, a fifth of its aluminum, and two thirds of its lead and rubber use.[14]

Automobile use was facilitated by—and drove—the expansion of roads, houses, and other infrastructure after mid-century. This construction boom prompted an eightfold increase in global cement production between 1957 and 1995, and a tripling of asphalt output worldwide since 1950. One third of this asphalt was poured into the giant U.S. network of interstate highways. Where this infrastructure supported extensive rather than intensive development, as in U.S. suburbs, more sewers, bridges, building foundations, houses, and telephone cables were needed to service a given number of people.[15]

By the late 1960s, a materials countertrend—recycling—began to develop in step with growing environmental awareness. The practice was not new: strategic materials were recycled during World War II, and organic material has been composted for centuries. But an attempt to root the practice more widely encountered difficulty, because industrial economies had long been tooled to depend on virgin materials, and markets could not easily absorb recyclable materials. Despite these deep-rooted obstacles, growth in recycling has been steady: in industrial countries, the share of paper and cardboard recycled grew from an average 30 percent in 1980 to 40 percent by the mid-1990s. Glass recycling levels rose from less than 20 percent to about 50 percent in the same period. And the share of U.S. metals consumption met by recycling rose from 33 percent in 1970 to almost 50 percent in 1998.[16]

Increased recycling, however, has not dampened the growth in world materials use. The developing world continues to industrialize, and more affluent nations show no sign of reducing overall materials consumption. In 1995, nearly 10 billion tons of materials—industrial and construction minerals, metals, wood products, and synthetic materials—entered the global economy. This is more than twice as much as in 1963, the first year for which global data are available for all major categories. (See Table 3–1 and Figure 3–1.) Global data for a true total of materials use—including the billions of tons that never entered the economy but were left at mine sites or smelters—would more than double this total.[17]

Production trends in the last half-century have varied by material and region. Fossil-fuel-based materials, led by plastics, have grown at more than twice the pace of other major materials categories since 1960, largely because of their light weight, versatility, and cheap availability. Metals

Table 3–1. Growth in World Materials Production, 1960–95

Material	Production in 1995[1]	Increase Over Early 1960s[2]
	(million tons)	(factor of change)
Minerals[3]	7,641	2.5-fold
Metals	1,196	2.1-fold
Wood Products[3]	724	2.3-fold
Synthetics[4]	252	5.6-fold
All Materials	9,813	2.4-fold

[1]Marketable production only; does not include hidden flows. [2]Minerals and total materials data are for 1963; forest products data are for 1961. [3]Nonfuel. [4]Fossil-fuel-based.
SOURCE: See endnote 17.

grew at a slower pace, but substantially nonetheless: globally, metals production doubled between 1920 and 1950, and has quadrupled since mid-century. The use of wood products has marched steadily upward since 1961 (see also Chapter 4), but in industrial nations the trend is more complex: wood has been replaced by other materials in many cases, but paper production has surged.[18]

Perhaps the greatest variation this century is found across regions. The United

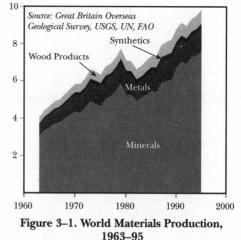

Figure 3–1. World Materials Production, 1963–95

States was the materials behemoth this century, towering above every other nation in its appetite for raw materials of all kinds. (See Table 3–2.) Its 18-fold increase in materials consumption since 1900 is globally important in two ways. First, the United States has accounted for a dominating share of the world total, some 43 percent in 1963 and 30 percent in 1995. And its economic and ideological power has made the high-consumption, materials-intensive economic model the desired development path for dozens of countries and billions of people around the world.[19]

Today residents of Brazil, Chile, and South Korea buy new television sets at rates comparable to their industrial-nation counterparts, at about 4–6 sets per 100 individuals each year. In China, purchases of refrigerators, washing machines, and television sets rose 8–40 times between 1981 and 1985—reminiscent of Japan's consumer goods rush in the 1960s. On the whole, however, with roughly 20 percent of global population, industrial countries still devour far more materials and products than developing nations—using, for example, 84 percent of the world's paper and 87 percent of the cars each year.[20]

Table 3–2. Growth in U.S. Materials Consumption, 1900–95

Material	Growth	Consumption, 1995
	(factor of change)	(million tons)
Minerals[1]	29-fold	2,410
Wood Products[1]	3-fold	170
Metals	14-fold	132
Synthetics[2]	82-fold	131
All Materials	18-fold	2,843

[1]Nonfuel. [2]Fossil-fuel-based.

SOURCE: Data supplied by Grecia Matos, Minerals and Materials Analysis Section, United States Geological Survey, Reston, VA, 27 July 1998.

THE SHADOW SIDE OF CONSUMPTION

In the early 1990s, researchers at the University of British Columbia began to measure the land area needed to supply national populations with resources (including imported ones), and the area needed to absorb their wastes. They dubbed this combined area the "ecological footprint" of a population. In some countries, the United States among them, the footprint is larger than the nation's area, because of a net dependence on imports or because resources or waste absorption capacity are overexploited. Indeed, the researchers determined that sustaining the entire world at an American or Canadian level of resource use would require the land area of three Earths. Materials use strongly influences the size of a population's footprint: in the U.S. case, materials are conservatively estimated to account for more than a fifth of the total footprint area. (Fossil fuel use and food production are other major components.) And other research implicates materials even more heavily. When measured by weight, materials account for 44 percent of the U.S. resource use, 58 percent in the case of Japan, and as much as 68 percent of Germany's resource burden.[21]

More direct evidence of the unsustainability of today's material flows is found in the environmental damage done by materials extraction, processing, and disposal. Demand for wood and paper products—from construction lumber to packaging material to newsprint—continues to strip forests, with serious environmental consequences. Indeed, the World Resources Institute estimates that logging for wood products threatens more than 70 percent of the world's large intact virgin forests. And in many parts of the world, single-species timber plantations have replaced old-growth forests—eroding species diversity, introducing toxic insecticides, and displacing local peoples.[22]

Healthy forests provide vital ecosystem services, including erosion control, provision of water across rainy and dry seasons, and regulation of rainfall. The loss of these services can devastate local watersheds, as China learned in 1998, when deforestation reduced the capacity of hillsides to hold water, leaving the Yangtze River basin vulnerable to the worst flooding in more than 40 years. Forests also provide habitat to a diverse selection of plant and animal life; tropical forests, for example, are home to more than 50 percent of the world's species. The impact of the loss of these vital ecosystems was underlined in 1998 when a majority of biologists polled in the United States agreed that the world is in the midst of a mass extinction, the first since dinosaurs died out 65 million years ago. The connection between these environmental calamities and the surging demand for wood and paper products—especially in industrial countries—is increasingly difficult to ignore.[23]

Mineral and metals extraction also leaves a lasting and damaging environmental footprint. Mining requires removing from the earth both metal-bearing rock, called ore, and overburden, the dirt and rock that covers the ore. Very little of this material is used: some 110 tons of "overburden" earth and an equal amount of ore are excavated to produce just a ton of copper. (See Table 3–3.) Not surprisingly, the quantities of waste generated are enormous: Canada's mining wastes are 58 times greater than its urban refuse. Indeed, few newlyweds would guess that their two gold wedding rings were responsible for six tons of waste at a mining site in Nevada or Kyrgyzstan. These mind-boggling movements of material now exceed that of natural systems: mining alone strips more of the Earth's surface each year than the natural erosion by rivers.[24]

Mines use toxic chemicals, including

Table 3–3. World Ore and Waste Production for Selected Metals, 1995

Metal	Ore Mined	Share of Ore That Becomes Waste[1]
	(million tons)	(percent)
Iron	25,503	60
Copper	11,026	99
Gold[2]	7,235	99.99967
Lead	1,077	97.5
Aluminum	856	70

[1] Does not include overburden.   [2]1997 data.
SOURCE: See endnote 24.

cyanide, mercury, and sulfuric acid, to separate metal from ore. Tailings, the toxin-laced ore that remains once the metal is separated, are often dumped directly into lakes or rivers, with devastating consequences. Tailings from the Ok Tedi mine in Papua New Guinea, for instance, have decimated the fish, crocodiles, crustaceans, and turtles that once thrived in the 70 kilometers of the Ok Tedi River downstream. Moreover, the mining wastes have changed the course of the river, which now floods riverside farms with poisonous waters. And damage to the watershed has disrupted the health and livelihoods of the indigenous Wopkamin people.[25]

Toxic meltdowns can occur even when tailings are contained rather than dumped. In 1998, a tailings reservoir in Spain collapsed, spewing 5 million cubic meters of mining sludge onto 2,000 hectares of cropland and killing fish and wildlife in the neighboring Doñana National Park, a World Heritage Site. Mining is implicated in the contamination of more than 19,000 kilometers of U.S. rivers and streams, some virtually permanently. The Iron Mountain mine in northern California continues to leach pollutants into nearby streams and the Sacramento River more than 35 years after being closed. Water downstream of the mine is 10,000 times more acidic than car battery acid. The area is now a Superfund site (a high priority for cleanup), but if remediation fails, experts estimate that leaching at present rates will continue for at least 3,000 years before the pollution source is depleted. The U.S.-based Mineral Policy Center estimates that the U.S. government will have to spend $32–72 billion cleaning up the toxic damage left at thousands of abandoned mines across the country.[26]

Industrial activity this century has sent millions of tons of lead, zinc, and copper into the environment; global industrial emissions of lead now exceed natural rates by a factor of 27. The impacts of this pollution are grave: the area within 15 kilometers of old smelters in the former Soviet Union, for example, is entirely devoid of vegetation because of metals contamination. Exposure to mercury, which is widely used by miners in the Amazon Basin and West Africa, increases cancer risk and can damage kidneys and nervous systems. And lead, a neurotoxin, is known to stunt children's intellectual development.[27]

Resource extraction and processing also degrade the environment indirectly. In the United States, materials processing and manufacturing alone claimed 14 percent of the country's energy use in 1994. Most of this energy is generated from the burning of fossil fuels, implicating everyday products in global climate change. In addition, cement production contributes about 5 percent of the world's emissions of carbon, again contributing to climate change.[28]

This century, modern chemistry introduced new synthetic chemicals, often with unknown consequences, into the remotest corners of the world. In 1995, scientists studying the global reach of organochlorine pesticides reported that almost all of those they studied were "ubiquitous on a global scale." Other evidence supports this conclusion: researchers looking for a control population of humans free of chemical contamination turned to the native peoples of the Canadian Arctic, only to find that these remote peoples carried chemical contaminants at levels higher than people who live in St. Lawrence, Canada, the original focus of the research. Chemicals had reached the indigenous people through wind, water, and their food supply.[29]

Part of the reason for this worrying development is that many chemicals cannot be controlled once emitted to the environment. Chlorofluorocarbons, for instance, which were long used as refrigerants and solvents, are implicated in the decay of stratospheric ozone. A large share of pesticides used in agriculture—roughly 85–90 percent—never reach their targets, dispersing instead through air, soil, and water and sometimes settling in the fatty tissues of animals and people.[30]

Many synthetic chemicals are not just ubiquitous but long-lived. Persistent organic pollutants (POPs), including those used in electrical wiring or pesticides, remain active in the environment long after their original purpose is served. Because they are slow to degrade, POPs accumulate in fatty tissues as they are passed up the food chain. They have been shown to disrupt endocrine and reproductive systems—implicated in miniature genitals in Florida alligators, for example—often a generation or more after exposure. The delay in appearance of POPs' health effects raises questions about the wisdom of heavy dependence on tens of thousands of newly synthesized chemicals whose effects are poorly understood. And the long list of unknowns surrounding POPs is just a small indication of our chemical ignorance. The U.S. National Academy of Sciences reports that insufficient information exists for even a partial health assessment of 95 percent of chemicals in the environment.[31]

The dramatic increase since mid-century in another dispersed material, nitrogen fertilizer, along with the increased combustion of fossil fuels, has made humans the planet's leading producers of fixed nitrogen (the form that plants can use), essentially raising the fertility of the planet. But this fertility windfall favors some species at the expense of others. Grasslands in Europe and North America, for instance, are now less biologically diverse as nitrogen deposition has allowed a few varieties—often invasive species—to crowd out many others. And algae blooms in waterways as diverse as the Baltic Sea, the Chesapeake Bay, and the Gulf of Mexico—the result of fertilizer runoff—have led to fish and shrimp kills as algae rob other species of the water's limited supply of oxygen. Scientists are just beginning to comprehend the full effects of disrupting the global flow of nitrogen, one of four major elements (along with carbon, sulfur, and phosphorus) that lubricate essential planetary systems.[32]

Mountains of materials have been discarded this century, typically in the cheapest way possible. In a 1991 waste survey of more than 100 nations by the International Maritime Organization, more than 90 percent of responding countries said that uncontrolled dumping of industrial wastes was a problem. Nearly two thirds said that hazardous industrial waste is disposed of at uncontrolled sites, and nearly a quarter reported dumping industrial waste in the oceans. The casual treatment of industrial waste has had terrible environmental, health, and economic consequences in much of the world. One quarter of the Russian population, for example, reportedly lives in areas where pollution concentrations exceed standards by 10 times. In the United States, some 40,000 locations have been listed as hazardous waste "Superfund" sites, and the Environmental Protection Agency estimates that cleanup of just the 1,400 priority sites will cost $31 billion.[33]

Finally, municipal solid waste—a relatively small, but high-profile waste flow—generates its own set of problems. In developing countries, this material is often dumped at sites near cities, sometimes within congested neighborhoods, where it draws rats and other vermin that pose a health threat to nearby residents. In industrial countries, the material is typically landfilled or incinerated, each of which has environmental consequences. Unless they are lined, for example, landfills often leach acidic juices downward, contaminating groundwater supplies. And rotting organic matter in landfills often generates methane, a greenhouse gas with 21 times the global warming potential of carbon dioxide. Methane is sometimes tapped for energy use, but this is not the typical practice. Landfills are responsible for a third of U.S. methane emissions, and 10 percent of methane emissions from human sources worldwide.[34]

The casual treatment of industrial waste has had terrible environmental, health, and economic consequences.

Incineration, a common disposal method, also carries a long string of liabilities. Municipal waste incinerators are the single largest source of mercury emissions in the northeastern United States, contributing nearly half of all human-induced emissions in that region. And as incineration reduces piles of waste, it increases emissions of dioxin, a POP, and generally concentrates toxicity in the remaining hazardous waste.[35]

As more countries aggressively apply the materials-intensive economic model, episodes of environmental destruction will only multiply. Indeed, if the entire world lived at the materials-intensiveness of the average American, materials use would grow severalfold, and environmental damage would increase at least correspondingly. (See Table 3–4.) In some

Table 3-4. Hypothetical Global Materials Use in 1995, Based on U.S. Per Capita Consumption Levels

Material	Increase If World Consumed at U.S. Levels
	(factor of change)
Minerals[1]	7-fold
Metals	2-fold
Wood Products[1]	5-fold
Synthetics[2]	11-fold
Total	6-fold

[1]Nonfuel. [2]Fossil-fuel-based.

SOURCE: Grecia Matos, Minerals and Materials Analysis Section, USGS, Reston, VA, 27 July 1998; United Nations, *World Population Prospects: The 1996 Revision* (New York: 1996); U.S. Bureau of the Census, *International Data Base*, electronic database, Suitland, MD, updated 15 June 1998.

cases, the increase in damage could outpace the growth in materials use. To cite just one example, as the quality of ore grades declines into the twenty-first century, more waste will be generated per ton of metal mined than was the case 100 years ago.

A MATERIAL REVOLUTION

The environmental problems associated with intensive materials use led to calls in the early 1990s for a "dematerialization" of industrial countries: a reduction in the materials needed to deliver the services people want. Using calculations that show global, human-induced flows of materials to be twice as high as natural flows, German researchers recommended in 1993 that global materials flows be cut in half. But because most developing countries need to increase materials flows just to meet people's basic needs, the researchers concluded that the global reduction in materials use would have to be shouldered by the world's heaviest

consumers, industrial nations. Indeed, by the researchers' estimates, this responsibility implies a 90-percent decrease in materials use by industrial nations over the next half-century.[36]

This bracing estimate is not meant as a prescription for reductions in all types of materials. Some materials, especially toxic ones, may need to be eliminated entirely, while others can be used sustainably at reduction levels short of 90 percent. But the estimate is credible enough to be taken seriously by many officials, especially in Europe. Austria has incorporated a "Factor 10" (90 percent) reduction into its National Environmental Plan, and the Dutch and German governments, along with the Organisation for Economic Co-operation and Development (OECD), have expressed interest in pursuing radical reductions.[37]

How can such monumental gains be achieved? Some would argue that materials reductions will occur naturally as an economy matures. Indeed, since 1970, when global materials use was first tracked, materials use per dollar of gross world product has fallen by 18 percent. While the drop is quite modest—and was entirely canceled by increases in total materials use and materials use per person—the factors that prompted it do offer a foundation for radical reductions in the coming decades.[38]

As with most efficiency increases in industrial economies since the Industrial Revolution, the modest decrease in materials intensity since 1970 was largely an unplanned spinoff of other economic and social developments. In industrial countries, roads, houses, bridges, and other major works of infrastructure were largely completed, lighter materials were substituted for heavier ones, recycling programs kicked into gear, and service companies like banks, restaurants, and insurance companies—whose "products" are less materials-intensive than the goods pumped out by factories—grabbed a larger share of the economy.[39]

Because materials savings was not the goal of these initiatives, however, the incidental gains made to date only hint at the reduction potential. Infrastructure was not designed to last centuries, as castles and cathedrals once were, and had to be replaced more often. Materials gains from lighter products were often offset by other developments, especially increased consumption. (See Table 3–5.) Recycling was limited to materials that were mostly pure and easily collected, and for which a market already existed. And service firms, while not heavy producers of materials, often promote materials use either by trading in or financing it—the case for retailers or financial institutions—or by consuming materials voraciously themselves: the construction industry and water utilities, for example, use enormous quantities of materials. In short, incremental efficiency gains were made, but total materials use continued to climb.[40]

Indeed, it is the absolute levels of materials use that matter from an environmental perspective. Beetles and spider monkeys in South American forests do not care if the trees lost in their habitat were pulped into millions instead of thousands of newspapers. From their perspective, the loss of habitat is not cushioned by the greater efficiency of material use. Decreases in materials intensity,

Table 3–5. Gains in Materials Efficiency of Selected Products and Factors That Undercut Gains

Product	Efficiency Gains	Factors That Undercut Efficiency Gains
Plastics in cars	Use of plastics in U.S. cars increased by 26 percent between 1980 and 1994, replacing steel in many uses, and reducing car weight by 6 percent.	Cars contain 25 chemically incompatible plastics that, unlike steel, cannot be easily recycled. Thus most plastics in cars wind up in landfills.
Bottles and Cans	Aluminum cans weigh 30 percent less today than they did 20 years ago.	Cans replaced an environmentally superior product—refillable bottles; 95 percent of soda containers were refillable in the United States in 1960.
Lead batteries	A typical automobile battery used 30 pounds of lead in 1974, but only 20 pounds in 1994—with improved performance.	U.S. domestic battery shipments increased by 76 percent in the same period, more than offsetting the efficiency gains.
Radial Tires	Radial tires are 25 percent lighter, and last twice as long, as bias-ply tires.	Radial tires are more difficult to retread. Sales of passenger car retreads fell by 52 percent in the United States between 1977 and 1997.
Mobile Phones	Weight of mobile phones was reduced 10-fold between 1991 and 1996.	Subscribers to cellular telephone service jumped more than eightfold in the same period, nearly offsetting the gains from lightweighting. Moreover, the mobile phones did not typically replace older phones, but were additions to a household's phone inventory.

SOURCE: See endnote 40.

while important, are always insufficient if rising consumption offsets them, requiring the continued logging of forests, opening of new mines, and pollution of air and water.

A host of infrequently used goods— lawn mowers, for example—might be provided by a service firm.

Thus, "natural dematerialization" is unlikely to deliver overall reductions in materials use. But even deliberate initiatives may be insufficient, if they do nothing to change existing industrial structures. The OECD estimates that under current market conditions and environmental policies, firms in industrial nations can make profitable reductions in materials (and energy) use of 10–40 percent. It cites a study of 150 businesses in Poland, for example, showing that waste could be reduced by 30 percent just from equipment modernization. While welcome, such reductions would leave industrial systems—with their dependence on virgin materials and massive generation of waste—essentially intact. In the face of a projected 150-percent expansion of the global economy by 2020, and given the need for developing countries to lift themselves out of poverty, revolutionary thinking will be required to achieve overall reductions—not just relative efficiency gains—in materials use.[41]

For this reason, some analysts predict a wholesale remaking of industrial economies. Many use as their model the natural world, and envision economies that operate with little virgin material, that introduce no hazardous materials into the air, soil, or water, and that generate no waste that cannot be used elsewhere in the economy or safely and easily absorbed by the environment. Whether such a systematic overhaul can be fully achieved is unclear, but a series of initiatives could bring such a world much closer to reality.[42]

A key to radical reductions in materials use is to sever its link to economic activity. Perhaps the most revolutionary step in this direction is to shift to a true service economy. Unlike today's service firms, which often fuel materials excesses, low materials throughput would be at the core of a redesigned service economy. Companies would earn their profits not by selling goods (such as washing machines or cars) but by providing the services that goods currently deliver (convenient cleaning of clothes or transportation). They would be responsible for all the materials and products used to provide their services as well as for maintaining those goods and taking them back at the end of their useful lives. Service firms would thus have a strong incentive to make products that last and that are easily repaired, upgraded, dismantled, and reused or recycled.[43]

In effect, many service-provider firms would become lessors rather than sellers of products. The Xerox corporation is a widely cited example. The company now leases most of its office copy machines as part of a redefined mission: to provide document services rather than to sell photocopiers. This arrangement has given the company a strong incentive to maximize the use of its machines; between 1992 and 1997 Xerox doubled the share of copiers that are remanufactured—to 28 percent—a strategy it says kept 30,000 tons of material from returned machines out of landfills in 1997 alone. Each remanufactured machine meets the same standards, and carries the same warranty, as a newly minted one. The company has only begun to implement the program; it expects eventually to boost the remanufactured share of its machines to 84 percent, and the recycled share of its material to 97 percent.[44]

Some services would save on materials by eliminating goods that spend most of their time idle. One study estimates that over a set period, the use of laundry services rather than home washing machines could cut resource use per wash between 10- and 80-fold, depending on how the material is disposed of. If landfilled, for instance, household machines would be 80 times more materials-intensive than commercial laundry machines; if perfectly dismantled and recycled, household machines would still use 10 times more materials per wash. The example also illustrates the power of front-end rather than the end-of-pipe efforts that have characterized recycling to date. While washing may be a function that consumers would prefer to retain in their home (an option that could still be accommodated by a service firm, if the machine were leased), a host of other infrequently used goods—lawn mowers, for example—might be provided by a service firm.[45]

In essence, service providers replace some materials with intelligence or labor. As the computer revolution continues to unfold, digital technology—basically embodied intelligence—can be used to breathe new life into rapidly obsolescent products such as cameras and televisions. By upgrading product capabilities through the replacement of a computer chip, perfectly good casings, lenses, picture tubes, and other components can avoid a premature trip to the landfill. Similarly, labor can be used to extend the useful life of products: service providers need workers to disassemble, repair, and rebuild their leasable goods, saving materials and increasing employment at the same time.

Some questions may need to be resolved before switching to a service economy, however. There may be unanticipated social effects. What happens to low-income people, for example, when the supply of secondhand products dries up as more and more goods become leased? A service economy could take from them a key survival strategy, forcing them to pay monthly lease rates or eliminating their durable goods use altogether. But the subsidies that now aid powerful materials producers—fueling wasteful materials use—might instead finance access to essential services. Another concern is that product leasing might edge out smaller firms in favor of those that vertically integrate product design, manufacture, and repair. Forestalling these inequities is a challenge for societies making the leap to a services economy.[46]

Revamped efforts in recycling offer the possibility of reducing the materials load of a service economy still further. The scope of recycling, for example, is being broadened as products are designed with recycling in mind. Computer cases are now often made with single materials, and use no glues, paints, or composites that might impede recycling. Producers of cars and television sets increasingly build their products for easy disassembly. Xerox's ambitious plan to have 84 percent of its copiers be remanufactured is possible because in 1997 the company shifted to redesigned, easily disassembled machines. Widespread adoption of these "design for environment" initiatives could boost recycling rates economy-wide: today, just 17 percent of these durable goods are recycled in the United States.[47]

With the right incentives, even greater materials reductions are possible. In Germany, a revolutionary packaging waste ordinance that went into effect in early 1993 holds producers accountable for nearly all the packaging material they generate. The new law dramatically increased the rate of packaging recycling, from 12 percent in 1992 to 86 percent in 1997. Plastic collections, for example, jumped nearly 19-fold, from 30,000 tons in 1991 to 567,000 tons in 1997. Better yet, the law gave producers a strong incentive to cut their use of packaging, which dropped 17 percent for households and small businesses between 1991 and 1997. Use of secondary packaging—outer containers like the box around a tube of toothpaste—has especially declined. Several countries, including Austria, France, and Belgium, have adopted similar legislation.[48]

Car-sharing operations in Berlin and Vancouver make cars available to people wo do not own an auto.

Other creative initiatives could expand recycling at the factory level. A cluster of industries in Kalundborg, Denmark, has championed the concept of industrial symbiosis, under which unusable discharges from each factory become inputs to other factories. Warm water from Kalundborg's power plant is used by a nearby fish farm, sludge from the fish farm fertilizes farmland, and fly ash from the power plant is used to make cement. The scheme saves the firms millions of kroner in raw materials costs, and annually diverts more than 1.3 million tons of waste from landfills or ocean dumping as well as some 135,000 tons of carbon and sulfur emissions from the atmosphere. Encouragingly, the concept is not limited to the industrial world. A similar setup in Fiji links together a brewery, a mushroom farm, a chicken raising operation, fish ponds, hydroponic gardens, and a methane gas production unit, all small in scale. Other waste-minimizing efforts are under way in places as diverse as Namibia and North Carolina.[49]

As with recycling and waste reuse, materials efficiency can be imaginatively rethought. If efficiency is measured not just at the factory gate but across the life of a product, characteristics such as dura-

bility and capacity for reuse suddenly become important. For example, doubling the useful life of a car may involve no increase in materials efficiency at the factory, but it cuts in half both the resources used and the waste generated per trip over the car's life—a clear increase in resource efficiency. Recognizing this, many companies are increasing the durability of the products they use. Toyota, for example, shifted to entirely reusable shipping containers in 1991, each with a potential lifetime of 20 years. A similar move at Xerox saved the company $2–5 million annually. Advances like these, expanded economy-wide, would sharply reduce container and packaging waste—which account for some 30 percent of inflows to U.S. landfills.[50]

Product life is also expanded through the remanufacture, repair, and reuse of spent goods. In nearly all cases, these strategies are more materials- and energy-efficient, and generate fewer wastes, than virgin materials production does. And remanufacture and repair options create more jobs than disposing of goods would. The Institute for Local Self-Reliance in Washington, D.C., estimates that computer repair and refurbishing create an estimated 68 times as many jobs as running a landfill does. Labor costs also make repair and remanufacturing expensive, however; an economy-wide shift to this approach would probably require a realignment of the relative costs of capital and labor.[51]

Widespread adoption of these "3R" measures would be a nostalgic step for some consumers. Most grandparents in industrial countries can remember an economy in which milk bottles and other beverage containers were reused, shoes were resoled and clothes mended, and machines were rebuilt. Some may remember that all but two of the U.S. ships sunk at Pearl Harbor were recovered, overhauled, and recommissioned, in part because of the savings in time and material that this option offered. That such practices seem revolutionary to new generations of consumers is a reflection of how far industrial economies have drifted from the careful use of material resources.[52]

Materials substitution can be made safer by introducing strict environmental criteria into substitution strategies. Because the use of nonrenewable materials—especially petrochemicals—is ultimately unsustainable, some analysts maintain that these should be replaced with biomass-based materials, shifting economies from a "hydrocarbon" base to a "carbohydrate" one. Biodegradable materials made from plant starches, oils, and enzymes can replace synthetics and eliminate toxic impacts. Enzymes have replaced phosphates in 90 percent of all detergents in Europe and Japan, and in half of those in the United States. Vegetable oils can replace mineral oils in paints and inks: three out of four American daily newspapers now use soy-based, biodegradable inks. And starch or sugar can substitute for petroleum in making plastics.[53]

The feasibility of such a shift remains questionable, however, especially because of land requirements in a world of increasingly scarce cropland. Some analysts argue that agricultural and pulping wastes can provide sufficient feedstocks needed to displace petrochemical-based materials. At a minimum, plant-based materials are a promising way to reduce many of the environmental and health hazards associated with petroleum-based materials.[54]

As in the past, the efficiency gains of a materials-light economy could be offset by increased consumption, resulting in continued environmental decline. Thus, consumers need to be involved if real reductions in materials use are to occur. One idea that could limit materials consumption, build community spirit, save money, and meet people's needs is the sharing of goods. Car-sharing operations in Berlin, Vancouver, and other cities make cars available to people who do not own an auto. Participants rely on public transportation, cycling, or walking for most of their transportation needs, but use a car from their co-op for special trips. In Switzerland, where car sharing has grown exponentially over the last 10 years, thousands have given up their cars and now drive less than half the distance they did each year before the switch. They report an improved quality of life and greater flexibility in personal mobility, without the stress of car ownership. Meeting the full market potential of car-sharing would eliminate an estimated 6 million cars from European cities.[55]

Another imaginative sharing initiative is the "tool libraries" sponsored by the cities of Berkeley, California, and Takoma Park, Maryland, in the United States. Participants have access to a wide range of power and hand tools—a materials-light alternative to owning that makes sense for people who use tools only occasionally.[56]

SHIFTING GEARS

Overhauling materials practices will require policies that steer economies away from forests, mines, and petroleum stocks as the primary source of materials, and away from landfills and incinerators as cheap disposal options. Instead, businesses and consumers need to be encouraged to reduce dependence on virgin materials and to tap the rich flow of currently wasted resources through product reuse, remanufacturing, or sharing, or through materials recycling.

Probably the single most important policy step in this direction is the abandonment of subsidies that make virgin materials seem cheap. Whether in the form of direct payments or as resource giveaways, assistance to mining and logging firms makes virgin materials artificially attractive to manufacturers. The infamous 1872 Mining Law in the United States continues to give mining firms access to public lands for just $12 per hectare, without requiring payment of royalties or the cleanup of mining sites. The effect is to encourage virgin materials use at the expense of alternatives such as recycling. By closing the subsidy spigot for extractive activities, policymakers can earn double dividends. The environmental gains would be substantial, because most materials-driven environmental damage occurs at the extractive stage. And the public treasury would be fattened through payments from mining and logging operations that remain open.[57]

Higher targets for recycled content in products would ease the pressure on virgin materials.

Like virgin materials extraction, waste generation can also be substantially curtailed, even to the point of near-zero waste in some industries and cities. A handful of firms report achieving near-zero waste levels at some facilities. The city of Canberra, Australia, is pursuing a "No Waste by 2010" strategy. And the Netherlands has set a national waste reduction goal of 70–90 percent. A key instrument for meeting such ambitious targets is to tax waste in all its forms, from smokestack emissions to landfilled solids. Pollution taxes in the Netherlands, for example, were primarily responsible for a 72–99 percent reduction in heavy metals discharges into waterways between 1976 and the mid-1990s. High landfill taxes in Denmark have boosted construction debris reuse from 12 to 82 percent in eight years—heads and shoulders above the 4-percent rates seen in most industrial countries. Such a tax

could bring huge materials savings in the United States, for example, where construction materials use between 2000 and 2020 is projected to exceed total use in the preceding century.[58]

At the consumer level, a waste tax can take the form of higher rates for garbage collection or, better still, fees that are assessed based on the amount of garbage generated. Cities that have shifted to such a system have seen a substantial reduction in waste generation. "Pay as you throw" programs in which people are charged by the bag or by volume of trash illustrate the direct effect of taxes on waste. Dover, New Hampshire, and Crockett, Texas, for instance, reduced household waste by about 25 percent in five years after such programs were introduced. These initiatives are most effective when coupled with curbside recycling programs: as disposal is taxed, people recycle more. Eleven of 17 U.S. communities with record-setting recycling rates have pay-as-you-throw systems.[59]

A modified version of a waste tax is the refundable deposit—essentially a temporary tax that is returned to the payer when the taxed material is brought back. High deposits for refillable glass bottles in Denmark have yielded huge paybacks: return rates are around 98–99 percent, implying that bottles could be reused 50–100 times.[60]

Some waste is so harmful that regulation rather than taxes may be needed to ensure that it is controlled. The outlawing in the United States of lead emissions, which were found to be damaging to the intellectual development of children, is a case in point. Likewise, the international phaseout of ozone-depleting substances has reduced their use substantially—by 88 percent in the case of chlorofluorocarbons, chemicals that were commonplace in refrigerators and air conditioners just a few years ago. And under negotiation is an international phaseout of 12 persistent organic pollutants. Where the human and environmental costs of using particular materials is just too high, a ban may be the only way to effectively reduce the threat they pose.[61]

As brakes are applied to extraction, to waste disposal, and to toxic emissions, the incentive to shift to new modes of production and consumption begins to increase. But other government initiatives can facilitate the shift as well. If producers, for example, were made legally responsible for the materials they use over the entire life of those materials, they would have a strong incentive to cut usage to a minimum and to make the materials they continue to use durable and recyclable. Some 28 countries have implemented "take back" laws for packaging materials, 16 have done so for batteries, and 12 are planning similar policies for electronics. The best-documented of these is the 1991 German packaging ordinance. Not only did it lead to substantial cuts in packaging, it also prompted the production of long-lasting products. The International Fruit Container Organization, born out of the 1991 law, became the leading manufacturer and lessor of reusable shipping crates, which now carry 75 percent of all produce shipped through Germany. Expansion of the concept of producer responsibility economywide could have a profound effect on materials use.[62]

In addition to stepping up recycling, economies can set higher targets for recycled content in products. This would ease the pressure on virgin materials, and would also raise the value of recycled materials. In the United Kingdom, the world's fifth highest paper consumer, a bill under debate would increase the recycled content of newspapers from 40 to 80 percent. And by making wood panels with a 70-percent recycled content, the United Kingdom could reduce primary wood use in panels by up to 20 percent.[63]

Building codes can also be revised to permit the use of recycled material in construction. Out-of-date building codes often require the use of particular materials for a job, rather than specifying a particular standard of performance. Innovations such as drainage pipes made of recycled plastic are not widely adopted in the United States, for example, often because safety and performance standards for their use have not been set. Revision of these codes—after adequate testing to ensure safety—could open the door to safe and extensive use of recycled building materials and alternative building methods.[64]

Waste exchanges—information centers that help to match suppliers of waste material with buyers—can be promoted as a way to increase recycling rates of a diverse set of materials. Authorities in Canberra have set up a regional resource exchange on the Internet as part of their campaign to eliminate waste by 2010. The government encourages local businesses to use the exchange, which handles material as diverse as organic waste and cardboard boxes. A private-sector initiative in the border region centering on Matamoros, Mexico, and Brownsville, Texas, is even more ambitious. It uses a computer model to analyze the waste flows and material needs of hundreds of businesses in the region, identifying potential supply matches that businesses were unaware of.[65]

Meanwhile, the very purpose of materials consumption is being questioned by some researchers. A new study from the University of Surrey in the United Kingdom indicates that between 1954 and 1994, British consumers attempted to fulfill nonmaterial needs such as affection, identity, participation, and creativity with material goods—despite little evidence that this is possible. This questionable consumption pattern thus represents a grossly inefficient use of resources. Civic entities—from religious groups to environmental organizations—are well suited to articulate the social and environmental costs of these excesses.[66]

Community and neighborhood-based organizations can help develop strategies for reducing materials consumption. One particularly successful approach is the Eco-Team Program of the international organization Global Action Plan for the Earth (GAP). More than 8,000 neighborhood teams in Europe and 3,000 in the United States, each consisting of five or six households, meet regularly to discuss ways to reduce waste, use less water and energy, and buy "green" products. GAP reports that households completing the program have reduced landfilled waste by 42 percent, water use by 25 percent, carbon emissions by 16 percent, and fuel for transportation by 15 percent. They also report annual savings of $401 per household.[67]

Youth in America using cell phone

Religious groups are well positioned to warn of the dangers of making goods into gods.

24/7/365/366 in 21st Century ~
as/like a god...??
I thought much cell phone usage increase waste &
                              adjacent concrete

Religious groups might reflect on the relationship between excessive consumption and the modern decline in spiritual health. They are well positioned to warn of the dangers of making goods into gods, and their influence in many societies is tremendous. They are also qualified to deliver the positive side of the consumption message: that healthy consumption—moderation in purchasing, with an emphasis on goods and services that foster a person's growth—feeds the spirit and helps people achieve their fullest potential.

In addition to these changes in policies and behaviors—each of which could have an immediate effect on materials use—policymakers need to pay close attention to the consequences of other decisions with profound yet indirect materials impacts. Indeed, these societal choices—

from the way land is used to the price of energy, labor, and materials—can affect levels of materials use for decades.

Consider, for example, the question of land use. The gangly suburbs of the United States use more kilometers of pavement, more sewer, water, and telephone lines, and more schools and police and fire stations to service a given population than if development patterns were denser. The Center for Neighborhood Technology in Chicago recently studied seven counties surrounding that city and found that low-density development was about 2.5 times more materials-intensive per inhabitant than high-density development.[68]

While the vast openness around many U.S. cities makes sprawl possible, it is political choices that activate this pattern of resource-intensive development. Zoning laws and building codes, for instance, encourage low-density development. And as noted earlier, fossil fuel subsidies make petroleum-based construction products—from asphalt to plastic water lines—artificially cheap. More than $100 billion in subsidies mask the cost of driving in the United States, reducing a natural disincentive to live far from work and other important destinations. The full materials implications of these political decisions and subsidies extend well beyond heavy infrastructure demands: distant residential development often makes two cars a necessity, while large homes and yards encourage the purchase of more goods to fill them.[69]

Most urban planners, zoning officials, and politicians are unaware of the materials impact—and the full environmental impact—of their land use decisions. But this is just one of many political decisions that heavily influence levels of materials use. The relative prices of labor and capital are also important. Key elements of a sustainable materials economy, such as sorting of recyclable material and disassembly of products for recycling, are often labor-intensive and therefore pro-hibitively expensive in an economy based on high wages and cheap raw materials. In a 1998 survey of U.S. consumers, for example, half of those who threw out appliances cited the high cost of repair and a third cited the low cost of replacement as principal reasons behind their decision to junk the goods.[70]

Other policy choices also have far-reaching effects: it is materially relevant, for example, whether a society chooses cars or a bicycle/rail combination as the center of its transportation system. Energy pricing matters too, as cheap energy extends the material base of nearly everything in the economy.

And some analysts worry that workers' limited freedom to choose shorter working hours over pay increases fosters a consumer mentality that boosts materials use. Indeed, most economic activities have profound materials consequences.[71]

Recognizing the absurdity of our materials-intensive past is a first step in making the leap to a rational, sustainable materials economy. Once this is grasped, the opportunities to dematerialize our economies are well within reach. Societies that learn to shed their attachment to things and to focus instead on delivering what people need might be remembered 100 years from now as creators of the most durable civilization in history.

4

Reorienting the Forest Products Economy

Janet N. Abramovitz and Ashley T. Mattoon

In the 1850s, massive white pine trees—up to 2 meters in diameter—were so abundant in North America's Great Lakes region that tree cutters considered any log less than a meter in diameter to be "undersized." Today the trees are harvested at one third that size. Despite predictions by chroniclers of the day that the forests were too vast to be depleted, the "limitless" supply of white pines did indeed fall, as did the local industries that had been built on these invaluable resources.[1]

Such boom-and-bust patterns began millennia ago in ancient Greece and Rome. They continue today as the search for timber pushes into the world's last old-growth forest frontiers—from the temperate and boreal forests of Canada, Russia, and Chile, to the tropical forests of Brazil, Indonesia, Papua New Guinea, Cambodia, and Cameroon. Nearly half of the forests that once covered the Earth are gone. Between 1980 and 1995 alone, at least 200 million hectares of forest were lost—an area larger than Mexico.[2]

In industrial countries, where most of the world's commercial wood is produced, timber harvest is the primary cause of forest degradation. In developing nations, land clearing for agriculture and grazing combine with timber harvest to reduce forest area. Even there it is often timber harvesting, accompanied by roads that penetrate the forest and provide access to otherwise inaccessible places, that precipitates land clearing.[3]

Driving the timber harvest is growing demand for wood products. In the last three decades alone, industrial roundwood use has risen by almost one third, paper consumption has nearly tripled, and fuelwood and charcoal consumption have grown by almost two thirds. And as the world's most populous nations become more affluent, demand is likely to continue spiraling upward.[4]

The world's forests face other pressures as well—invasion by exotic species, air pollution, vast fires, and climate change. The health and quality of the remaining forests are declining, lessening their ability to support species and ecosystem services.[5]

When forests disappear, we lose more than just timber. The top 150 nonwood forests products traded internationally—such as rattan, cork, nuts, oils, and medicinals—are worth more than $11 billion a year. They provide even greater local benefits, including employing hundreds of millions of people.[6]

In addition, forests shelter countless species, including organisms that are useful in pollinating crops and controlling disease-carrying pests. And without forest cover to protect watersheds, rainfall erodes the denuded land; flooding and drought become more extreme. In 1998, heavy rains brought record-setting floods to many deforested regions, including India, Bangladesh, and Mexico. Flooding in China's Yangtze watershed—which has lost 85 percent of its forests to logging and agriculture—resulted in thousands of deaths, dislocated hundreds of millions of people, inundated tens of millions of hectares of cropland, and cost tens of billions of dollars.[7]

The apparent abundance of wood products in the marketplace may give consumers a false sense of complacency about the health of forests. Yet because the production and consumption of major forest products—timber, paper, and fuel—are principal forces driving the loss and degradation of forests, there is hope that these trends can be reversed by changing the way we produce and use these products.

Luckily, public concern about the fate of forests is rising along with demand. Indeed, this has happened in nearly every age. As ancient Rome's forests became scarce, "the value of trees rose in the opinion of both philosophers and thieves," noted John Perlin in his book on the role of wood in the development of civilization. While some of Rome's builders and industries shifted to more-efficient methods and farmers planted trees to

regain watershed protection services, the government secured timber from abroad and tried to keep supply steady and prices low in order to quiet discontent. Unfortunately, this shortsighted response to scarcity continues today.[8]

THE CHANGING TIMBER LANDSCAPE

The landscape of timber production, trade, and consumption has changed significantly during the past century. The tools of harvesting and processing have changed from axes and saws to mechanical harvesters and high-speed mills. The decreasing supply of larger trees and higher value species has led suppliers to turn to new regions, species, and processes to satisfy growing demand. And new ways of using wood have created a range of products—from paper to plywood—that were scarce or unimagined 100 years ago.

By the nineteenth century, most of the accessible timber in industrial nations had already been cut for fuel and building purposes. Merchant and military shipbuilding also consumed vast areas of timberland—from the ancient civilizations of the Mediterranean and Middle East to Britain in the last few hundred years. When Britain's native forests declined, shipbuilders, ironsmiths, and the like looked to Scandinavia, Ireland, and the American colonies for materials. Building one large sixteenth-century warship required 2,000 mature oak trees—more than 20 hectares worth. The expansion of railroads in the nineteenth and early twentieth centuries also consumed enormous volumes of wood for construction and fuel. By 1900, U.S. railroads, for example, used 20–25 percent of the country's annual timber production.[9]

While the wood on the market today comes from a variety of forest types and nonforest areas, relatively little comes from sustainably managed forests. Although a substantial share of wood still comes from primary forests, more now comes from secondary stands (those that have been harvested and regrown), mainly in the United States and Europe. Even though tree plantations are increasing in area, sometimes at the expense of natural forests, only 10 percent of today's industrial wood comes from tree farms. In many countries, the most valuable primary forests have been exploited, and there is public sentiment to reduce logging pressures on what remains.[10]

About 55 percent of the wood cut today is used directly for fuel, while the rest goes into industrial products like lumber and paper. (See Table 4–1.) Production of pulp for paper and wood-based panels like fiberboard has expanded far faster in recent decades than traditional products like sawnwood, which require the higher-quality wood that is in increasingly short supply.[11]

Almost half of the world's fuelwood is produced in five countries—India, China, Brazil, Indonesia, and Nigeria. And just five countries produce more than 45 percent of the world's industrial wood harvest. The United States, Canada, and Russia have remained among the top five producers for at least 40 years, while China and Brazil joined this group in the 1970s. Together, the top 10 (which

includes Sweden, Finland, Malaysia, Germany, and Indonesia) account for more than 71 percent of industrial production.[12]

The value of the wood trade (legal and illegal) makes this sector a potent economic force, one that has long influenced how forests are managed and how nations interact. More and more wood products enter the international market every year, reflecting a general trend toward trade globalization. (Very little of what the U.N. Food and Agriculture Organization (FAO) classifies as fuelwood moves across borders, so trade here refers almost exclusively to industrial wood.) Worldwide, the share of production that is exported has doubled since 1970. Between 1970 and 1995, the value of legal forest products exports worldwide almost tripled in constant dollars, to more than $142 billion a year.[13]

The effort to expand production and trade has come at a high cost to many nations that are cutting their forests at unsustainable levels. The Philippines provides a cautionary example of the consequences of this. In the 1960s and 1970s, the Philippines became one of the top four timber exporters in the world by liquidating 90 percent of its forests. Since then, however, the nation has turned into an importer, and 18 million forest dwellers have become impoverished. Since 1961, Canada more than tripled

Table 4–1. Production of Wood and Wood Products, 1965–95

Type	1965	1980	1995	Increase 1965–95
	(million cubic meters)			(percent)
Roundwood	2,231	2,920	3,331	49
Fuelwood and Charcoal	1,099	1,472	1,839	67
Industrial Roundwood	1,132	1,448	1,492	32
Sawnwood	384	451	427	11
Wood-based Panels	42	101	146	248
Pulpwood and Particles	238	370	419	76
	(million tons)			
Paper and Paperboard	98	170	282	189

SOURCE: U.N. Food and Agriculture Organization, *FAOSTAT Statistics Database*, <http://apps.fao.org>.

production, Brazil and Malaysia expanded production more than fivefold, and Indonesia increased output sevenfold. And these nations continue to cut their forests at unsustainable rates. Not coincidentally, Indonesia, Brazil, and Malaysia together accounted for 53 percent of the world's forest loss during the 1980s.[14]

A disproportionate share of the world's industrial wood is produced and used in industrial nations. (See Table 4–2.) Although developing countries have increased their rate and share of consumption in recent decades, these are still well below the levels of industrial nations. Indeed, consumption per person in industrial nations is 12 times higher than in developing ones. Fuelwood is the only wood product that developing countries use more of, and even then their consumption per person is less than twice that in industrial countries.[15]

The relative scarcity of large, high-quality timber has caused prices for many solid wood products to rise in some regions in the last 35 years. Yet the relentless search by the timber industry for new

sources of cheap raw material to bring to market has shielded many consumers from these price hikes and kept them unaware of the changes in quality and species. For consumers without access to products from distant markets, however, such scarcities are keenly felt.[16]

Rising consumption and declining forests, combined with economic and social pressures, have spurred improvements in how efficiently wood is used. Although wood was so abundant in North America through the nineteenth century that processors used only the straightest, clearest portion of a log and discarded the rest, such gross wastage is largely a thing of the past. Between 1945 and 1990, the amount of raw wood used to make each ton of industrial wood products fell by 23 percent. As a result, consumption of many finished products (like paper and plywood) has grown faster than the overall wood harvest.[17]

In the United States, for example, while population more than tripled since 1900, the total amount of wood used grew by just 63 percent. The net result is that

Table 4–2. Population and Industrial Roundwood Consumption in Industrial and Developing Countries, 1970 and 1990, With Projections for 2010

Population/Consumption	1970	1990	2010
	(percent)		
Population			
Industrial countries	27	22	17
Developing countries	73	78	83
Consumption			
Industrial countries	86	77	73
Developing countries	14	23	27
	(cubic meters per 1,000 people)		
Industrial countries	1,091	1,141	1,073
Developing countries	84	95	87
World	410	322	259

SOURCE: Population from United Nations, *World Population Prospects: The 1996 Revision* (New York: 1996); consumption from U.N. Food and Agriculture Organization (FAO), *FAOSTAT Statistics Database*, <http://apps.fao.org/>; 2010 from FAO, *Provisional Outlook for Global Forest Product Consumption, Production, and Trade to 2010* (Rome: 1997).

wood use per person has actually declined there by 52 percent since 1900. Most of the increase in U.S. wood consumption in this century has occurred since 1950, as usage for buildings and paper exploded.[18]

The rise in efficiency has been made possible in part by improvements in forest practices and by new technologies in harvesting, processing, and recycling. Many mills are now using computer-guided machines to maximize the value and amount of usable product from each log. In industrial countries, 40–50 percent of the wood that enters a sawmill ends up as solid lumber (although in much of the developing world the figure is still only 25–30 percent). Further, in industrial countries virtually all of the residues are used for other products like pulp, new composite wood products, or fuel to run the mills. (See Table 4–3.) U.S. timber mills reduced their waste (the material unaccounted for or dumped) from 14 percent in 1970 to just 1.5 percent in 1993.[19]

As large trees have become more scarce and technologies have improved, entirely new wood products have been developed to meet demand. Many of these use smaller-diameter trees, formerly underused species, or wood waste that was once destined for the burn pile. Oriented strand board (OSB), for exam-ple, is made of layers of small wood chips glued together. This new panel first appeared in the 1980s, and already accounts for almost one third of the growing panel market.[20]

Some newer products are replacing other wood-based products—like OSB for plywood—while others are substituting for nonwood products, as rayon (a fabric made from wood pulp) does for silk or cotton. Still other wood-based products are being put to entirely new uses, such as combining wood fiber and plastic to make stronger automobile door panels. Even making paper from trees, which now takes almost one fifth the total timber harvest, was developed only 150 years ago.[21]

Wood composites—including panels like OSB, particleboard, medium-density fiberboard, laminated veneer lumber, and I-joists—can be used for structural purposes in buildings as well as for cabinets, furniture, and doors. Many composites are actually stronger that their solid wood counterparts.[22]

In most timber-processing operations, short pieces of wood are considered waste and are burned to power the plant or ground up for pulp. Many processors, however, have found ways to turn this "trash" into cash by making higher value-added products that do not need long pieces of wood, such as desk organizers,

Table 4–3. United States: Use of Wood Fiber and Roundwood, 1993

Product	Share of Harvest That Goes Directly to Product[1]	Share of Wood That Is Ultimately Used[2]
	(percent)	
Solid wood (lumber, plywood, panels)	48	23
Pulp/paper	26	41
Fuelwood	18	27
Miscellaneous/unused/exported	8	8

[1]About 28% of wood that is cut never enters the commercial flow and in not included in these figures.
[2]Accounts for flow of residues from processing.
SOURCE: Peter J. Ince, "Recycling of Wood and Paper Products in the United States" (Madison, WI: USDA Forest Service, Forest Products Laboratory, January 1996).

mouse traps, and sushi trays. One of the most valuable uses of these scraps is to "finger-joint" short lengths together to create long pieces that can be used for doors, windows, and molding. In the United States, scraps used as boiler fuel fetch $14–24 per million board feet; for papermaking, $50–125; and as shipping pallets, up to $200. But when they are converted to finger-jointed moldings, they command $1,250–1,350.[23]

Reduction in the waste and pollution generated by processors is another part of the changing timber landscape in the last few decades, thanks to technological advances spurred largely by public concern and government regulation. Pulp and paper mills in Sweden, for example, have reduced their sulfur emissions by about 90 percent, and chlorine bleaching has been eliminated.[24]

Of course, technology also has negative effects. Expensive new machines allow vast areas to be quickly cleared, bundled, and chipped in around-the-clock operations that employ few workers. Mills, too, are now bigger and faster. And as products are produced more cheaply, consumption is encouraged, feeding into the false sense of abundance.[25]

Consumption increases have been at least tempered by efficiency improvements and recycling, which helps stem demand for virgin materials. Worldwide, 41 percent of all paper and paperboard is recovered for recycling. Despite this, further expansion of recycling is needed. In the United States, for instance, the volume of municipal solid waste has doubled in the last 30 years, disposal options are closing down, and costs are rising. Since more than half of the waste (by weight) sent to landfills or incinerators is still paper and wood, significant opportunities exist to reclaim this lost resource and at the same time reduce the burdens of waste disposal and ease pressures on forests.[26]

Unfortunately, greater processing effi-

ciency and expanded recycling have not been able to keep pace with overall growth in consumption—in other words, wood use is still rising. Further reductions in consumption are needed—from eliminating unnecessary purchases to buying products that have less packaging and using more-sustainable building methods.

THE TREES IN OUR HOMES

Today, about 40 percent of the world's industrial roundwood is used to make sawnwood and panels—materials that are largely used in construction, shipping, and manufacturing. Wood has long been a favored building material because it is aesthetically pleasing, highly workable, widely available, and relatively inexpensive. Its production requires less energy and generates fewer toxic pollutants and less waste than does production of metals, concrete, or plastics.[27]

In the United States, consumer of nearly one fourth of the world's industrial roundwood, at least 40 percent is used for construction. Manufacturing of furniture and the like uses about 9 percent, and shipping, about 6 percent. Ultimately, about 10 percent of the world's industrial wood is used by the U.S. construction industry, and most of that goes into home building.[28]

In virtually every industrial nation over the last few decades, the size and number of dwellings has increased and the number of people in each home has declined due to growing affluence. Single-family homes in the United States have more than doubled in size since 1950, for instance. As a result of expanding house size and shrinking family size, the area occupied on average by Americans has increased by 79 percent in the last three decades—to more than 72 square meters per person, at least twice the average space in Japan. Even in land-starved

Japan, the area per occupant has increased by 44 percent since 1970.[29]

Of course, these larger homes not only require more material to construct and maintain, they are also filled with more materials—furniture, floor coverings, appliances—much of which is made from wood fiber. In the last three decades, three times as many homes were built in the United States as in the preceding 30 years.[30]

During construction, 10 percent of the wood used in new U.S. buildings ends up as construction waste.

Timber availability and quality have long influenced construction. When, for example, ancient civilizations in Knossos, Babylon, Greece, and Rome exhausted their forests, the shortages and expense of imports brought about changes in the design of buildings to minimize the amount of lumber used for construction and heating. Even the stick frame house, which now dominates construction in western societies, was developed in the nineteenth century as an alternative to using whole logs for construction.[31]

This pattern of evolving construction technologies and materials efficiency continues. In recent years, higher prices for traditional solid wood products combined with declining quality and availability (as well as concerns for rapid forest loss) have led some builders, architects, foresters, and environmentalists to look for other ways to design and build structures that are resource-efficient, economical, and comfortable. Alternative products and building techniques are being used more widely to meet growing demand. These include engineered and nontraditional wood products as well as nonwood products. Builders are developing new meth-

ods that make optimal use of wood and other materials, and even rediscovering and adapting old methods such as adobe and rammed earth construction.

Rethinking construction methods offers additional opportunities to save materials. Techniques like optimum value engineering, or advanced framing, have been developed by the National Association of Home Builders and others. They involve using wood products in standard increments to produce less waste, not using a larger dimension than is actually needed, and spacing studs farther apart. Building with such an approach to engineering can reduce wood use by nearly 20 percent and cut costs by 8–17 percent per house—saving several thousand dollars. It also reduces waste and saves energy.[32]

Prefabricated components like trusses and building panels can also save materials and money. Trusses are constructed of pieces of wood assembled to form structural members capable of carrying far greater loads than comparable amounts of solid lumber. They are used to support roofs and floors. Structural insulated panels can incorporate the interior and exterior sheathing and insulation as well. A comparison of standard framing versus prefabricated components found that a house built with the new components used 26 percent less wood, was built faster, and saved thousands of dollars. Indeed, the U.K. government estimated that the slower adoption of prefabricated components in that country has meant office building costs are 30 percent above where they would be otherwise.[33]

Another way to reduce materials use is to improve recycling and reuse at each stage of a building's life. During construction, 10 percent of the wood used in new buildings in the United States ends up as construction waste. Reusing materials on-site—for example, using plywood concrete forms several times and then using them as roofing—sorting materials to make reuse easier, and selling or donating waste materials can cut project costs and divert substantial amounts of material from landfills to productive uses.[34]

Proper building maintenance can also save materials and money. And a study for Friends of the Earth calculated that one third of the demand for new homes in the United Kingdom could be met by renovating existing buildings and reducing vacancy rates.[35]

Salvaged wood from older structures can be a valuable resource. In many cases, the beams, rafters, doors, trims, and flooring in old buildings are of sizes, species, and quality that are now too costly or impossible to obtain from forests (for example, heartwood pine and chestnut floors, or large redwood timbers). Although this is a small sector of the wood market, it illustrates the value and creative potential embodied in many old structures slated for demolition or allowed to decay.[36]

Typically, much of the wood that comes from demolition is not of sufficient quality to be remilled and reused directly. But some can be used as the raw material for composite wood products or paper, or as mulch or fuel. Demolition wood is already burned for fuel in many Asian cities, in Sweden, and in the Netherlands, for example.[37]

When new wood is needed, builders and manufacturers can turn to certified wood products that are produced with less impact on the forests. Products labeled by the Forest Stewardship Council (the largest and most recognized third-party certifier) as originating in well-managed forests are increasingly available, although still only a small portion of the market. By the end of 1998, nearly 11 million hectares in 27 countries have been certified. Networks such as the Certified Forest Products Council in North America and the U.K. 1995 Plus Buyers Group make it easier for commercial and individual buyers to locate sources of certified and recycled wood products.[38]

Using reclaimed and certified wood products can be cost-effective and affordable, especially when combined with wood-efficient building methods. The Natural Resources Defense Council noted in a recent study that new homes built in California using these methods cost several thousand dollars less than standard new homes.[39]

PAPER: FROM FISHING NETS TO SILICON

The paper we use today bears little resemblance to the paper first produced in China nearly 1,900 years ago, made of tree bark, hemp, old rags, and used fishing nets. Papermaking spread to Europe by the end of the ninth century, and began in North America in 1690. Well into the nineteenth century, the primary source of fiber for paper in the western world was rags and cloth.[40]

As paper demand started to outstrip rag supply in the late eighteenth century, a search for substitutes began. By the mid-1800s the invention of wood pulping techniques paved the way for an increased role of wood in papermaking. Today, wood fibers account for nearly 91 percent of the fiber used in making paper, more than one third of which is in the form of recycled paper. (See Figure 4–1.) A mere 9 percent comes from various nonwood fibers that were the predominant source for more than 1,700 years.[41]

As the use of wood in papermaking expanded by vast proportions over the last 150 years, so did the use of paper itself. In the United States, for example, paper production rose from a meager 1 million tons in 1889 to nearly 85 million tons in 1997. While paper was once used almost solely for printing and writing purposes, technological innovations and falling costs during this century expanded its role in our daily lives. Today there are more than 450 grades of paper—used for purposes as diverse as filtering coffee, covering electrical cables, clothing surgeons, carrying groceries, and shipping goods across the globe.[42]

The virgin wood fiber used to make paper accounts for close to 18 percent of the world's total annual wood harvest. In 1993, 618 million cubic meters of wood went to making paper. Of this, nearly two thirds came from wood harvested specifically for pulp, and the rest was from manufacturing residues such as wood chips and sawdust. Given this substantial use of residues, the share of the world's wood that is used to make paper is often underestimated. Although mill residues have long been used as a fiber source for paper, their contribution to the world's pulp supply has grown so much in recent decades that they represent a valuable commodity in their own right. Indeed, due to the integration of fiber sources for lumber, plywood, and pulp, distinguishing the wood flows among the various sectors is difficult. Today, trees are less likely to be harvested for one particular purpose.[43]

During the past century, most of the world's wood supply for paper has come from old-growth and second-growth forests of Canada, the United States, Scandinavia, and the former Soviet Union. Although these areas are still major sources, new players have emerged in recent decades as pulp capacity in countries such as Brazil, New Zealand, Indonesia, and Chile has expanded with the cultivation of fast-growing eucalyptus and pine plantations. In some cases, these plantations have replaced natural forests. For example, many of the fires that consumed vast swaths of forests in Indonesia in recent years were set to clear land for pulp and palm oil plantations.[44]

Many paper companies based in the United States, Europe, and Japan are investing heavily in overseas plantation development. Warmer climates, available land, and cheap labor have encouraged this trend. Forest management for pulp has shifted toward a more agricultural model: genetic strains are carefully bred and selected, and seedlings are planted and developed into single-species, single-aged stands that are treated with fertilizers and pesticides. Crops are harvested in 10–30 year rotations. The uniform, predictable fiber source thus produced is extremely attractive to an industry whose expensive machinery requires a steady flow of easily managed fiber inputs.[45]

Over the past three decades, international trade in pulp and paper products has tripled. Today about one fifth of pulp production and one fourth of paper production is traded internationally, accounting for roughly 44 percent of the value of world forest product exports. Although the world's pulpwood production is shifting south, northern producers continue to dominate the paper industry. In 1995, the world's largest paper producer—the United States—accounted for nearly 30 percent of global production. Japan was ranked second, at nearly 11 percent. Japan is somewhat unusual, however, as its industry depends substantially on raw material imports. In 1994, Japan imported

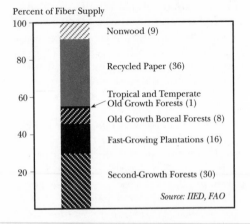

Percent of Fiber Supply

Nonwood (9)

Recycled Paper (36)

Tropical and Temperate Old Growth Forests (1)

Old Growth Boreal Forests (8)

Fast-Growing Plantations (16)

Second-Growth Forests (30)

Source: IIED, FAO

Figure 4–1. Fiber Sources for Global Paper Production, Mid-1990s

70 percent of the world's trade in wood chips and 12 percent of the traded pulp.[46]

Global consumption of paper is growing faster than use of most other major wood products. Between 1950 and 1996, paper consumption increased six times, to 281 million tons. By 2010, it is expected to reach nearly 400 million tons. Nearly half of the world's paper is used for packaging, such as cardboard boxes and food containers. Printing and writing papers account for another 28 percent, newsprint's share is about 13 percent, and sanitary and household papers use 6 percent.[47]

Industrial nations use the lion's share of the world's paper—close to 75 percent in 1994—and will continue to do so well into the future. But paper consumption is growing at a faster rate in developing nations, and by 2010 these countries are expected to use almost 33 percent, up from 15 percent in 1980. In recent years, Southeast Asia has been home to the world's fastest-growing paper market, increasing at approximately 10 percent a year. Due to weakened Asian markets, annual growth in world paper demand is projected to slow in 1998.[48]

On a per capita basis, differences in consumption trends are even more pronounced. Per capita consumption in industrial nations was about 160 kilograms in 1995, compared with 17 kilograms in developing nations. (See Figure 4–2.) In the United States, the per capita figure is over 330 kilograms of paper a year—roughly seven times the global average.[49]

Cycles of overcapacity have helped fuel the rapid growth in paper production and consumption. As mill size has grown during the last century, the industry has become less able to adjust to market signals. New mills can take three to four years to come on-line, and once built they must run almost constantly to pay off investments. Supply and demand fall out of sync, as huge quantities of pulp are dumped on the market, creating gluts

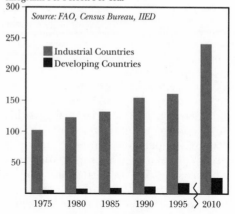

Kilograms Per Person Per Year

Source: FAO, Census Bureau, IIED

Industrial Countries
Developing Countries

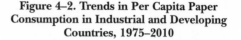

Figure 4–2. Trends in Per Capita Paper Consumption in Industrial and Developing Countries, 1975–2010

and large price swings.[50]

There are many parts of the world that need greater access to paper and the services it provides. Paper provides a means for communication and education as well as having important sanitary uses. But much of the paper use in industrial nations is excessive, wasteful, and simply unnecessary. For example, the average U.S. household receives 553 pieces of junk mail each year, a figure that is expected to triple by 2010. Nearly 10 billion mail-order catalogs are discarded each year in the United States. Indeed, paper and paperboard account for nearly 40 percent of the municipal solid waste generated there, and the U.S. Environmental Protection Agency (EPA) expects that paper, paperboard, and wood waste will continue to grow faster than population in the future.[51]

Years ago, when it became clear that computers were going to be information and communication tools, it was widely believed that paper use would drop precipitously. The dream of the "paperless office," however, has not been realized. In fact, some analysts consider the rise in electronic communications to have been "a great blessing to the paper industry." It is possible that new technologies could still reduce the need for printing and writing paper—with electronic books and "electric paper" (made of silicon, and able to be reused up to a million times).[52]

Paper recycling is considered one of the environmental success stories of our time. Between 1970 and 1995, the world's use of wastepaper more than tripled, and recovered paper now makes up nearly 36 percent of the total fiber supply for paper. FAO predicts that by 2010 the share of recycled paper in the fiber supply for paper will increase to 46 percent—which would cut wood pulp demand 17 percent below what it would otherwise be.[53]

Expanded recycling has been an important factor in slowing the growth in demand for woodpulp, but it has served more as a supplement than a substitute for fiber supply to industry. Global paper consumption is increasing at such a rapid rate that it has overwhelmed many of the gains achieved by recycling, and virgin wood pulp consumption continues to expand roughly 1–2 percent a year. In addition, recycled fibers cannot replace virgin fiber entirely, since paper fibers can only be recycled five or six times before they become too weak for further use.[54]

The tree bark and fishing nets used for papermaking 1,900 years ago are no longer a major constituent in the world's fiber supply for paper. But as noted earlier, nonwood sources do account for 9 percent of the supply today. There are two main types of nonwood fibers for paper: agricultural residues from crops such as wheat, rice, and sugarcane, and crops that can be grown specifically for pulp, such as kenaf and industrial hemp.[55]

Developing nations account for 97 percent of the world's nonwood pulp production and consumption. In the United States, nonwood fibers account for less than 1 percent of the paper industry feedstock, whereas in China nonwoods—primarily straw—make up nearly 60 percent.

In fact, China, the world's third largest paper producer, accounts for 75 percent of the world's nonwood pulping capacity.[56]

Currently, the world's nonwood pulp capacity is centered where there are limited forest resources, such as China, India, and Pakistan. In countries where forest resources seem relatively plentiful and where billions of dollars have been invested in wood pulp mills, there is little incentive to expand the use of nonwood fibers. Yet a growing body of research suggests that a strong case can be made for increasing the share of nonwood fibers in paper to as much as 20–30 percent. Much of this increase could be met with agricultural residues. Although a substantial portion—often about half—of these residues are and should be reincorporated into the soil to maintain soil quality, surplus residues are often burned in the field, resulting in polluted air and a wasted resource.[57]

WOOD ENERGY

Long before wood was used so extensively for purposes such as paper production, it was used as fuel. Since the discovery of the first fire-making technologies, humans have depended on fuelwood and charcoal to cook food, heat homes, and power industries. With the emergence of fossil fuel as a major energy source in the nineteenth and twentieth centuries, the relative role of wood as a fuel supply in industrial economies steadily declined. Its primary uses there today are to heat homes and provide a source of energy for forest products industries that use scraps from mills to fuel their plants.[58]

Yet wood still remains an important source of energy in developing countries, where at least 2 billion people depend on fuelwood or charcoal as their primary or sole source of domestic energy, and where it powers industry. In developing nations, fuelwood and charcoal account for approximately 15 percent of total energy use (compared with 1–2 percent in industrial countries). These numbers mask enormous variations among different countries, however. In 40 of the world's poorest nations, wood meets more than 70 percent of energy needs.[59]

Fuelwood is not simply a developing-country issue, however. For one thing, an important source of fuelwood in industrial countries is not usually accounted for in energy and forest product statistics. In countries with large forest products industries, secondary fuel supplies—such as wood chips, sawdust, and pulping liquors—are produced as byproducts of milling processes. In the United States, lumber and plywood mills meet at least 70 percent of their energy needs and paper mills meet more than half of theirs with wood residues and pulping liquors. These secondary sources add close to 300 million cubic meters of wood to the 200 million that are consumed directly for fuel in industrial countries.[60]

A recent study sheds further light on the often overlooked sources of woodfuel. The European Timber Trends Study found that out of Europe's "total wood energy" supply in 1990, 44 percent came from primary sources of fuelwood, while processing byproducts provided an equal share. When all these sources are accounted for, it turns out that fuel is the predominant use of wood in Europe—accounting for more than 45 percent of the region's total wood consumption. Likewise, in the United States, although only 18 percent of wood is harvested directly for fuel, when residues are included the proportion used for fuel tops 27 percent.[61]

Although industrial countries ultimately use more wood for energy than commonly thought, the dependence is greatest and scarcity has the largest impact in developing nations. During the 1970s and early 1980s it was widely

believed that the world was headed for a "fuelwood crisis," and that severe shortages were in store. This was based on the assumption that fuelwood collection and deforestation were directly linked and that increasing fuelwood needs would inevitably surpass forests' ability to meet demand. In recent years, however, many studies have reexamined these predictions and have improved our understanding of the sources of fuelwood in specific regions and the impact on forests. FAO's *State of the World's Forests 1997* summed up this new understanding succinctly: "Without doubt, fuelwood shortages and overcutting can have negative economic, environmental and social effects. But, in most cases, fuelwood collection is not a primary cause of deforestation. Furthermore, it is now clear that fuelwood production and harvesting systems can be, and often are, sustainable."[62]

Fuel is the predominant use of wood in Europe—accounting for more than 45 percent of the region's wood consumption.

Much of today's fuelwood does not come directly from primary forests. What does come from these areas is often dead twigs and branches or trees cut down initially to clear land for agriculture. Other major sources of fuelwood include tree plantations and "nonforest areas" such as village lands, agricultural land, coconut and rubber plantations, and trees along roadsides. Recent studies by the Regional Wood Energy Development Programme in Asia (RWEDP) have concluded that in many of the 15 countries studied, as much as 50 percent of fuelwood is derived from nonforest areas.[63]

In India, recent studies have indicated that the role of forests in providing fuelwood has often been overestimated and that nonforest resources—especially in more recent years—are of greater importance. In the state of Kerala, for example, 80 percent of wood supply came from "homestead trees" cultivated in conjunction with agricultural crops to provide fruit, shade, protection against erosion, and a source of firewood. Another report on fuelwood sources in India found that between the periods 1978–79 and 1992–93, the percentage of households collecting firewood from their own farms increased from 35 to 49 percent and from roadside bushes and trees from 24 to 30 percent, while the collection from forests dropped from 35 to 17 percent.[64]

Deforestation and forest degradation are often more closely associated with urban use of fuelwood than rural use. In rural areas, fuelwood is gathered locally, and collectors are more conscientious about harvesting in a sustainable manner. Fuel suppliers for urban areas, on the other hand, sometimes clearcut woodland areas and make little attempt to conserve the resource base.[65]

In addition to household use, consumption of fuelwood by small industries can account for a large share of fuelwood use in certain areas. In Zimbabwe, the brick-making industry consumes the same amount of wood as is used for cooking in all rural areas of the country. In Burkina Faso, rural beer brewing industries use about 1 kilogram of fuelwood for each liter of beer. And tobacco growers in Brazil use about 5 million cubic meters (enough to fill about 100,000 logging trucks) of wood every year just for curing or drying tobacco. In some cases, small businesses obtain their wood from common lands or unprotected forests. In cases where rural industries are required to pay for the wood consumed, they may maintain their own plantations of fast-growing trees to sustain their woodfuel needs on a consistent basis.[66]

Although fuelwood collection is no longer considered to be a major cause of deforestation, there are still areas where its collection does contribute to forest loss and degradation. And in regions of scarcity, fuelwood shortages pose a significant problem for people and for forests. A recent FAO report estimated that as much as half of the world's 2 billion fuelwood users face fuel shortages and as many as 100 million "already experience virtual 'fuelwood famine'." Of the 15 Asian countries examined under RWEDP assessments, fuelwood consumption exceeded potential sustainable supply in Bangladesh, Pakistan, and Nepal. The gap between demand and potential sustainable supply is expected to grow wider in these countries by 2010. Several regions of sub-Saharan Africa also face fuelwood shortages, largely due to an increase in fuelwood use, expansion of agriculture into forests and woodlands, and overgrazing by growing cattle populations.[67]

In responding to today's fuelwood shortages, analysts frequently call attention to the failures of some of the top-down approaches pursued in the 1970s. Designers of some of these initiatives were often not aware of the wide variation in local needs, the role of women as primary users, and the volume of wood consumed by local industries in some areas. Through close examination of the efforts that succeeded in recent decades, it has become clear that locally based, community-generated approaches to fuel supply are most effective. Fuelwood production can be sustainable if it is done through small-scale, carefully managed plantation, woodlot, or agroforestry projects.[68]

Production of fuelwood can provide both local and global benefits. As concern about carbon emissions from the burning of fossil fuels has grown, many scientists claim that the substitution of biofuels (such as wood) for fossil fuels could be a substantial aid in mitigating climate change. Assuming replanting, the biomass burned is potentially "carbon-neutral" as it releases gases that it absorbed out of the atmosphere during its growth. As a potential means of easing climate change and improving supplies to regions where wood-fuel is scarce, this approach is worth careful consideration.[69]

THE FUTURE OF FOREST PRODUCTS

When the European Forestry Institute recently examined future prospects for the world's wood supply, it asked, Will the world run out of wood? The answer was, Not likely. Indeed, the more profound and far-reaching issues to be faced in coming decades are what kind of forest will remain, at what cost, for whose benefit, and will the forests be able support the diversity of life and provide the other services that people need.[70]

If current trends continue, according to FAO, by 2010 paper consumption will increase by 49 percent, fuelwood consumption will rise by 18 percent, and overall wood consumption will increase by 20 percent. Industrial nations are expected to continue their already disproportionately high levels of consumption, and developing nations are expected to increase their demand. Some analysts have predicted that in some major timber-producing nations, such as the United States, growth in consumption may outstrip the production capacity of domestic timberlands in the next decade, and they will begin "spending down" their forests.[71]

What might happen if the developing world reached the high consumption levels of industrial nations? If wood use accelerates to the point where everyone consumes as much as the average person in an industrial country does today, by 2010 the world would consume more than twice as much wood as it does today. And if by 2010 everyone in the world consumed as much paper as the average American does today, total paper consumption would be more than eight times current world consumption. To meet that demand, the harvest would have to increase severalfold—a pressure the world's forests are unlikely to withstand if they are to continue providing essential ecosystem services.[72]

Such scenarios are not inevitable or even reasonable. It is possible to balance people's needs for forest products while still sustaining the forests. New techniques in sustainable forest management, as well as a broader appreciation of forests' nontimber services, offer promise. Furthermore, there are a number of ways that we could meet future demand without increasing harvest levels. Indeed, it may be possible to actually reduce harvest levels.

There are many ways to reduce wood use by lowering consumption levels. If, for example, total paper consumption in industrial countries stayed at current levels rather than increasing as predicted, world paper consumption in 2010 would increase by 24 percent rather than 49 percent. If industrial nations reduced their predicted consumption of industrial roundwood by 8 percent, this would offset FAO's projected rise in developing nations.[73]

It is also possible to reduce wood use by improving efficiency at every step of the production process. In the United States and the United Kingdom, about 30–50 percent of the wood that is cut—during land clearing, the thinning of commercial stands, or logging—never even enters the commercial flow. While some of it needs to be left in the forest, this "waste" offers opportunities for local industries and for reducing the overall harvest.[74]

In many developing countries, large efficiency gains are possible. The amount of finished product that leaves the mills is a fraction of what it is elsewhere, and the residues (sawdust, scraps, and so on) are generally underused. In Brazil, for example, two thirds of the wood that is commercially harvested is discarded, and only one third ends up as sawnwood. By one estimate, improving equipment maintenance and worker training could increase processing efficiency by 50 percent. Combined with better forest management practices, Brazil could produce the same amount of timber while disturbing one third as much forestland.[75]

If developing nations increased their processing efficiency to the current level of industrial nations by using the newest technologies, they could nearly meet their projected 2010 demands for processed wood without increasing harvest levels.[76]

Brazil could produce the same amount of timber while disturbing one third as much forestland.

Increasing pre- and post-consumer recovery and recycling could prove to be a fruitful source of materials and could reduce the waste burden. For example, 10 percent of all the wood consumed to build new houses in the United States ends up as construction debris. And, worldwide, more than half of all paper is still not recycled.[77]

There are ecologically friendly materials that could replace wood in many applications. There is room to expand the use of agricultural residues and other non-woods as a substitute for or supplement to wood in paper, construction materials, and fuel. In the United States, for example, 350 million tons of agricultural residues are available each year, even after 60 percent is returned to soils. The demand for wood pulp for paper could be almost cut in half if the fiber supply for paper shifted to 30 percent wood pulp (from 56 percent today), 50 percent recovered paper, and 20 percent nonwood fibers.[78]

Designing for durability rather than disposability and extending the useful life of finished products could help reduce the demand for more timber. As described earlier, there are also less demanding ways to meet the needs that forest products now fill.

There are clearly many opportunities to bring about a new forest economy. Unfortunately, many of these steps have yet to be scaled up to the necessary level. Most individuals and institutions do not recognize the excessive use of wood—a "renewable resource"—as a problem. One of the primary obstacles is inertia. The status quo is comfortable and familiar, institutions are heavily invested in existing technologies and practices, and governments are wedded to current policies. Another barrier is the reluctance of most industrial nations to even contemplate a fundamental question: How much do we really need?

High-consuming nations have a special role to play in reducing the pressure they are putting on the world's forests. Not only do their purchases and habits directly affect forests, but their technologies and lifestyles are often exported (either directly or through the media) and adopted by developing countries. So far, European nations have been leaders in environmental certification of forest products, reducing demand, and increasing recycling—all while maintaining a high standard of living.

Individual consumers can make a difference through their purchasing decisions—or their decisions not to purchase. Their lifestyle decisions—from the type and size of home they live in to its contents—their recycling habits, and the laws they support are all part of the forest economy. Educating consumers about the impacts of their consumption patterns can help them make better informed choices.[79]

In the office, where the speed and ease of computers, printers, and copiers have dramatically increased paper use (and the money spent on paper and mail), there are opportunities for reduction. Electronic mail and computers still have the potential to reduce paper use in communications—and save money. One major insurance company saves 14 tons of paper yearly by publishing its manuals on-line. In the United States, EPA cut its paper consumption by 16 percent in just two years—by using double-sided copying and increasing the use of computers for communication.[80]

Companies that buy forest products—from builders to publishers to manufacturers—can also shift the forest economy in a more sustainable direction. Their decisions send signals to suppliers and regulators. Commitment by some large consumers, like newspapers and magazines, for example, has already begun to have such an effect in Germany and the United Kingdom. BBC magazines, for one, which prints 15 trillion pages a year, audits its suppliers and has stated that it would buy paper certified from sustainable forestry when it becomes available in sufficient quantity. The companies in the UK 1995 Plus Buyers Group, which the BBC belongs to, represent about 25 percent of the U.K. market for wood products.[81]

Builders and architects can specify reclaimed or certified wood, set goals and targets for purchases and waste recovery, and use efficient and durable designs. They can work to make building regulations responsive to the principles of sustainable development. Those who commission buildings can ask builders to follow these practices. Microsoft, for instance, directed that construction waste at its new office complex be recycled. In doing so the company recycled 78 percent of the waste and saved almost $168,000. Although the savings are small for such a large company, it demonstrates to others that such an approach is practical and profitable. Perhaps the biggest obstacle to overcome is the reluctance of builders and construction workers to adopt new techniques.[82]

In the pulp and paper industry, major obstacles to change are the capital-intensive nature of the industry and scant research on alternative fibers. Thus the industry is inflexible to changes in market conditions or fiber sources. As noted earlier, agricultural residues are an underused fiber source that could make a substantial contribution to the feedstock for paper in some areas. A company in Nebraska has recognized the value of this "waste" and in the year 2000 plans to start annual production of 140,000 tons of high-quality paper pulp from corn stalks.[83]

Some companies are realizing that the way to higher profits is not through increasing the volume of wood cut or processed but through producing higher-value products. People who make their living from the forest also benefit from a volume-to-value shift because more jobs, and higher skilled jobs, are created per unit of wood in value-added processing than in less labor-intensive areas (such as logging and chip mills). (See Table 4–4.) Workers and communities gain because the forest will be sustained, and with it the jobs.

Of course, not all livelihoods and benefits come from these sorts of commercial forest operations. Smaller-scale nonwood forest product operations, such as rattan harvesting, have long provided a sustainable stream of goods and livelihoods for hundreds of millions of people. But these benefits are often lost when forests are logged.

Job creation is often used as the rationale for increasing harvest levels and government subsidies to the forest industry. Ironically, in recent decades there has been a general decline in number of jobs generated in extractive forestry, despite record harvests. In Sweden, about half of all jobs in the forest products industry have been lost since 1980, a time when production increased by more than 17 percent largely as a result of increased

Table 4–4. United States: Employment Created by Various Timber Products

Process	Additional Jobs Created
Logs to lumber	3 jobs per million board feet
Lumber to components (furniture parts, for example)	another 20 jobs per million board feet
Components to high-end consumer goods (furniture, for example)	another 80 jobs per million board feet

SOURCE: Catherine Mater, "Emerging Technologies for Sustainable Forestry," in Sustainable Forestry Working Group, ed., *The Business of Sustainable Forestry: Case Studies* (Chicago: John D. and Catherine T. MacArthur Foundation, 1998).

mechanization. In Canada, the world's biggest timber exporter, the number of jobs per volume harvested has fallen by 20 percent in the last 20 years, despite a substantial rise in harvest levels. There have also been job declines in other sectors that relied on forests that were no longer healthy—fisheries, for instance.[84]

Further, many of these extractive industries generate relatively little employment, especially when compared with other options for forest use. For example, the U.S. National Forests are currently managed primarily for timber supply, despite the fact that recreational use of these woodlands generates nearly 2.6 million jobs and adds $97.8 billion to the national economy. Logging, on the other hand, adds only 76,000 jobs and $3.5 billion.[85]

The most important reform governments can make is to end long-standing policies of encouraging and subsidizing high-volume extractive industries under the assumption that this use of the forests is the most profitable. Subsidies have helped create unrealistically low prices that do not reflect the true value of forest resources and the costs of squandering them. Timber subsidies also make it difficult for other materials (such as recycled or nonwood fiber for paper) to compete fairly and drive down prices that private landowners can get for their timber. Overcoming this barrier is essential to creating a sustainable forest economy—and putting a nation's economy on a sounder footing.

Underpricing and lost revenue from timber harvest on public land can be so substantial that governments in effect pay private interests to take public timber. In Canada, stumpage rates are half what they are in the United States. And from 1992 to 1994 the U.S. timber sales program lost $1 billion in direct costs alone (such as road-building and mapping), not including the costs of reforestation, stream erosion, and lost fisheries, water supply, recreation, and so on. Similarly, Indonesia lost $2.5 billion in 1990.[86]

Many publicly funded services to the forest industry evolved to facilitate industrial forestry—schools, research, extension, product testing, marketing assistance, sector promotion, and so on. If more of this funding were directed to efforts to develop sustainable forest management, alternative fibers for buildings and paper, uses for recycled materials, and so forth, it could help shift the forest industry in a environmentally sustainable direction while creating jobs and economic growth.

In many countries, state control of forestland helps extractive industries—and indeed, it was often established to do just that. Examples include the systems started in India under British colonial rule, in British Columbia earlier in this century, and in modern Indonesia. When the Indonesian government declared in 1967 that it had sole legal jurisdiction over the nation's forests, customary rights that had evolved as a complex and sustainable management system over many generations were no longer legally recognized. As elsewhere, by removing power from local communities, a real-life "tragedy of the commons" was created—the government, which has the authority, is unable to police the nation's vast forests, and the communities who are in the forest have no power to stop exploitation by outsiders.[87]

Control also brought revenues that the government now depends on, creating a conflict of interest. This cozy relationship is clear in British Columbia, where the government owns 94 percent of the forestland, including First Nations' (indigenous peoples') land; most of the long-term leases have been given to a handful of companies, and the government sets revenue targets.[88]

Weak laws or failure to enforce laws have encouraged vast forest resources to be squandered. Brazil, which finally granted enforcement authority to its environment agency in 1998 after stalling for nine years, repealed the authority just a few months later. British Columbia, Cambodia, and Russia, to name a few, also have poor records of ensuring compliance with weak laws. In response to 1998's devastating floods, the Chinese government finally began enforcing a logging ban in the upper reaches of the Yangtze and reforesting the watershed, which has lost 85 percent of its forest cover. It acknowledges that the water storage value of forests is worth three times as much as the cut timber.[89]

Domestic and international laws and regulations can be used to spur innovation. Some cities, for example, have developed programs and set goals to increase recycling, foster green building programs, and establish guidelines for wood-use efficiency. A 1994 European Union Directive targeted a 50–65 percent recovery rate for all packaging waste by 2001. And a 1996 law in Japan set a target of 60 percent for consumption of recovered paper by 2000, to reduce its fiber imports and the amount of waste sent to scarce landfills.[90]

The U.N. Framework Convention on Climate Change could encourage reforestation for carbon sequestration, and sustainable woodfuel plantations as a substitute for fossil fuels. Trade rules could be reformed to allow nations to halt the importation of timber known to be illegally harvested in the country of origin, and to allow for labeling by species, nation of origin, and method of production. The World Bank and other lenders can help ensure that sustainable forest management and efficient processing and energy industries are pursued. The International Monetary Fund, for example, in its 1998 bailout of the Indonesian economy did stipulate that the corrupt plywood cartel be abolished. However, it also encouraged the expansion of palm oil plantations—one of the main culprits in the recent devastating fires.[91]

While there are many pressures on forestlands, the production and consumption of wood products is a major force driving forest loss and degradation. And it is the pressure that is perhaps the most amenable to change—where individuals and businesses have a direct role and where we can see results quickly. It is possible to envision and achieve a forest products economy that provides all the things people need from forests—goods, livelihoods, and services—and ensures that healthy forest ecosystems survive into the next millennium.

5

Charting a New Course for Oceans

Anne Platt McGinn

For much of human history the oceans have been viewed as infinite and free for the taking. In his inaugural address to the 1883 International Fisheries Exhibition in London, British scientific philosopher Thomas Huxley argued that "all the great sea-fisheries are inexhaustible." Huxley assumed that natural checks—that is, temporary population crashes in fish stocks—were strong enough to withstand a full-fledged human assault. Although these opinions were challenged at the time by a few people, and were couched in qualifications by Huxley himself, the view of oceans as a resource of unending bounty and a frontier for exploitation prevailed.[1]

Today we depend on oceans as a source of food and fuel, a means of trade and commerce, and a base for cities and tourism. Worldwide, people on average obtain 16 percent of their animal protein from fish. Ocean-based deposits meet one fourth of the world's annual oil and gas needs, and more than half of world trade travels by ship. Currently, more than 2 billion people—many of them urbanites—live within 100 kilometers of a shoreline. And millions more crowd the world's beaches and coastal areas each year, bringing in billions of dollars in tourism revenues.[2]

At its high point in the late 1980s, combined spending on fisheries, ocean transport, offshore oil and gas drilling, and navies contributed about $821 billion (in 1995 dollars) to the world economy. Although the net worth of these industries has since declined to about $609 billion due to a drop in navy budgets, oil prices, and valuable marine fish stocks, it will likely increase in the decades ahead with the development of ocean thermal and tidal energy, further exploration of untapped marine resources, and rapidly expanding aquaculture.[3]

More important than these economic figures, however, is the fact that humans depend on oceans for life itself.

We are grateful to the Curtis and Edith Munson Foundation for its support of our research on oceanic fisheries.

Harboring a greater variety of animal body types (phyla) than terrestrial systems and supplying more than half of the planet's ecological goods and services, the oceans play a commanding role in the Earth's balance of life. Due to their large physical volume and density, oceans absorb, store, and transport vast quantities of heat, water, and nutrients. The world's oceans store about 1,000 times more heat than the atmosphere does, for example. Through processes such as evaporation and photosynthesis, marine systems and species help regulate the climate, maintain a livable atmosphere, convert solar energy into food, and break down natural wastes. The value of these "free" services far surpasses that of ocean-based industries: coral reefs alone, for instance, are estimated to be worth $375 billion annually by providing fish, medicines, tourism revenues, and coastal protection for more than 100 countries.[4]

Despite the importance of healthy oceans to our economy and well-being, we have pushed the world's oceans perilously close to—and in some cases past—their natural limits. The warning signs are clear. The share of overexploited marine fish species, for instance, has jumped from almost none in 1950 to 35 percent in 1996, with an additional 25 percent nearing full exploitation. More than half of the world's coastlines and 60 percent of the coral reefs are threatened by human activities, including intensive coastal development, pollution, and overfishing.[5]

Most scientists today reject Huxley's notion that humans are incapable of harming the oceans. In January 1998, as the United Nations was launching the Year of the Ocean, more than 1,600 marine scientists, fishery biologists, conservationists, and oceanographers from across the globe issued a joint statement entitled "Troubled Waters." They agreed that the most pressing threats to ocean health are human-induced, including species overexploitation, habitat degrada-

tion, pollution, introduction of alien species, and climate change. The impacts of these five threats are exacerbated by poorly planned commercial activities and coastal population growth. One marine scientist has summed up the current state of affairs simply: "Too much is taken from the sea and too much is put into it."[6]

Yet many people still consider the oceans as not only inexhaustible, but immune to human interference. In part, the vast seascape is far removed from everyday life and therefore remains separate and disconnected from the more familiar landscape. Much of the ocean environment is relatively inaccessible to scientists, let alone the general public. Because scientists have only begun to piece together how ocean systems work, society has yet to appreciate—much less protect—the wealth of oceans in its entirety. Indeed, our current course of action is rapidly undermining this wealth. Overcoming ignorance and apathy is never easy, but educating people about our collective dependence on healthy oceans will help build support for marine conservation. And that is just what the oceans need.

ECONOMIC AND ECOLOGICAL VALUES

From the Greeks in the Mediterranean to the Chinese on the Yellow Sea, marine environments have provided the backbone for food security, commerce, trade, and transportation for centuries. Ancient civilizations sprang up on coasts of inland seas and oceans where fish were abundant and trade was relatively easy to arrange. Archaeological evidence from the western Pacific reveals that *Homo erectus* began building boats as far back as 800,000 years ago, suggesting that people turned to the sea for food long before agricultural fields were plowed. Fossilized piles of shells along coastal Peru indicate that people harvested shellfish from tidal pools some 12,000 years ago.[7]

Today, on average, people receive about 6 percent of total protein and 16 percent of their animal protein from fish. Nearly 1 billion people, predominantly in Asia, rely on fish for at least 30 percent of their animal protein supply. Most of these fish come from oceans, but with increasing frequency they are cultured on farms rather than captured in the wild. Aquaculture, based on the traditional Asian practice of raising fish in ponds, has begun to explode in recent years. It now constitutes one of the fastest growing sectors in world food production.[8]

Today, on average, people receive 16 percent of their animal protein from fish.

In addition to harvesting food from the sea, people have traditionally relied on oceans as a transportation route. Metal tools found along Yemen's coastal plain and stone tablets uncovered in Egypt reveal a thriving maritime trade in and around the Mediterranean and Red Seas dating back to the Bronze Age, some 5,000 years ago. By harnessing the strong trade winds and seasonal monsoons in the Indian Ocean, Arabs established long-lasting trade routes around 100 B.C.[9]

A far cry from these early centers of ocean commerce, the hubs of modern-day sea trade are dominated by multinational companies that are more influenced by the rise and fall of stock prices than by the tides and trade winds. Modern fishing trawlers, oil tankers, aircraft carriers, and container ships follow a path set by electronic beams, satellites, and computers. Of course, technological

change poses challenges as well as potential innovations: two recently constructed ocean cruise liners are too large to fit through the Panama Canal.[10]

Society now derives a substantial portion of energy and fuel from the sea—a trend that was virtually unthinkable a century ago. (See Table 5–1.) And in an age of falling trade barriers and mounting pressures on land-based resources, new ocean-based industries such as tidal and thermal energy production promise to become even more vital to the workings of the world economy. Having increased sixfold between 1955 and 1995, the volume of international trade is expected to triple again by 2020, according to the U.S. National Oceanographic and Atmospheric Administration—and 90 percent of it is expected to move by ocean.[11]

In contrast to familiar fishing grounds and sea passageways, the depths of the ocean were long believed to be a vast wasteland that was inhospitable, if not completely devoid of life. Since the first deployment of submersibles in the 1930s and more advanced underwater acoustics and pressure chambers in the 1960s, scientific and commercial exploration has helped illuminate life in the deep sea and the geological history of the ancient ocean. Mining for sand, gravel, coral, and minerals (including sulfur and, most recently, petroleum) has taken place in shallow waters and continental shelves for decades, although offshore mining is severely restricted in some national waters.[12]

Isolated but highly concentrated deep sea deposits of manganese, gold, nickel, and copper, first discovered in the late 1970s, continue to tempt investors. These valuable nodules have proved technologically difficult and expensive to extract, given the extreme pressures and depths of their location. An international compromise on the deep seabed mining provisions of the Law of the Sea in 1994 has opened the way to some mining in international waters. But it appears unlikely to lead to

Table 5–1. Ocean-Based Industries, by Trends and Value, 1995

Industry	Key Trends	Value in 1995
Fisheries	Fish catch up fivefold since 1950; global per capita supplies up from 8 kilograms in 1950 to 15 kilograms in 1996; currently 200 million people rely on fishing for livelihood; 83 percent of fish by value imported to industrial countries.	$80 billion
Seaborne Trade and Shipping	Since 1955, the annual volume of shipments is up six-fold to 5 billion tons of oil, dry bulk goods, and other cargo transported in 1995; 27,000 vessels—each larger than 1,000 gross tons—registered; half of cargo loaded in industrial countries, while three fourths unloaded in industrial countries.	$155 billion
Navies	For years, military spending was larger than other ocean-dependent activities combined; has declined due to end of cold war.	$242 billion
Offshore Oil and Gas Extraction	About 26 percent of the world's oil and natural gas comes from offshore drilling installations in Middle East, United States, Latin America, North Sea waters.	$132 billion

SOURCE: See endnote 11.

much soon, as long as mineral prices remain low, demand is still largely met from the land, and the cost of underwater operations remains prohibitively high.[13]

Perhaps more valuable than the mineral wealth in oceans are still undiscovered living resources—new forms of life, potential medicines, and genetic material. For example, in 1997 medical researchers stumbled across a new compound in dogfish that stops the spread of cancer by cutting off the blood supply to tumors. The promise of life-saving cures from marine species is gradually becoming a commercial reality for bioprospectors and pharmaceutical companies as anti-inflammatory and cancer drugs have been discovered, for example, and other leads are being pursued.[14]

Tinkering with the ocean for the sake of short-sighted commercial development, whether for mineral wealth or medicine, warrants close scrutiny, however. Given how little we know—only 1.5 percent of the deep sea has ever been explored, let alone adequately inventoried—any development could be potentially irreversible in these unique environments. Although seabed mining is now subjected to some degree of international oversight, prospecting for living biological resources is completely unregulated.[15]

During the past 100 years, scientists who work both underwater and among marine fossils found high in mountains have shown that the tree of life has its evolutionary roots in the sea. For some 3.2 billion years, all life on Earth was marine. A complex and diverse food web slowly evolved from a fortuitous mix there of single-celled algae, bacteria, and several million trips around the sun. Life remained sea-bound until some 245 million years ago, when the atmosphere became oxygen-rich.[16]

Thanks to several billion years' worth of trial and error, the oceans today are home to a variety of species that have no descendants on land. Thirty-two out of 33 animal life forms are represented in marine habitats. (Only insects are missing.) Fifteen of these are exclusively marine phyla, including those of comb jellies, peanut worms, and starfish. Five phyla, including that of sponges, live predominantly in salt water. Although on an individual basis marine species count for just 9 percent of the 1.8 million species described for the entire planet, there may be as many as 10 million species in the sea that have not been classified.[17]

In addition to hosting a vast array of biological diversity, the marine environment performs such vital functions as oxygen production, nutrient recycling, storm protection, and climate regulation—services that are often taken for granted. The coastal zone is disproportionately valuable: marine biological activity is concentrated along the world's coastlines (where sunlit surface waters receive nutrients and sediments from land-based runoff, river deltas, and rainfall) and in upwelling systems (where cold, nutrient-rich deep-water currents run up against continental margins). It provides 25 percent of the planet's primary biological productivity and an estimated 80–90 percent of the global commercial fish catch. One recent study estimated that coastal environments alone account for 38 percent of the goods and services provided by the Earth's ecosystems, while open oceans contribute an additional 25 percent. The value of all marine goods and services is estimated at

$21 trillion annually, 70 percent more than terrestrial systems. (See Table 5–2.).[18]

Oceans are vital to both the chemical and the biological balance of life. The same mechanism that created the present atmosphere—photosynthesis—continues today to feed the marine food chain. Phytoplankton—tiny microscopic plants— take carbon dioxide (CO_2) from the atmosphere and convert it into oxygen and simple sugars, a form of carbon that can be consumed by marine animals. Other types of phytoplankton process nitrogen and sulfur, and thereby help the oceans function as a biological pump.[19]

The oceans also serve as a net sink for CO_2. Although most organic carbon is consumed in the marine food web and eventually returned to the atmosphere via respiration, the unused balance rains down to the deep waters that make up the bulk of the ocean, where it is stored temporarily. Over the course of millions of years, these deposits have accumulated to the point that most of the world's organic carbon, some 15 million gigatons, is sequestered in marine sediments, compared with just 4,000 gigatons in land-based reserves. On an annual basis, about one third of the world's carbon emissions—some 2 gigatons—is taken up by oceans, an amount roughly equal to the uptake by land-based resources. If deforestation continues to diminish the ability of forests to absorb carbon, oceans are expected to play a more

Table 5–2. Ecological Goods and Services, by Ecosystem, Area, and Value

Ecosystem	Area (million hectares)	Total Value (dollars per hectare per year)	Global Flow Value (billion dollars per year)	Global Value (percent)
Marine	36,302	577	20,949	63
Open Ocean	33,200	252	8,381	25
Coastal	3,102	4,052	12,568	38
Terrestrial	15,323	804	12,319	37
Global	51,625	—	33,268	100

SOURCE: Robert Costanza et al., "The Value of the World's Ecosystem Services and Natural Capital," *Nature*, 15 May 1997.

important role in regulating the planet's CO_2 budget in the future as human-induced emissions keep rising.[20]

Perhaps no other example so vividly illustrates the connections between the oceans and the atmosphere than El Niño. Named after the Christ Child because it usually appears in December, the El Niño Southern Oscillation takes place when trade winds and ocean surface currents in the eastern and central Pacific Ocean reverse direction. Scientists do not know what triggers the shift, but the aftermath is clear: warm surface waters essentially pile up in the eastern Pacific and block deep, cold waters from upwelling, while a low pressure system hovers over South America, collecting heat and moisture that would otherwise be distributed at sea. This produces severe weather in many parts of the world—increased precipitation, heavy flooding, drought, fire, and deep freezes—which in turn have enormous economic impact. During the 1997–98 El Niño, for example, Argentina lost more than $3 billion in agricultural products due to these ocean-climate reactions, and Peru reported a 90-percent drop in anchovy harvests compared with the previous year.[21]

Fortunately, the scientific map of the ocean realm is becoming more accurate. But we still have a lot to learn about marine life. And the more we learn, the better we understand the role of oceans in sustaining humanity, and how human beings are unwittingly undermining this role.

A SEA OF PROBLEMS

As noted earlier, the primary threats to oceans—overfishing, habitat degradation, pollution, alien species, and climate change—are largely human-induced and synergistic. Fishing, for example, has drastically altered the marine food web and underwater habitat areas. Meanwhile, the ocean's front line of defense—the coastal zone—is crumbling from years of degradation and fragmentation, while its waters have been treated as a waste receptacle for generations. The combination of over-exploitation, the loss of buffer areas, and a rising tide of pollution has essentially suffocated marine life and the livelihoods based on it in some areas. Upsetting the marine ecosystem in these ways has, in turn, given the upper hand to invasive species and changes in climate.[22]

The health of marine fisheries is an important yardstick for the health of the oceans. On the surface, all appears well. World fish production—wild catches and farmed fish combined—reached an all-time high in 1996 of 120 million tons, up sixfold from 1950. But beneath the surface, things are not so bright. Years of relentless exploitation in the oceans have taken their toll: 11 of the world's 15 most important fishing areas and 70 percent of the major fish species are either fully or overexploited, according to the U.N. Food and Agriculture Organization (FAO).[23]

This apparent contradiction can be explained by two factors. The appearance of steadily growing aquaculture products—from 7 million tons of fish in 1984 to 23 million tons in 1996—masks sharp declines in most of the world's valuable fish stocks. Sharks—heir to an ancient lineage of vertebrates dating back some 400 million years—are at their lowest point of all time. Their longevity and low rates of reproduction make sharks especially vulnerable to overexploitation. Other top marine predators, including tuna, swordfish, and cod, are suffering a similar fate.[24]

In the course of depleting prized species, fishers are taking smaller fish that tend to reproduce at a younger age, and are generally less commercially valuable. During the 1980s, for instance, five low-value open-sea species—the Peruvian anchovy, South American pilchard, Japanese pilchard, Chilean jack mackerel, and Alaskan pollock—accounted for 73 percent of the increase in world landings. But unless the volume of fishing is reduced, the cycle of overfishing soon repeats itself with new prey: excessive fishing can trigger abrupt declines in these lower-level species, leaving fishers only steps away from the base of the food chain.[25]

In the South Pacific, the catch of orange roughy plummeted by 70 percent in just six years.

Fishers are now so efficient that they can—and do—wipe out entire populations of fish and then move on either to a different species or to a fishing area in some other part of the world. Following the decline of groundfish stocks in the late 1980s and early 1990s, for instance, fishers still working in the Grand Banks region off the Atlantic coast of Canada started catching dogfish (a type of shark), skate, monkfish, and other species once considered trash. And in the South Pacific, the catch of orange roughy—no match against modern vessels and high-tech gear—plummeted by 70 percent in just six years.[26]

Overfishing poses a serious biological threat to ocean health. For one, the resulting reductions in the genetic diversity of the spawning populations make it more difficult for the species to adapt to future environmental changes. Species such as the orange roughy, for instance, may have been fished down to the point where future recoveries are impossible. Second, declines in one species can alter predator-prey relations and leave ecosystems vulnerable to invasive species. The overharvesting of triggerfish and pufferfish for souvenirs on coral reefs in the Caribbean has sapped the health of the

entire reef. As these fish declined, populations of their prey—sea urchins—exploded, damaging the coral by grazing on the protective layers of algae and hurting the local reef-diving industry.[27]

These trends have enormous social consequences as well. The welfare of more than 200 million people around the world who depend on fishing for their income and food security is severely threatened. As the fish disappear, so too do the coastal communities that depend on fishing for their way of life. Subsistence and small-scale fishers, who catch nearly half of the world's fish, suffer the greatest losses as they cannot afford to compete with large-scale vessels or changing technology. Furthermore, the health of more than 1 billion poor consumers who depend on minimal quantities of fish in their diets is at risk as a growing share of fish—83 percent by value—is exported to industrial countries each year.[28]

Despite a steadily growing human appetite for fish, large quantities are wasted each year because the fish are undersized or a nonmarketable sex or species, or because a fisher does not have a permit to catch them and must therefore throw them out. FAO estimates that discards of fish alone—not counting marine mammals, seabirds, and turtles—total 20 million tons, equivalent to one fourth of the annual marine catch. Many of these fish do not survive the process of getting entangled in gear, being brought onboard, and then tossed back to sea. The resulting loss of biodiversity is particularly striking in shrimp fisheries. Working with fine-mesh nets and in areas of high species diversity, shrimp trawlers on average take 5 kilograms of innocent bystanders for every kilogram of shrimp they keep.[29]

In addition to causing overexploitation and waste, careless fishing practices also damage the very areas that fish rely on for their most vulnerable stages of life—breeding, spawning, and maturation. Tropical coral reefs of Southeast Asia bear the scars from fishers who squirt sodium cyanide poison at fish to stun them, making it easier to trap them alive. Almost unheard of 15 years ago, cyanide poison fishing is now reported in reef fisheries from Eritrea to Fiji. Though it involves too little poison to harm people who later eat the fish, over time this practice can kill most reef organisms and convert a productive community into a graveyard.[30]

Another threat to habitat areas stems from trawling, the process in which nets and chains are dragged across vast areas of mud, rocks, gravel, and sand, essentially sweeping—in some cases, mining—everything in the vicinity. By recent estimates, all the ocean's continental shelves are trawled by fishers at least once every two years, with some areas hit several times a season. Now considered a major cause of habitat degradation, trawling disturbs benthic (bottom-dwelling) communities as well as localized species diversity and food supplies.[31]

The conditions that make coastal areas so productive for fish—proximity to nutrient flows and tidal mixing and their place at the crossroads between land and water—unfortunately also make them vulnerable to human assault. Today, nearly 40 percent of the world lives within 100 kilometers of a coastline. Moreover, two thirds of the world's largest cities are coastal. Population densities in China's 11 coastal provinces average more than 600 people per square kilometer, for example, and in the rapidly growing city of Shanghai, more than 2,000 people crowd into each square kilometer of land along the sea. To keep up with demand for housing, buildings, and industries, coastal land in China that used to be cultivated is now developed.[32]

A similar situation is occurring worldwide, as more people move to coastal areas and further stress the seams between land and sea. Not surprisingly, coastal ecosystems are losing ground. (See Table 5–3.) Between 1983 and 1994, more than 90,000 hectares of seagrasses were destroyed worldwide. Data from just four countries—Malaysia, the Philippines, Thailand, and Viet Nam—reveal a cumulative loss of about 7,500 square kilometers of mangroves, many of which were cleared to make way for shrimp ponds and tourism developments. This represents 10 percent of all remaining mangrove forests in South and Southeast Asia.[33]

Human activities on land also cause a large portion of offshore contamination. An estimated 44 percent of marine pollution comes from land-based pathways, flowing down rivers into tidal estuaries, where it bleeds out to sea; an additional 33 percent is airborne pollution that is carried by winds and deposited far offshore. From nutrient-rich sediments, fertilizers, and human waste to toxic heavy metals and synthetic chemicals, the outfall from human society ends up circulating in the fluid and turbulent seas.[34]

Excessive nutrient loading has left some coastal systems looking visibly sick. Seen from an airplane, the surface waters of Manila Bay in the Philippines resemble green soup due to dense carpets of algae. Of course, nitrogen and phosphorus are necessary for life, and in limited quantities they can help boost plant productivi-

Table 5–3. Status of Coral Reefs, by Region, Mid-1990s

Region	Total Reef Area	Share of Total at High or Medium Risk
	(square kilometers)	(percent)
Middle East	20,000	61
Caribbean	20,000	61
Atlantic	3,100	87
Indian Ocean	36,100	54
Southeast Asia	68,100	82
Pacific	108,000	41
Global	255,300	58

SOURCE: World Resources Institute et al., *Reefs At Risk: A Map-Based Indicator of Threats to the World's Coral Reefs* (Washington, DC: 1998).

ty. But too much of a good thing can be bad. Excessive nutrients build up and create conditions that are conducive to outbreaks of dense algae blooms, also known as "red tides" for their colorful displays, which actually range from green to brown or red depending on the species of phytoplankton. The blooms block sunlight, absorb dissolved oxygen, and disrupt food-web dynamics. Large portions of the Gulf of Mexico are now considered a biological "dead zone" due to algal blooms.[35]

Although these are a naturally occurring phenomenon, the frequency and severity of red tides has increased in the past couple of decades, as has the appearance of novel toxic species. Some experts link the recent outbreaks to increasing loads of nitrogen and phosphorus from nutrient-rich wastewater and agricultural runoff in poorly flushed waters. Between 1976 and 1986, the population living in the vicinity of Tolo harbor, Hong Kong, increased sixfold, for instance, while nutrient loadings rose 2.5-fold and the annual incidence of red tides jumped eightfold. In other cases, red tides follow in the footsteps of fish farms, thriving on the waste- and feed-infested waters. Concerted efforts to contain aquacultural waste have helped, but poorly managed operations still offer an effective conduit. Whatever the cause, the public health and economic costs of red tides are substantial. (See Table 5–4.) Between 1970 and 1990, the incidence of paralytic shellfish poisoning doubled worldwide, for instance, as the plankton carrying the responsible toxin spread from the northern to southern hemisphere.[36]

Unlike red tides, which date back to Biblical times, organochlorines are a fairly recent addition to the marine environment. But they, too, are proving to have pernicious effects. First manufactured in the 1930s, synthetic organic compounds such as chlordane, DDT, and PCBs are used for everything from electrical wiring to pesticides. Indeed, one reason

Table 5–4. Economic Losses from Red Tides in Fisheries and Aquaculture Facilities

Year	Location	Species	Loss (million dollars)
1972	Japan	Yellowtail	~47
1977	Japan	Yellowtail	~20
1978	Japan	Yellowtail	~22
1978	Korea	Oyster	4.6
1979	Maine	Many species	2.8
1980	New England	Many species	7
1981	Korea	Oyster	>60
1985	Long Island, NY	Scallops	2
1986	Chile	Red salmon	21
1987	Japan	Yellowtail	15
1988	Norway, Sweden	Salmon	5
1989	Norway	Salmon, rainbow trout	4.5
1989–90	Puget Sound, WA	Salmon farms	4–5
1991	Washington state	Oysters	15–20
1991–92	Korea		133
1996	Texas	Oysters	24
1998	Hong Kong	Farmed fish	32

SOURCE: See endnote 36.

they are so difficult to control is that they are ubiquitous. The organic form of tin (tributyltin), for example, is used in most of the world's marine paints to keep barnacles, seaweed, and other organisms from clinging to ships. Once the paint is dissolved in the water, it accumulates in mollusks, scallops, and rock crabs, which are consumed by fish and marine mammals. Recent sea otter die-offs in California have been linked to the immune system suppression effect of having several milligrams of tributyltin in the animal's liver. North Sea waters alone receive about 68 tons of this substance every year.[37]

As part of a larger group of chemicals known collectively as persistent organic pollutants (POPs), these compounds are difficult to control because they do not degrade easily. (POPs include both chlorinated and brominated chemicals.) Highly volatile in warm temperatures, POPs tend to circulate toward colder environments where the conditions are more stable, such as the Arctic Circle. Moreover, they do not dissolve in water, but are lipid-soluble, which means that they accumulate in the fat tissues of fish that are then consumed by predators at a more concentrated level. Thus scientists have found accumulations of 100 to 1,000 times the input level in species at the top of the food chain—from seabirds and seals to polar bears and people.[38]

A recent survey on Baffin Island, Canada, of Inuit people who consume large quantities of walrus and seal meat and blubber found blood levels 20 times higher than the tolerable daily intake of toxaphene and chlordane, two insecticides that have been banned in the United States for more than 15 years. POPs have been implicated in a wide range of animal and human health problems—from suppression of immune systems, leading to higher risk of illness and infection, to disruption of the endocrine system, which is linked to birth defects and infertility. Their continued use in many parts of the world poses a threat to marine life and fish consumers everywhere.[39]

Heavy metal contamination is another lasting legacy of the industrial age. In the Baltic Sea, concentrations of mercury have increased fivefold during the last 50 years, largely due to the air deposition resulting from fossil fuel burning. Many fish in the Baltic are blacklisted because they contain too much mercury for safe human consumption. A similar trend has occurred in the U.S. Great Lakes.[40]

Heavily stressed aquatic environments are more susceptible to rapidly colonizing species. Already weakened by a combination of overfishing, coastal habitat degradation, and increasing agricultural and industrial pollution, the Black Sea, for instance, was ripe for an exotic species introduction in the 1980s. With no natural enemies in the Azov and Black Seas, and with a taste for fish eggs, larvae, and other zooplankton, the Atlantic comb jelly—probably released in a ship's ballast water—helped wipe out life in the Black Sea. An estimated 85 percent of the marine species there—including a majority of commercial fish stocks—have disappeared.[41]

Globally, several thousand species are estimated to be in ships' ballast tanks at any given time. U.S. waters alone are thought to receive at least 56 million tons of discharged ballast water a year. The combination of ships in motion and regular flushing means that species get a free one-way ticket to a foreign destination, such as the Black Sea. In San Francisco Bay, for instance, researchers catalogued 234 exotic species, concluding that one foreign species takes hold in the bay every 14 weeks, often through ships' ballast water. Based on sampling in these and other areas, the researchers identify marine bioinvasions as "a major global environmental and economic problem."[42]

Because marine species are extremely sensitive to changes in temperature, changes in climate and atmospheric conditions pose high risks to them. Recent evidence shows, for example, that the thinning ozone layer above Antarctica has allowed more ultraviolet-B (UV-B) radiation to penetrate the waters. This has affected photosynthesis and the growth of phytoplankton and macroalgae. But the effects are not limited to the base of the food chain: increased intensity of UV-B radiation damages the larval development of crabs, shrimp, and some fish. By striking aquatic species during their most vulnerable stages of life and reducing their food supply at the same time, increases in UV-B could have devastating impacts on world fisheries production.[43]

Among the early signs of human-induced climate change in the oceans are coral bleaching, stronger storms, sea level rise, and ice cap melting. When corals are subjected to any number of stresses, such as warmer water or lower than normal tides, they expel symbiotic zooxanthellae (tiny plants). This gives them a bright white or bleached look, first documented in the mid-1980s, and also means that the corals cannot grow or reproduce. In spring 1998, marine scientists reported a massive area of bleached coral throughout the tropics, including, for the first time, reefs in the Indian Ocean. Scientists have linked the latest bleaching events to an increase in sea surface temperature of 1 degree Celsius due to El Niño, although other instances are related to a complex mix of monsoonal, oceanographic, and climatic variables.[44]

Because higher temperatures cause water to expand, a warming world may trigger more frequent and damaging storms. In 1995, scientists recorded the highest sea surface temperature in the north Atlantic Ocean ever, the same year the region was hit with 19 tropical storms—twice the previous 49-year average. Ironically, the coastal barriers, seawalls, jetties, and levies that are designed to protect human settlements from storm surges likely exacerbate the problem of coastal erosion and instability, as they create deeper inshore troughs that boost wave intensity and sustain winds.[45]

Depending on the rate and extent of warming, global sea levels may rise 5–95 centimeters by 2100—up to five times as much as during the last century. The effects of this shoreline migration would be dramatic: a 1-meter rise would flood most of New York City, including the entire subway system and all three major airports. Economic damages and losses could cost the global economy up to $970 billion in 2100, according to the Organisation for Economic Co-operation and Development. Of course, the human costs would be unimaginable, especially in the low-lying, densely populated river deltas of Bangladesh, China, Egypt, and Nigeria.[46]

These damages could be just the tip of the iceberg. Warmer temperatures will likely accelerate polar ice cap melting and could boost this rising wave by several meters. Just four years after a large portion of Antarctica melted, another large ice sheet fell off into the Southern Sea in February 1998, rekindling fears that global warming could ignite a massive thaw that would flood coastal areas worldwide. Because oceans play such a vital role in regulating the Earth's climate and maintaining a healthy planet, minor changes in ocean circulation or in its temperature or chemical balance could have repercussions many orders of magnitude larger than the sum of human-induced wounds.[47]

While understanding past climatic fluctuations and predicting future developments is an ongoing challenge for scientists, there is clear and growing evidence of the overuse—indeed abuse—that many marine ecosystems and species are currently suffering from direct human actions. And the situation is probably much worse than these snapshots would have us believe, for many sources of danger are still unknown or poorly monitored. The need to take preventive and decisive action on behalf of oceans is more important than ever.[48]

OCEAN GOVERNANCE

Military personnel have long realized the practical aspects of controlling the oceans. "Armies have little to fight for unless they control the sea," noted the ancient Greek philosopher Thucydides. For centuries, controlling the ocean frontier meant exploiting it for economic and military gain. Indeed, a mere 30 years known as the European Age of Exploration, from 1492 to 1522, virtually ensured that the next 500 years would be ones of mounting societal dependence on oceans for transportation, commerce, and food.[49]

Triggered by the blockade of the port of Constantinople in 1453, which signaled the fall of the Byzantine Empire, European merchants were forced to find new trade routes to the East. In the process, they opened the world to the modern era of global trade, travel, cultural exchange, and colonization. The voyages of Vasco da Gama to India, Christopher Columbus to the "New World," and Ferdinand Magellan around the world showed that oceans could serve as a vital link to unexplored lands and resources. What had previously been identified as *terra incognito* on European maps now became a bit more familiar. The notion that oceans provide limitless resources and are something to be conquered and controlled has persisted ever since.[50]

The frontier mentality also played itself out in legal doctrine. In 1604, the Dutch attorney Hugo Grotius wrote *Mare Liberum* (Freedom of the Seas) on behalf of a Dutch trading company. Angered by Portuguese and Spanish exclusive claims to trade with the Spice Islands, Grotius argued in favor of open and free access for all, especially the Dutch: "The sea is common to all, because it is so limitless that it cannot become a possession of one…whether…from the point of view of navigation or of fisheries." This concept dates back to early Roman law and was long practiced in Asian maritime societies. Indeed, the reason that the Portuguese and Dutch had the dispute in the first place is that Asian societies welcomed all who sought peaceful trade.[51]

Although Grotius did not originate the concept, the arguments he made on behalf of seventeenth-century mercantile interests dominate maritime law nearly to this day. In part this is because the nations that advanced colonialism—Britain, Spain, Portugal, and later Germany— relied on navigational freedom to control

people and resources. As long as the sea was the primary means of transporting armed forces, these countries tried to limit other nations' territorial water claims to the recognized 3–12 miles offshore well into this century. More important, the oceans themselves were not considered a source of wealth until after World War II.[52]

By the early twentieth century, fisheries already showed signs of strain, rapidly changing technology expanded the uses of oceans and accelerated the rate at which damage could occur, and more nations and interest groups became involved in disputes over access rights. The difficult question was—and remains—how to limit access.

In 1945, the United States was the first country to extend its control from the traditional 12-mile territorial zone to the contiguous high seas. Under the Truman Proclamation, U.S. officials justified the move as a way to protect fisheries better, establish conservation zones, and exploit seabed minerals of the continental shelf. Many fishing-dependent countries soon followed suit, triggering a global "sea grab." Within a decade several Latin American countries, including Argentina, Peru, Chile, and Honduras, had extended their jurisdiction to 200 nautical miles to protect their fisheries from outside intrusions and to claim resources of the continental shelf.[53]

What began as an isolated trend in the 1950s and 1960s quickly grew into a global phenomenon. By 1973, nearly 35 percent of the ocean's area—equal to the Earth's entire land mass—was claimed by coastal states, many of them developing countries. These claims led to the 1982 U.N. Convention on the Law of the Sea (UNCLOS), although the treaty did not formally enter into force until 60 countries had ratified it in November 1994.[54]

Known as the "constitution of the oceans," this U.N. treaty marked the end of an era: resources in the 200 nautical miles closest to shore were now under national jurisdiction; only the high seas remained open to all. Under UNCLOS, coastal nations were granted rights to use and develop fisheries within a 200-nautical-mile exclusive economic zone (EEZ). With the privilege of controlling access came the responsibility to protect and conserve marine resources. In part, the 1982 convention merely formalized what was already accepted as customary international law—most notably, the right of national claims over the EEZ. But it also went far beyond existing practices.[55]

A landmark FAO study in 1992 argued that the global fishing industry was losing $54 billion a year.

By redistributing control away from powerful fishing nations to coastal countries worldwide, the Law of the Sea reallocated world marine resources. In the early 1950s, for example, about 80 percent of the world's fish catch was taken by industrial countries. Forty years later, 64 percent of the catch was in the hands of developing countries. UNCLOS also established a comprehensive framework governing ocean use and set such use in the context of environmental protection. Rather than trying to address individual concerns, the convention recognized the need for parties to negotiate additional complementary and more specific agreements. Despite these benefits, the process of nationalizing waters conflicted with the multinational reality created by transboundary pollution problems. And it neither solved the issue of overfishing nor simplified the protection of marine resources.[56]

In 1967, well before the final UNCLOS text was approved, the Liberian oil tanker *Torrey Canyon* ran aground off Britain's southwest coast, dumping 120,000 tons of crude oil (three times as much as the infamous *Exxon Valdez* spilled in Alaska 22 years later). The largest in a series of highly visible disasters during the 1960s, this incident brought the horror of marine pollution to headlines worldwide and helped spark international action. Working with national governments, the U.N. International Maritime Organization (IMO) imposed strict safety and environmental regulations on the growing tanker industry during the 1970s and 1980s in an effort to stop ocean dumping and ship-based discharges, and to prevent accidental spills. Thanks to new rules requiring double-hulled construction, improved cargo handling procedures, and cautious operations at port and at sea, the volume of oil spilled into the oceans has dropped 60 percent since 1981, even though the amount of oil shipped has almost doubled. But industry representatives and government regulators have only begun to contain the damages from more routine shipping and tanker operations.[57]

The IMO is slowly becoming an ocean steward by recognizing the risks of biological and genetic pollution from shipping. To address the role of ballast water in the spread of alien species, the IMO's Marine Environment Protection Committee is drafting a legally binding Annex to the 1973 International Convention for the Prevention of Pollution from Ships that is expected to call for open-water ballast exchange.[58]

In similar fashion, other key international organizations, including FAO, the U.N. Environment Programme (UNEP), and even the World Trade Organization (WTO), have recently become involved in marine biological diversity issues. Traditionally an advocate for fisheries development, FAO has become a voice of concern about the effects of overexploitation and habitat degradation on fisheries production. A landmark FAO study in 1992 argued that, 10 years after UNCLOS, many fisheries were at risk of biological collapse, the global fishing industry was losing $54 billion a year, and people were losing jobs and food. The report described the role that subsidies, overinvestment and excessive capacity, and other economic trends play in overfishing. FAO has since initiated a series of consultations on particular aspects of the global overfishing problem—from subsidies and overcapacity to shark mortality—that can provide useful consensus statements, albeit without enforcement provisions.[59]

During the 1990s, UNEP has supported efforts to move toward ecosystem-based management of oceans. Country representatives at a November 1995 meeting of the UNEP-sponsored Global Program of Action for the Protection of the Marine Environment from Land-Based Activities strongly supported a global but nonbinding ban on persistent organic pollutants. Advocates of the ban have singled out 12 POPs for elimination, several of which are already restricted in some countries; others will be added in the future. A global ban would help ensure that such chemicals are eliminated from use completely, rather than trying to contain damages later. Indeed, a global ban on POPs could do for the marine environment what the oil spill regulations of the 1970s and 1980s did—it could shift the burden of proof away from "innocent until proven guilty" toward a more precautionary approach that puts the burden of proof on the user.[60]

International trade rules are likely to become more widely used for purposes of marine conservation, although they are also the subject of some controversy. The United States, for example, has enacted laws that restrict or prohibit the importation of fish and wildlife products from other countries that do not meet certain environmental criteria. Two of them—the Marine Mammal Protection Act (MMPA) and the Sea Turtle Conservation

Amendments to the the U.S. Endangered Species Act—illustrate how trade restrictions can be used to promote the conservation of marine resources.[61]

The MMPA prohibits imports of yellowfin tuna into the United States from countries whose tuna fishing vessels operating in the eastern Pacific Ocean do not meet U.S. dolphin protection standards. Trade embargoes resulting from MMPA led to two separate challenges before dispute resolution panels of the General Agreement on Tariffs and Trade—by Mexico in 1991 and by the European Union in 1993. In each case, the panel ruled in favor of foreign tuna fishers, holding that trade regimes (particularly unilateral ones) do not permit distinctions between otherwise "like" products on the basis of how they were produced. Although neither decision was implemented, the cases prompted the United States and 11 other countries whose vessels fish in the region to negotiate a multilateral agreement establishing an International Dolphin Conservation Program, overseen by the Inter-American Tropical Tuna Commission. The new agreement sets common standards for dolphin protection and provides for comprehensive monitoring and observation of the fishery. U.S. legislation has since been changed to coincide with this agreement.[62]

The law protecting sea turtles prohibits U.S. imports of shrimp captured in ways that harm these animals, requiring the use of turtle excluder devices or some comparable gear. Embargoes resulting from this law have encouraged some Latin American and Asian countries that wish to keep selling their shrimp in the lucrative U.S. market to improve sea turtle protection measures. India, Malaysia, Pakistan, and Thailand have challenged the law in the World Trade Organization. In October 1998, the Appellate Board of the WTO ruled that the particular way in which the United States was implementing the law was discriminatory. One of the WTO's concerns was that it is preferable for environmental standards—such as those relating to the protection of sea turtles—to be established on a multilateral basis, rather than unilaterally.[63]

What has replaced freedom of the seas falls short of what is needed to protect ocean resources.

Although the WTO frowns on using trade restrictions to promote environmental goals, it also takes a dim view of subsidies. Its Committee on Trade and the Environment issued a policy statement on fishing subsidies in March 1998, a topic receiving increasing scrutiny from national governments, regional organizations, and the FAO. The possibility thus exists to use WTO rules to push for the removal of subsidies that promote overfishing. At the very least, member states can press the WTO to make global fishing subsidies data public.[64]

Having witnessed the effects of fishery stock collapses and resource degradation when the oceans are seen as a frontier for exploitation, we now need to move rapidly into an era of precautionary management based on an ecosystem approach. Policymakers, commercial interests, individual resource users, and the public at large need to come to terms with the reality that oceans are both a resource to be used and an environment to be protected. Fortunately, a series of UNCLOS-related agreements have begun to lay the groundwork for this new course. (See Table 5–5.)[65]

Further progress toward an ecologically based approach comes from the endorsement of the Global Environment Facility (GEF) and World Bank of a conservation system based on regions known as large marine ecosystems. Based on their biolog-ical, chemical, and physical characteristics, 49 of these ecosystems have been designated worldwide. The GEF has pledged $200–300 million to support country-specific projects dealing with transboundary international waters issues. To date, 58 developing countries have submitted proposals, each with the approval of their Ministers of Environment, Fisheries, and Finance. The U.S. Congress, the Ecological Society of America, and North Sea environment ministers have called for a similar approach to marine ecosystem protection.[66]

Although recent policy initiatives help fill the void in international law, what has replaced the freedom of the seas nevertheless falls short of what is needed to protect ocean resources and systems. Complementary actions at the regional and national levels are still lacking in many areas, as are more localized and site-specific programs. As they did 400 years ago, commercial interests and merchant industries still hold powerful sway over the terms of ocean governance. Scientists' calls for precaution and protective measures are largely ignored by policymakers, who focus on enhancing commerce, trade, and market supply and who look to extract as much from the sea as possible, with little regard for the effects on marine species or habitats. Overcoming the interest groups that favor the status quo will require engaging all potential stakeholders and reformulating the governance equation to incorporate the stewardship obligations that come with the privilege of use.

BUILDING POLITICAL WILL

Fortunately, a new sea ethic is emerging. From tighter dumping regulations to recent international agreements, policymakers have made some initial progress toward the goal of cleaning up our act.

Table 5–5. Strengths and Weaknesses of International Oceans Policies in the 1990s

Policy	Strength	Weakness
U.N. Global Driftnet Moratorium, 1991	Outside of a few areas, use of driftnets has ended on the world's oceans.	Fishers use longlines and other damaging fishing methods to evade the specifics of the moratorium, often with similar effects on marine wildlife.
Oceans Chapter in Agenda 21, 1992 Earth Summit	Addresses the sustainable use and conservation of marine resources and habitat areas; U.N. Commission on Sustainable Development to address oceans and seas in 1999.	Language with respect to conservation is weak; lacks specific commitments.
FAO High Seas Fishing Vessel Compliance Agreement, 1993	Global binding agreement; countries with vessels on the high seas must ensure that they do not undermine agreed fishing rules; requires countries to provide FAO with comprehensive information about vessel operation.	Not yet in force, as only 12 of necessary 25 countries have ratified it.
U.N. Convention on the Law of the Sea, 1982 (entered into force, 1994)	Global agreement; comprehensive framework for ocean development; calls for balance between use and conservation; ratified by more than 60 nations.	Conservation obligations weak.
FAO Code of Conduct for Responsible Fisheries, 1995	Agreed to by more than 60 fishing nations; contains principles for sustainable fisheries management and conservation; highlights aquaculture, bycatch, and trade.	Voluntary code; no punishment for ignoring it; no mention of of subsidies.
U.N. Agreement on Straddling Fish Stocks and Highly Migratory Fish Stocks, 1995	Prescribes precautionary approach to fishery management both inside and outside EEZ; vessel inspection rights in accordance with regional agreements; provides binding dispute resolution.	Not yet in force, as falls short of the required 30 ratifications; ratified by only 4 of the top 20 fishing nations.
Jakarta Mandate, Convention on Biological Diversity, 1995	Adopted guidelines and general principles on the protection of marine biological diversity and sustainable use of marine and coastal resources; puts ocean use in broader context of biological and social goals.	General guidelines only.

SOURCE: See endnote 65.

But much more is needed in the way of public education to build political support for marine conservation. To boost ongoing efforts, two key principles are important. First, any dividing up of the waters should be based on equity, fairness, and need as determined by dependence on the resource and the best available scientific knowledge, not simply on economic might and political pressure. In a similar vein, resource users should be responsible for their actions, with decisionmaking and accountability shared by stakeholders and government officials. Second, given the uncertainty in our scientific knowledge and management capabilities, we must err on the side of caution and take a precautionary approach.[67]

One tool that can help engage people in problem-solving is integrated coastal management (ICM). Through community-based planning, ICM brings together diverse groups of people—fishers, politicians, tourism operators, traders, and the general public—to identify shared problems and goals and to define solutions that build on their common interests. Discussions, mapping exercises, and site visits all help people make the connections between land and water use and the health of the marine environment. Active involvement in defining the problem, proposing solutions, and overseeing implementation is critical to making sure people are committed to the success of a project.[68]

Pressure from consumers, watchdog groups, and conscientious business leaders can help develop voluntary codes of conduct and standard industry practices.

Replanting mangroves and constructing artificial reefs are two concrete steps that help some fish stocks rebound quickly while letting people witness firsthand the results of their labors. Once people see the immediate payoff of their work, they are more likely to stay involved in longer-term protection efforts, such as marine sanctuaries, which involve removing an area from use entirely.

Marine protected areas are an important tool to help marine scientists and resource planners incorporate a more holistic, ecologically based approach to oceans protection. By limiting accessibility and easing pressures on the resource, these areas allow stocks to rebound and profits to return. Globally, more than

1,300 marine and coastal sites have some form of protection. But most lack effective on-the-ground management.[69]

Furthermore, efforts to establish marine refuges and parks lag far behind similar efforts on land. The World Heritage Convention, which identifies and protects areas of special significance to humankind, identifies only 31 sites that include either a marine or a coastal component, out of a total of 522. John Waugh, Senior Program Officer of the World Conservation Union–U.S. and others argue that the World Heritage List could be extended to a number of marine hotspots and should include representative areas of the continental shelf, the deep sea, and the open ocean. Setting these and other areas aside as off-limits to commercial development can help advance scientific understanding of marine systems and provide refuge for threatened species.[70]

To address the need for better data, coral reef scientists have recently enlisted the help of recreational scuba divers. Sport divers who volunteer to collect data are given basic training to identify and survey fish and coral species and to conduct rudimentary site assessments. The data are then compiled and put into a global inventory that policymakers use to monitor trends and to target intervention. More efforts like these—that engage the help of concerned individuals and volunteers—could help overcome funding and data deficiencies and build greater public awareness of the problems plaguing the world's oceans.[71]

Promoting sustainable ocean use also means shifting demand away from environmentally damaging products and extraction techniques. To this end, market forces, such as charging consumers more for particular fish and introducing industry codes of conduct, can be helpful. In April 1996, the World Wide Fund for Nature teamed up with one of the world's largest manufacturers of seafood products, Anglo-Dutch Unilever, to create economic incentives for sustainable fishing. Implemented through an independent Marine Stewardship Council, fisheries products that are harvested in a sustainable manner will qualify for an ecolabel. Similar efforts could help convince industries to curb wasteful practices and could generate greater consumer awareness of the need to choose products carefully.[72]

Away from public oversight, companies engaged in shipping, oil and gas extraction, deep sea mining, bioprospecting, and tidal and thermal energy represent a coalition of special interests whose activities help determine the fate of the oceans. It is crucial to get representatives of these industries engaged in implementing a new ocean charter that supports sustainable use. Their practices not only affect the health of oceans, they also help decide the pace of a transition toward a more sustainable energy economy, which in turn affects the balance between climate and oceans.

Making trade data and industry information publicly available is an important way both to build industry credibility and to ensure some degree of public oversight. While regulations are an important component of environmental protection, pressure from consumers, watchdog groups, and conscientious business leaders can help develop voluntary codes of action and standard industry practices that help move industrial sectors toward cleaner and greener operations. Economic incentives targeted to particular industries, such as low-interest loans for thermal projects, can help companies make a quicker transition to sus-tainable practices.

The fact that oceans are so central to the global economy and to human and planetary health may be the strongest motivation for protective action. For although the range of assaults and threats to ocean health are broad, the benefits that oceans provide are invaluable and shared by all. These huge bodies of water represent an enormous opportunity to forge a new system of cooperative, international governance based on shared resources and common interests. Achieving these far-reaching goals, however, begins with the technically simple but politically daunting task of overcoming several thousand years' worth of ingrained behavior. It requires us to see oceans not as an economic frontier for exploitation but as a scientific frontier for exploration and a biological frontier for careful use.

For generations, oceans have drawn people to their shores for a glimpse of the horizon, a sense of scale and awe at nature's might. Today, oceans offer careful observers a different kind of awe: a warning that our impacts on the Earth are exceeding natural bounds and in danger of disrupting life. Unfortunately, protection efforts already lag far behind what is needed. How we choose to react will determine the future of the planet. Precisely because so little is known about the condition of the oceans, we must approach the challenge with precaution and care. Oceans are not simply one more system under pressure—they are critical to our survival. As Carl Safina writes in *The Song for the Blue Ocean,* "we need the oceans more than they need us."[73]

6

Appreciating the Benefits of Plant Biodiversity

John Tuxill

At first glance, wild potatoes are not too impressive. Most are thin-stemmed, rather weedy-looking plants that underground bear disappointingly small tubers. But do not be deceived by initial appearances, for these plants are key allies in humankind's ongoing struggle to control late blight, a kind of fungus that thrives on potato plants. It was late blight that, in the 1840s, colonized and devastated the genetically uniform potato fields of Ireland, triggering the infamous famine that claimed more than a million lives. The disease has been controlled this century largely with fungicides, but in the mid-1980s farmers began reporting outbreaks of fungicide-resistant blight. These newly virulent strains have cut global potato harvests in the 1990s by 15 percent, a \$3.25-billion yield loss; in some regions, such as the highlands of Tanzania, losses to blight have approached 100 percent. Fortunately, scientists at the International Potato Center in Lima, Peru, have located genetic resistance to the new blight strains in the gene

pools of traditional Andean potato cultivars and their wild relatives, and now see hope for reviving the global potato crop.[1]

Wild potatoes are but one manifestation of the benefits humans gain from biological diversity, the richness and complexity of life on Earth. Plant biodiversity, in particular, is arguably the single greatest resource that humankind has garnered from nature during our long cultural development. Presently, scientists have described more than 250,000 species of mosses, ferns, conifers, and flowering plants, and estimate there may be upwards of 50,000 plant species yet to be documented, primarily in the remote, little-studied reaches of tropical forests.[2]

Within just the hundred-odd species of cultivated plants that supply most of the world's food, traditional farmers have selected and developed hundreds of thousands of distinct genetic varieties. During this century, professional plant breeders have used this rich gene pool to create the high-yielding crop varieties responsible for much of the enormous productivity of modern farming. Plant diversity also provides oils, latexes, gums, fibers, dyes, essences, and other products that clean, clothe, and refresh us and that have many industrial uses. And whether we are in the 20 percent of humankind who open a bottle of pills when we are feeling ill, or in the 80 percent who consult a local herbalist for a healing remedy, a large chunk of our medicines comes from chemical compounds produced by plants.[3]

Yet the more intensively we use plant diversity, the more we threaten its long-term future. The scale of human enterprise on Earth has become so great—we are now nearly 6 billion strong and consume about 40 percent of the planet's annual biological productivity—that we are eroding the very ecological foundations of plant biodiversity and losing unique gene pools, species, and even entire communities of species forever. It is as if humankind is painting a picture of the next millennium with a shrinking palette—the world will still be colored green, but in increasingly uniform and monocultured tones. Of course, our actions have produced benefits: society now grows more food than ever before, and those who can purchase it have a material standard of living unimaginable to earlier generations. But the undeniable price that plant diversity and the ecological health of our planet are paying for these achievements casts a shadow over the future of the development path that countries have pursued this century. To become more than a short-term civilization, we must start by maintaining biological diversity.[4]

INTO THE MASS EXTINCTION

Extinction is a natural part of evolution, but it is normally a rare and obscure event; the natural or "background" rate of extinction appears to be about 1–10 species a year. By contrast, scientists estimate that extinction rates have accelerated this century to at least 1,000 species per year. These numbers indicate we now live in a time of mass extinction—a global evolutionary upheaval in the diversity and composition of life on Earth.[5]

Paleontologists studying Earth's fossil record have identified five previous mass extinction episodes during life's 1.5 billion years of evolution, with the most recent being about 65 million years ago, at the end of the Cretaceous period, when the dinosaurs disappeared. Earlier mass extinctions hit marine invertebrates and other animal groups hard, but plants weathered these episodes with relatively little trouble. Indeed, flowering plants, which now account for nearly 90 percent of all land plant species, did not begin their diversification until the Cretaceous—relatively recently, in evolutionary terms.[6]

In the current mass extinction, however, plants are suffering unprecedented losses. According to a 1997 global analysis of more than 240,000 plant species coordinated by the World Conservation Union–IUCN, one out of every eight plants surveyed is potentially at risk of extinction. (See Table 6–1.) This tally includes species already endangered or clearly vulnerable to extinction, as well as those that are naturally rare (and thus at risk from ecological disruption) or extremely poorly known. More than 90 percent of these at-risk species are endemic to a single country—that is, found nowhere else in the world.[7]

The United States, Australia, and South Africa have the most plant species at risk (see Table 6–2), but their high standing is partly due to how much better-known their flora is compared with that of other species-rich countries. We have a good idea of how many plants have become endangered as the coastal sage scrub and perennial grasslands of California have been converted into sub-

Table 6–1. Threatened Plant Species, 1997

Status	Total	Share
	(number)	(percent)
Total Number of Species Surveyed	242,013	
Total Number of Threatened Species	33,418	14
Vulnerable to Extinction	7,951	3
In Immediate Danger of Extinction	6,893	3
Naturally Rare	14,505	6
Indeterminate Status	4,070	2
Total Number of Extinct Species	380	<1

SOURCE: Kerry S. Walter and Harriet J. Gillett, eds., *1997 IUCN Red List of Threatened Plants* (Gland, Switzerland: World Conservation Union–IUCN, 1997).

urban homes and cropland, for example. But we simply do not know how many species have dwindled as the cloud forests of Central America have been replaced by coffee plots and cattle pastures, or as the lowland rainforests of Indonesia and Malaysia have become oil palm and pulpwood plantations.

Increasingly, it is not just individual species but entire communities and ecosystems of plants that face extinction. The inter-Andean laurel and oak forests of Colombia, the heathlands of western Australia, the seasonally dry forest of the Pacific island of New Caledonia—all have been largely overrun by humankind. In the southeast corner of Florida in the United States, native plant communities, such as subtropical hardwood hammocks and limestone ridge pinelands, have been reduced to tiny patches in a sea of suburban homes, sugarcane fields, and citrus orchards. These irreplaceable remnants are all that is left of what southeast Florida once was—and they are now held together only with constant human vigilance to beat back a siege of exotic plants, such as Brazilian pepper and Australian casuarina.[8]

Biodiversity is also lost when gene pools within species evaporate. The closest wild ancestor of corn is a lanky, sprawling annual grass called teosinte, native to

Mexico and Guatemala, where it occurs in eight separate populations. Botanist Garrison Wilkes of the University of Massachusetts regards seven of these populations as rare, vulnerable, or already endangered—primarily due to the abandonment of traditional agricultural practices and to increased livestock grazing in the field margins and fallow areas favored by teosinte. Overall, teosinte is not yet threatened with extinction. But because

Table 6–2. Top 10 Countries with the Most Threatened Plants

Country	Total	Percentage of Country's Total Flora Threatened
	(number)	
United States	4,669	29
Australia	2,245	14
South Africa	2,215	11.5
Turkey	1,876	22
Mexico	1,593	6
Brazil	1,358	2.5
Panama	1,302	13
India	1,236	8
Spain	985	19.5
Peru	906	5

SOURCE: Kerry S. Walter and Harriet J. Gillett, eds., *1997 IUCN Red List of Threatened Plants* (Gland, Switzerland: World Conservation Union–IUCN, 1997).

the plant hybridizes readily with domesticated corn, every loss of a unique teosinte population reduces genetic diversity that may one day be needed to breed better-adapted corn plants.[9]

OF FOOD AND FARMERS

Nowhere is the value of biodiversity more evident than in our food supply. Roughly one third of all plant species have edible fruits, tubers, nuts, seeds, leaves, roots, or stems. During the nine tenths of human history when everyone lived as hunter-gatherers, an average culture would have had knowledge of several hundred edible plant species that could provide sustenance. Today, wild foods continue to supplement the diet of millions of rural poor worldwide, particularly during seasonal periods of food scarcity. Tuareg women in Niger, for instance, regularly harvest desert panic-grass and shama millet while migrating with their animal herds between wet and dry-season pastures. In rural northeast Thailand, wild foods gathered from forests and field margins make up half of all food eaten by villagers during the rainy season. In the city of Iquitos in the Peruvian Amazon, fruits of nearly 60 species of wild trees, shrubs, and vines are sold in the city produce markets. Residents in the surrounding countryside are estimated to obtain a tenth of their entire diet from wild-harvested fruits.[10]

For the last 5–10 millennia, we have actively cultivated the bulk of our food. Agriculture arose independently in many different regions, as people gradually lived closer together, became less nomadic, and focused their food production on plants that were amenable to repeated sowing and harvesting. In the 1920s the legendary Russian plant explorer Nikolai Vavilov identified geographic centers of crop diversity, including Mesoamerica, the central Andes, the Mediterranean Basin, the Near East, highland Ethiopia, and eastern China. He also inferred correctly that most centers correspond to where crops were first domesticated. For instance, native Andean farmers not only brought seven different species of wild potatoes into cultivation, they also domesticated common beans, lima beans, passion fruit, quinoa and amaranths (both grains), and a host of little-known tuber and leaf crops such as *oca*, *ulluco*, and *tarwi*—more than 25 species of food plants in all.[11]

Over the millennia, farmers have developed a wealth of distinctive varieties within crops by selecting and replanting seeds and cuttings from uniquely favorable individual plants—perhaps one that matured slightly sooner than others, was unusually resistant to pests, or possessed a distinctive color or taste. Subsistence farmers have always been acutely attentive to such varietal diversity because it helps them cope with variability in their environment, and for most major crops, farmers have developed thousands of folk varieties, or "landraces." India alone, for instance, probably had at least 30,000 rice landraces earlier this century.[12]

On-farm crop selection remains vital in developing countries, where farmers continue to save 80–90 percent of their own seed supplies. In industrial nations, by contrast, the seed supply process has become increasingly centralized during this century, as professional plant breeders have taken up the job of crop improvement and as corporations have assumed responsibility for supplying seeds. The power and promise of scientifically based plant breeding was confirmed by the 1930s, when the first commercial hybrid corn was marketed by the Pioneer Hi-Bred Company. Hybrids are favored by seed supply companies because they tend to be especially high-yielding (the bottom line for commercial farming) and because "second-generation" hybrid seeds do not retain the traits of their parents. This means that farmers must purchase hybrid seed anew from the supplier rather than saving their own stock. Some farmers have also been legally disenfranchised from seed-saving; under European Union law, it is now illegal for farmers to save and replant seed from plant varieties that have been patented by breeders.[13]

Traditional crop varieties are indispensable for global food security.

Although farmers can now purchase and plant seeds genetically engineered with the latest molecular techniques, the productivity of our food supply still depends on the plant diversity maintained by wildlands and traditional agricultural practices. Wild relatives of crops continue be used by breeders as sources of disease resistance, vigor, and other traits that produce billions of dollars in benefits to global agriculture. Imagine giving up sugarcane, strawberries, tomatoes, and wine grapes; none of these crops could be grown commercially without the genetic contribution of their respective wild relatives. With the rescue mission of their wild kin now under way, we can also place potatoes on this list.[14]

Traditional crop varieties are equally indispensable for global food security. Subsistence farmers around the world continue to grow primarily either landraces or locally adapted versions of professionally bred seed. Such small-scale agriculture produces 15–20 percent of the world's food supply, is predominantly performed by women, and provides the daily sustenance of roughly 1.4 billion rural poor. Moreover, landraces have contributed the genetic infrastructure of the intensively bred crop varieties that feed the rest of us. More than one third of the

U.S. wheat crop owes its productivity to landrace genes from Asia and other regions, a contribution worth at least $500 million annually.[15]

As we enter the next millennium, agricultural biodiversity faces an uncertain future. The availability of wild foods and populations of many wild relatives of crops is declining as wildlands are converted to human-dominated habitats and as hedgerows, fallow fields, and other secondary habitats decline within traditional agricultural landscapes. In the United States, two thirds of all rare and endangered plants are close relatives of cultivated species. If these species go extinct, a pool of potentially crucial future benefits for global agriculture will also vanish.[16]

There is also grave concern for the old crop landraces. By volume, the world's farmers now grow more sorghum, spinach, apples, and other crops than ever before, but they grow fewer varieties of each crop. Crop diversity in industrial nations has undergone a massive turnover this century; the proportion of varieties grown in the United States before 1904 but no longer present in either commercial agriculture or any major seed storage facility ranges from 81 percent for tomatoes to over 90 percent for peas and cabbages. Figures are less comprehensive for developing countries, but China is estimated to have gone from growing 10,000 wheat varieties in 1949 to only 1,000 by the 1970s, while just 20 percent of the corn varieties cultivated in Mexico in the 1930s can still be found there—an alarming decline for the cradle of corn.[17]

Crop varieties are lost for many reasons. Sometimes an extended drought destroys harvests and farmers must consume their planting seed stocks just to survive. Long-term climate change can also be a problem. In Senegal, two decades of below-normal rainfall created a growing season too short for traditional rice varieties to produce good yields. When fast-maturing rice cultivars became available through development aid programs, women farmers rapidly adopted them because of the greater harvest security they offered.[18]

In the majority of cases, however, farmers voluntarily abandon traditional seeds when they adopt new varieties, change agricultural practices, or move out of farming altogether. In industrial countries, crop diversity has declined in concert with the steady commercialization and consolidation of agriculture this century: fewer family farmers, and fewer seed companies offering fewer varieties for sale, mean fewer crop varieties planted in fields or saved after harvest. The seed supply industry is now dominated by multinational corporations; increasingly, the same companies that sell fertilizers and pesticides to farmers now also promote seeds bred to use those products.[19]

In most developing countries, diversity losses were minimal until the 1960s, when the famed international agricultural development program known as the Green Revolution introduced new high-yielding varieties of wheat, rice, corn, and other major crops. Developed to boost food self-sufficiency in famine-prone countries, the Green Revolution varieties were widely distributed, often with government subsidies to encourage their adoption, and displaced landraces from many prime farmland areas.[20]

In areas where agriculture is highly mechanized and commercialized, crops now exhibit what the U.N. Food and Agriculture Organization (FAO) politely calls an "impressively uniform" genetic base. A survey of nine major crops in the Netherlands found that the three most popular varieties for each crop covered 81–99 percent of the respective areas planted. Such patterns have also emerged on much of the developing world's prime farmland. One single wheat variety blanketed 67 percent of Bangladesh's wheat acreage in 1983 and 30 percent of India's the following year.[21]

The ecological risks we take in adopting such genetic uniformity are enormous, and keeping them at bay requires an extensive infrastructure of agricultural scientists and extension workers—as well as all too frequent applications of pesticides and other potent agrochemicals. A particularly heavy burden falls on professional plant breeders, who are now engaged in a relay race to develop ever more robust crop varieties before those already in monoculture succumb to evolving pests and diseases, or to changing environmental conditions.[22]

Breeders started this race earlier this century with a tremendous genetic endowment at their disposal, courtesy of nature and generations of subsistence farmers. Despite major losses, this wellspring is still far from empty—estimates are that plant breeders have used only a small fraction of the varietal diversity present in crop gene banks (facilities that store seeds under cold, dry conditions that can maintain seed viability for decades). At the same time, we can never be sure that what is already stored will cover all our future needs. When grassy stunt virus began attacking high-yielding Asian rices in the 1970s, breeders located genetic resistance to the disease in only a single collection of one population of a wild rice species in Uttar Pradesh, India—and that population has never been found again since. Conserving and reinvigorating biodiversity in agricultural landscapes remains essential for achieving global food security.[23]

OF MEDICINES AND MATERIAL GOODS

In a doctor's office in Germany, a man diagnosed with hypertension is prescribed reserpine, a drug from the Asian snakeroot plant. In a small town in India, a woman complaining of stomach pains visits an

Ayurvedic healer, and receives a soothing and effective herbal tea as part of her treatment. In a California suburb, a headache sufferer unseals a bottle of aspirin, a compound originally isolated from European willow trees and meadow herbs.[24]

People everywhere rely on plants for staying healthy and extending the quality and length of their lives. One quarter of the prescription drugs marketed in North America and Europe contain active ingredients derived from plants. Plant-based drugs are part of standard medical procedures for treating heart conditions, childhood leukemia, lymphatic cancer, glaucoma, and many other serious illnesses. Worldwide, the over-the-counter value of these drugs is estimated at more than $40 billion annually. Major pharmaceutical companies and institutions such as the U.S. National Cancer Institute implement plant screening programs as a primary means of identifying new drugs.[25]

The World Health Organization estimates that 3.5 billion people in developing countries rely on plant-based medicine for their primary health care. Ayurvedic and other traditional healers in South Asia use at least 1,800 different plant species in treatments and are regularly consulted by some 800 million people. In China, where medicinal plant use goes back at least four millennia, healers employ more than 5,000 plant species. At least 89 plant-derived commercial drugs used in industrial countries were originally discovered by folk healers, many of whom are women. Traditional medicine is particularly important for poor and rural residents, who typically are not well served by formal health care systems. Recent evidence suggests that when economic woes and structural adjustment programs restrict governments' abilities to provide health care, urban and even middle-class residents of developing countries also turn to more affordable traditional medicinal experts.[26]

Traditional herbal therapies are growing rapidly in popularity in industrial countries as well. FAO estimates that between 4,000 and 6,000 species of medicinal plants are traded internationally, with China accounting for about 30 percent of all such exports. In 1992, the booming U.S. retail market for herbal medicines reached nearly $1.5 billion, and the European market is even larger.[27]

Despite their demonstrable value, medicinal plants are declining in many areas. Human alteration of forests and other habitats all too often eliminates sites rich in wild medicinal plants. This creates an immediate problem for folk healers when they can no longer find the plants they need for performing certain cures—a problem commonly lamented by indigenous herbalists in eastern Panama, among others. Moreover, strong consumer demand and inadequate oversight of harvesting levels and practices mean that wild-gathered medicinal plants are commonly overexploited.[28]

In Cameroon, for example, the bark of the African cherry is highly esteemed by traditional healers, but most of the country's harvest is exported to Western Europe, where African cherry is a principal treatment for prostate disorders. In recent years Cameroon has been the leading supplier of African cherry bark to international markets, but clearance of the tree's montane forest habitat, combined with the inability of the government forestry department to manage the harvest, has led to widespread, wanton destruction of cherry stands.[29]

In addition to the immediate losses, every dismantling of a unique habitat represents a loss of future drugs and medicines, particularly in species-rich habitats like tropical forests. Fewer than 1 percent of all plant species have been screened by chemists to see what bioactive compounds they may contain. The nearly 50 drugs already derived from tropical rainforest plants are estimated to represent only 12 percent of the medically useful compounds waiting to be discovered in rainforests.[30]

Most tragically of all, many rural societies are rapidly losing their cultural knowledge about medicinal plants. In communities undergoing accelerated westernization, fewer young people are interested in learning about traditional healing plants and how to use them. From Samoa to Suriname, most herbalists and healers are elderly, and few have apprentices studying to take their place. Ironically, as this decline has accelerated, there has been a resurgent interest in ethnobotany—the study of how people classify, conceptualize, and use plants—and other fields of study related to traditional medicinal plant use. Professional ethnobotanists surveying medicinal plants used by different cultures are racing against time to document traditional knowledge before it vanishes with its last elderly practitioners.[31]

For the one quarter of humanity who live at or near subsistence levels, plant diversity offers more than just food security and health care—it also provides a roof over their heads, cooks their food, provides eating utensils, and on average meets about 90 percent of their material needs. Consider palms: temperate zone dwellers may think of palm trees primarily as providing an occasional coconut or the backdrop to an idyllic island vacation, but tropical peoples have a different perspective. The babassu palm from the eastern Amazon Basin has more than 35 different uses—construction material, oil and fiber source, game attractant, even as an insect repellent. Commercial extraction of babassu products is a part or full-time economic activity for more than 2 million rural Brazilians.[32]

Indigenous peoples throughout tropical America have been referred to as "palm cultures." The posts, floors, walls, and beams of their houses are made from the wood of palm trunks, while the roofs are thatched with palm leaves. They use baskets and sacks woven from palm leaves to store household items, including

food—which may itself be palm fruits, palm hearts (the young growing shoot of the plant), or wild game hunted with weapons made from palm stems and leaves. At night, family members will likely drift off to sleep in hammocks woven from palm fibers. When people die, they may be buried in a coffin carved from a palm trunk.[33]

One quarter of the prescription drugs marketed in North America and Europe contain active ingredients derived from plants.

Palms are exceptionally versatile, but they are only part of the spectrum of useful plants in biodiverse environments. In northwest Ecuador, indigenous cultures that practice shifting agriculture use more than 900 plant species to meet their material, medicinal, and food needs; halfway around the world, Dusun and Iban communities in the rainforests of central Borneo use a similar total of plants in their daily lives. People who are more integrated into regional and national economies tend to use fewer plants, but still commonly depend on plant diversity for household uses and to generate cash income. In India, at least 5.7 million people make a living harvesting nontimber forest products, a trade that accounts for nearly half the revenues earned by Indian state forests.[34]

Those of us who live in manicured suburbs or urban concrete jungles may meet more of our material needs with metals and plastics, but plant diversity still enriches our lives. Artisans who craft musical instruments or furniture, for instance, value the unique acoustic qualities and appearances of the different tropical and temperate hardwoods that they work with—aspects of biodiversity that ultimately benefit anyone who listens to classical music or purchases handcrafted furniture. Among the nonfood plants traded internationally on commercial levels are at least 200 species of timber trees, 42 plants producing essential oils, 66 species yielding latexes or gums, and 13 species used as dyes and colorants.[35]

As with medicinals, the value that plant resources have for handicraft production, industrial use, or household needs has often not prevented their local or regional decline. One of the most valuable nontimber forest products is rattan, a flexible cane obtained from a number of species of vine-like palms that can grow up to 185 meters long. Asian rattan palms support an international furniture-making industry worth $3.5–6.5 billion annually. Unfortunately, rattan stocks are declining throughout much of tropical Asia because of the loss of native rainforest and overharvesting. In the past few years, some Asian furniture makers have even begun importing rattan supplies from Nigeria and other central African countries.[36]

On a global level, declines of wild plants related to industrial crops such as cotton or plantation-grown timber could one day limit our ability to cultivate those commodities by shrinking the gene pools needed for breeding new crops. More locally, declines of materially useful species mean life gets harder and tougher in the short term. When a tree species favored for firewood is overharvested, women must walk longer to collect their family's fuel supply, make due with an inferior species that does not burn as well, or spend scarce money purchasing fuel from vendors. When a fiber plant collected for sale to handicraft producers becomes scarce, it is harder for collectors to earn an income that could help pay school fees for their children. Whether we are rich or poor, biodiversity enhances the quality of our lives—and many people already feel its loss.

BIO-UNIFORMITY RISING

The cumulative effects of human activities on Earth are evident not just in declines in particular species, but in the increasingly tattered state of entire ecosystems and landscapes—and when large-scale ecological processes begin to break down, conservation and management become all the more complicated. Take the problem of habitat fragmentation, when undisturbed wildlands are reduced to patchwork, island-like remnants of their former selves. Natural islands in oceans or large lakes tend to be impoverished in species; their smaller area means they usually do not develop the ecological complexity and diversity characteristic of more extensive mainland areas. Moreover, when an island population of a species is eradicated, it is harder for adjacent mainland populations to recolonize and replace it.[37]

As a result, when development—large-scale agriculture, settlements, roads—sprawls across landscapes, remaining habitat fragments usually behave like the islands they have become: they lose species. In western Ecuador, the Río Palenque Science Center protects a square-kilometer remnant of the lowland rainforest that covered the region a mere three decades ago; now the center is an island amid cattle pasture and oil palm plantations. Twenty-four species of orchids, bromeliads, and other plants at Río Palenque have already succumbed to the "island effect" and can no longer be found there. One vanished species, an understory shrub, has never been recorded anywhere else and is presumed extinct.[38]

Even with these drawbacks, small areas of native habitat can have enormous conservation value when they are all that is left of a unique plant community or rare habitat. But waiting to protect them until only patches remain carries an unmistakable tradeoff: smaller holdings require more-intensive management than larger ones. In smaller reserves, managers often must simulate natural disturbances (such as prescribed burns to maintain fire-adapted vegetation); provide pollination, seed dispersal, and pest control services in place of vanished animals; reintroduce desirable native species when they disappear from a site (perhaps due to a series of poor breeding seasons); and perform other duties the original ecosystem once did free of charge. Governments and societies that are unwilling or unable to shoulder these management costs will soon find that the biodiversity they intended to protect with nature reserves has vanished from within them.[39]

Invasive species that crowd out native flora and fauna are one of the biggest headaches for managing biodiversity in disturbed landscapes. In certain susceptible habitats, such as oceanic islands and subtropical heathlands, controlling invasives may be the single biggest management challenge. South Africa has one of the largest invasive species problems of any nation, and has a great deal at stake: the fynbos heathlands and montane forest of the country's Cape region hold more plant species—8,600, most of them endemic—in a smaller area than anywhere else on Earth. Fortunately, South Africans are increasingly aware of the threat that exotics pose, and in 1996 the government initiated a program to fight invasives with handsaw and hoe. Some 40,000 people are employed to cut and clear Australian eucalypts, Central American pines, and other unwanted guests in natural areas. It is a measure of the scale and severity of the invasive problem that this effort is South Africa's single largest public works program.[40]

Large-scale ecological alterations also have great potential to combine their effects in unpredictable and damaging ways. For instance, much of the world is now saturated in nitrogen compounds (an essential element required by all plants for growth and development) because of our overuse of nitrogen-based synthetic fertilizers and fossil fuels. Studies of North American prairies found that the plants that responded best to excess nitrogen tended to be weedy invasives, not the diverse native prairie flora. Likewise, plant and animal species already pressed for survival in fragmented landscapes may also have to contend with altered rainfall patterns, temperature ranges, seasonal timing, and other effects of global climate change.[41]

Scientists are already detecting what could be the first fingerprints of an altered global atmosphere on plant communities.

Already, scientists are detecting what could be the first fingerprints of an altered global atmosphere on plant communities. Data from tropical forest research plots worldwide indicate that the rate at which rainforest trees die and replace each other, called the turnover rate, has increased steadily since the 1950s. This suggests that the forests under study are becoming "younger," increasingly dominated by faster-growing, shorter-lived trees and woody vines—exactly the kinds of plants expected to thrive in a carbon dioxide–rich world with more extreme weather events. Without major reductions in global carbon emissions, forest turnover rates will likely rise further, and over time could push to extinction many slower-growing tropical hardwood tree species that cannot compete in a carbon-enriched environment.[42]

Global trends are shaping a botanical world that is most striking in its greater uniformity. The richly textured mix of native plant communities that evolved over thousands of years is increasingly frayed, replaced by extensive areas under intensive cultivation or heavy grazing, lands devoted to settlements or industrial activities, and secondary habitats—partially disturbed areas dominated by shorter-lived, "weedy," often non-native species. A 1994 mapping study by the organization Conservation International estimated that nearly three quarters of our planet's habitable land surface (that which is not bare rock, drifting sand, or ice) already is either partially or heavily disturbed. Moreover, within human-dominated landscapes, relatively diverse patchworks of small-scale cultivation, fallow fields, seasonal grazing areas, and managed native vegetation are being replaced by large, uniform fields or by extensive denuded and degraded areas.[43]

The mixtures of species in different regions are becoming more similar as well. Lists of endangered plants are dominated by endemic species—those native to a relatively restricted area such as a country or state, an isolated mountain range, or a specific soil type. When endemic plants vanish, the remaining species pool becomes more uniform. Finally, the spectrum of distinct populations and varieties within plant species is shrinking, a problem most advanced in our endowment of domesticated plants.[44]

Countries that emerged in a world filled with biodiversity now must gain and maintain prosperity amid increasing bio-uniformity. We are conducting an unprecedented experiment with the security and stability of our food supply, our health care systems, and the ecological infrastructure upon which both rest. To obtain the results we desire, we must conserve and protect the plant biodiversity that remains with us, and manage our use of natural systems in ways that restore biodiversity to landscapes worldwide.

STORED FOR SAFEKEEPING

Broad recognition of the need to safeguard plant resources is largely a twentieth century phenomenon. The first warnings about the global erosion of plant diversity were voiced in the 1920s by scientists such as Harry Harlan of the United States and Nikolai Vavilov, who realized the threat posed by farmers' abandonment of landraces in favor of newer varieties that were spreading widely in an increasingly interconnected world.[45]

The dominant approach to conserving plant varieties and species has involved removing them from their native habitat or agricultural setting and protecting them at specialized institutions such as botanical gardens, nurseries, and gene banks. Most off-site collections of wild species and ornamental plants are in the custody of the world's 1,600 botanical gardens. Combined, they tend representatives of tens of thousands of plant species—nearly 25 percent of the world's flowering plants and ferns, by one estimate.[46]

Most botanical gardens active today were established by European colonial powers to introduce economically important and ornamental plants throughout the far-flung reaches of empires, and to promote the study of potentially useful plants. Nowadays many botanical gardens have reoriented their mission toward species preservation, particularly in their research and education programs. Since the late 1980s, botanical gardens have coordinated efforts through an international conservation network, which helps ensure that the rarest plants receive priority for propagation and, ultimately, reintroduction.[47]

Gene banks have focused almost exclusively on storing seeds of crop varieties and their immediate wild relatives. (The principal exception is the Royal Botanic Garden's Millennium Seed Bank in

England, which holds more than 4,000 wild species and is expanding toward a collection of one quarter of the world's flora.) Gene banks arose from plant breeders' need to have readily accessible stocks of breeding material. Their conservation role came to the forefront in the 1970s, following large losses linked to genetic uniformity in the southern U.S. corn crop in 1970 and the Soviet winter wheat crop of 1971–72.[48]

In 1974, governments and the United Nations established the International Board for Plant Genetic Resources (now known as the International Plant Genetic Resources Institute, or IPGRI), which cobbled together a global network of gene banks. The network includes university breeding programs, government seed storage units, and the Consultative Group on International Agricultural Research (CGIAR), a worldwide network of 16 agricultural research centers originally established to bring the Green Revolution to developing countries, and funded primarily by the World Bank and international aid agencies.[49]

The number of unique seed samples or "accessions" in gene banks now exceeds 6 million. The largest chunk of these, more than 500,000 accessions, are in the gene banks of CGIAR centers such as the International Rice Research Institute in the Philippines and the International Wheat and Maize Improvement Center (CIMMYT) in Mexico. At least 90 percent of all gene bank accessions are of food and commodity plants, especially the world's most intensively bred and economically valuable crops. (See Table 6–3.) By the late 1980s, IPGRI regarded a number of these crops, such as wheat and corn, as essentially completely collected; that is, nearly all of the known landraces and varieties of the crop are already represented in gene banks. Others have questioned this assessment, however, arguing that the lack of quantitative studies of crop gene pools makes it difficult to ascer-

Table 6–3. Gene Bank Collections for Selected Crops

Crop	Accessions in Gene Banks	Estimated Share of Landraces Collected
	(number)	(percent)
Wheat	850,000	90
Rice	420,000	90
Corn	262,000	95
Sorghum	168,500	80
Soybeans	176,000	70
Common Beans	268,500	50
Potatoes	31,000	80–90
Cassava	28,000	35
Tomatoes	77,500	90
Squashes, Cucumbers, Gourds	30,000	50
Onions, Garlic	25,000	70
Sugarcane	27,500	70
Cotton	48,500	75

SOURCE: Donald L. Plucknett et al., *Gene Banks and the World's Food* (Princeton, NJ: Princeton University Press, 1987); Brian D. Wright, *Crop Genetic Resource Policy: Toward A Research Agenda*, EPTD Discussion Paper 19 (Washington, DC: International Food Policy Research Institute, 1996); U.N. Food and Agriculture Organization, *The State of the World's Plant Genetic Resources for Food and Agriculture* (Rome: 1996).

tain whether even the best-studied crops have been adequately sampled.[50]

There are additional reasons for interpreting gene bank totals conservatively. The total annual cost of maintaining all accessions currently in gene banks is about $300 million, and many facilities, hard-pressed for operating funds, cannot maintain seeds under optimal physical conditions. Seeds that are improperly dried or kept at room temperature rather than in cold storage may begin to lose viability within a few years. At this point, they must be "grown out"—germinated, planted, raised to maturity, and then reharvested, which is a time-consuming and labor-intensive activity when repeated for thousands of accessions per year. These problems suggest that an unknown fraction of accessions is probably of questionable viability.[51]

Only 13 percent of gene-banked seeds are in well-run facilities with long-term storage capability—and even the crown jewels of the system, such as the U.S. National Seed Storage Laboratory, have at times had problems maintaining seed viability rates. For extensively gene-banked crops (primarily major grains and legumes) where large collections are duplicated in different facilities, the odds of losing the diversity already on deposit are reduced. But for sparsely collected crops whose accessions are stored at just one or two sites, the possibility of genetic erosion remains disquietingly high.[52]

Despite such drawbacks, off-site facilities remain indispensable for conservation. In some cases, botanical gardens and gene banks have rescued species whose wild populations are now gone. They can also help return diversity to its proper home through reintroduction programs. Although the uplands of East Africa are not the center of domestication for common beans, the farmers of the region adopted them as their own several centuries ago, and have developed the world's richest mix of local bean varieties. When Rwanda was overwhelmed by civil conflict in 1994, the height of the genocidal violence occurred during the February-to-June growing season, greatly reducing harvests and raising the prospect of widespread famine. Amid the relief contributions that flowed into the country once the situation had stabilized were stocks of at least 170 bean varieties that had been previously collected in Rwanda and stored in gene banks worldwide. These supplies helped ensure that Rwandan farmers had stocks of high-quality, locally adapted beans for planting in the subsequent growing season.[53]

Still, even the most enthusiastic boosters of botanical gardens and gene banks

recognize that such facilities, even when impeccably maintained, provide only one piece in the conservation puzzle. Off-site storage takes species out of their natural ecological settings. Wild tomato seeds can be sealed in a glass jar and frozen for safekeeping, but left out of the cold are the plant's pollinators, its dispersers, and all the other organisms and relationships that have shaped the plant's unique evolution. Gene banks and botanical gardens only save a narrow—albeit valuable—slice of plant diversity. When stored seeds are grown out over several generations offsite, in time they can even lose their native adaptations and evolve to fit instead the conditions of their captivity.[54]

KEEPING DIVERSITY IN PLACE

In the end, plant diversity can be securely maintained only by protecting the native habitats and ecosystems where plants have evolved. Countries have safeguarded wildlands primarily through establishing national parks, forest reserves, and other formally protected areas. During this century, governments have steadily increased protected area networks, and they now encompass nearly 12 million square kilometers, or about 8 percent of the Earth's land surface. Many protected areas guard irreplaceable botanical resources, such as Malaysia's Mount Kinabalu National Park, which safeguards the unique vegetation of southeast Asia's highest peak. A few reserves have been established specifically to protect useful plants, such as the Sierra de Manantlan biosphere reserve in Mexico, which encompasses the only known populations of perennial wild corn.[55]

Yet current protected area networks also have major limitations. Many highly diverse plant communities, such as tropical deciduous forests, are greatly under-protected. In addition, many protected areas officially decreed on paper are minimally implemented by chronically underfunded and understaffed natural resource agencies. But perhaps the most fundamental limitation of national parks, wilderness areas, and similarly strict designations arises when they conflict with the cultural and economic importance that plants hold for local communities.[56]

A great deal of the natural wealth that conservationists have sought to protect is actually on lands and under waters long managed by local people. Indigenous societies worldwide have traditionally protected prominent landscape features like mountains or forests, designating them as sacred sites and ceremonial centers. In parts of West Africa, sacred groves hold some of the last remaining populations of important medicinal plants. On Samoa and other Pacific islands, communities manage forests to produce wild foods and medicines, raw materials for canoes and household goods, and other benefits.[57]

Not surprisingly, actions such as evicting long-term residents from newly designated forest reserves, or denying them access to previously harvested plant stands, have generated a great deal of ill will toward protected areas worldwide. Fortunately, workable alternatives are emerging in a number of cases where long-term residents have been made equal partners in managing protected lands. In the Indian state of West Bengal, 320,000 hectares of semi-deciduous sal forest is managed jointly by villagers and the state forestry department, with villagers taking primary responsibility for patrolling nearby forest stands. Since joint management began in 1972, the status of the sal forests has improved, and regenerating stands now provide villagers with medicines, firewood, and wild-gathered foodstuffs. Medicinals also feature prominently in a 4,000-hectare rainforest reserve in Belize, which is government-owned but managed by the Belize Associa-

tion of Traditional Healers.[58]

Such collaboration between locals and professional resource managers is also crucial to reversing the overexploitation of valuable wild plants. Very few commercially marketed wild species are harvested sustainably, in ways or at levels that do not degrade the plant resource. Despite the lack of progress, however, the foundations of sustainability are becoming increasingly clear. Secure and enforceable tenure is essential—either in the form of rights to harvest a plant or tenure over the land it grows on. Harvesters also need enough economic security to be able to afford the tradeoffs involved in not harvesting everything at once. Access to fair and open markets is important, as is having technology appropriate for the harvesting task. Information about the ecology and productivity of a plant can make a big difference. Consumers willing to pay a premium for well-harvested products also help—like those generated through certification programs for "environmentally friendly" products.[59]

Few wild harvests meet all these criteria, but a growing number of initiatives are coming close. In Mexico, ancient cone-bearing plants called cycads have been heavily exploited for their ornamental value, both for sale domestically and for horticultural export to the United States, Japan, and Europe. Most cycads are wild-harvested by uprooting or cutting, but a botanical garden in the state of Veracruz is working with local villagers to reduce pressures on several overexploited species. In one community, Monte Oscuro, residents set aside a communal plot of dry forest to protect a relict population of cycads in exchange for help with building a community plant nursery. Seeds are collected from the wild plants, then germinated and tended in the nursery by villagers who have received training in basic cycad propagation. Some of the young cycads are returned to the forest to offset any potential downturn in the wild population from the seed harvest. The rest are sold and the profits deposited in a community fund.[60]

Presently the largest hurdle is finding good markets for the young plants the communities are producing; cycads are slow-growing, and horticultural buyers prefer larger plants. Better monitoring and enforcement of the international ornamental plant trade would help, for Mexican cycad species are listed with the Convention on International Trade in Endangered Species of Wild Fauna and Flora (CITES) of 1973, which provides a powerful legal tool for controlling international trade in threatened plants and animals. CITES is generally regarded as one of the more effective international environmental treaties. It prohibits trade in the most highly endangered species (listed in the Treaty's Appendix I), and keeps watch on vulnerable species (listed in Appendix II) by requiring that countries issue a limited number of permits for the species' export and import between signatory countries. Although CITES provides powerful tools for enforcing sustainable harvests, it is still up to the countries involved to use them.[61]

In some rural communities in Zimbabwe, villagers contribute seeds annually to a community seed stock.

Combining local and international strengths also is crucial for sustaining the genetic diversity of our food supply. What is needed most is agricultural development that strengthens rather than simplifies plant diversity to meet the needs and goals of farmers—especially subsistence farmers in developing countries who still maintain diverse agricultural landscapes.

Meeting this challenge requires understanding the particular cultural, economic, and technological reasons why farmers maintain elements of traditional farming, such as unique crop variety mixtures. For instance, native Hopi communities in the southwest United States maintain indigenous corn and lima bean varieties because the germinating seeds are indispensable for religious ceremonies. Mende farmers in Sierra Leone continue to grow native red-hulled African rice for the same reason. Andean peasant farmers still grow pink and purple potatoes, big-seed corn, quinoa, and other traditional crops because that is what they themselves prefer to eat; the commercial varieties they grow are strictly to sell for cash income.[62]

One option to help farmers maintain crop diversity could involve supporting farmers' informal networks of seed exchange and procurement, so as to improve their access to diverse seed sources. In some rural communities in Zimbabwe, villagers contribute seeds annually to a community seed stock. At the start of the planting season, the seeds are redistributed to all community members, a step that gives villagers access to the full range of varietal diversity present in the immediate vicinity and ensures that no one goes without seeds for planting. Grassroots organizations in Ethiopia, Peru, Tonga, and many other countries have sponsored community seed banks, regional agricultural fairs, seed collection tours, demonstration gardens, and similar projects to promote informal seed exchange between farmers, increase their access to crop diversity, and help them replenish seed stocks after poor harvests.[63]

Another approach to maintaining varietal diversity involves reorienting formal plant breeding toward the local needs of farmers. Typically plant breeders create uniform, widely adaptable "pure-bred" varietal lines, and only toward the end of the process are the lines evaluated with farmers. Participatory plant breeding methods involve farmers at all stages. In the most advanced programs, breeders and farming communities work together over several crop generations to evaluate, select, combine, and improve a wide range of varieties, both those available locally and those from other regions. In this way, participatory plant breeding can improve the suite of locally preferred varieties without resorting to varietal uniformity; this approach maintains—or potentially even enhances—the genetic diversity present in farmers' fields.[64]

Participatory plant breeding has been pioneered primarily by grassroots development organizations and innovative national plant breeding programs in developing countries; it has not been taken up by commercial seed producers, perhaps because its benefits tend to be diffuse and not easily appropriated for commercial gain. The CGIAR centers are exploring participatory approaches, but also remain heavily involved in standard breeding programs. For instance, the corn and wheat center CIMMYT recently collaborated with university breeders and seed companies to develop better-yielding corn varieties targeted for highland Mexico—areas where corn landraces continue to be grown by small-scale farmers under diverse environmental conditions. In doing so, CIMMYT chose to focus on hybrid corn varieties. If well tailored to the environmental and economic constraints facing highland Mexican farmers, the new hybrids could boost crop yields— but farmers will be unable to save their seeds and adapt them further to local conditions. The seed companies involved will surely benefit, but past experience suggests that local plant biodiversity may pay the price.[65]

As this last example shows, the most fundamental changes to be made in protecting crop genetic diversity—and plant biodiversity in general—involve changing policies. Governments are often biased toward promoting intensive agriculture dependent on high inputs and genetically uniform crops. Farmers in most south-ern African countries, for instance, are only eligible for government agricultural credit programs if they agree to plant modern improved varieties. International development aid and structural adjustment policies commonly promote nontraditional export crops, which can trigger habitat conversion (erasing wild plant diversity) and replace indigenous crop mixtures. Until fundamental policy changes are taken to heart by governments, international lenders, and related institutions, the path to sustaining plant biodiversity—wild or domesticated—will remain difficult.[66]

SHARING THE BENEFITS

Governments can begin to chart a new course by resolving the most prominent policy issue affecting plant diversity today: how to distribute biodiversity's economic benefits fairly and equitably. Establishing a system of intellectual property rights to plant resources has proved contentious because of a simple pattern—plant diversity (both wild and cultivated) is held mostly by developing countries, but the economic benefits it generates are disproportionately captured by industrial nations. For most of this century, plant diversity has been treated as the "common heritage" of humankind, freely available to anyone who can use it, with proprietary ownership only granted via patent law to individuals who demonstrate trade secrets or uniquely improve a crop variety or other plant.[67]

Since the early 1980s, however, there has been widening agreement that indigenous people and traditional farmers deserve compensation for their long-standing generation, management, and knowledge of biodiversity. Grassroots advocates argue that indigenous people deserve "traditional resource rights" to the plants they cultivate and know how to use, rights that would have the same international legal standing as that afforded to patent rights. Recognition of such rights requires, at a minimum, negotiating equitable benefit-sharing agreements at the community level whenever plants or indigenous knowledge about them is collected by researchers. An additional way to acknowledge the world's debt to rural communities who safeguard plant biodiversity would be to establish an international fund supporting continued local management of plant resources. Such a step appears the most practical means of compensation for the large amount of plant biodiversity that is already in the public domain (such as the millions of seed accessions in gene banks or plants widely used as herbal medicines), since establishing exactly who deserves compensation for commercial innovations from these plant resources is a Herculean task.[68]

To date, formal agreements for sharing the benefits of plant diversity have been negotiated most extensively in the search for new pharmaceuticals from plants in biodiversity-rich developing countries. The first such "bioprospecting" agreement was announced in 1991 between Merck Pharmaceuticals and Costa Rica's nongovernmental National Institute of Biodiversity (InBio), in which Merck paid InBio $1.1 million for access to plant and insect samples, and promised to share an undisclosed percentage of royalties from any commercial products that resulted.[69]

There are now at least a dozen bioprospecting agreements in place worldwide, involving national governments, indigenous communities, conservation groups, start-up companies, and established corporate giants. Most legitimate agreements have followed the Merck-InBio model, with a modest up-front payment and a promise to return between one quarter of 1 percent and 3 percent (depending on the project) of any future royalties to the biodiversity holders. Bioprospecting proponents argue that with the huge cost ($200–350 million) of bringing a new drug to market, companies cannot afford to share a higher percentage of royalties. Critics, however, suspect many bilateral bioprospecting agreements are not negotiated on an even footing; when a biotechnology firm approached the U.S. government about prospecting for unique microbes inhabiting the geysers and hot springs of Yellowstone National Park, for instance, the Park Service negotiated a royalty share of 10 percent. Moreover, not all bioprospecting agreements automatically uphold traditional resource rights; many have been negotiated on a national rather than community level, involving governments who many indigenous people think do not adequately represent—indeed, sometimes actively undermine—their interests.[70]

In contrast with bioprospecting, resolving who owns the world's crop genetic resources is being negotiated multilaterally, in factious diplomatic arenas. In 1989 FAO adopted a Farmers' Rights proposal that would compensate farmers for their contribution to biodiversity via an international trust fund to support the conservation of plant genetic resources. The 1992 Convention on Biological Diversity also called for incorporating Farmers' Rights, subsequent to further international negotiations. There has been no official endorsement of this concept, however, from the industrial nations who would provide the compensation, and the fund has remained unimplemented. During the most recent round of international negotiations, in June 1998, the European Union appeared ready to support Farmers' Rights, but Australian, U.S., and Canadian diplomats continued to stonewall the issue.[71]

Meanwhile, the intellectual property agenda of industrial countries is being advanced by the World Trade Organization (WTO). All countries acceding to the General Agreement on Tariffs and

Trades are required to establish a system for protecting breeders' rights through plant variety patents. They can either adopt the system of administering patents and breeders' rights followed by industrial nations under the International Union for the Protection of New Varieties of Plants (UPOV), or instead design their own unique system. The UPOV Convention was established in 1978 and substantially revised in 1991; initially it gave farmers the right to save commercial seed for their own use, but the 1991 version allowed signatory countries to revoke this right. Some countries, including India, are looking at structuring their own plant patent systems to also acknowledge farmers' rights, but it is unclear whether the WTO will approve such arrangements.[72]

Despite the foot-dragging in international arenas, de facto boundaries are emerging for what will and will not be tolerated in the expropriation of crop genetic resources. In May 1997, two Australian agricultural centers applied for proprietary breeders' rights on two varieties of chickpeas. Their application sparked an international uproar because the Australian breeders had obtained both varieties from a CGIAR gene bank, which had provided the seeds with the understanding they were to be used for research and not for direct financial gain. Moreover, the Australians did little breeding to improve the two chickpeas, one of which was a landrace widely grown by Indian farmers, and they even appeared to be laying the groundwork to market the chickpeas in India and Pakistan. Ultimately, the Australian government bowed to international pressure and rejected the patent application. The CGIAR subsequently called for a moratorium on all claims for proprietary breeding rights involving germplasm held in trust by CGIAR or FAO-sponsored gene banks.[73]

While blatant gene grabs like that of the Australians may now be beyond the international pale, the current situation remains far from ideal. The lack of a clear, multilateral system of intellectual property rights for plant genetic resources distracts governments from the task of conserving these resources for future generations. The right of subsistence farmers to save and adapt the seeds they plant—arguably the most important mechanism for sustaining crop genetic diversity in fields—still has not been recognized by many governments. Without clear ground rules established, institutions and industries that depend directly on biodiversity for their well-being have little incentive to invest in strategies to help sustain plant diversity in the fields and wildlands where it originates. All countries must redouble their efforts to surmount the political logjam over plant genetic resources, for continued delay puts biodiversity at risk, and ultimately serves no one's interest.[74]

The right of subsistence farmers to save and adapt the seeds they plant still has not been recognized by many governments.

For all of human history, we have depended on plants and the rest of biodiversity for our soul and subsistence. Now the roles are reversed, and biodiversity's fate depends squarely on how we shape our own future. From reducing over-exploitation of wild plants to establishing traditional resource rights for biodiversity stewards, many options are available for developing cultural links that support plant diversity rather than diminish it. Such steps are not just about meeting international treaty obligations or establishing new protected areas, but rather are part of a larger process of shaping ecologically literate civil societies that are in balance with the natural world. To maintain biodiversity's benefits, what matters most is how well we meet the challenges of living sustainably with our deeds as well as our words.

7

Feeding Nine Billion

Lester R. Brown

When this century began, each American farmer produced enough food to feed seven other people in the United States and abroad. Today, a U.S. farmer feeds 96 people. Staggering gains in agricultural productivity in the United States and elsewhere have underpinned the emergence of the modern world as we know it. Just as the discovery of agriculture itself set the stage for the emergence of early civilization, these gains in agricultural productivity have facilitated the emergence of our modern global civilization.[1]

This has been a revolutionary century for world agriculture. Draft animals have largely been replaced by tractors; traditional varieties of corn, wheat, and rice have given way to high-yielding varieties; and world irrigated area has multiplied sixfold since 1900. The use of chemical fertilizers—virtually unheard of in 1900—now accounts for an estimated 40 percent of world grain production.[2]

Technological advances have tripled the productivity of world cropland during this century. They have helped expand the world grain harvest from less than 400 million tons in 1900 to nearly 1.9 billion tons in 1998. Indeed, farmers have expanded grain production five times as much since 1900 as during the preceding 10,000 years since agriculture began.[3]

A CENTURY OF GROWTH

The advances in agriculture that have underpinned the near quintupling of the grain harvest during the twentieth century have come from essentially five technologies, four of which were available before 1900. Irrigation, one of the key contributors, goes back several thousand years, but the other advances are historically much more recent. In 1847 Justus von Leibig, a German agricultural chemist, demonstrated that all the nutri-

We are grateful to the Winslow Foundation for its support of our research on the world food prospect.

ents that plants take from the soil could be replaced in mineral form. This second advance set the stage for the worldwide use of chemical fertilizer to boost land productivity by ensuring that nutrient shortages did not restrict yields.[4]

In the 1860s, Gregor Mendel, an Austrian monk breeding garden peas discovered the basic principles of genetics. This third advance laid the groundwork for the spectacular gains in plant breeding of this century. And fourth, the Japanese succeeded in dwarfing cereals in the 1880s, which eventually led to the highly productive short-strawed wheats and rices that are widely used throughout the world today.[5]

The health effects of being overfed and underfed are the same— increased susceptibility to illness, reduced life expectancy, and reduced productivity.

The fifth major technology that has contributed to major advances in grain production is the development of hybrid corn, a breakthrough that came in 1917 at the University of Connecticut Agricultural Experiment Station. This highly productive hybrid grown throughout the world today helped make corn one of the big three cereals, along with wheat and rice. While wheat and rice are consumed largely by humans, most of the world's corn harvest is fed to livestock and poultry.[6]

Another source of agricultural growth in this century is the exchange of crops between the Old World and the New that was set in motion by Christopher Columbus. Wheat and other small grains were introduced into the New World by the early European settlers. Corn, which was domesticated by the New World farmers, is now grown on every continent. The

potato, first domesticated by the Incans in the Andes, is today a food staple in nearly all temperate-zone countries. The soybean, which has surpassed the wheat crop in value in the United States, was introduced from China. Meanwhile in China, the production of corn has expanded to 120 million tons per year, only slightly less than its 135-million-ton rice harvest.[7]

With livestock and poultry, the flow was pretty much one way, since the only resident of the farmyard that was domesticated in the New World is the turkey. All other livestock and poultry—cattle, sheep, goats, pigs, horses, chickens, and ducks—came from the Old World. This exchange of crops and livestock that began five centuries ago contributes both to the productivity of world agriculture and to the diversity of modern diets.[8]

This impressive century of growth unfortunately has not translated into adequate food supplies for all the Earth's inhabitants. An estimated 841 million people remain hungry and undernourished, a number that approaches the population of the entire world when Thomas Malthus warned about the race between food and people some 200 years ago. Unless the world can move quickly to stabilize population, the ranks of the hungry and undernourished could increase as the new millennium unfolds.[9]

Historically, we have depended on three basic systems for our food supply: oceanic fisheries, rangelands, and croplands. With oceanic fisheries and rangelands, two essentially natural systems, the world appears to have "hit the wall." After increasing nearly fivefold since mid-century, the oceanic fish catch appears to be at or near its sustainable yield limit. Overfishing is now the rule, not the exception. The same can be said about the world's rangelands: after tripling from 1950 to 1990, the production of beef and mutton has increased little in recent years as overgrazing has lowered rangeland productivity in large areas of the world.[10]

Continued population growth is the dominant source of mounting pressure on these natural systems. Some countries, such as Ethiopia, Nigeria, and Pakistan, are projected to nearly triple their populations by 2050. Nigeria is expected to have 339 million people in 2050—more than there were in all of Africa in 1950. Ethiopia, controlling a large share of the headwaters of the Nile, which is in effect the food lifeline for the Sudan and Egypt, is projected to increase its population from 62 million at present to 213 million in the year 2050. India, a country with nearly a billion people and water tables falling almost everywhere, is due to add another 600 million by 2050. And China, even with its efforts to slow population growth, is still slated to add some 300 million people, more than currently live in the United States, before its population stabilizes in 2040.[11]

OVERFED AND UNDERFED

We live today in a nutritionally divided world, one where some people eat too much and others too little. Both are forms of malnutrition. Ironically, those who are overfed and overweight and those who are underfed and underweight face similar health problems. And the health effects are the same—increased susceptibility to illness, reduced life expectancy, and reduced productivity.

Worldwide, the number of overweight people could total 600 million. In the United States, the world's largest industrial country, 97 million adults now fall into this category, representing 55 percent of those 20 years of age or older. Other countries with a particularly large share of overweight people include Russia, at 57 percent, and the United Kingdom, at 51 percent; other European societies are not far behind. There are also substantial num-

bers of overweight people within some developing countries. In Brazil, for example, more than 30 percent of the population is overweight. For China and India, in contrast, the figures are 8 and 7 percent, and for Ethiopia, a meager 2 percent.[12]

Unfortunately, the share of the population that is overweight in industrial societies has increased in recent decades as lifestyles have become more sedentary. In simplest terms, obesity occurs when food energy intake exceeds energy use. It can result from too much food, too little exercise, or both. In the United States, the share of those overweight is highest among minority groups—those with low incomes and limited education, whose diets are often high in fat and sugar.[13]

U.S. government researchers report that being overweight raises the risk of mortality from high blood pressure, coronary heart disease, stroke, diabetes, and various forms of cancer. In the United States, obesity is the second leading cause of preventable deaths after smoking. Dr. Robert Eckel, speaking for the American Heart Association, says that "obesity is becoming a dangerous epidemic."[14]

At the other end of the scale are those who get too little to eat. The U.N. Food and Agriculture Organization, using national nutritional surveys, estimates that 841 million people living in developing countries suffer from basic protein-energy malnutrition—they do not get enough protein, enough calories, or enough of both. Infants and children lack the food they need to develop their full physical and mental potential. Most of the adults and children in this group do not have the energy to maintain normal levels of physical activity.[15]

As the world has become more economically integrated, the face of famine has changed. Whereas famine was once geographically defined by poor harvests, today it is also economically defined by low productivity and incomes. It is found among those who are on the land but cannot produce enough food or who are in the cities and cannot buy enough. Famine concentrated among the poor is less visible than the more traditional geographically focused version, but it is no less real. Malnutrition weakens the body's immune system to the point where common childhood ailments such as measles and diarrhea are often fatal. Each day 19,000 children die as a result of malnutrition and related illnesses.[16]

The world's hungry children are concentrated in two areas: the Indian subcontinent, where three fifths of all children suffer from malnutrition, and sub-Saharan Africa, where the equivalent figure is 30 percent. Malnutrition among infants and children is of particular concern because anything that stunts their physical development may also stunt their mental development. Malnutrition not only exacts a high social cost, as measured in human suffering, it also depreciates a country's human capital, its most valuable resource.[17]

Many developing countries have socially damaging levels of malnutrition, as measured by the share of children under age five that are underweight. (See Table 7–1.) Among major countries, Bangladesh and India are at the top of the list. Other populous countries with a large percentage of underweight children are Viet Nam, Ethiopia, Indonesia, Pakistan, and Nigeria.

Over the last half-century, the share of the world that is malnourished has declined substantially. More than anything else, this has been due to rising food production per person. Using grain production per person as the indicator, the world has made substantial progress in raising food consumption since 1950. There has been, however, a loss of momentum since 1984. World grain consumption per person, which averaged 247 kilograms in 1950, had climbed to 342 kilograms by 1984, a gain of 38 percent. (See Figure 7–1.) During the 14 years

Table 7–1. Share of Children Under Five Years of Age Who Are Underweight in Selected Countries

Country	Share of Underweight
	(percent)
Bangladesh	66
India	64
Viet Nam	56
Ethiopia	48
Indonesia	40
Pakistan	40
Nigeria	36
Philippines	33
Tanzania	29
Thailand	26
China	21
Zimbabwe	11
Egypt	10
Brazil	7

SOURCE: World Health Organization, *Global Database on Child Growth*, Geneva, 1997, based on national surveys taken between 1987 and 1995.

since then it has declined to 319 kilograms, a drop of 7 percent. Although there are obvious limitations to using average grain supply as a measure, it is nonetheless much easier in a low-income society to eliminate malnutrition when grain production per person is rising than when it is falling. Since more people are involved in grain production than in any other economic activity in developing countries, a rise in grain output per person means gains in both productivity and consumption.[18]

This rising global tide of grain production from 1950 to 1984 lifted food consumption for many to a nutritionally adequate level, but the extent of the rise varied widely by country and region of the world. The trends in the two population giants—China and India—that together contain 35 percent of humanity contrast sharply. Although India has made impressive progress in raising grain production, the growth in output has been largely offset by that of population, leaving nearly two thirds of its children malnourished.

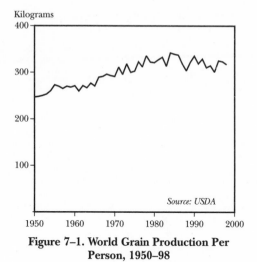

Kilograms

Figure 7–1. World Grain Production Per Person, 1950–98

Source: USDA

As a result, the annual grain harvest per person is still slightly less than 200 kilograms per person, providing the average Indian with little more than a starch-dominated subsistence diet. At 200 kilograms, or roughly one pound per day, nearly all grain must be consumed directly just to satisfy basic food energy needs, leaving little to convert into animal protein.[19]

In China, by contrast, the impressive progress in boosting agricultural output after the economic reforms of 1978, combined with a dramatic slowing of population growth, raised grain production per person from roughly 200 to nearly 300 kilograms. This increase, accompanied by record gains in income, let China both raise the amount of grain consumed directly and convert substantial quantities of grain into pork, poultry, and eggs, thus eliminating much of the protein-calorie malnutrition of two decades ago. While the share of underweight children in India remains at 64 percent, that in China had dropped to 21 percent by the late 1980s, when the last nutritional surveys were taken in these two countries. Given the doubling of incomes in China during the 1990s, continuing impressive gains in agriculture, and the latest life expectancy esti-

mate of 71 years, the portion of children malnourished has likely dropped much further. Many of those still malnourished in China live in the interior of the country, often in semiarid regions where rainfall is so low that modern agricultural technologies can make only a modest contribution to raising food output.[20]

Grain consumption per person varies widely by country (see Table 7–2), providing a rough indicator of nutritional adequacy. The annual consumption figure, including grain consumed indirectly in the form of livestock products, ranges from just under 200 kilograms to more than 900 kilograms. Ironically, the healthiest people in the world are not those at the top of this ladder, but rather those in the middle. Life expectancy in Italy, for example, where on average people get 400 kilograms of grain per year, is higher than in the United States, which uses twice as much grain and has much higher health care expenditures per person. The health of those who live too high on the food chain often suffers from excessive consumption of fat-rich livestock products.[21]

The continued existence of hunger today is largely the result of low productivity, which manifests itself in low incomes and poverty. For the world as a whole, incomes have risen dramatically over the last century, climbing from $1,300 per person in 1900 to more than $6,000 per person in 1998 (in 1997 dollars). This rising economic tide has lifted most of humanity out of poverty and hunger, but unfortunately it has been uneven, leaving many still suffering from poverty and from hunger and malnutrition.[22]

The World Bank estimates that 1.3 billion people live in absolute poverty, with incomes of $1 a day or less. Most of these people live in rural areas. Many try to gain a livelihood from plots of land that have been divided and subdivided as population has increased. Others have too little land to make a living because landownership is concentrated in the hands of a

Table 7–2. Annual Per Capita Grain Use and Consumption of Livestock Products in Selected Countries, 1998

Country	Grain Use[1]	Consumption					
		Beef	Pork	Poultry	Mutton	Milk[2]	Eggs
	(kilograms)	(kilograms)					(number)
United States	900	44	31	47	1	264	284
Italy	400	25	35	19	2	215	215
China	300	5	35	10	2	6	289
India	200	1	—	1	1	75	30

[1]Rounded to nearest 100 kilograms.   [2]Total consumption, including that used to produce cheese, yogurt, and ice cream.

SOURCE: U.S. Department of Agriculture, *Production, Supply, and Distribution*, electronic database, Washington, DC, updated October 1998.

small segment of the population. Still another group consists of rural landless—those who have no land of their own but who work on that of others, often on a seasonal basis. For other individuals, soil erosion and other forms of land degradation are undermining rural livelihoods. Perhaps the fastest growing segment of the absolute poor are those who live in the squatter settlements that ring so many Third World cities.[23]

Consumers the world over have benefited from declining real grain prices over the last half-century, but there is now a possibility that this trend could be reversed as aquifer depletion spreads, shrinking irrigation water supplies. This is particularly important in major countries such as China and India, which rely on irrigated land for half or more of their food and where groundwater depletion will inevitably lead to irrigation cutbacks. There are also scores of smaller countries faced with aquifer depletion, many of them in North Africa and the Middle East, where most of the food comes from irrigated land.

Fortunately for those on the lower rungs of the global economic ladder, the declining real price of grain created an ideal environment for easing hunger and malnutrition. If this twentieth-century trend of falling grain prices is reversed as

we enter the new millennium, as now seems likely, it could impoverish more people in a shorter period of time than any event in history.

If a strategy to eliminate hunger is to succeed, it must simultaneously focus on accelerating the shift to smaller families in order to stabilize population sooner rather than later, raise investment in the rural areas where poverty is concentrated, and design economic policies to distribute wealth more equitably. Any strategy that does not focus on the social investment needs in education and health and in new investments that create productive employment is not likely to accomplish its goal.

LAND: A FINITE RESOURCE

The option of expanding world grain production by cultivating more land has virtually disappeared. The world's grain harvested area increased from 587 million hectares in 1950 to the historical high of 732 million hectares in 1981, a gain of 25 percent. Since then, however, the grain area has shrunk to 690 million hectares, a 6-percent drop, as it was converted to non-farm uses, abandoned because of soil erosion, or shifted to other crops such as soybeans. During the next half-century the grain harvested area is not expected to change much, with gains and losses essentially offsetting each other.[24]

Gains in the grain harvested area in the last 50 years have come from clearing new land for agriculture and from expanding irrigation, which both allowed arid land to be brought under cultivation and also facilitated an increase in multiple cropping. In the Indian Punjab, for example, irrigation and earlier-maturing varieties have made the double cropping of winter wheat and rice commonplace. Similarly, large areas of central China grow winter wheat and corn as a summer crop. These gains have partly offset land losses from the conversion to nonfarm uses and from soil erosion and other forms of degradation.

In the next 50 years, some further gains in cultivated area are likely. If grain prices rise in Brazil, for instance, parts of the cerrado—a semiarid region in the east central part of the country—will likely be brought under the plow. In Africa, there are opportunities for expanding the cultivated area in the Congo River basin, particularly on its outer fringes. And in Asia, the outer islands of Indonesia offer some opportunities for increasing cultivation, although as in Brazil, the additional land is typically marginal in nature. The inherent fertility of nearly all this land is low, requiring special efforts to maintain productivity.

Heavy cropland losses during the next half-century are expected in countries such as India, where the construction of housing alone will claim a substantial area of cropland. Other countries are losing cropland because of degradation. Kazakhstan, for example, abandoned nearly half its grainland between 1980 and 1998 as a result of soil erosion and other forms of land degradation, letting it revert to rangeland. Other countries in Central Asia, North Africa, and the Andean countries of Latin America are

also losing cropland to degradation.[25]

Between 1950 and 1998, the grain harvested area per person worldwide shrank from 0.23 hectares to 0.12 hectares. (See Figure 7–2.) For most countries this was not a problem because unprecedented rises in land productivity more than offset the shrinkage. Given the marked loss of momentum in raising land productivity since 1990, however, there is reason to doubt whether future increases can offset the projected shrinkage in cropland per person to 0.07 hectares by 2050.[26]

A look at this situation for individual countries is both illuminating and worrying. Assume, for purposes of projection, that India's cropland area will not change by 2050; the addition of 600 million people there and the land they need for housing and to meet other nonfood needs, plus land required for industrialization, will almost certainly reduce cropland area per person below 0.07 hectares. (See Table 7–3.) India—which has already tripled its wheat yields and doubled its rice yields—will find it difficult to sustain the rises in land productivity needed to offset the continuing shrinkage in per capita grain area.[27]

China is in a somewhat better position

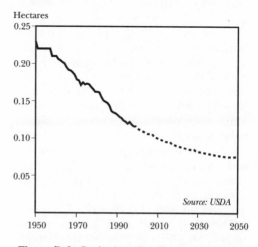

Figure 7–2. Grain Area Per Person, 1950–98, With Projections to 2050

Table 7–3. Grain Harvested Area Per Person in Selected Countries in 1950, With Projections for 2000 and 2050[1]

Country	1950	2000	2050
	(hectares)		
United States	0.41	0.23	0.19
Brazil	0.34	0.11	0.08
India	0.28	0.10	0.07
Bangladesh	0.29	0.10	0.06
China	0.16	0.07	0.06
Iran	0.61	0.13	0.06
Nigeria	0.52	0.13	0.05
Indonesia	0.18	0.07	0.04
Ethiopia	0.39	0.11	0.03
Pakistan	0.31	0.08	0.03

[1]1998 grain area used for all years.

SOURCE: U.S. Department of Agriculture, *Production, Supply, and Distribution*, electronic database, Washington, DC, updated October 1998; United Nations, *World Population Prospects: The 1996 Revision* (New York: 1996).

because its projected population growth is much lower than that of India. Its grainland per person is expected to shrink from 0.07 to 0.06 hectares. The question for China is not so much whether its land and other agricultural resources will enable it to feed 1.5 billion people, but whether it can feed 1.5 billion affluent people who are consuming large quantities of livestock products.

The countries likely to be in the most trouble over the next half-century are those in the second tier in terms of size—nations that are projected to surpass the 300 million mark before 2050 (Pakistan, Nigeria, and Indonesia), plus Ethiopia, which will cross the 200 million threshold. Pakistan—with 357 million people in 2050, more than live in the United States and Canada combined today—will see its grain harvested area shrink to 0.03 hectares per person, or less than one tenth of an acre. Every seven Pakistanis will have just one fifth of a hectare or half an acre on which to produce their entire food supply—less than a typical suburban building lot in the United States. Nigeria,

whose current population of 115 million is projected to expand to 339 million, will see its grainland per person shrink to 0.05 hectares.[28]

Bangladesh, Ethiopia, and Iran are also facing shrinkages of their grain harvested area per person to dangerously small areas. Egypt, too, will be facing a difficult situation. As its population climbs to 114 million, its grainland per person will shrink from 0.04 hectares to 0.02 hectares. Since it is already importing nearly half its grain, its dependence on grain from abroad seems certain to climb.[29]

Aside from the loss of grainland to nonfarm uses and to soil erosion and other forms of degradation, a substantial area of grainland is being lost to oilseeds, importantly the soybean. As incomes have risen in lower-income countries, the demand for vegetable oil for cooking has escalated. This, combined with the rapidly rising demand for soybean meal among the more affluent as a protein supplement for livestock and poultry feeds, has increased the demand for soybeans nearly ninefold since 1950. Because soybeans are a legume and therefore not as responsive as grains are to applications of nitrogen fertilizer, their yield per hectare has risen much more slowly. To satisfy this enormous growth in the global appetite for soybeans, the area planted in this crop has jumped from 14 million hectares in 1990 to 69 million hectares in 1997, with much of the growth coming at the expense of grain. (See Figure 7–3.)[30]

In the last 50 years, world agriculture has been dominated by surplus capacity. As a result, farmers in the United States were paid to idle part of their cropland under commodity supply-management programs until 1995, when the programs were dismantled. A much smaller area idled in Europe beginning in the early 1990s has now been largely returned to production. One of the legacies of this long-standing surplus production capacity is that land is often thought of as a sur-

Million Hectares

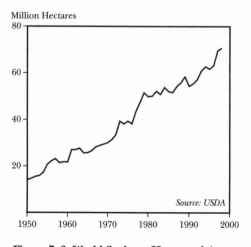

Figure 7–3. World Soybean Harvested Area, 1950–98

plus commodity. Given this prevailing psychology, the world may have difficulty coming to grips with the prospect of a worldwide scarcity of cropland, and of the need to protect this resource from conversion to nonfarm uses.[31]

The effects of the acute cropland scarcity emerging in some countries could affect many other areas of human activity. For example, it could fundamentally alter transportation policy, favoring the development of more land-efficient bicycle-rail transport systems at the expense of the automobile. It could affect the conversion of cropland to recreational uses, such as golf, one of the more land-intensive sports. Indeed, Viet Nam has already banned the construction of more golf courses because of land scarcity.

WATER: EMERGING CONSTRAINT ON GROWTH

The first farmers were concerned about the amount of grain produced relative to the amount that they sowed. For them, seed was the scarce resource. Later it was

the availability of fertile land to till that constrained growth in output. As land became scarce, farmers began to calculate yield in terms of the grain produced per unit of land cultivated, and grain yields today are routinely reported in tons per hectare or bushels per acre. As we move into the new millennium, with water scarcity emerging as the dominant constraint on efforts to expand food production, we may see another shift in the focus of yield calculations—namely to the amount of water required per ton of grain produced.

From the beginning of irrigated agriculture several thousand years ago in the Middle East until 1900, the world's irrigated area expanded to an estimated 48 million hectares. Then growth in irrigation began to accelerate, nearly doubling by 1950 to 94 million hectares. But the big growth has come during the last half of this century as the irrigated area increased to some 260 million hectares, nearly tripling the mid-century level. Now 40 percent of world food production comes from irrigated land. The growth in irrigation has permitted the expansion of agriculture into arid regions, increased multiple cropping in monsoonal climates by facilitating cropping during the dry season, and allowed a substantial expansion in fertilizer use.[32]

The remarkable growth in irrigated agriculture since mid-century divides into two distinct eras—from 1950 to 1978, when irrigation was expanding faster than population, and since 1978, when its growth has fallen behind that of population. The irrigated area per person reached a historic high in 1978 of 0.047 hectares. (See Figure 7–4.) It then began to decline slowly, falling to 0.044 hectares in 1997, a drop of 6 percent.[33]

Irrigated agriculture is concentrated in Asia, which has some of the world's great rivers—the Indus, the Ganges, the Yangtze, the Yellow, and the Brahmaputra. Originating at high elevations and

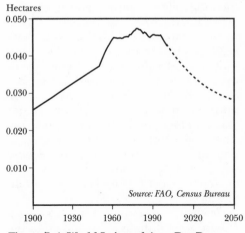

Hectares

Source: FAO, Census Bureau

Figure 7–4. World Irrigated Area Per Person, 1900–98, With Projections to 2050

traveling long distances, they provide an abundance of opportunities for dams and the diversion of water into networks of gravity-fed canals and ditches. Two thirds of the world's irrigated area is in Asia. Roughly 70 percent of the grain harvest in China comes from irrigated land, while the equivalent figure in India is 50 percent and in the United States, 15 percent.[34]

As the 1990s have unfolded, evidence of water scarcity is mounting. Water tables are falling on every continent—in the southern Great Plains of the United States, the southwestern United States, much of North Africa and the Middle East, most of India, and almost everywhere in China that the land is flat. A survey covering 1991 to 1996, for instance, indicates that the water table under the north China plain is dropping an average of 1.5 meters, or roughly 5 feet, a year. Since this area accounts for nearly 40 percent of China's grain harvest, this is a matter of some concern to the leaders in Beijing.[35]

A similar situation exists in India. David Seckler and his colleagues at the International Irrigation Management Institute in Sri Lanka estimate that underground water withdrawals in India are at

least double the rate of aquifer recharge. They report that water tables are falling at 1–3 meters (3–10 feet) per year almost everywhere in India. Seckler describes India as being on a free ride, expanding its agriculture by depleting underground water reserves. At some point, he says, this "house of cards" will collapse. When it does, India's grain harvest could fall by as much as 25 percent. In a country where the supply and demand for food is already precariously balanced, and where 18 million people are added each year, this is not a happy prospect.[36]

Many major rivers run dry before they reach the sea. Some have disappeared entirely. In the southwestern United States, the Colorado River rarely ever reaches the Gulf of California. In Central Asia, the Amu Darya, one of the two rivers feeding the Aral Sea, is drained dry by Uzbek and Turkmen cotton farmers long before it gets to the sea. As a result, the Aral Sea is shrinking and may eventually disappear, known to future generations only from old maps.[37]

The Yellow River, the cradle of Chinese civilization, ran dry for the first time in China's 3,000-year history in 1972, failing to reach the sea for some 15 days. Over the next dozen years, it ran dry intermittently, but since 1985 has run dry for part of each year. In 1997, it failed to reach the sea for seven months out of the year. Originating on the Tibetan Plateau, the Yellow River flows through eight provinces en route to the sea. The last of these, Shandong Province, which accounts for a fifth of China's corn harvest and a seventh of its wheat harvest, gets half of its irrigation water from the Yellow River. The remaining half comes from irrigation wells.[38]

With hundreds of major projects planned in upstream provinces to withdraw water for industrial and urban use, for power projects, and for irrigation, the Yellow River could one day become an inland river, never reaching the sea.

Official policy stresses the need to develop the economically depressed interior provinces, and Beijing is letting these projects continue even though it may mean the eventual sacrifice of irrigated agriculture in the lower reaches of the Yellow River basin.

Little water from the Nile makes it to the Mediterranean, and the Ganges barely makes it to the Bay of Bengal in the dry season. With the collective population of Ethiopia, the Sudan, and Egypt—the three dominant countries in the Nile River basin—projected to grow from 157 million today to 388 million over the next half-century, competition for the Nile waters is certain to intensify. The same can be said about the Ganges, where there is keen rivalry between India and Bangladesh for water.[39]

Historically, land scarcity traditionally shaped grain trade patterns. Now water scarcity is beginning to shape them as well. North Africa and the Middle East, a region where every country faces water shortages, has become the world's fastest growing grain import market during the 1990s. To import a ton of wheat is to import 1,000 tons of water. In effect, for countries facing water shortages, the most efficient way to import water is to import grain. In 1997, the water required to produce the grain and other farm products imported into North Africa and the Middle East was roughly equal to the annual flow of the Nile River.[40]

Worldwide, roughly 70 percent of all water diverted from rivers or pumped from underground is used for irrigation, while 20 percent goes to industry, and 10 percent to residential uses. As countries push up against the limits of their water supplies, the contest between these three end-use sectors intensifies. A thousand tons of water can be used in agriculture to produce a ton of wheat worth $200, or it can be used in industry to expand output by $14,000—70 times as much. Similarly, if the goal is to produce jobs, using scarce

water in industry is far more productive than using it for irrigation. Because the economics of water use do not favor agriculture, this sector almost always loses.[41]

In an effort to assess the water prospect in China more precisely, Dennis Engi at Sandia National Laboratory has modeled the supply/demand balances of all the river basins in the country, projecting them into the future. His figures show huge water deficits developing in some key river basins. The combination of aquifer depletion and diversion of irrigation water to nonfarm uses indicates that irrigated agriculture may be phased out in some of the more water-short regions of China. By 2010, for example, irrigated agriculture could virtually disappear in China's Hai river basin as growing urban and industrial water demand in Beijing, Tianjin, and other cities in the basin absorbs the water now used in agriculture.[42]

Perhaps more than anything else, growing water shortages may hamstring future efforts to expand food production. Water used for irrigation raises land productivity both directly and indirectly, by raising the potential for using fertilizer. And in arid regions it determines the amount of land that can be cultivated. The bottom line is that if we are facing a future of water scarcity, we are also facing a future of food scarcity.

RAISING LAND PRODUCTIVITY

When the last half of this century began, the average world grain yield per hectare was just over one ton—1.06 tons, to be precise. By 1998, it had climbed to 2.73 tons per hectare. Grain yields vary widely among countries. But in a world where farmers everywhere are drawing on the same backlog of agricultural technology, the variations that were once explained largely by uneven levels of economic development are today explained largely by differences in natural conditions, such as temperature, rainfall, day length, solar intensity, and inherent soil fertility.[43]

Take wheat, for example. Three developing countries—Egypt, Mexico, and China—are in the top five listed in Table 7–4 in wheat yield per hectare. And two industrial countries—Canada and Australia—are in the bottom five. This is because Egypt, Mexico, and China irrigate most of their wheat, while in Canada and Australia the wheat is rainfed and grown in areas of low rainfall.

The threefold yield difference between the United Kingdom and the United States is also largely a difference in rainfall. Soil moisture conditions are simply much more favorable in the United Kingdom. The two countries at the top of the list—the United Kingdom and France—are blessed with fertile soils, good rainfall, and, because of their northerly latitude, long days during the summer growing season.

Table 7–4. Wheat Yield Per Hectare in Key Producing Countries, 1997[1]

Country	Tons
United Kingdom	7.7
France	7.2
Egypt	5.7
Mexico	4.1
China	3.8
Poland	3.4
United States	2.7
Ukraine	2.6
India	2.6
Argentina	2.4
Canada	2.3
Pakistan	2.1
Australia	2.0
Russia	1.4
Kazakhstan	0.7

[1]Yield shown for 1997 is the average of 1996–98.
SOURCE: U.S. Department of Agriculture, *Production, Supply, and Distribution,* electronic database, Washington, DC, updated October 1998.

By contrast, Kazakhstan—at the bottom of the list—relies on some of the most marginal cropland in the world. It was the site of the Soviet Virgin Lands Project in the 1950s, a project that pushed cultivation into a semiarid grassland region that could neither produce high yields nor sustain cultivation over the long term. Much of the land plowed in the 1950s is so vulnerable to wind erosion that it is being given over to grazing sheep. Although Kazakhstan has since 1980 abandoned almost half its grainland (the more marginal land), the average yield on the land that remains in cultivation, the more productive land, is only 0.7 tons per hectare.[44]

Solar intensity is another explanation of differences in yields. For example, rice yields even in an agriculturally advanced country like Japan are scarcely 5 tons per hectare, even though all the rice there is irrigated. The principal constraint on yields in Japan, and indeed in much of the rest of Asia, is solar intensity. Because rice is grown during the summer monsoon season, there is extensive cloud cover during the growing season. This helps explain why rice yields in California are 30 percent higher than those in Japan. It is not that California's farmers are more skilled at growing rice; they just have the advantage of intense sunlight throughout the entire growing season.[45]

The three keys to the rises in land productivity since mid-century are plant breeding, the spread of irrigation, and growth in the use of fertilizers. The principal contribution of plant breeders has been to increase the share of photosynthate, the product of photosynthesis, that goes into seed production. Originally domesticated wheats converted roughly 20 percent of photosynthate into seed, with the remainder used to sustain leaves, stem, and roots. With the more productive modern wheat varieties now converting more than 50 percent of photosynthate into seed, there is not much remaining potential for increase, since scientists estimate that the absolute upper limit is 62 percent. Anything beyond that would begin to deprive the rest of the plant of the energy needed to function, thus reducing yields. Whether even 60 percent can be reached in practice remains to be seen.[46]

A lack of understanding of the physiology of increasing crop yields has led some observers to conclude that biotechnology could yield another generation of high-yielding varieties—ones that could again double or triple yields of existing varieties. Unfortunately, traditional plant breeders have done most of the things that are physiologically possible to raise the yield potential of the principal crops such as wheat, corn, and rice. The main contribution of genetic engineering to agriculture in the future is likely to be in the breeding of disease- and insect-resistant varieties. This will contribute to additional production only if these biological pest controls are more effective than the chemical controls now used.[47]

Another area in which biotechnology might be able to contribute to greater production is in breeding crop varieties that are more drought-resistant or salt-tolerant. In each of these, however, there may be some physiological constraints on how far genetic engineers can go. This is certainly true with increasing the water efficiency of crops, since water use is tied so directly to the basic physiological processes of plants, such as photosynthesis, nutrient uptake, and plant temperature regulation.

Some of the natural constraints on land productivity can be alleviated. For example, soil moisture can be increased by irrigation. Soil fertility can be increased by fertilization. Indeed, one constraint, the availability of nutrients, has been eliminated in much of the world by fertilizer use. Between 1950 and 1998, world fertilizer use increased from 14 million tons to roughly 130 million tons, an increase of more than ninefold. But in many agriculturally advanced countries fertilizer use is leveling off as the response to additional applications diminishes. In some countries—including the United States, Japan, and most of those in Western Europe—fertilizer use has plateaued, and it may soon do so in China. In a country like the United States, where fertilizer use has not increased since 1980, applying more fertilizer has little or no effect on yields.[48]

California's rice farmers have the advantage of intense sunlight throughout the entire growing season.

[handwritten note: + Iso Mertanuska Valley near Anchorage: "midnight sun"]

In assessing the future prospect for raising land productivity, it is useful to contrast conditions at the middle of this century with those as we prepare to begin the next half-century. In 1950, farmers were gaining access to new high-yielding varieties, including hybrid corn, followed shortly thereafter by widely adapted dwarf wheats and rices. Since then, as noted, world irrigated area nearly tripled and fertilizer use increased ninefold. The share of photosynthate going to seed was raised to more than half in the most productive varieties. New varieties and rapidly expanding irrigation and fertilizer use enabled many countries to double or triple their yields of wheat, corn, and rice.

In looking ahead at the next 50 years, there is little potential for further increasing the share of photosynthate going to seed. World irrigated area is not expected to grow very much, if at all, since it seems certain to shrink in some countries. And world fertilizer use will continue to grow, albeit much more slowly, with the remaining growth concentrated in the Indian subcontinent, Africa, and Latin America. The net effect of these conditions is that the rise in land productivity that has slowed so dramatically in the 1990s will probably slow further as the next century gets under way. Already some countries have experienced a plateauing or near plateauing of the rise in yields, such as with wheat in the United States and rice in Japan. Some developing countries, such as Mexico with wheat and South Korea with rice, are also seeing their yield rises taper off.[49]

An analysis of the trend in world grain yield from 1950 through 1998 shows this half-century span dividing into two distinct eras. Between 1950 and 1990, the yield per hectare climbed by 2.1 percent a year, but during the 1990s it has increased by only 1.1 percent a year. (See Table 7–5.)

History will likely see the four-decade span from 1950 to 1990 as the golden age in raising world cropland productivity. But the slowdown since then does not come as a surprise, given the inability of scientists to develop a second generation of high-yielding grain varieties that will again double or triple yields. With the share of photosynthate going to seed already quite high and approaching the physiological limit in some situations, raising yields becomes ever more difficult. The key question the world must now face is, Will the deceleration in the rise in grainland productivity that has been under way since 1990 continue, falling

Table 7–5. World Grain Yield Gains, 1950–90 and 1990–97

	Yield[1]	Annual Increase
	(tons per hectare)	(percent)
1950	1.06	
1990	2.48	2.1
1997	2.70	1.1

[1]Yields for 1990 and 1997 are three-year averages.
SOURCE: U.S. Department of Agriculture, *Production, Supply, and Distribution*, electronic database, Washington, DC, updated October 1998.

further and further behind population growth as we move into the next century?

CHANGING COURSE

As we prepare for the new millennium, there is a rising tide of concern about the long-term food prospect. This can be seen in the frustration of plant breeders who are running into physiological constraints as they attempt to develop the new higher-yielding varieties needed to restore rapid growth in the world food supply. And it can be seen in the apprehensiveness of political leaders in countries where the food supply depends heavily on irrigation but the aquifers are being depleted.

This mounting concern is also evident in the intelligence community in Washington, where the National Intelligence Council (NIC), the umbrella over all U.S. intelligence agencies, has commissioned a major interdisciplinary assessment of China's food prospect by a prominent group of scientists. This research effort was triggered by the realization that if China were to turn to the world market for massive quantities of grain, it could drive world grain prices up to a level that would create unprecedented political instability in Third World cities. The NIC study—the most comprehensive interdisciplinary assessment ever undertaken of China's food prospect— concluded in its "most likely" scenario that by 2025 China would need to import 175 million tons of grain. This quantity, which approaches current world grain exports of 200 million tons, could overwhelm the capacity of exporting countries.[50]

Two major food issues face the world as it enters the twenty-first century. One is how to feed adequately those who suffer from chronic hunger and malnutrition, people who do not get enough protein and energy to develop their full physical and mental potential. The second is how to maintain the price stability needed in world grain markets if economic progress is not to be disrupted.[51]

The worst mistake political leaders can make entering the new millennium is to underestimate the dimensions of the food challenge. To begin with, oceanic fisheries and rangelands—the two leading sources of growth in the animal protein supply over the last half-century—have both apparently reached their limits. This means that all future growth in the world food supply must come from croplands, but irrigation water supplies may not expand much further and the response to additional fertilizer is diminishing in many countries. The backlog of unused technology to raise land productivity is shrinking. This does not mean that food production cannot be increased. It can be and it will. But it is becoming much more difficult to sustain the rapid growth needed to keep up with increased demand.

Given these challenging new dimensions of the food prospect, governments facing continuing population growth need to calculate their future population carrying capacity by projecting the land available for crops, the amount of water that will be available for irrigation over the long term, and the likely yield of crops, based on what the most agriculturally advanced countries with similar growing conditions have achieved. This will provide the basis for a public dialogue on population policy. Once projections of future food supplies are completed, societies can consider what combination of population size and consumption levels they want, recognizing that there are tradeoffs between the two.

Supply-side initiatives are still important in achieving an acceptable balance between food and people. But victory in the battle to eradicate hunger and malnutrition may now depend heavily on demand-side initiatives. The world still needs to invest more in agricultural research, in agricultural infrastructure, and in providing credit to small farmers, especially women in agriculture. But in addition, there is now a need for substantial demand-side initiatives in slowing population growth and using grain and water more efficiently.

Once projections of future food supplies are completed, societies can consider what population size and consumption levels they want.

The most recent U.N. population projections show the world adding 3.3 billion people during the first half of the next century. All these people will be added in the developing world, with a disproportionate share being added in countries that are already densely populated. A review of the U.N. projections shows some of the biggest increases slated for the Indian subcontinent and sub-Saharan Africa—the two regions where most of the world's hungry people are concentrated. As noted earlier, India is projected to add nearly 600 million people to its current population during the next half-century. Pakistan, meanwhile, will go from 148 million to 357 million by 2050. In Africa, Nigeria will go from 122 million at present to 339 million, while Ethiopia will more than triple its population, going from 62 million to 213 million.[52]

Given the limits to the carrying capacity of each country's land and water resources, every national government needs a carefully articulated and adequately supported population policy, one that takes into account the country's carrying capacity at whatever consumption level citizens decide on. As Harvard biologist Edward O. Wilson observes in his landmark book *The Diversity of Life*, "Every nation has an economic policy and a foreign policy. The time has come to speak more openly of a population policy. ...what, in the judgment of its informed citizenry, is the optimal population?"[53]

Making sure that couples everywhere have access to family planning is one key step in achieving an acceptable balance between food and people. The International Conference on Population and Development held in Cairo in 1994 concluded that providing quality reproductive health care services to all those in need in developing countries would cost about $17 billion in the year 2000. By 2015, this would climb to $22 billion. The agreement was for donor countries to provide one third of the funds, with developing countries providing the remaining two thirds. Unfortunately, industrial countries—most importantly, the United States—have reneged on this commitment.[54]

Restructuring the world water economy holds the key to eliminating hunger.

Educating young females is a key to accelerating this shift to smaller families. In every society for which data are available, the more education women have, the fewer children they have. Closely related to the need for education of young females is the need to provide equal opportunities for women in all phases of national life.[55]

Another demand-side initiative to lighten pressure on world food supplies is for those who are consuming health-damaging quantities of fat-rich livestock products to move down the food chain. As noted earlier, the healthiest people in the world are not those whose diets are dominated by livestock products but those who

consume livestock products in moderation, thus satisfying needs for protein in a way that does not damage their health. In societies with a high incidence of obesity, such as the United States, a government-sponsored nutritional education program to encourage the obese to eat less meat and other foods rich in fats could improve health, increase life expectancy, and reduce health care costs.

A closely related demand-side initiative that can help alleviate long-term pressures on land and water resources is to accelerate the shift to more-efficient means of converting grain into animal protein. Now that there is little prospect of increasing the animal protein yield of oceanic fisheries and rangelands, nearly all future gains must come from feeding, whether it be fish in ponds or cattle in feedlots. At this point, relative conversion efficiencies come into play. For cattle in feedlots, an additional kilogram of live weight requires roughly 7 kilograms of grain. For pork, it is close to 4 kilograms of grain per kilogram of live weight. For poultry, it is just over 2, and for the leading species used for fish farming, such as carp, catfish, and tilapia, it is less than 2.[56]

Water scarcity is becoming a more central constraint than land scarcity on efforts to expand food production. There is a lot of land, including deserts, that could be made to bloom if water were available for irrigation, but the potential for developing new water resources is so limited that future gains in irrigation now depend more on increasing the efficiency of water use than on increasing supply. This means both using more water-efficient irrigation technologies and shifting to more water-efficient food staples. In some countries, for example, this may mean eating more wheat and sorghum and less rice. And since water efficiency in effect equals grain efficiency, responding to water scarcity also argues for encouraging the production of poultry and fish over beef and pork—trends that are already in evidence. If poultry and fish production are twice as grain-efficient as pork production, they are also twice as water-efficient, since grain equals water.

Thus, restructuring the world water economy holds the key to eliminating hunger. One of the most frequently proposed remedies for water scarcity is water pricing—charging users enough for water to ensure that it is used efficiently. Although there is wide agreement among water analysts of the need to shift to this system, few governments have adopted effective water pricing policies. Water pricing would enhance the use of irrigation practices such as sprinklers, which can substantially boost efficiency over the traditional flood or furrow irrigation now widely used, especially in Asia. Drip irrigation, a technology pioneered in Israel, is not economical for use on grain, but on high-value fruit and vegetable crops it can cut water use by up to 70 percent.[57]

The risk for countries that are likely to become heavily dependent on grain imports for their food supply is perhaps greater than most realize simply because the collective import needs of potentially grain-deficit countries promises to overwhelm the capacity of exporters. A little noticed change that affects the prospects for eradicating hunger is the leveling off since 1980 of grain exports among the principal exporting countries, which account for 85 percent of world exports. (See Figure 7–5.) After climbing from 60 million tons in 1950 to 200 million tons in 1980, there has been little gain since then. U.S. grain production during the last 18 years has increased roughly 1 percent annually, the same or slightly less than the growth in domestic demand. Unable to raise land productivity faster than the growth in demand, the exportable surplus has not increased. The United States, which supplies roughly half of the world's 200 million tons of grain exports, is projected to add 74 million people to its pop-

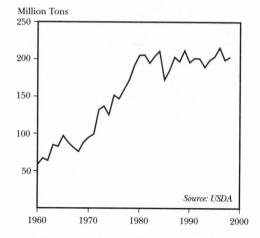

Figure 7–5. Grain Exports from Argentina, Australia, Canada, European Union, and the United States, 1960–97

ulation over the next 50 years, so it will take some effort to expand production fast enough merely to satisfy its growing domestic needs—much less the escalating needs of the rest of the world.[58]

Two of the other five major exporters—Canada and Australia—are severely restricted in their efforts to expand production by the lack of soil moisture. Little growth can be expected from them. For the European Union, where yields are already at record levels, the potential for further gains appears to be limited. The only one of the major exporters that might be able to expand grain exports substantially is Argentina. Its current exports, running around 20 million tons a year, could conceivably double. Still, this would be a rather minor increase in a world where the need for imported grain could easily jump from 200 million to 400 million tons in the decades ahead. One region not now contributing in a major way is Eastern Europe. Countries such as Poland, the Ukraine, Hungary, and Romania can expand their grain exports, at least modestly, if they adopt the economic policies needed to realize their full agricultural potential.[59]

Adequately feeding the projected increases in population poses one of the most difficult challenges that modern civilization faces. With little prospect of achieving an acceptable balance between food and people by supply-side initiatives alone, the time has come to focus on the demand side of the food equation as well. This means finding ways to accelerate the shift to smaller families, particularly in those countries where many are already hungry and malnourished, and it means moving down the food chain for those who are consuming unhealthily large amounts of livestock products.

8

Exploring a New Vision for Cities

Molly O'Meara

"It was a town of unnatural red and black like the painted face of a savage," wrote Charles Dickens in his 1854 novel *Hard Times*. "It was a town of machines and tall chimneys, out of which interminable serpents of smoke trailed themselves for ever and ever, and never got uncoiled." Although Dickens showed a brighter side to urban life in some of his earlier work, from the 1850s onward his characters were increasingly worn down by the industrial city's untamed filth.[1]

This shift in Dickens's stories coincided with a turning point in the history of cities. In 1850, the United Kingdom became the first nation to have a mainly urban population, and it was followed by a score of industrial countries in Europe, then North America, and later Japan. Booming industrial cities required tremendous quantities of water, food, fuels, and building materials. Pollution and waste were evident everywhere, as Dickens so vividly described.[2]

As the nineteenth century came to a close, the ills of the industrial city prompt-

ed visions of a new urban form. Engineers were already building bigger water and waste systems. And innovations such as the telephone, automobile, and skyscraper inspired futuristic thinking. Among the most influential visionaries was Ebenezer Howard, a British stenographer-turned-reformer. "Ill-ventilated, unplanned, unwieldy, and unhealthy" cities, Howard declared in 1902, had no place in a more humane future. Instead, a network of clean, self-sufficient "garden cities" would marry the best social aspects of city life to the beauty of nature. French architect Le Corbusier, a generation after Howard, was also offended by the industrial cities of his time: "They are ineffectual, they use up our bodies, they thwart our souls." Le Corbusier envisioned gleaming skyscrapers surrounded by parks and wide motorways that would shape a "radiant city" worthy of the new century.[3]

Today, cities around the world have some of the forms prescribed by Howard and Le Corbusier but not the function they intended: sustaining a more equitable society in harmony with nature. Chaotic suburban development in the United States, for instance, is a caricature of Howard's garden city ideal. Gated enclaves and congested roads have degraded rather than enhanced public space. Towering office blocks, Le Corbusier's "islands in the sky," were supposed to allow more room for nature below. But most skyscrapers tend to be built without regard to the local environment—heating or air conditioning must make up for shortfalls in design—and so take a heavy toll on natural resources.[4]

Twentieth-century cities fail to meet the needs of the present while at the same time compromising the ability of future generations to meet their own needs— the exact opposite of "sustainable development" as defined by the Brundtland Commission's 1987 landmark report, *Our Common Future.* Plato's observation in 400 B.C. that "any city, however small, is in fact divided into two, one the city of the poor, the other of the rich" holds true today. And the most basic requirements of the urban poor, particularly in the developing world, go unfulfilled. At least 1.1 billion choke on unhealthy levels of air pollution, 220 million lack clean drinking water, 420 million do not have access to the simplest latrines, and 600 million do not have adequate shelter.[5]

At the same time, resource use by the rich threatens the security of future generations. Although cities have always relied on their hinterlands, wealthy urbanites today draw more heavily on far-flung resources—quickening the pace of climate change, deforestation, soil erosion, and loss of biological diversity worldwide. London, for example, now requires roughly 58 times its land area just to supply its residents with food and timber. Meeting the needs of everyone in the world in the same way that the needs of Londoners are met would require at least three more Earths.[6]

The search for a new vision for cities has even more urgency now. In 1900, only 160 million people, one tenth of the world's population, were city dwellers. By shortly after 2000, in contrast, half the world (3.2 billion people) will live in urban areas—a 20-fold increase in numbers. The challenge for the next century will be to improve the environmental conditions of cities themselves while reducing the demands that they make on Earth's finite resources.[7]

AN URBANIZING WORLD

Although urban areas have existed for millennia, we still do not have a good definition of "the city" because its shape and role keeps changing from place to place and over time. Around 4000 B.C., farming villages in Mesopotamian river valleys grew into the world's first cities. These settlements culminated in the Sumerian city-state—with its elaborate temples, stratified social classes, advanced technology, extended trade, and military fortifications. Many of these early cities had walls that formally set the town off from the countryside. Over the years, these walls were often rebuilt to accommodate larger populations, as rural dwellers sought a better life in the city and as births within the city began to outnumber deaths.[8]

The Industrial Revolution brought the next major urban transformation. By the eighteenth century, industrializing cities in Europe were spilling over their confines. In the late nineteenth and early twentieth centuries, western urban populations surged beyond administrative limits as well. In many cities in Europe and North America, the number of people living within the political boundaries of major city centers declined, particularly after 1950, but roads and buildings continued to pave over surrounding forest and farmland. New technologies and government policies helped create this sprawl. The most extreme examples of widely dispersed suburban "edge cities" are found in the United States. Between 1950 and 1990, for instance, greater Chicago's population grew by 38 percent but spread over 124 percent more land; metro Cleveland's population increased by 21 percent during these years, but the city ate up 112 percent more land.[9]

As the shape of cities has changed, so have notions about what constitutes an "urban area." Today, cities swell not only from an influx of newcomers and births within the city but also from reclassification of rural areas. Urban population statistics may correspond to the political boundaries of an old city center or extend to some part of the greater metropolitan region, which may have numerous centers of employment. Thus, depending on where the lines are drawn, Tokyo's population ranges from 8 million to 39 million and Mexico City's from 2 million to 18 million. This chapter uses the U.N. definition for "urban agglomerations," which incorporates the population in a city or town plus the adjacent suburban fringe.[10]

Economic forces underlie the ongoing changes in the role of cities. In the past half-century, many cities in the develop-

ing world have grown as industrialization has brought both the prospect of urban jobs and the degradation of rural areas. In the 1950s, most of the world's jobs were in agriculture; by 1990, most were in services—an outgrowth of industrialization. Cities still provide a marketplace for food and other items produced in the surrounding region, but a growing number also serve as global bazaars. Telephones, satellites, and computer links are among the technologies that allow today's network of "global" cities to reach beyond their immediate hinterlands. Elites in Seoul and Stockholm may have more in common with each other than with their rural compatriots.[11]

Much modern urban infrastructure was built in response to nineteenth-century problems in the western industrial city, which dominated history for a brief moment. In 1800, just 3 of the 10 largest cities were in Europe (see Table 8–1); by 1900, 9 were in Europe or North America; but by 2000, there will only be 2. Asia, which led world urbanization between 800 and 1800, again today has half of the 10 largest cities. India's urban population alone—256 million—could constitute the world's fourth most populous nation.[12]

Table 8–1. Population of World's 10 Largest Metropolitan Areas in 1000, 1800, and 1900, With Projections for 2000

1000		1800		1900		2000	
			(million)				
Cordova	0.45	Peking	1.10	London	6.5	Tokyo	28.0
Kaifeng	0.40	London	0.86	New York	4.2	Mexico City	18.1
Constantinople	0.30	Canton	0.80	Paris	3.3	Bombay	18.0
Angkor	0.20	Edo (Tokyo)	0.69	Berlin	2.7	São Paulo	17.7
Kyoto	0.18	Constantinople	0.57	Chicago	1.7	New York	16.6
Cairo	0.14	Paris	0.55	Vienna	1.7	Shanghai	14.2
Bagdad	0.13	Naples	0.43	Tokyo	1.5	Lagos	13.5
Nishapur	0.13	Hangchow	0.39	St. Petersburg	1.4	Los Angeles	13.1
Hasa	0.11	Osaka	0.38	Manchester	1.4	Seoul	12.9
Anhilvada	0.10	Kyoto	0.38	Philadelphia	1.4	Beijing	12.4

SOURCE: 1000–1900 from Tertius Chandler, *Four Thousand Years of Urban Growth: An Historical Census* (Lewiston, NY: Edwin Mellen Press, 1987); 2000 from United Nations, *World Urbanization Prospects: The 1996 Revision* (New York: 1998).

With North America, Europe, and Japan already highly urbanized, most city growth will continue to occur in developing countries. The pace of urbanization today in places such as Lagos and Bombay echoes that of Chicago and New York a century ago. The big difference lies in the absolute population increase, however, which is much higher. (See Table 8–2.) Between 1990 and 1995, 263 million people were added to the cities of the developing world—the equivalent of another Los Angeles or Shanghai forming every three months. Indeed, population increase in developing-country cities will be the distinguishing demographic trend of the next century, accounting for nearly 90 percent of the 2.7 billion people due to be added to world population between 1995 and 2030.[13]

Regional variations within the Third World are striking. Some 73 percent of Latin Americans now live in cities, making the region roughly as urbanized as Europe and North America. Thus, the most explosive growth in the future is expected in Africa and Asia, which are still only 30–35 percent urbanized. (See Table 8–3.) In many parts of the developing world, particularly Southeast Asia and West Africa, urban numbers are hard to gauge as "circular" migrants—people who move to the city temporarily—elude census takers. In general, cities with more than 1 million people are often called large, while membership in the "megacity" club generally requires a population of 10 million. By this definition, Africa has just one megacity, Lagos. But burgeoning African cities of several hundred thousand are "mega-villages" that are growing too fast for local authorities to manage.[14]

As urban numbers swell, cities present not only problems but also opportunities. For millennia, cities have been the cultural centers and engines of creativity that advance civilization. They remain magnets that draw people and ideas. Urban environmental stewardship can improve local conditions, resulting in clean public spaces, services, and access to places of employment—all of which help ease inequities between rich and poor. The sheer size and reach of cities means that

Table 8–2. Rate and Scale of Population Growth in Selected Industrial Cities, 1875–1900, and Developing Cities, 1975–2000

City	Annual Population Growth (percent)	Population Added (million)
Industrial Cities (1875–1900)		
Chicago	6.0	1.3
New York	3.3	2.3
Tokyo	2.6	0.7
London	1.7	2.2
Paris	1.6	1.1
Developing Cities (1975–2000)		
Lagos	5.8	10.2
Bombay	4.0	11.2
São Paolo	2.3	7.7
Mexico City	1.9	6.9
Shanghai	0.9	2.7

SOURCE: Industrial cities from Tertius Chandler, *Four Thousand Years of Urban Growth: An Historical Census* (Lewiston, NY: Edwin Mellen Press, 1987); developing cities from United Nations, *World Urbanization Prospects: The 1996 Revision* (New York: 1998).

Table 8–3. Percentage of Population Living in Urban Areas, by Region, 1950–95, With Projections for 2015

Region	1950	1975	1995	2015
Africa	14.6	25.2	34.9	46.4
Asia[1]	15.3	22.2	33.0	45.6
Latin America	41.4	61.2	73.4	79.9
Industrial Countries[2]	54.9	69.9	74.9	80.0
World	29.7	37.8	45.3	54.4

[1]Excluding Japan. [2]Europe, Japan, Australia, New Zealand, and North America excluding Mexico.
SOURCE: United Nations, *World Urbanization Prospects: The 1996 Revision* (New York: 1998).

they will have a profound effect on the global environment—for better or worse. Today's cities take up 2 percent of the world's surface but consume 75 percent of its resources. Thus, increased efficiency in a relatively small part of the world would yield big results. The remainder of this chapter provides examples of changes in urban water, waste, transportation, and buildings that can benefit both people and the planet.[15]

IMPROVING WATER SUPPLY AND QUALITY

Most human settlements have been sited to take advantage of water for agriculture and transportation. The world's earliest cities arose in the valleys of great rivers: the Nile, the Tigris-Euphrates, the Indus, and the Yellow. But the rivers and streams that provide drinking water also receive household and industrial wastes, so the flow of water into a city and the flow of wastes out are intimately linked.[16]

Nineteenth-century engineers constructed vast water and sewer systems in industrial countries. The goal was twofold: to meet growing water demand by boosting supplies, and to channel wastewater and rainwater away from people as quickly as possible. These systems were an unquestionable boon to health. With better water and sanitation, life expectancy in French cities, for instance, shot up from 32 years in 1850 to 45 years by 1900.[17]

But large, costly projects have failed to reach many rural areas and poor urban districts. Despite gains during the 1980s, which was designated by the United Nations as the International Water Supply and Sanitation Decade, 25 percent of the developing world remains without clean water and 66 percent lacks sanitation. Waterborne diarrheal diseases, which

arise from poor water and waste management, are the world's leading cause of illness. Each year, 5 million children die from diarrheal ailments; most come from poor urban families.[18]

Moreover, technologies designed to promote health now contribute to broader environmental ills. The first class of problems occurs in bringing water into cities. The architect Vitruvius wrote in the first century B.C. that finding water was the first step in planning a new city. But his contemporary colleagues today assume water is a secondary consideration, relying instead on engineers to divert rivers or pump water over great distances. Thus, cities have extended their reach for water, destroying fragile ecosystems and reducing the water available for crops. Prime examples include the western United States, where water battles are being waged, and northern China, where 108 cities report shortages. Since the turn of the century, municipal use of water worldwide has grown 19 times and industrial use has grown 26 times while agricultural use has increased only 5 times.[19]

Another set of damaging effects occurs as water is hurried away from cities. When rainwater is channeled through pipes and gutters, less water infiltrates the soil to recharge underground supplies. Roads also prevent water from seeping into the ground. Thus rain runs off pavement straight into channels, where it speeds into rivers and streams, causing more severe floods than would occur if plants or soil soaked up some of the deluge. Moreover, without enough water to recharge underground supplies, the land may subside, causing rail tracks to buckle, water pipes to burst, and building foundations to crack. And in coastal areas, salt water may leak into wells, ruining drinking supplies.[20]

A dramatic image of subsidence appears in a 1995 report on Mexico City's water supply. At first, the photo of a small boy apparently leaning against a telephone pole looks out of place in a book about water. But the pole is actually a well casing that was once underground. Excessive withdrawal of groundwater has caused parts of Mexico City to sink more than 9 meters in the last century, so now the pipe towers some 7 meters above ground. Local children reportedly mark their height on it to see if they grow faster than the ground sinks.[21]

Water-short cities in the next century will be pressed to slake their thirst in ways that cause less ecological destruction and require less money. Conservation may be a large part of the solution. Unlike energy, water has yet to become a major target for efficiency gains. Complementary approaches include restricting development near drinking water sources and using low-cost methods of wastewater treatment.[22]

Metropolitan Boston provides an example of successful water conservation. Since 1987, the Massachusetts Water Resources Authority has managed to avoid diverting two large rivers to augment supply, as engineers had initially prescribed. For a third to half the cost of the diversions, the government has reduced total water demand by 24 percent by repairing leaky pipes, installing water-saving fixtures, and educating everyone from schoolchildren to plant managers on water-saving measures.[23]

Conservation is not only for the rich; developing countries also stand to save money. In the Third World, as much as 60 percent of water is lost through leaky pipes and theft. In Manila, for example, 58 percent of the drinking water is forfeited to leaks or illegal tapping, whereas Singapore, where pipes are better maintained, loses only 8 percent.[24]

A key to water conservation is removing incentives for profligate use. Lack of meters, inordinately low prices, and prices that decline as use increases all encourage wastefulness. As underpricing causes excessive use, the problem feeds

on itself. With the cash-strapped water agency unable to maintain its pipes, more water is lost to leaks. This causes the agency to lay claim to additional water supplies, diverting them from agriculture. And as farms fail without irrigation, more people migrate to cities, raising the demand for water. Bogor, Indonesia, took its first steps to break this cycle in 1988, when it installed meters and hiked prices to encourage households to conserve. Demand initially fell by one third, allowing the utility to connect more families to the system.[25]

Although pricing the poor out of water is a concern, artificially low prices may hurt this group even more. Prices that do not reflect the true cost of water discourage utilities from extending service. It would be a losing proposition. Thus many of the poor in developing countries end up paying much more for water from private vendors, who charge anywhere from 4 to 100 times the public rate that wealthy citizens pay. In Istanbul, water from vendors is 10 times the public rate; in Bombay, it is 20 times higher.[26]

Making better use of rainwater is another conservation technique that doubles as a flood-control strategy. Metropolitan Tokyo, with 82 percent of its land surface covered by asphalt or concrete, suffers from torrential runoff that causes floods and depletes underground water supplies. The city has thus turned to rainwater as a supplemental source. Tanks atop 579 city buildings capture this free resource for use in washrooms, gardens, air-conditioning systems, and fire hoses. Now rain that falls on the giant Kokugikan sumo wrestling stadium supplies 70 percent of the water in the building that is not used for drinking.[27]

Other forms of water recycling also hold potential to enhance city water supplies. Municipal wastewater can be used instead of high-quality drinking water to flush toilets or to water lawns. If treated, it may be used to irrigate some types of crops or to raise fish. Some 70 percent of Israeli wastewater is recycled in this way. Treatment is made easier if wastewater from industry is kept separate from the residential flow. In most countries, the flows are combined, however. Thus as cities in developing countries build sewage infrastructure, they will save money and water if they keep flows separate.[28]

Just as conservation of water can boost water supplies, conservation of land can protect water quality. A number of cities are finding that cooperating with neighboring regions, industries, and agriculture to protect watersheds is ultimately less costly than trying to make polluted water safe for drinking. New York City, for instance, plans to buy $300 million worth of land upstate to protect the watersheds that deliver the city's drinking water. The tactic is part of a comprehensive watershed protection strategy that, while costly at $1.4 billion, will save the city from having to pay $3–8 billion for a new filtration system.[29]

Limiting development near important water sources not only preserves water quality, it also prevents floods and provides a connection to nature. In the 1880s, landscape architect Frederick Law Olmsted persuaded Boston that keeping buildings away from floodplains by establishing riverfront parks would ultimately prove cheaper than keeping floods away from buildings through huge public works projects. The result was the verdant Back Bay Fens, a park that protected the neighborhood from flooding. In contrast, Los Angeles has paid for failing to heed similar warnings made by Olmsted's son in the 1930s—the city has little parkland and faced $500 million in damages from three major floods in the early 1990s alone.[30]

In addition to improving water supply and quality, cities can also treat wastewater at lower economic and environmental cost. One time-honored biological approach—wetlands treatment—uses more land but is also much less expensive

and does not produce toxic sludge. Vegetation in stabilization ponds or modified wetlands extracts contaminants such as nitrates and mercury, while bacteria and other organisms break down toxic compounds. Phoenix, Arizona, is creating wetlands to clean a portion of its sewage because the option is much cheaper than a $625-million upgrade of its wastewater treatment plant.[31]

Many of the poor in developing countries end up paying much more for water from private vendors.

Where cities have been unable or unwilling to extend sewers to the poorest people, some communities have stepped into the breach with low-cost solutions. The most famous example is in the Orangi district of Karachi, Pakistan, home to nearly 1 million "squatters." In the early 1980s, Akhter Hameed Khan, a dynamic community organizer, formed a nongovernmental research institute called the Orangi Pilot Project. Between 1981 and 1996, this group helped neighborhoods to organize, collect money, and manage construction of sewers that serve some 90 percent of Orangi's residents.[32]

Increasingly, cities are looking to tap the resources of the private sector, as governments alone will be unable to come up with the billions of dollars needed over the next decade for reliable water systems. Water privatization is most extensive in the United Kingdom and France, and companies from these countries are beginning to ply their trade abroad. Only 5 percent of the financing for water worldwide comes from private sources, but privatization, in various degrees, is a growing trend. Between 1990 and 1997, the number of private water projects in developing countries increased more than 10-fold, mainly in Latin America and East Asia. In Buenos Aires, for instance, an international consortium led by the French firm Lyonnaise des Eaux-Dumez renovated thousands of kilometers of pipes in the water system, expanding coverage and lowering rates.[33]

Still, privatization is not a panacea. Water supply and sanitation are important public services, so some form of public control or regulation will always be needed to make sure that quality and prices are reasonable. Unfortunately, few cities have regulations in place yet to make privatization work fairly.

MINING URBAN WASTE

Remains from some of the earliest cities suggest that residents there at first took a *laissez-faire* approach to waste disposal, simply raising the roofs of their houses as mounting garbage caused street levels to rise. In eighteenth-century Boston, when refuse threatened to impede industrial progress, the city's first "paved" roads were built: wooden planks placed on top of the garbage. A century later, Charles Dickens spoke to both the water and waste problems of nineteenth-century New York when he referred to it as "a city without baths or plumbing, lighted by gas and scavenged by pigs."[34]

Today, garbage is most voluminous in rich countries but most visible in cities of developing countries. In the 1950s, Manila began to dump much of its garbage in a poor neighborhood, laying the foundation for what would become the city's most striking topographical feature—"Mount Smoky." Methane from the rotting refuse burned in an acrid haze, lending the summit its name. Until a newly elected Philippine president razed the garbage mountain in the early 1990s, it towered 40 meters above sea level in Manila Bay and was home to some 20,000

people who made a living from scavenging the refuse.[35]

Like water, waste profoundly affects human health. Hazards are most pronounced in the developing world, where between one third and half of city trash goes uncollected. Open piles of garbage attract disease-carrying rats and flies, and often wash into drainage channels, where they contribute to floods and waterborne disease. And even the most expensive methods of waste disposal—high-tech "sanitary" landfills and incinerators—are not completely free of health risks. Toxins from landfills can leach into groundwater, and heavy metals, chlorine compounds, and dioxin are among the hazards in incinerator ash.[36]

City waste has many broader environmental implications. Just as storm drains short-circuit the water cycle, urban waste disposal systems designed to speed wastes away from people actually interrupt the nutrient cycle. Trucks, planes, and trains haul food into cities from great distances, but the nutrients rarely make it back to farmland. Roughly half of the 20,000 tons of food that New York City receives each day is transformed into human energy; the other half is shunted to sewers or trucked to increasingly remote landfills. Not only does this add to the waste disposal burden, it also heightens the demand for manufactured fertilizer, a major source of nitrogen pollution, which is a growing global threat.[37]

Moreover, throwing items away instead of reusing or recycling them increases the demand for new resources obtained by environmentally destructive mining and logging. (See also Chapter 3.) In 1895, George Waring, New York City's commissioner of street cleaning, recognized that the "out of sight, out of mind" approach to trash "is an easy one to follow, but it is not an economical one, nor a decent one, nor a safe one." His prescient warning went unheeded. In the industrial world, waste collection has improved public

health, but the problem of waste generation has only worsened. Urbanites in industrial countries generate up to 100 times more refuse per person than their counterparts in developing countries.[38]

But cities have the potential to shift from being repositories of waste to great sources of raw materials. The farms, forests, and mines of the twenty-first century may well be found in our urban centers—in the form of city gardens and recycling plants. Local authorities can spur the transition by providing incentives for composting, recycling, and waste-based industries.

Organic waste—paper, food scraps, lawn clippings, and even human waste—is a valuable resource. In industrial countries, food and yard waste alone account for some 36 percent of the municipal waste stream. European cities are leading a trend toward composting, which transforms this organic waste into a product that invigorates agricultural soils. Cities in seven countries—Austria, Belgium, Denmark, Germany, Luxembourg, the Netherlands, and Switzerland—collect these wastes separately, recovering more than 85 percent of them.[39]

Composting can also boost urban food security by enriching city gardens. The U.N. Development Programme (UNDP) estimates that 800 million urban farmers harvest 15 percent of the world's food supply. In parts of Africa, urban agriculture is a survival strategy. Some 68 percent of families in Dar es Salaam, Tanzania grow vegetables or raise livestock. City farmers also tend 80,000 gardens in Berlin as well as crops in Buenos Aires that meet one fifth of that city's nutritional needs.[40]

To keep paper and inorganic materials such as metals, glass, and plastics from landfills, a number of cities have found ways to promote recycling and waste-based industries. They can charge a fee for the collection of unsorted garbage, for example, while picking up for free refuse that has been separated for recycling. By

adopting "pay-as-you-throw" systems, at least 11 U.S. cities have boosted recycling rates to the 45–60 percent range, well above the national average of 27 percent.[41]

Some cities have gone a step further, to engage the industries that create disposable goods or generate waste. In 1997, Tokyo municipal officials—looking for new waste disposal options in land-short Japan—announced that they would require makers and distributors of plastic bottles to recover and recycle their products. And Graz, Austria, has created a labeling program to spur small- and medium-sized industries to reduce waste: companies receive the city's Ecoprofit label if they reduce solid waste by 30 percent and hazardous waste by 50 percent.[42]

While the private sector is a newcomer to water supply and sanitation, it has a long history in waste collection and disposal. In some developing-country cities, local authorities have struck recycling deals with private companies and even self-employed wastepickers. (See Table 8–4.) City officials in Bandung, Indonesia, are working with a local nongovernmental organization (NGO) to employ a group of scavenger families. The families receive financial and technical support to separate recyclables more safely and efficiently, compost organic wastes, and create businesses that use the wastes they collect as raw materials. They make money—and the city reduces the cost of waste management.[43]

A handful of cities are moving beyond recycling to "industrial symbiosis," where one company's waste becomes another's input. (See Chapter 3.) The first eco-industrial park began to evolve more than 20 years ago in Kalundborg, Denmark. Today, waste gases from an oil refinery there are burned by a power plant, waste heat from the plant warms commercial fish ponds, and other companies use byproducts of combustion to make wallboard and concrete. According to one calculation, Kalundborg's waste-saving

Table 8-4. Community Waste-Based Industries

Location	Description
Santos, Brazil	Calculating that scavengers were collecting about 1,200 tons of recyclable materials per month, compared with the city's 200, Santos authorities began to pay scavengers to collect recyclables; the scavengers also share in the profits from sale of the materials.
Dakar, Senegal	Dakar officials divided the city into collection zones with subsectors and invited companies to bid for contracts to collect waste from a maximum of three zones. Companies must subcontract in each sector with community groups that collect garbage from inaccessible areas and educate their neighbors. The new system costs less, covers 80 percent of the city (15 percent more than before), and provides 1,000 new jobs.
Cairo, Egypt	The Zabbaleen have been garbage pickers since they began coming to Cairo in mid-century. With the help of aid agencies, the city and the community launched a program in 1981 to improve city collection service and boost the Zabbaleen's income and standard of living. Today, the Zabbaleen sew rags into quilts and compost animal waste to sell to farmers.

SOURCE: International Council for Local Environmental Initiatives (ICLEI), "Santos, Brazil: Recycling, Dignity, and Citizenhood," *Members in Action, 1996–1997* (Toronto: 1997); ICLEI, *Urban Community of Dakar, Senegal: Participatory Solid Waste Management,* Case Study 45 (Toronto: January 1997); Richard Gilbert et al., *Making Cities Work: The Role of Local Authorities in the Urban Environment* (London: Earthscan, 1996); Akhtar Badshah, *Our Urban Future* (London: Zed Books, 1996).

approach translates into $120 million in savings and revenues on a $60-million investment over a five-year period. Since 1993, more than 20 U.S. cities hoping to revive stagnant economies have announced plans for similar parks.[44]

MOVING PEOPLE AND GOODS

Transportation shapes cities. While walking distances constrained life in the earliest cities, by the end of the nineteenth century electric trolley and rail tracks stretched growing industrial cities into radial spokes. Early twentieth-century "streetcar suburbs" in North America and Europe were initially compact, with houses a short walk from the stations.[45]

The automobile allowed the city to spread out in a more random fashion

than ever before—a trend the United States was quickest to adopt. By the 1930s, developers were building houses and roads between the rail spokes for people with cars. Bangkok has experienced a speeded-up version of this phenomenon. As recently as 1959, a group of U.S. consultants noted: "To a person accustomed to Western standards, [Bangkok] is remarkable for its compactness. A vigorous walker can traverse it from north to south in three hours or less." But as population soared and a city built for canal traffic became a city dominated by motorized vehicles, Bangkok's built-up area mushroomed from 67 square kilometers in 1953 to 426 square kilometers in 1990. Today even the most vigorous walker would probably not contemplate a cross-city voyage on foot; in fact, it can take three hours to cross Bangkok by car.[46]

The shape of a city, in turn, influences livability and demands on natural resources. Sprawling conurbations threaten both human and environmental health. By the mid-1920s, Le Corbusier was lamenting the destruction wrought by car fumes: "On the Champs Elysees, half the chestnuts lining the avenue have their leaves withered….Our lungs absorb these dangerous gases. But the martyred trees cry out, 'Beware!'" Today, vehicle exhaust is often the dominant ingredient in urban air pollution, which takes at least 3 million lives worldwide each year.[47]

Roads designed to hasten the speed of cars are often dangerous. Traffic accidents kill some 885,000 people each year—equivalent to 10 fatal jumbo jet crashes per day—and injure many times this number. Another health threat is less obvious: by replacing short trips that could be made by bicycle or on foot, cars promote sedentary lifestyles. Even in the United Kingdom's most hostile traffic, the health benefits of cycling—reduction in coronary heart disease, obesity, and hypertension—outweigh the risks of accidents by around 20 to 1, according to the British Medical Association.[48]

Car dependency also breeds social inequities. One third of the U.S. population is too young, too old, or too poor to drive. Some 98 percent of Boston's welfare recipients live within walking distance of public transit, but only 32 percent of potential employers are that close to a transit station. In the developing world, as much as 80 percent of the population can afford a bicycle, but only 5–10 percent earn enough to buy a car.[49]

Some technical fixes, already adopted in most industrial nations, are urgently needed in many developing countries. The reduced health risks and car maintenance costs that follow from removing lead from gasoline and requiring catalytic converters far outweigh the expense. The World Bank estimates that in Manila, basic improvements in vehicles and fuels alone would save more than 2,000 lives and at least $200 million a year in avoided health costs. Even more efficient cars and cleaner fuels are on the horizon—in the form of ultra-efficient cars powered by emissions-free hydrogen fuel cells, for instance. (See Chapter 2.) While promising, these innovations will still only address pollution, leaving accidents, congestion, and social inequities untouched.[50]

Greater reliance on cars in cities cannot be sustained. In the United States, suburban roads and houses supplant more than 1 million hectares of farmland each year. According to government estimates, some 200,000 hectares of arable land in China disappear each year under city streets and developments in China. Today, transportation accounts for 15–20 percent of the annual 6 billion tons of carbon emissions from human activities that are leading to climate change. By 2030, China is expected to have 828 million city dwellers. If they were to drive as much as the average American, the carbon emissions from transportation in urban China alone would exceed 1 billion tons, roughly as much as released from all transportation worldwide today.[51]

Transportation and land-use decisions by city officials can shape an alternative to the car-reliant city: a cleaner, greener, and more equitable urban form. Some of the best examples come from Western Europe and Scandinavia. The Netherlands has 128 cars per square kilometer, one of the highest densities in the world. But nationwide spatial planning gives priority to bike paths, allowing Dutch cities to achieve some of the world's highest rates of bicycle use. Some 30 percent of all urban trips there are made by bike, compared with less than 1 percent in U.S. cities. In Stockholm, the city council has orchestrated "transit villages" around suburban rail stations, allowing homes to sprout only a short walk from offices and stores. The walkability of these neighborhoods prompted car trips to fall by 229 kilometers per person between 1980 and 1990 as transit use rose.[52]

Curitiba, Brazil, is famous for both its busways and its bikeways. In the early 1970s, the city designated several main roadways radiating from the city center as structural axes for busways. Through zoning laws, the city encouraged construction of high-density buildings along these transit corridors. Since then, innovations such as extra-large buses for popular routes and tube-shaped shelters where passengers pay their fares in advance have added to the system's speed and convenience. The bus stations link to a 150-kilometer network of bike paths. Although Curitiba has one car for every three people, two thirds of all trips in the city are made by bus. Car traffic has declined by 30 percent since 1974, even as the population doubled.[53]

In cities where public support for transit and cycling is strong, some interesting private initiatives are beginning to flourish. Car-sharing networks, for example, have grown in popularity in Europe since the late 1980s. Each member pays for a card that opens the lockers that hold keys to cars parked around the city. Members who call the network to reserve a car are directed to the closest one. The European Car Sharing Network now has more than 100,000 participants in 40 organizations in 230 cities in Germany, Austria, Switzerland, and the Netherlands. One of the largest groups is Stattauto, headquartered in Berlin, which estimates that each of their vehicles replaces five private cars; altogether the fleet eliminates 510,000 kilometers of driving each year.[54]

The private sector has been involved in financing city transport for a long time. In the late nineteenth century, private companies would foot the bill for urban rail construction in return for development rights near the stations. Public funds have paid for such construction in recent years. But now a company in Portland is negotiating construction of a light rail track to the airport in exchange for a lease to air-port land. At the same time, an elevated rail system through Bangkok will get much of its revenue from property development under the route, and numerous other projects are under way elsewhere. The private sector can help operate public transit as well. In Curitiba, private companies pay for bus operating costs; the city pays for the roads, lighting, bus stops, and staff to monitor the companies.[55]

Copenhagen has even extended the public-private partnership idea to bicycles. The city maintains a fleet of bikes for public use that is financed through advertising on the wheel surfaces and bicycle frames. The system is popular: organizers estimate that the 2,300 bicycles are used on average once every 8 minutes.[56]

BUILDING BETTER NEIGHBORHOODS

The layout of neighborhoods goes hand-in-hand with transportation in shaping cities. By building roads, rail lines, or bike paths, cities decide not only how people will move around, but where the accessible and desirable buildings will be and where new services will be needed. And by mandating where new buildings can be built and what kind of uses—residential, retail, industrial—are allowed, land-use and zoning laws influence how far people must travel to get to work, buy food, and go about their daily business.[57]

Responding to pollution and overcrowding in the early twentieth century, local governments in the United States adopted zoning laws that limited residential density and placed restrictions on land use that separated houses from businesses. The car helped make such land use possible, and ever greater distances between houses, stores, and jobs made the car more essential. That feedback effect has helped to make U.S. cities among the least compact and most car-dependent in the world. (See Table 8–5.)

Much of the chaotic urban development in developing countries occurs because 30–60 percent of city populations live in squatter settlements and 70–95 percent of new housing is technically outside the law. In Cairo, to cite just one case, informal settlements have grown rapidly, turning a cemetery in the city's eastern section into the "City of the Dead," where poor families squeeze into the small care-takers' rooms in the tombs. At the same time, more than a half-million apartments stand empty because the poor cannot afford the public housing and because the private sector caters to the upper class.[58]

The arrangement of buildings helps determine the livability of a city. Streets come alive with pedestrians when shops, factories, offices, and houses are all within walking distance of each other. And city greenery and parks between buildings cool streets and soothe the spirit. In contrast, public life diminishes when architects design office parks and shopping malls to be enjoyed from the inside, and gaping parking lots to welcome cars but not pedestrians. Crime often plagues fragmented cities, which isolate the poor in distinct pockets. Brazilian scholar Raquel Rolnick has exposed the link between ter-ritorial exclusion and violence in cities within the state of São Paulo. On the other hand, urban analyst Jane Jacobs noted an advantage to diverse street life when she wrote about Manhattan in the early 1960s: many "eyes on the street" deter crime.[59]

Neighborhood layout also influences the resource demands of a city. Changes in the layout can lower energy demands from transportation by a factor of 10. And trees that block buildings from the sun or wind lower the energy the residents need for heating and cooling. Moreover, when neighborhoods are spread out at low density, they require more water, sewer pipes, power lines, and roads. Sprawling cities also use more building materials. Buildings, which consume roughly 40 percent of materials in the global economy, represent one fourth of the demand for wood worldwide.[60]

Economic concerns are forcing a number of local authorities in the United States to face up to these realities. A Rutgers University study found that compact growth instead of sprawl-as-usual would save New Jersey taxpayers $1.3 billion in infrastructure costs over 20 years. Similarly, another study predicted that if rapid suburban development continued apace in Maryland between 1995 and 2020, the new sewers, water pipes, schools, and roads to support it would cost about $10 billion more than if population growth were accommodated by more condensed development. And the U.S. Forest Service estimated that planting 95,000 trees in metropolitan Chicago would yield a net benefit of $38 million in energy savings over 30 years.[61]

A few cities are beginning to rein in rapacious development, boost parkland, and even improve the quality of buildings that do get constructed. Their tools include regulations or incentives that push developers to build on vacant land within the city rather than outlying green areas, setting aside land for informal settlements,

Table 8–5. Population Density and Car Use in Selected Cities, by Regional Average, 1990

Location of Cities	Population Density	Private Car Use Per Capita
	(persons per hectare)	(kilometers driven per person)
United States	14.7	10,870
Canada	26.2	6,946
Europe	49.9	4,519
Wealthy Asia	163.9	1,487
Developing Asia	162.8	1,611

SOURCE: Peter Newman and Jeffrey Kenworthy, *Sustainability and Cities: Overcoming Automobile Dependence* (Washington, DC: Island Press, in press).

and changing city building codes.

The U.S. city with the most success at stemming sprawl is Portland, Oregon. A 1973 state law requires the metropolitan area to demarcate an urban growth boundary to allow for future growth without encroaching too far into agricultural or forestland. Planners are now trying to reduce the need for cars within the boundary. New rules require 85 percent of new building to be within a five-minute walk of a transit stop. Revised codes allow for mixed-use development of apartments above stores and forbid "snob zoning" that prohibits the denser type of housing—townhouses and apartment buildings—that can support transit.[62]

In Kimberly, South Africa, a private developer teamed up with local residents to replace shacks with a low-cost "solar neighborhood" for 200 families.

Compact cities need not be forbidding concrete jungles. Portland has fortified its ties to nature by removing freeways that blocked access to the Willamette River and requiring buildings to step down as they approach the city's eastern edge, in order to protect "view corridors" of Mount Hood. And because suburban development is confined, Portlanders do not have to travel far to enjoy the wilderness. Peter Newman and Jeff Kenworthy, Australian researchers who have analyzed transportation in cities extensively, point out that some of the most population-dense and least car-reliant European hubs, such as Paris and Vienna, are among the most aesthetically pleasing cities in the world.[63]

To reduce fringe development, a number of older industrial cities are offering incentives to redevelop vacant or abandoned parcels of land within the metropolitan area. Some of the most sought-after new housing in southern England, for instance, is on such "infill" sites. One concern, however, is that a former occupant may have been an industrial polluter who left the land contaminated. By offering tax credits and funds for environmental cleanup, cities and higher forms of government can entice buyers to take the risk—a strategy that benefits the region in the long term. Following the U.S. Environmental Protection Agency's announcement of a federal "brownfields" initiative, some 228 pilot redevelopment efforts have been proposed in U.S. cities.[64]

Increasingly, local authorities in developing countries recognize the truth of a point made a decade ago by researchers Jorge Hardoy and David Satterthwaite: "the unnamed millions who build, organize and plan illegally are the most important organizers, builders and planners of Third World cities." Those who cannot afford a house on the formal market seek out the most precarious slopes and river valleys. Squatters are unlikely to receive an eviction notice—but they probably will never see water pipes and electricity lines either. However, most cities contain places where low-income sites could be developed, at lower cost, because they are already close to transportation and services. In Curitiba, the city set aside such tracts for informal settlements.[65]

Not only can neighborhoods be laid out better, buildings themselves can be constructed better. Buildings—which have their own water, waste, and energy flows—are actually microcosms of the city. They are particularly well suited to use the new decentralized energy technologies such as solar panels that generate electricity and natural gas turbines that generate both heat and electricity. (See Chapter 2.) Cities can support green construction by setting codes that require buildings to be energy-efficient, and by requiring green design for public construction. The Danish Planning Institute has published a guide to urban ecology in Copenhagen that highlights 45 projects in the city that use much less water and energy than conventional buildings and that contain facilities to compost organic waste.[66]

In the much less affluent city of Kimberly, South Africa, a private developer teamed up with local residents to replace tin and mud shacks with a low-cost "solar neighborhood" for 200 families. Based on that success, the developer is planning a similar project for the smaller town of Ugie, where homes using passive solar design and solar ovens will be clustered in groups of six to share gardens. Household organic waste, composted on-site, will be used in the gardens, as will filtered wastewater. The basic home costs no more than the $3,200-government subsidy for first-time home buyers— a state-assisted "self-help" program designed to address the legacy of apartheid. Costs stay low because residents do the construction themselves.[67]

REALIZING THE VISION

At the end of her classic 1984 book on the urban environment, *The Granite Garden*, Anne Whiston Spirn reminds us that "in the present lies not only the nightmare of what the city will become if current trends continue, but also the dream of what the city could be." Taking today's urban problems to an apocalyptic conclusion, Spirn envisions an "infernal city" that has disintegrated following uprisings by city dwellers denied adequate food, water, and work. Social and environmental ills have followed those fleeing cities into a countryside ravaged by suburban development.[68]

The innovations in water, waste, transportation, and neighborhoods described

in this chapter help shape an alternative "sustainable city" vision. It is a city with a unique sense of place. Architects and engineers design buildings and transportation systems in response to citizens' requests and local climate. Rich and poor alike share clean air and water and vibrant public spaces. John Eberhard of the Massachusetts Institute of Technology suggests that just as the industrial city supplanted the preindustrial, a "third generation" of urban systems will arise. In the sustainable city, these new systems mimic the metabolism of nature. Rather than devouring water, food, energy, and processed goods and belching out the remains as noxious pollutants, the city controls its appetites and puts its waste to use. Rainwater and filtered wastewater are used to water gardens. Food scraps become compost that sustains the city's vegetable crops. Roofs are adorned with water tanks, vegetation, and solar panels.[69]

In June 1996, representatives from 171 nations and 579 cities met in Istanbul for the second U.N. Conference on Human Settlements (Habitat II) to endorse the broad outlines of the sustainable city vision: "the universal goals of ensuring adequate shelter for all and making human settlements safer, healthier and more livable, equitable, sustainable and productive." Delegates signed on to a Habitat Agenda that complemented the call for sustainable development made four years earlier in Rio, at the U.N. Conference on Environment and Development. Some 127 governments arrived in Istanbul with five-year national action plans; they agreed that a key to implementing their proposals would be support of the city-level Local Agenda 21 plans called for in Rio. These conferences—which included record numbers of NGOs—shone a spotlight on problems of environment and development, from the global to the local level. And in doing so, they helped reveal two key obstacles to progress in sustainable urban planning:

lack of political will and lack of money.[70]

Lack of political will may relate to insufficient understanding of local problems. Cities highlighted in this chapter for their "eco-innovations" succeeded because they identified problems and the links between them. A charismatic mayor in Curitiba, for instance, saw that chaotic development and poor public transportation conspired to worsen air pollution: car use increased as buildings sprouted far from bus stops. When citizens understand such connections, they often support or even demand change. Yet most poor cities lack the basic demographic and environmental data necessary to unveil the links between problems. The Habitat Agenda charges the U.N. Centre on Human Settlements (Habitat) with helping in such data gathering, in order to review post-conference progress. Since 1995, Habitat has been compiling data, which now includes indicators on population, income, water, waste, housing, and transportation for 237 cities in 110 countries. To expand the effort, Habitat has been assembling government experts, university scholars, and independent researchers in a Global Urban Observatory Network.[71]

Yet even when data on local problems are adequate, cities may face a dearth of ideas for solutions. Inspiration from other cities may help bolster political will. Nineteenth-century sanitary reforms gained momentum as scientists and local authorities from different cities compared notes. Such exchange is just as essential today. In 1990, the Toronto-based International Council on Local Environmental Initiatives (ICLEI) was formed to serve as the environmental arm of the world's oldest association of municipalities, the International Union of Local Authorities. As a clearinghouse, ICLEI disseminates information about the 2,000-plus cities in 64 countries that are now working on Local Agenda 21 initiatives. In a similar vein, one of the most immediate outcomes of the Istanbul meeting was a database of "Best Practices," which now contains more than 650 urban success stories. Each city is unique, so an innovation from one might be adapted, rather than precisely replicated, in another.[72]

Direct contact between local authorities from different cities can speed such information exchange. In recent years, networks for sustainable cities have proliferated, organized by existing municipal associations, NGOs, national governments, or international agencies. The New York-based Mega-Cities Project, one of the most prominent NGOs, was founded in 1987 to promote exchange between officials from the world's largest cities. Europe has some of the strongest city exchange programs. More than 100 European city leaders convened in Aalborg, Denmark, in 1994 to inaugurate the European Sustainable Cities and Towns Campaign, which is supported by several municipal associations in Europe, as well as ICLEI and the World Health Organization. Networks linked to governments or international agencies may have a funding component. For instance, the World Bank and the European Investment Bank brought mayors of cities bordering the Mediterranean together in Barcelona in 1991 to launch the Mediterranean Coastal Cities Network. The lending institutions, along with UNDP, help the cities gather data on environmental problems and devise solutions, as well as exchange information.[73]

Even when political will exists in one part of a city, fragmented governance often inhibits political action. Rarely does one government structure correspond to an entire metropolitan region. As districts within a metropolis compete with each other for development that will boost tax revenue, they push built-up areas over forests and farmland, pave over watersheds, and invite air pollution from increased car use. In the United States, the city that has made the most notable progress toward sustainability, Portland, is also the only one with an elected metropolitan government. David Rusk, former mayor of Albuquerque, New Mexico, has shown that regions with strong metropolitan cooperation are also less segregated along lines of race and class and are economically healthier. And Myron Orfield, a legislator from Minnesota, has helped galvanize "metropolitanism" in the United States—a movement that includes inner-city boosters and residents of decaying older suburbs seeking to direct investment toward existing infrastructure, as well as environmentalists trying to protect fringe areas from development.[74]

National and subnational policies can make or break a city's efforts to develop sustainably. Only higher levels of government can subdue the rivalry that spawns urban sprawl. State law requires Portland, for instance, to constrain its metropolitan boundary. Similarly, national policies that integrate environmental and spatial planning in Denmark and the Netherlands restrict new urban development in cities such as Copenhagen and Amsterdam to preserve green space. A city council can enact building codes to improve water and energy efficiency, but its conservation efforts will be undermined if the national government continues subsidizing the use of these resources. Cities with Local Agenda 21s are generally those that have strong support from the national level. A 1997 survey showed that 82 percent of known Local Agenda 21 initiatives were concentrated in 11 countries with national campaigns sponsored by government or country-wide municipal associations.[75]

The second main obstacle, lack of money, is often exacerbated by such disconnections between different levels of government. National governments in both industrial and developing countries have continued to shift functions to subnational and city governments in recent years, relying on local authorities to find

the money to do the job. Yet city governments are generally not allowed to levy taxes high enough to yield the needed revenue. The challenge for cities is to mobilize existing revenue and local resources to provide needed services.[76]

National policies that integrate environmental and spatial planning restrict new urban development in Copenhagen and Amsterdam to preserve green space.

If cities have control over services that draw on natural resources, they may be able to raise fees to meet both economic and environmental goals. Fees for unsorted household garbage have bolstered urban recycling efforts in a number of industrial countries. The success of water conservation programs from Bogor to Boston has hinged on higher prices—a standby of energy efficiency as well. Rather than maintain artificially low prices for all, water authorities or electric utilities can provide targeted subsidies, such as a loan or grant for the poorest families to pay for the initial hook-up, which is often the most prohibitive cost. Another tactic is to raise fees on parking to discourage driving and help fund public transportation.

In seeking to fund a sustainable city, local authorities have increasingly relied on the resourcefulness of local communities and NGOs, as well as the profit-making ability of the private sector. Both types of alliances work best if they are actual partnerships, in which local authorities acknowledge their responsibility for safeguarding public welfare. When the resources of the private sector far outweigh those of the city, local authorities may be unable to oversee the companies' activities and to insist on service provision to all. These concerns are not new: in the industrial cities of the nineteenth century, people complained that rail companies neglected projects that would benefit the public. UNDP's recently established Public Private Partnerships for the Urban Environment program emphasizes the importance of public oversight. It aims to help cities in developing countries turn environmental problems into viable business opportunities in water, waste, and energy services.[77]

Some cities have found a novel way to use one of the most widespread forms of local revenue, the property tax, to promote development of vacant lots within urban areas. Taxes on buildings tend to raise rents and discourage urban redevelopment, so shifting property taxes from buildings to land can stimulate construction on central sites, and can encourage speculators to develop empty city lots to help pay their taxes. But such a shift will only work if complementary policies protect surrounding forests and farmland from development. Thus, metropolitan areas subject to spatial restrictions on growth may be best equipped to make use of this tactic.[78]

Higher service fees and targeted tax policies will not achieve their desired effect if people cannot pay bills or taxes. Pervasive unemployment and poverty often keep cash-strapped cities in the red. Most mayors, according to a recent survey by UNDP, cite job creation as their most pressing concern. The need for environmental services can match up with the demand for jobs, as the experience with community waste-based industries in cities such as Cairo demonstrates. Small-scale lending programs—"microcredit"—can also help alleviate the poverty that blights cities. Small loans give a chance to poor entrepreneurs who lack the collater-al a traditional bank would require. In the United States, there were 250 microcredit programs in 1996, twice as many as in 1992. According to the World Bank, 30–80 percent of workers in the developing world work in the microenterprise sector.[79]

Rectifying local finances and improving the ability of citizens to pay local taxes frees up money for environmental protection. In Ahmedabad, India, a talented municipal commissioner began a campaign in the early 1990s to balance the city's budget by eliminating costly corruption, raising utility rates, and collecting taxes. By 1996, the city boasted a substantial surplus, as revenues shot past expenditures. With the new funds, the city initiated a host of projects to improve the local environment and public health. As environmental health rebounded, so too did the climate for private investment, which may ultimately attract even more money to solving Ahmedabad's problems. With advice from the U.S. Agency for International Development, the city has floated India's first municipal bond, which will finance improvements in water and sewer infrastructure.[80]

In the late nineteenth and early twentieth centuries, those who reflected on life-threatening urban pollution—Dickens, Howard, and Le Corbusier among them—feared that cities might eventually self-destruct. Today, it is not only inhumane living conditions but also unsustainable resource use that pose a threat. Efforts to overcome the political and financial barriers to sustainable city planning have one thing in common: the dynamism of committed people trading ideas and working together. It is this concentration of human energy that allowed cities to give birth to human civilization—and that may ultimately save it.

9

Ending Violent Conflict

Michael Renner

"This conference could augur well for the coming century. It would unite into one mighty whole the efforts of all States sincerely striving to make the great idea of universal peace triumph over strife and discord." Count Mikhail Nikolayevich Muravyov, Russia's Foreign Minister, expressed the hopes of many when he spoke of the prospects for the First Hague International Peace Conference in 1899.[1]

Called on the initiative of Czar Nicholas II of Russia, who expressed concern that the armed peace of the time constituted a "crushing burden," the event brought together representatives from 26 countries. The international peace movement, which had worked hard for the gathering to take place, but whose representatives were not allowed to participate, placed high hopes in the event, anticipating progress on disarmament and the establishment of a permanent court of arbitration to settle international conflicts by peaceful means. But the conference—and a follow-up gathering in 1907—succeeded mostly in codifying the rules of warfare rather than making war itself less likely.[2]

Indeed, the two Hague peace conferences proved incapable of stopping Europe and the world from marching toward the general war that was the opening event of what British historian Eric Hobsbawm has called "the age of extremes." The twentieth century was to become the most violent of all human ages, unprecedented in the scale and intensity of killing and destruction. Around the turn of the century, preparations for war intensified and soon turned feverish. "In the 1900s war drew visibly nearer, in the 1910s its imminence could and was in some ways taken for granted," observes Hobsbawm. From 1880–1914, the six leading European powers tripled their military expenditures. Their armies almost doubled in size—from 2.6 million to 4.5 million—and their navies, measured in tonnage, grew more than fivefold. Out of the Industrial Revolution emerged a military-industrial complex capable of churning out massive quantities of weapons, ready and eager to profit from an insecure and belligerent world.[3]

Some, including the Swedish industrialist Alfred Nobel, who invented dynamite in 1867, put faith in the argument that the destructive power of his explosives and of other new armaments was so immense as to render future warfare more and more unthinkable. Others, like Polish-Russian industrialist Ivan Bliokh, who in 1898 published *Technical, Economic and Political Aspects of the Coming War*, predicted the horrors of trench warfare and the political and social convulsions that would follow the mass slaughter of World War I.[4]

No one was more ardent in warning against the coming war or worked harder to prevent it than Bertha von Suttner, one of the most well known pacifists of her time. Her anti-war novel, *Die Waffen Nieder* (Lay Down Your Arms), published in 1889, became one of the most influential books of the nineteenth century. Translated into many languages, it helped spread the pacifist idea throughout the world at a time when peace societies in the different European countries were small and splintered, and lacked coordination.

Von Suttner worked hard to convince her close friend Alfred Nobel to devote his wealth to the cause of peace. It was her influence that made the Swedish industrialist establish, posthumously, the Nobel Peace Prize, which she then received in 1905.[5]

Von Suttner was in many ways ahead of her time. She prophesied the enormity of destruction in World War I, warned of coming weapons of mass destruction, argued for peacekeeping forces, demanded the establishment of a United Nations–type organization, and supported a "European Confederation of States." Imbued by her era's sense of the inevitability of progress, she held that peace was a condition "that would necessarily result from the progress of culture." But von Suttner became more anxious and pessimistic in the last years of her life, as

Europe and the world lurched toward war. When she passed away on 21 June 1914, it seemed that the hope for peace died with her. Seven days later, the heir to the throne of the Habsburg empire and his wife were killed by a Serb nationalist in Sarajevo—the event that triggered World War I.[6]

A third Hague Peace Conference, scheduled for 1915, never took place. Yet the Hague Conference process has remained a milestone event in human efforts to tame the beast of warfare. One hundred years later, its legacy is being revived. In an effort to take care of unfinished business, the Hague Appeal—a major citizens' peace conference to be held in May 1999—will bring together citizen activists, political leaders, and others to develop global strategies for disarmament and an end to nuclear arms, the peaceful settlement of disputes, and international humanitarian law.[7]

WAR IN THE TWENTIETH CENTURY

Although militarism was an ingrained habit of many societies 100 years ago, the preambles of nineteenth-century humanitarian law nevertheless frequently invoked the need for civilization to restrain warfare. The 1868 St. Petersburg Declaration Renouncing the Use, in Time of War, of Certain Explosive Projectiles recognized that there was a limit "at which the necessities of war ought to yield to the requirements of humanity."[8]

During our century, however, killings, expulsions, and wholesale destruction have been conducted with such ruthlessness and on such an astronomical scale that new words had to be invented to describe them: genocide was coined in 1944 to talk about the deliberate and systematic destruction of a racial, political, or cultural group, and overkill was first used in 1957 to describe the obliteration of a target with far greater destructive force than required. Until the sixteenth century, fewer than 1 million persons were killed in battle or due to war-related causes during any 100-year stretch. From then on, the pace accelerated. Three times as many people fell victim to war in our century than in all the wars from the first century A.D. until 1899. (See Table 9–1.)

So immense was the killing during World War I that its individual battles inflicted casualties as large as those suffered in entire wars of earlier eras. (See Table 9–2.) The French lost almost 20 percent of their men of military age, and the Germans 13 percent. All in all, an estimated 26 million people died during the Great War; at least another 20 million or so were maimed, permanently shell-shocked, or otherwise disabled. Civilians accounted for half of all war deaths, killed mostly by malnutrition, lack of medical care, crowding, and the breakdown of social services.[9]

One reason World War I was so devastating was the enormous size of the armies that were mobilized. Governments had begun to use standing armies in the seventeenth century, and universal conscription had become the rule in most

Table 9–1. War-Related Deaths Over the Centuries

Years	War Deaths	Deaths per 1,000 People
	(million)	
0–1499	3.7	n.a.
1500–99	1.6	3.2
1600–99	6.1	11.2
1700–99	7.0	9.7
1800–99	19.4	16.2
1900–95	109.7	44.4

SOURCE: William Eckhardt, "War-Related Deaths Since 3000 BC," *Bulletin of Peace Proposals*, December 1991; Ruth Leger Sivard, *World Military and Social Expenditures 1996* (Washington, DC: World Priorities, 1996).

countries by the end of the nineteenth century. Some 20 million Europeans went off to fight in August 1914, and by 1918 a total of 65 million soldiers had been mobilized on all sides. Compared with just 1 percent in the wars of 100 years earlier, 14 percent of Europe's population was pulled directly into the fighting. And soldiers were armed far more formidably. World War I saw the first substantial use of war planes, tanks, and chemical warfare.[10]

World War II, however, dwarfed World War I in scale. It signaled a new era of warfare—total war, waged not just against military forces, but mercilessly against a country's economy, infrastructure, and civilian population. The Allied military forces reached a peak strength of 46.9 million soldiers, and the Axis powers, 21.7 million. At least 45 million persons were involved in arms manufacturing. Between a third and half of the major combatant states' labor forces were directly or indirectly involved in the war effort. (See Table 9–3.)[11]

The nations at war thus devoted the lion's share of their industrial strength and economic wealth to this gargantuan all-or-nothing struggle. The Soviet Union suffered by far the most from the fighting; not only did 17 million of its inhabitants perish, but 25 percent of its prewar capital assets were destroyed, compared with 13 percent in Germany, 7 percent in France, and 3 percent in the United Kingdom.[12]

The five major combatants in World War II—the United States, the Soviet Union, Germany, the United Kingdom, and Japan—were producing armaments in fearful quantities, including at least 220,000 tanks and 780,000 aircraft. Just in the European "theater" of the war, the Allies and Axis together used more than $2.5 trillion worth of munitions during World War II. The United States geared up from producing a negligible share of global arms production in 1939 to 40 percent by 1944.[13]

Table 9–2. Death Tolls of Selected Wars, 1500–1945

Conflict	Time Period	Number Killed	Civilian Victims (percent)
Peasants' War (Germany)	1524–1525	175,000	57
Dutch Independence War (vs. Spain)	1585–1604	177,000	32
30-Year War (Europe)	1618–1648	4,000,000	50
Spanish Succession War (Europe)	1701–1714	1,251,000	n.a.
7-Year War (Europe, North America, India)	1755–1763	1,358,000	27
French Revolutionary/Napoleonic Wars	1792–1815	4,899,000	41
Crimean War (Russia, France, Britain)	1854–1856	772,000	66
U.S. Civil War	1861–1865	820,000	24
Paraguay vs. Brazil and Argentina	1864–1870	1,100,000	73
French-Prussian War	1870–1871	250,000	25
U.S.-Spanish War	1898	200,000	95
World War I	1914–1918	26,000,000	50
World War II	1939–1945	53,547,000	60

SOURCE: Calculated from Ruth Leger Sivard, *World Military and Social Expenditures 1991* (Washington, DC: World Priorities, 1991).

Statistics about the war's human impact tend to be numbing, so immense was the scale. Almost 54 million people are believed to have perished in frontline fighting, aerial bombardment, concentration camp mass murders, repressions of uprisings, and disease and hunger. War deaths were equivalent to 10–20 percent of the total population in the Soviet Union, Poland, and Yugoslavia, and 4–6 percent in Germany, Italy, Japan, and China. World War I had generated perhaps 4–5 million refugees. At the end of World War II, by comparison, an estimated 40 million people were uprooted in Europe alone—not including 11 million foreign forced laborers stranded in Germany or 14 million Germans expelled from Eastern Europe. In Asia, the Japanese occupation of China left about 50 million Chinese homeless.[14]

The final acts of hostility of World War II—the dropping of atomic bombs over Hiroshima and Nagasaki—also heralded the beginning of the nuclear age and the coming cold war. After this, another world war would not just have been "a war to end all wars," as the euphemism at the start of World War I had it, but more likely a war to end all civilizations. Huge resources went to develop, build, and maintain nuclear arsenals. The United States alone is thought to have spent at least $5.5 trillion (in 1996 dollars). How much the Soviet Union and the other nuclear powers spent may never be known, though one estimate says a grand total of $8 trillion may be a reasonable, though conservative, assumption.[15]

With the help of 2,046 test explosions, the United States, the Soviet Union, and the smaller nuclear weapons states developed and deployed huge armaments. (See Figure 9–1.) The global stockpile of nuclear warheads peaked at 69,490 in

Table 9–3. Share of Working Population in War Effort, 1943

Country	Arms Industry	Armed Forces
Soviet Union	31	23
United Kingdom	23	22
Germany	14	23
United States	19	16

SOURCE: Alan L. Gropman, *Mobilizing U.S. Industry in World War II*, McNair Paper 50 (Washington, DC: Institute for National Strategic Studies, August 1996).

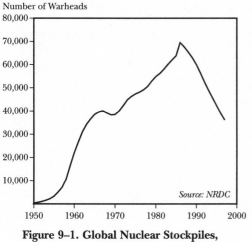

Number of Warheads

Source: NRDC

Figure 9–1. Global Nuclear Stockpiles, 1950–97

1986, containing an explosive yield of 18 billion tons of TNT (3.6 tons for every human being), compared with 6 million tons of explosive force used in all of World War II.[16]

Not only has the firepower of weapons, nuclear and non-nuclear, multiplied. Their speed, range, maneuverability, and accuracy have soared as well. Governments have spent lavishly on military research and development to produce these technical breakthroughs. Extrapolating from U.S. data, cumulative worldwide resources devoted to military innovation may have amounted to some $3.5 trillion during the last half-century.[17]

Despite some ups and downs, the overall trend in twentieth-century global military spending has been one of strong growth. Total expenditures by all combatants in 1914–19 ran to about $1.4 trillion. During the 1930s, annual world military spending increased from about $50–60 billion to about $150 billion on the eve of World War II. Military spending during that conflict may have come to something on the order of $7–8 trillion, or about $1.3 trillion a year. Considering that global military expenditures toward the end of the cold war peaked at roughly $1.3 tril-

lion a year, it is clear that maintaining the armed peace of the 1980s came with an annual price tag as large as that for waging the largest war in human history.[18]

While the superpowers were arming themselves for doomsday, they and their allies also spread arms across the planet in unprecedented quantity and quality. Since 1960 alone, the global arms trade amounted to at least $1.5 trillion (in 1996 dollars). Perhaps as much as two thirds of that went to developing countries—often indebting the recipients and skewing their national budget priorities in the process. From 1984 to 1995 alone, for instance, the developing world received about 15,000 tanks, 34,000 artillery pieces, 27,000 armored personnel carriers and armored cars, close to 1,000 warships and submarines, 4,200 combat aircraft, more than 3,000 helicopters, some 48,000 missiles, and millions of small-caliber arms.[19]

This massive infusion of arms helped destabilize countries and regions that were in the throes of anti-colonial struggles, ethnic battles, and numerous other unresolved conflicts. It is little wonder, then, that the number of conflicts in the post–World War II era surged, from 12 in 1950 to a peak of 51 in 1992. Only after the end of the cold war was it possible to bring several long-running hostilities to an end, bringing the number of armed conflicts down to 25 in 1997. None of the post-1945 wars could measure up to the earlier global conflicts, but together they have killed almost as many people as died during World War I. And some of them were incredibly destructive: Korea lost 10 percent of its population to war in the early 1950s, and Viet Nam lost 13 percent in the 1960s and 1970s. (See Table 9–4.) And the share of civilians among the victims has risen to ever higher levels: perhaps 70 percent of all war casualties since World War II, but more than 90 percent in the 1990s.[20]

From the beginning of the modern

Table 9–4. Death Tolls of Largest Armed Conflicts Since 1945[1]

Conflict	Time Period	Number Killed	Civilian Victims (percent)
Chinese civil war	1946–50	1,000,000	50
Korea	1950–53	3,000,000	50
Viet Nam (U.S. intervention)	1960–75	2,358,000	58
Biafra (Nigerian civil war)	1967–70	2,000,000	50
Cambodian civil war	1970–89	1,221,000	69
Bangladesh secession	1971	1,000,000	50
Afghanistan (Soviet intervention)	1978–92	1,500,000	67
Mozambican civil war	1981–94	1,050,000	95
Sudanese civil war	1984 onward	1,500,000[2]	97

[1]Conflicts that killed 1 million persons or more.   [2]Numbers up to 1995 only.
SOURCE: Ruth Leger Sivard, *World Military and Social Expenditures 1996* (Washington, DC: World Priorities, 1996).

state system some 350 years ago, states have put great energy and enormous resources into developing ever more sophisticated and destructive weapons, in the process building up relentlessly toward ever higher levels of organized violence. Weapons now can traverse the entire planet and extinguish all life; military satellites can pry into the most remote corners of the world; alliances have spanned continents. Yet with the end of the cold war, this buildup reached its anticlimactic denouement: violence between sovereign states, though not unthinkable, has become less likely and far less frequent, whereas violence within societies has become depressingly commonplace.

PEACE AND DISARMAMENT IN THIS CENTURY

Prior to the twentieth century, recourse to force was seen as the sovereign right of governments. But the experience of 1914–45—of total uninhibited global warfare—underscores the fact that efforts to regulate conduct during war alone are sorely inadequate. In order to survive, humanity needs international norms pro-

hibiting the use of force in the first place. It is one of the accomplishments of the twentieth century—though one still being violated—that the use of force by states is now considered illegal except in self-defense. The U.N. Charter states unambiguously that: "All Members shall refrain in their international relations from the threat or use of force against the territorial integrity or political independence of any state." The use of force domestically, meanwhile, is also less and less seen as acceptable, though governmental opinions diverge widely, and the international community has shown itself to be highly selective in addressing the issue.[21]

Throughout human history, nations have made repeated efforts to promote the rule of law in international relations, provide for avenues of peaceful settlement of conflicts, govern the conduct of warring parties (codifying the expected behavior of combatants toward each other and specifying the need to spare noncombatants), regulate armaments, and create institutions for the common good. During the twentieth century, a series of rules and norms have been formulated (see Table 9–5), with the two Hague Peace Conferences being milestone events. All in all, some 41 international "humanitarian laws" are currently in force, though hardly respected universally.[22]

The rule-writing has not only sought to deal with the age-old, intrinsic savagery of warfare, but also to catch up with new realities—such as new means of waging war and the changing nature of conflicts. The 1977 Environmental Modification Convention, for instance, instructs states not to engage in any military use of environmental modification techniques that have "widespread, long-lasting or severe effects." And whereas war laws had traditionally covered interstate wars, the Second Protocol Additional to the 1949 Geneva Conventions, adopted in 1977, addressed the protection of victims in internal conflicts, in recognition that these are the dominant forms of war in our time.[23]

The twentieth century is also the cen-tury of human rights advocacy. The advancement of human rights—initially focused on civil and political rights, and followed by so-called second-generation (economic, social, and cultural) and third-generation rights (right to development, right to peace, and right to a decent environment)—implicitly annuls warfare as a legitimate tool, since warfare denies the enjoyment of these rights. The 1968 Teheran Human Rights conference stated quite unambiguously that "Peace is the underlying condition for the full observance of human rights and war is their negation." Today there are more than 70 international and regional conventions, agreements, and declarations on human rights. Although the number of countries that have signed and ratified these legal instruments is still limited—let alone

Table 9–5. Selected Humanitarian, Human Rights, and Arms Control Treaties of the Twentieth Century

Humanitarian/Laws of War	Human Rights	Arms Control/Disarmament
1907 Hague Conventions	1948 Universal Declaration of Human Rights	1959 Antarctic Treaty
1925 Protocol Prohibiting Use of Poison Gas	1951 Convention Relating to the Status of Refugees	1967 Outer Space Treaty
1929 Geneva Conventions	1966 Covenant on Economic, Social, and Cultural Rights	1969/1995 Nuclear Non-Proliferation Treaty
1948 Genocide Convention	1966 Covenant on Civil and Political Rights	1971 Seabed Treaty
1949 Geneva Convention	1984 Anti-Torture Convention	1972 Biological Weapons Convention
1976 Environmental Modification Convention		1993 Chemical Weapons Convention
1977 Protocols Additional to 1949 Geneva Convention		1996 Nuclear Test-Ban Treaty
1980/1995 Inhumane Weapons Convention		1997 Anti-Personnel Landmine Convention

SOURCE: United Nations Treaty Collection Web page, <http://www.un.org/Depts/Treaty/overview.htm>, viewed 19 August 1998; Ian Browline, ed., *Basic Documents on Human Rights* (Oxford, U.K.: Clarendon Press, 1992); Dieter Fleck, ed., *The Handbook of Humanitarian Law in Armed Conflicts* (New York: Oxford University Press, 1995); "Multilaterals Project Chronological Index," <http://tufts.edu/fletcher/multi/chrono.html>, viewed 20 July 1998.

those that live up to their commitments—there can be no doubt that human rights advocacy has been one of the most transforming factors of our age.[24]

An important part of the efforts to limit the use of force has been the creation of international organizations through which states could discuss and regulate their affairs. Reflecting the growing complexity of global human society, the twentieth century has witnessed a proliferation of intergovernmental organizations, such as the League of Nations and the United Nations, growing from just 37 in 1909 to more than 400 by 1997. In part through these organizations, a total of some 50,000 bilateral and multilateral treaties have been negotiated in all spheres of life.[25]

The end of the cold war permitted the world to climb down from the extreme heights of overkill arsenals.

The most important and representative body is the United Nations, whose membership grew from an original 51 states in 1945 to 185 today. Established "to save succeeding generations from the scourge of war," as the famous passage from the U.N. Charter puts it, much of the peace and security machinery of the United Nations was deadlocked by the cold war. When that ended, however, the Security Council entered a period of frenzied activity. The number of resolutions, official statements, and consultations skyrocketed, and only a few vetoes were cast by the permanent members.[26]

Forced by cold war strictures to improvise, the United Nations came up with an important innovation when it "invented" peacekeeping—the dispatch of unarmed or lightly armed U.N. personnel initially to help patrol tense border areas and monitor ceasefire lines, and later to supervise the implementation of complex peace treaties, including such tasks as disarming and demobilizing combatants, and monitoring elections and human rights violations. Despite sudden (and short-lived) growth in the 1990s, however, peacekeeping was and still is being run on an ad hoc basis, and hobbled by unreliable financing.[27]

While the U.N.'s involvement in military and security matters remained limited throughout the cold war years, it has been clear from the start that many of its other activities—from promoting antipoverty and child survival programs to assisting education efforts, advocating women's rights, encouraging fair elections and human rights adherence, and promoting sustainable development—have a significant bearing on peace. This is based on the recognition that true peace requires justice and equity, and a sufficient degree of human well-being. The UNESCO charter, for instance, states that "Since wars begin in the minds of men, it is in the minds of men that the defenses of peace must be constructed." U.N. agencies and officials have been awarded a total of 11 Nobel Peace prizes.[28]

As part of the United Nations system, the World Court was established as a forum in which nations could search for peaceful settlement of their disputes. The Court is the product of 200 years of efforts at international arbitration. Disputes can be brought before the court in one of three ways. First, several hundred international commercial, economic, environmental, and other treaties give the Court jurisdiction to iron out any differences in interpretation. Second, countries may agree bilaterally to submit an already existing dispute. Third, they may decide to accept the Court's compulsory jurisdiction beyond any particular case. Despite considerable hopes, however, only a relatively small number of countries have accepted this latter role for the Court. By 1996 the number had reached 59, but 12 countries, the United States among them, had withdrawn their one-time consent.

Although the Court has enjoyed a significant rise in the numbers of disputes brought before it since 1986, on the whole it remains sorely underused: it has so far delivered 61 judgments in response to a total of 74 cases considered, and it has rendered 23 advisory opinions. Cases actually brought before it have often involved minor matters instead of the kind of high-profile issues that could establish the Court as a key organ in regulating international affairs. Only when the United States and others decide that an effective World Court is far better than a pliant one will the institution finally be unshackled.[29]

Near the close of the twentieth century, the international community is also belatedly making progress on another front: the establishment of an International Criminal Court (ICC). (See Table 9–6.) This is, in a sense, the crowning event of a long historical struggle concerning the legality of war itself and the conduct of warfare. In 1946, the victors of World War II established an International Military Tribunal to prosecute Nazi leaders for crimes against peace (that is, waging a war of aggression), war crimes (violating accepted norms limiting the conduct of war), and crimes against humanity (genocide and other systematic and widespread persecutions of civilian populations). But the cold-war rivalry blocked any effective action on establishing an international criminal court. The end of the East-West standoff permitted the adoption of at first a stop-gap measure—ad hoc tribunals in 1993 and 1994 for the former Yugoslavia and Rwanda—and then the resumption of serious work on setting up a permanent court, which led to the adoption of its founding statute in the summer of 1998.[30]

Another area in which some progress has been achieved is disarmament. During the first half of the century, governments talked about disarmament but never achieved it. During the cold war, the world had to content itself with weak arms control measures that barely restrained the dynamic of the arms race. But after accumulating armaments in unparalleled quantity and unprecedented sophistication, the end of the cold war—and several hot wars—permitted the world to climb down from the extreme heights of overkill arsenals.

Military expenditures have declined by some 40 percent from their mid-1980s peak. The ranks of the armed forces have been trimmed by about 20 percent from their high point in 1988 of 28.7 million. Worldwide holdings of tanks and armored vehicles, artillery, combat aircraft, and major fighting ships have fallen about 19 percent between 1990 and 1995. Meanwhile, the conventional arms trade, running amok in the 1980s, has taken a nosedive. From a peak of $82 billion in 1987 (in 1995 dollars), the value of weapons transfers fell to less than $27 billion in 1994, then rose to $32 billion in 1995. Nuclear arsenals, too, have been trimmed, from a peak of close to 70,000 warheads to just under 40,000 by 1996—although the equivalent of 8 billion tons of TNT assembled in these weapons is still far more than necessary to destroy the entire planet, and hopes for deeper cuts appear distant and uncertain. Four nations actually relinquished their nuclear arms: Belarus, Kazakhstan, and Ukraine transferred their Soviet-era arsenals to Russia, and South Africa dismantled warheads as the apartheid regime came to an end.[31]

The post–cold war reduction in armaments is best seen as a "thinning out" of arsenals—akin to pruning badly overgrown weeds. The Chemical Weapons Convention is one of few instances in which a whole class of weapons has actu-

Table 9–6. Pluses and Minuses of the New International Criminal Court

Pluses	Minuses
Jurisdiction over genocide, crimes against humanity, and war crimes.	But states can reject the court's jurisdiction over war crimes for the first seven years.
Aggression is included as a core crime.	But a legal definition of aggression has yet to be agreed.
Jurisdiction over crimes committed in international and internal wars.	But the list of specific prosecutable crimes for internal conflicts is more limited (does not include forced starvation of civilians or gassing of civilians).
ICC prosecutor can initiate investigations on his/her own, based on information from victims, NGOs, or any other reliable source.	Court cannot act unless the state of the accused person's nationality, or the state where the crimes took place, have ratified the treaty.
The U.N. Security Council does not have a veto over the ICC's proceedings.	But the Council, if unanimous, can request a one-year delay of prosecution, and renew the request indefinitely, in one-year segments.
States are required to comply with the Court's requests for cooperation.	But states can withhold cooperation on national security grounds.
Civilian and military commanders can be held responsible for crimes of their subordinates.	But there is a limited right to assert the existence of orders from one's superior as a defense.
States that ratify the treaty cannot create reservations (by declaring that certain portions do not apply to them).	
Court can prosecute as a war crime the use of children under 15 as soldiers, rape, sexual slavery, or enforced pregnancy.	

SOURCE: Human Rights Watch, "Human Rights Watch Text Analysis International Criminal Court Treaty July 17, 1998," <http://www.hrw.org/hrw/press98/july/icc-anly.htm>, viewed 12 August 1998; "The Draft Statute at a Glance," *On the Record*, 27 July 1998; "A Court Is Born," *On the Record*, 17 July 1998.

ally been outlawed. Opened for signature in 1993 and entering into force in April 1997 (signed so far by 168 states), the convention bans the development, production, trade, possession, and use of chemical warfare agents and mandates that existing stockpiles and production facilities be eliminated.[32]

War may have reached the ultimate scale in our century, and peace may never have been more necessary for human survival, but musings about war and peace are nothing new. All through human history, lofty rhetoric about peace can be found, along with realism about the terrible impact of warfare and skepticism about its merit. What is perhaps different now is that civil society—peace movements and other citizens' groups—seems to be playing a more important role than in the past, trying to subject security policy to greater public scrutiny and to wrest it from the narrow control of military bureaucracies and defense intellectuals.[33]

As the destructive power of weaponry accelerated with the Industrial Revolution, the quest for peace became more urgent. Local or national peace societies were founded in Europe throughout the nineteenth century, although the earliest such groups appeared in New York in 1815 and in Britain. By 1886 there were some 36 peace societies worldwide. International contacts and coordination grew and improved with initiation of annual World Peace Congresses in 1889 and the establishment of the International Peace Bureau in Bern in 1891.[34]

As the power of weaponry accelerated, the quest for peace became more urgent.

The early peace movements, like those of our day, struggled with the ebb and flow of popular interest and support. The end of the East-West standoff has made it difficult to rally public opinion on issues of peace and disarmament. At the same time, however, the involvement of a broad variety of nongovernmental organizations (NGOs) has expanded the traditional peace agenda. In the 1980s, peace groups were consumed by such questions as the hair-trigger alert of nuclear strike forces and the circular-error probability of intercontinental missiles. Now, NGOs that are concerned with such varied issues as human rights, governmental transparency and accountability, environmental protection, human development, and justice and equity increasingly weigh in on matters of peace and war—reflecting a broadened understanding of peace and injecting a new dynamic. For instance, the successful anti-personnel landmines campaign and the NGO campaign for the International Criminal Court were spearheaded not by arms control groups but by human rights organizations and groups with social and humanitarian agendas.

THE CHANGING NATURE OF GLOBAL SECURITY

The second half of the twentieth century has witnessed two great paradoxes. One of them is that the most belligerent continent—Europe—became one of the most peaceful regions of the world, at least if peace is defined as the absence of war. The second paradox is that almost all conflicts now take place within rather than between nations. So large-scale investments in traditional military security to fend off potential outside invaders appear spectacularly misplaced.

What accounts for Europe's "success"? And can it be replicated elsewhere in the world? The horrors of twentieth-century warfare appear to have convinced a substantial portion of political leaders and the general public that Europe finally has to go down a different path if it is to survive. The experience of World War I alone would presumably have sufficed, but the 1919 Treaty of Versailles prevented the emergence of a European and global political system capable of reconciling former enemies and working to their common benefit. Instead, the penal peace imposed on Germany strengthened nationalist forces there and helped set the stage for World War II.

A crucial difference after World War II was that Germany was fully integrated into the postwar order, becoming a pillar of the European Community. Europe—or, to be more precise, Western Europe—has finally moved toward the confederation of states that Bertha von Suttner and others saw as indispensable for peace. In the process, strong and competent institutions emerged to regulate relations among European nations and resolve disputes that may arise. Economic links became so tight as to make peace infinitely more beneficial than gains anyone could hope to derive from rupturing these links. Cultural exchange programs and other efforts helped generate a growing sense of a common destiny instead of a purely national one. Equally important, democratic governance and respect for human rights grew far stronger. Finally, social welfare programs ensured a high degree of human well-being, greatly reducing the danger that social discontent could nourish violent conflict within countries.

Yet there is ambiguity. There is much talk these days about the "democratic peace," noting that democratic societies do not go to war against each other (though they may very well fight against nondemocratic states). Greater transparency and accountability in democratic societies can make it harder for governments to go to war by subjecting their policies and reasoning to scrutiny. But historian Eric Hobsbawm warns that in democratically governed societies, adversaries are "demonized in order to make them properly hateful or at least despicable." As the Gulf War showed, there may be a great aversion to putting your own soldiers in "harm's way," but little compunction about using overwhelming force to pulverize the military forces and the public infrastructure of the adversary. Democracy is a necessary but insufficient condition for peace.[35]

There is a similar degree of ambiguity about economic integration as an antidote to violent conflict. Leaders after World War II recognized that the "beggar-thy-neighbor" policies of the late 1920s and early 1930s—erecting trade barriers and engaging in competitive currency devaluations—caused a severe economic crisis that contributed to the undermining of the fledgling democracy in Germany and

helped lead to the outbreak of war. After 1945, economic integration was seen as a key remedy. When the fates of national economies are tied together closely in a global unregulated market, however, the ripple effects of economic trouble can be devastating—as developments in the late 1990s are showing so clearly. Moreover, moves by individual countries to protect their own economic base could set off a dynamic akin to that of the 1930s, with potentially worrisome ramifications in overall relations among nations.[36]

Integration also only works to further peace if it brings benefits to broad sections of society. The downside is that integration, as seen today under the banner of "globalization," can cause such dislocations, social pain, and growing uncertainty that integration itself can become a source of tension—if not between nations then within them. The issue is not just the degree of economic and other forms of interdependence, but the extent to which this integration is seen as accountable and experienced as beneficial to its constituent parts.[37]

A crucial question now is whether Russia will be treated like Germany after World War I or after World War II. There are mixed signals, with ominous implications. In security matters, NATO's decision to expand into Eastern Europe sent a message to Moscow that Russia is still regarded as a potential enemy. This problem could have been avoided by making the Organization for Security and Co-operation in Europe, rather than NATO, the cornerstone of a continent-wide security system.[38]

On the economic front, there has been less "integration" than an emergence of Russian dependence on the West: Russia is primarily exporting natural resources to western economies while importing consumer goods. Its domestic ability to produce goods and services has almost evaporated; during the 1990s, the gross domestic product has fallen by an estimated 50–80 percent and capital investment has dropped by 90 percent. Resurgent disease and malnutrition and massive poverty and inequality have sharpened social tensions. Where the country is headed and whether it will hold together are open questions. Also, since ill-informed western advice has played a significant role in the current situation, the country could turn decidedly anti-western in the future, perhaps reigniting East-West antagonism.[39]

Russia is not the only source of concern. Unlike Western Europe, national rivalries in other portions of the world may well result in armed conflict. Although war between France and Germany is no longer thinkable, it remains a constant threat or at least a distinct possibility between India and Pakistan, North and South Korea, Greece and Turkey, Israel and Syria, and Nigeria and Cameroon, among others. Some scholars wonder whether the Asia-Pacific region, plagued by a variety of disputes and antagonisms, will end up like Europe in 1914—the victim of destabilizing "balance-of-power" politics and a heavy infusion of weaponry.[40]

But most conflicts nowadays do not involve opposing armies equipped with fancy weapons. Instead, they take place within countries, among domestic opponents—often ragtag armies outfitted with unsophisticated small caliber arms, protagonists in a vast array of virulent social, ethnic, political, and other conflicts. Although a substantial share of the responsibility for these lies within these countries, outside factors play an important role.

The first is the cold war. East-West geopolitics ascribed "strategic" value to certain parts of the developing world; industrial countries accordingly intervened in a variety of ways and armed their protégés to the teeth. Once the cold war ended, however, the importance of many once-indispensable allies vanished.

Premier cold-war battlegrounds like Afghanistan, the Horn of Africa, or Central America reverted to "backwater" status. Recipients of aid and weapons from the North saw the flow of assistance dry up. But the legacy—the easy availability of weapons, a pervasive culture of violence, and a stunted political system—will likely be found in many of these countries for a long time to come.

When national economies are tied together closely in a global unregulated market, the ripple effects of economic trouble can be devastating.

The second factor is economic. Many developing countries were and are bound into the global economy as highly dependent sellers of raw materials or low-end manufactured goods. As advanced industrial countries move toward economies geared more toward information and communications technologies, these trading relations inevitably undergo structural change; economies dependent on the revenues that a single or a handful of commodities can fetch on the world market are naturally vulnerable to these changes. As painful social and economic adjustments must be made, internal contradictions erupt or are aggravated.

Many countries, particularly in the developing world, are facing a multitude of pressures that threaten to shred the weak fabric of their societies. Ethnic and sectarian cleavages are dividing communities and entire countries. But they are often the product of growing economic difficulties, especially the lack of employment and the widening discrepancies in wealth and power between rich and poor. In particular, the lack of adequate numbers of jobs in countries with burgeoning youthful populations is generating a minefield of social discontent and misery. State-centered economies are often not dynamic enough to generate sufficient employment; the capitalist global economy, on the other hand, may yield high growth but is promoting a type of economic development that favors those with modern skills—and leaves the many unskilled far behind.[41]

Equity issues also interact with growing resource scarcity and environmental degradation. The depletion of water resources and degradation of arable land, for instance, are playing an important role in generating or aggravating conflict. As Michael Klare of Hampshire College argues, "the damaging effects of environmental decline will not be felt uniformly by all peoples but will threaten some states and groups more than others—producing sharp cleavages in human society that could prove more destabilizing than the effects of the environment itself."[42]

Where governments show themselves unable or unwilling to deal with accelerating social, demographic, economic, and environmental pressures, people are trying to find support, identity, and security within their more immediate group or community. But individual groups feel they are competing against each other for scarce resources and services, and governments may even encourage such splits in classical divide-and-rule fashion. All too often, the end result is a polarization and splintering of societies, literally inviting violent responses to unresolved problems, and sometimes leading to the unraveling and collapse of society.

It is typically the weaker societies of the Third World that more readily fall victim to the multiple pressures at hand. What reaches the Western eye and ear is usually the symptoms of failures—the humanitarian fiascos, the flood of refugees—reinforcing the mistaken sense that industrial nations are not affected by some of the same underlying pressures, particularly growing social and economic polarization.

Western countries, not surprisingly, are attempting to insulate themselves from what they perceive as a suddenly "chaotic" world. Instead of the Soviet threat, discussions revolve around "rogue" states, the coming "clash of civilizations," or the supposed rise of China as a threatening world power. The West is working hard to establish or retain a monopoly on sophisticated arms (hence the strong emphasis on nonproliferation instead of global disarmament), pursuing ever newer arms technologies, building highly mobile intervention forces that can be deployed rapidly in far-flung places, retaining strong control over U.N. Security Council matters, and using punitive economic embargoes against "rogue" states.

SETTING THE NEW SECURITY AGENDA

Even during the cold war there was growing recognition that traditional security policies—building national or allied military muscle—often yielded insecurity. A series of independent international commissions headed by world leaders such as Willy Brandt of Germany, Olof Palme of Sweden, Julius Nyerere of Tanzania, Gro Harlem Brundtland of Norway, and Ingvar Carlsson of Sweden have promoted a fundamental rethinking of security. They advanced the concepts of "common security"—the view that in order for one state to be secure, its opponents must also feel secure—and "comprehensive security"—the notion that nonmilitary factors such as social inequities, poverty, environmental degradation, and migratory pressures are at least as important as military ones in determining the potential for conflict. The second concept in particular questions whether state security rather than security for people is the proper focus. It also implies that many sources of conflict today are not amenable to military "solutions," and that reliance on armaments, no matter how technologically sophisticated, can in fact be counterproductive.[43]

Security policy in the twenty-first century will have to deal both with the lingering legacies of the twentieth century and with the newly emerging, nonmilitary challenges. These two problems are intertwined: while the particular causes of our century's wars and arms races may quickly become history, the accumulated, leftover military equipment now makes for such easy availability of arms of all calibers that recourse to violent measures in future disputes is far too easy. To forestall the likelihood of endless skirmishes and wars in the coming century, governments and societies will have to pursue demilitarization, conflict prevention, more inspired and vigorous global institution-building, and a fundamental recalibration of their security investments.

As discussed earlier, the last few years have seen a reduction in military spending, in arms production, trade, and deployments, and in the size of armed forces. Yet progress has been highly uneven across the world, substantial arsenals remain in place, there is no letup in the drive toward more sophisticated weaponry, and business in transferring "surplus" weapons from one country to another is brisk. More fundamentally, there are few internationally accepted norms and standards to curb the production, possession, and trade of arms; the utility of military power has hardly been foresworn by the world's governments. Establishing effective restraints will be a key task in the twenty-first century. One measure long demanded by human rights organizations and other groups is a binding code of conduct to ensure that weapons are not exported to governments that fail to hold free elections, trample human rights, or engage in armed aggression.[44]

It is also time to rethink the utility of large standing military forces and to advance the norm that possession of an offensively armed military is unacceptable. Countries that face no obvious external adversaries may want to cut their militaries radically and to refocus remaining forces on purely defensive tasks; indeed, some may want to reconsider whether they need an army at all, joining the twentieth-century pioneers Costa Rica, Haiti, and Panama and the nineteenth century trailblazer Liechtenstein in abolishing their standing armed forces. Apart from any unilateral measures, a group of NGO experts has kicked off a project called Global Action to Prevent War that outlines a four-phase process over 20–40 years to achieve major multilateral reductions in armaments and armies and create an alternative security system.[45]

Countries that face no obvious adversaries may want to cut their militaries radically.

Denuclearization—the establishment of a timetable to phase out and eventually abolish all nuclear arms—is another pressing task. The nuclear "haves" insist that they will retain their arsenals. But the stakes are rising: India and Pakistan have joined the "nuclear club," and it is premature to assume that others will not eventually be tempted to acquire nuclear weapons as well. At the same time, pressure on the nuclear powers to fulfill their part of the bargain under the Nuclear Non-Proliferation Treaty and to begin serious negotiations for nuclear disarmament is rising. At the core of the nuclear issue lies an important general principle—that constraints on armaments be universal instead of allowing a select group of countries to hold on to certain kinds of weapons denied to all other states (as implied by current nonproliferation policies).[46]

What is needed in the twenty-first century is nothing short of a wholesale recalibration of our security investments.

If and when those who have nuclear weapons relent, these arms will join a still very short list of weapon types that have actually been outlawed since 1899, when the Hague International Peace Conference decided to ban expanding, or so-called dum dum bullets (a prohibition that was subsequently sidestepped by new technologies). Although the use of chemical weapons was banned in 1925, nearly another 70 years had to pass before the 1993 Chemical Weapons Convention outlawed their production as well. In 1995 the sale and use of blinding-laser weapons was outlawed, and in 1997 a treaty prohibiting anti-personnel landmines was signed.[47]

To deal with the security challenges of the twenty-first century, global institutions need to be strengthened and made more representative of the world's peoples. There is growing recognition that the U.N. Security Council is anachronistic in its composition and central workings—particularly the veto power held by the five permanent members. But there is no consensus on the specifics of reform, and the permanent members are highly reluctant to relinquish or water down any of their privileges. Yet this stance may well increase worldwide resentment; because the Council relies on the willing cooperation of at least a clear majority of the world's nations, it may also compromise the authority and effective-

ness of the Council.[48]

At least in the short term, it may be politically impossible to abolish the veto. But the veto right might be limited to issues concerning Chapter VII of the U.N. Charter (issues most directly concerned with threats to international peace and security), or the negative votes of two permanent members instead of just one might be required in order to veto a resolution. Likewise, the Council structure could be reformed by deciding on a set of criteria that any country hoping to remain or become a permanent member would have to meet.[49]

Peacekeeping and conflict prevention will also need an injection of new thinking. Experience has amply demonstrated the inadequacies of the current ad hoc U.N. peacekeeping infrastructure. There is a strong need to establish a more permanent, reliable system. Equally important is a far greater emphasis on conflict prevention—by building an early conflict warning network, providing for preventive deployments of peacekeepers, and establishing standing conflict resolution committees in every region of the world. Too little has been done so far: in 1997 the new U.N. Trust Fund for Preventive Action Against Conflicts received soaring rhetoric but scant funds.[50]

The wider United Nations needs reform as well. To make it truly the organization of the "peoples of the United Nations," as the U.N. Charter puts it—and hence more responsive to the kinds of conflicts that are typical of our age—the General Assembly needs to be supplemented by an assembly more representative of each society. This might be a chamber composed of national parliamentarians (akin to the European Parliament), or a forum of civil society that includes representatives of labor, environmental groups, and others. This would not be entirely a revolutionary concept: the International Labour Organisation has long had a tripartite structure, bringing together representatives of government, business, and labor.[51]

This and other steps would likely help move security policy away from its heavy state- and military-centered focus and toward an effort to address the numerous social, economic, demographic, and environmental pressures that many societies face. It would permit governments to devote greater resources and political will to such critical tasks both on the national and the global level. What is needed in the twenty-first century is nothing short of a wholesale recalibration of our security investments—reassessing the meaning of security, the means and tools of achieving and maintaining it, and the institutional arrangements necessary for success. This new understanding would be based on the realization that weapons are more often facilitators of violence and destabilization than they are guarantors of security.

A World Without Borders?

In the twentieth century, nation states reached the pinnacle of their power, concluding a process set in motion several centuries ago. But the forces of globalization and localization—transcending state borders from within and without—have made territorial concepts become less central. States continue to be important players, but they are increasingly challenged by footloose corporations operating across the planet, by international coalitions of NGOs, by the march of technology, and by the halting progress in creating and strengthening international organizations. In fact, added to the old spectacle of alliances of nation states there is now the new phenomenon of mixed coalitions that, on an issue-by-issue basis, bring together like-minded governments and civil society organizations, such as the campaign to ban anti-personnel landmines.

The upshot is that peace and security have become more complex and ambiguous objectives. We no longer live in a state-centric world, whether in its unipolar, bipolar, or multipolar form. The meaning of national borders is inevitably changed in an age when such boundaries can and are traversed with ever greater ease. Yet as James Rosenau of George Washington University argues, "It is an epoch of multiple contradictions....States are changing, but they are not disappearing. State sovereignty has eroded, but it is still vigorously asserted. Governments are weaker, but they can still throw their weight around....Borders still keep out intruders, but they are also more porous."[52]

In an increasingly interdependent world, it may appear that nations' inability to cope with social, economic, and environmental challenges on their own will of necessity lead to growing global cooperation. But such an outcome is by no means guaranteed. And while the inherent challenge to territoriality may over time help make traditional, military-centered concepts of security less relevant, we are already witnessing the emergence of private security organizations of all stripes. Their justification for existence is to protect the interests of a corporation, a privileged class, or an ethnic group; they may not defend borders, but they rely on the use of force—or the threat to use force—just as much as a state's armed forces.

Meanwhile, globalization—the massive expansion of the world economy—itself carries new conflict potential. Given spectacularly uneven economic benefits, heightened vulnerabilities and uncertainties for many communities and individuals, and the inherent challenge to local control and democratic accountability, economic globalization tears at the very fabric and cohesion of many societies. These processes may well trigger a backlash. James Rosenau calls this "fragmegration" (the parallel and interconnected processes of fragmentation and integration); Benjamin Barber of Rutgers University has given the phenomenon the more colorful title of "Jihad vs. McWorld."[53]

Whatever it should be called, it is clear that this new era, simply by attenuating the power of states, will not necessarily produce a more peaceful twenty-first century. Territorial contests and conflicts may become a thing of the past, and with them traditional wars. But new forms of conflict are not too difficult to imagine. Nevertheless, just as the world had an opportunity in 1899 to make war less likely, now we have a chance to prevent a twenty-first century marked by fighting that is driven by accelerating social and economic inequity, environmental depletion, and weapons left over from twentieth-century wars.

10

Building a Sustainable Society

David Malin Roodman

The last thousand years of history have changed the way many cultures see history itself. In traditional societies, where life's rhythms were set by the seasons and by the rituals of birth and death, time seemed cyclical. Technological innovation and cultural evolution occurred with imperceptible slowness, so the most dramatic changes most people experienced within their lives were drought, flood, famine, or war. Social change was transient—and dangerous. Thus the Chinese curse, "May you live in interesting times."

As the planet industrializes, all this is changing. The process of transformation that industrialization has unleashed in technology, society, and culture does not seem like a passing fad. And for billions of people, it holds out the hope of a better life. It represents a new kind of change, and is giving rise to a new perception of history, as linear and directed—as a march of progress. Diseases are being vanquished, child mortality is falling, incomes are rising, people are crossing oceans in mere hours. Chinese tradition

to the contrary, life for millions of people in this interesting time is much more a blessing than a curse.

But as we assess our era at this millennial moment, it becomes clear that the old view of history is still relevant. The changes under way are indeed dangerous for the planet and for humanity—not simply a process of perpetual advancement. In many respects, the process is transient and unstable, and threatens to give the lie to the very view of history it spawned.

Farmers in the Indian state of Gujarat, for example, are drilling their irrigation wells some 1.5 meters deeper each year, in ultimately futile pursuit of falling water tables. Mexico City is, for the moment, sinking, as residents pump up the water beneath them. The city has the misfortune of resting atop a geological sponge. Elevated train tracks, built flat in the 1960s, look like roller coasters now, and old churches are buckling. In the United States, populations of honeybees, essential for pollinating commercial crops, have shrunk precipitously, while frogs with extra legs and missing eyes have been found in northern states. Pesticides are a leading suspect behind both aberrations. On the northern Atlantic, Canadian warships have clashed with Spanish and Portuguese fishing trawlers in a "Turbot War," a bitter dispute reminiscent of debates over rearranging deck chairs on the Titanic. The fish stocks the boats are competing for are collapsing beneath them from overharvesting.[1]

All these trends are transient and dangerous. In Gujarat, for instance, either farmers will slow their pumping to restore balance within a few decades, or they will suck the aquifers dry. Either way, food production could plunge. Thus for all the talk of the march of progress, our era also echoes the dangerous times of war between ancient Chinese dynasties that inspired that curse.

If this is a transitional era, then the natural question is, What will the new dynasty look like? What sort of world are we headed toward? So far, the world order emerging is one almost no one wants. Human numbers are growing, forests are shrinking, species are dying, farmland is eroding, freshwater supplies are dwindling, fisheries are collapsing, rivers are constricting, greenhouse gases are accumulating, soot is contaminating the air, and lead is contaminating our blood.

It is not too late, however, to change the course of events, to build societies that are both environmentally sustainable and industrial (automated production is at the heart of many benefits of modern economic development). It is not too late to build a world where the air is safe to breathe, water is safe to drink, and resources are shared among all the world's people—to build a world, in other words, that most people recognize as the one they hope their children will inherit. That would be true progress.

Humanity's departure from environmental sustainability has been a complex historical process. Its roots reach back 11 millennia to the Agricultural Revolution, when people first modified the environment systematically and on a large scale. Restoring sustainability will be comparably complex—but it will need to occur much faster if we are to minimize harm to the planet and to ourselves. More than a matter of inventing cheap solar panels or recycling household trash, it will be a thoroughgoing process involving every sector of society. Only by envisioning this process can we develop a realistic understanding of what it will take—and find grounds for realistic hope.[2]

What, then, will it take to construct a sustainable, modern society? Governments will need to aggressively demarcate and defend environmental limits, working domestically and cooperating internationally. And they will have to do so in ways that stimulate rather than stifle the creativity of corporations. Businesses will need to anticipate the transition and position themselves to exploit the huge investment opportunities created. Nonprofit organizations ranging from international environmental groups to neighborhood churches—collectively called "civil society"—will need to press both governments and businesses forward. And undergirding all their efforts will be educated citizens operating in their capacities as voters, consumers, charitable donors, and owners of land and resources.

Each of these groups—governments, businesses, nonprofit groups, and citizens—can press the others toward the goal of sustainability, in a somewhat chaotic dynamic less reminiscent of an engine firing on all pistons than an organism working to survive. The odds of success may seem long, but the forces arrayed in defense of the status quo have never been weaker than they are today. Society has changed more profoundly during this century than in any before. If things keep changing as fast—but for the better—then the new millennium's history books will recall our generation as the one that showed the march of progress to be more than a myth.

GETTING THE SIGNALS RIGHT

There is little question that governments will have to apply much of the pressure that will move modern society onto a sustainable path. The paradox is that although they need to force major structural changes on economies, they cannot plan those changes, precisely because of the magnitude and complexity involved.

This is particularly clear for the problem of global climate change. The Intergovernmental Panel on Climate Change has conservatively estimated that the atmosphere can sustain carbon emissions of no more than 2 billion tons per year without serious disruption. Spreading that quota evenly among the 10 billion people projected to share the planet by 2100 yields a per-person quota of half a kilogram (a pound) a day. In a Range Rover, you could drive 4 kilometers (2.5 miles) on that amount before having to stop for the night. Not surprisingly, the United States, Japan, and other industrial nations are emitting carbon at a pace 12–27 times this figure—and climbing.[3]

Since these unsustainable emissions rates arise from the way industrial economies grow food, make things, and move products and people about, reversing the trends necessarily requires transforming many aspects of home and work life in the industrial world. And it will require the development of new, clean technologies, a process of discovery that is intrinsically unpredictable. In the case of carbon emissions, a 90–95 percent reduction per person is needed in industrial nations—an end, in other words, to the fossil fuel economy as we know it. (See Chapter 2.) No government can plan all that.[4]

Markets, on the other hand, excel at engineering systemic change. Markets helped make the Industrial and Information Revolutions possible. Properly harnessed, they can also guide the next Industrial Revolution, the one toward environmental sustainability. The key to making that happen is for governments to stop subsidizing environmental harm and start taxing it. That will translate environmental costs into the language of the market—prices—and help enforce the "polluter pays principle," which says that when people act in ways that hurt the environment, they should feel the costs of the damage they do.

So far, the world order emerging is one almost no one wants.

This commonsense proposal was first cloaked in the authority of economics 80 years ago by Cambridge don Arthur Cecil Pigou, and has become a textbook staple since. But "polluter pays" has been practiced much less than preached. As a result, when people flip on a light switch or get behind the wheel of a car, they are able to ignore the costs they impose on others—their neighbor's asthma, or the minute addition they make to the atmosphere's thickening blanket of greenhouse gases.[5]

Worldwide, subsidies worth at least $650 billion—equivalent to 9 percent of all government revenue—support logging, mining, oil drilling, livestock grazing, farming, fishing, energy use, and driving. That amount far exceeds what is spent on environmentally protective subsidies, such as for soil-conserving farming practices. The U.S. government, for instance, effectively spends tens of millions of dollars each year paying loggers to clearcut some of the country's only rainforest, in the Tongass National Forest in

Southeast Alaska. The government covers such costs as building logging roads, but then charges far less for the trees hauled out on those roads. Towering, ancient Sitka spruces have sold for $2 each.[6]

In India, state governments give cheap or free electricity to farmers, who use it to pump water out of underground aquifers faster than rain is recharging them. Though the subsidies are often defended in the name of the poor farmer or urban food buyer, most of the money ends up in the pockets of richer farmers, who can afford electric pumps. Similarly, governments in industrial nations effectively gave farmers $284 billion in 1996, through government spending and price supports. Though this money flow is usually justified as helping small farmers, most of it goes to larger farms, which produce most of the food. Of U.S. agricultural support payments, 61 percent went to the 18 percent of farms grossing more than $100,000 a year (and typically netting at least $50,000). The aid also helps lock in an industrial style of agriculture that depends heavily on pesticides and contributes to soil erosion and water pollution.[7]

Fortunately, governments have recently cut some environmentally harmful subsidies. In 1988, Brazil ended the generous investment tax credits it had once offered to ranchers and farmers who cleared land in the Amazon; officials believe this change contributed to the temporary deforestation slowdown at the time. In the United States, the Congress has yet to reform an 1872 law that gives miners first rights to millions of hectares of public land, but it has at least placed a temporary moratorium on new claims every year since 1994.[8]

Since the mid-1980s, Belgium, France, Japan, Spain, and the United Kingdom have all eliminated or radically reduced once-high coal subsidies. The combined coal output of these five countries sank by half between 1986 and 1995. Meanwhile, the fossil fuel subsidies in nations outside the industrial West, though still high, are less than half what they were a few years ago, mainly because of halting, sometimes painful steps away from central government planning. (See Table 10–1.)[9]

Still, there are nearly $650 billion more in environmentally harmful subsidies. Cutting most of the remaining ones could pay for an effective 8-percent cut in the global tax burden. Most of these cuts would occur in industrial nations, which subsidize pollution the most. In the United States, Germany, and Japan, where taxes average $6,000–7,000 a person, there would be a net tax cut of roughly $500 per person or $2,000 per family of four.[10]

Subsidy reform, moreover, is only the first step in making prices tell the environmental truth. If governments are to make visible the full environmental costs of many products and activities, they need to

Table 10–1. Subsidies for Fossil Fuel Use in Selected Developing and Former Eastern Bloc Countries, 1990–91 and 1995–96

Region/ Country	Subsidies		Change
	1990–91	1995–96	
	(billion 1997 dollars per year)		(percent)
China	25.7	10.8	–58
Egypt	1.9	1.4	–28
India	4.5	2.8	–37
Iran	12.2	10.1	–17
Mexico	5.0	2.4	–53
Russia[1]	62.5	14.8	–76
Venezuela	3.2	2.5	–22
All Developing and Former Eastern Bloc Countries[1]	202.5	84.2	–58

[1]Estimates for Eastern bloc nations are particularly rough because of hyperinflation in the early 1990s and because widespread nonpayment of energy bills in some of these nations created hard-to-measure de facto subsidies.

SOURCE: Worldwatch Institute, based on World Bank; see endnote 9.

tax pollution and resource depletion, as some increasingly are. (See Table 10–2.)[11]

One established and effective environmental tax regime is the system of water pollution charges in the Netherlands. Since 1970, gradually rising charges on emissions of organic materials and heavy metals into canals, rivers, and lakes have spurred companies to cut emissions—but without dictating how. Between 1976 and the mid-1990s, emissions of cadmium, chromium, copper, lead, mercury, nickel, and zinc into waters managed by regional governments (which adopted the charges earliest) plummeted 72–99 percent, and primarily because of the charges.[12]

The Dutch example illustrates the strengths of environmental taxes at their best. Companies that could prevent pollution most cheaply presumably did so most. Companies would also have passed part of the taxes on to their customers through higher prices, causing them to switch to less-pollution-intensive products. And demand for pollution control equipment has spurred Dutch manufacturers to develop better models, triggering innovations that governments could never have planned, lowering costs, and turning the country into a global leader in the market. The taxes have in effect sought the path of least economic resistance—of least cost—in cleaning up the country's waters.[13]

Tax increases sound like the bad news in "polluter pays." But the good news, ironically, is that tax burdens are already substantial in most countries. So there are plenty of taxes that could be cut with the money raised from environmental taxes. A tax shift would result—not a tax increase. Today, nearly 95 percent of the $7.5 trillion in tax revenues raised each year worldwide comes from levies on payrolls, personal income, corporate profits, capital gains, retail sales, trade, and built property—all of which are essentially penalties for work and investment. It violates common sense to tax heavily the activities societies generally want while taxing lightly the activities they do not want.[14]

One of the world's most environmentally proactive nations, Sweden, became the first to take up the tax-shifting idea. (See Table 10–3.) In 1991 the government took $2.4 billion from new taxes on carbon and sulfur dioxide emissions, equal to 1.9 percent of all tax revenues, and used the money to cut income taxes. As concern grew over unemployment in Western Europe, additional shifts in the mid-1990s—in Denmark, Finland, and the Netherlands, Spain, and the United Kingdom—focused more on cutting wage

Table 10–2. Experiences with Selected Environmental Tax Systems

Policy, Country, Year Initiated	Description, Effect
Toxic waste tax, Germany, 1991	Toxic waste production fell more than 15 percent in 3 years.
Water pollution taxes, Netherlands, 1970	Main factor behind 72–99 percent drop in industrial discharges of heavy metals into regionally managed waters.
Sulfur oxide tax, Sweden, 1991	One third of 40-percent emissions drop during 1989–95 attributed to charge.
Ozone-depleting substance tax, United States, 1990	Smoothing and enforcing phaseouts.
Carbon dioxide tax, Norway, 1991	Emissions appear to be 3–4 percent lower than they would be without the tax.

SOURCE: See endnote 11.

Table 10–3. Tax Shifts from Work and Investment to Environmental Damage

Country, Year Initiated	Taxes Cut On	Taxes Raised On	Revenue Shifted[1]
			(percent)
Sweden, 1991	Personal income	Carbon and sulfur emissions	1.9
Denmark, 1994	Personal income	Motor fuel, coal, electricity, and water sales; waste incineration and landfilling; motor vehicle ownership	2.5
Spain, 1995	Wages	Motor fuel sales	0.2
Denmark, 1996	Wages, agricultural property	Carbon emissions; pesticide, chlorinated solvent, and battery sales	0.5
Netherlands, 1996	Personal income and wages	Natural gas and electricity sales	0.8
United Kingdom, 1996–97	Wages	Landfilling	0.2
Finland, 1996–97	Personal income and wages	Energy sales, landfilling	0.5
Germany, 1999[2]	Wages	Energy sales	2.6

[1]Expressed relative to tax revenue raised by all levels of government.   [2]Planned but not enacted as of October 1998.
SOURCE: See endnote 15.

taxes. And in 1998, the new, left-of-center government of Germany announced plans to shift 2.6 percent of taxes from wages to energy.[15]

Though significant, these shifts only hint at the long-run potential in tax shifting, especially if greenhouse gas emissions are taxed. Studies suggest that if carbon taxes were phased in worldwide over 50 years, reaching $250 a ton in 2050, global emissions might roughly plateau by then, as people and businesses used fossil fuels more efficiently and shifted to solar and other energy sources. (The full tax would add as much as 18¢ to the pump price of a liter of gasoline, or 69¢ for a gallon.) If the tax kept rising after 2050, emissions might almost halt by 2100. Climate models suggest that the amount of carbon dioxide in the air would stabilize at about 65 percent above the preindustrial level, which is as small

an increase as can realistically be hoped for. (The concentration is already up 30 percent.) Revenues would peak mid-century at roughly $700 billion to $1.8 trillion a year, enough to pay for cuts of perhaps 15 percent in conventional taxes on work and investment. Such taxes would also move the world a huge step closer to environmental sustainability.[16]

REINVENTING REGULATION

Though fiscal tools are powerful, it would be a mistake for governments to expect that they can simply get the environmental prices right, and then let the market take care of any problems. Even the most diligent tax authorities could not reach all the places they would need to in order to safeguard the environment single-handedly. For example, it is impractical to measure—and thus tax—the smog-producing chemicals spewing from each of a city's million cars. Regulations, in contrast, have slashed tailpipe emissions in many countries by simply requiring that companies make cleaner cars.

Still, there is considerable room for improving regulations. Much of the first generation of environmental policy in industrial countries, starting in the 1970s, was born out of environmentalists' deep distrust of businesses, and seemed founded on the belief that the best way to make sure firms clean up was to tell them exactly how to do it. But by focusing on means rather than ends—for example, by prescribing water filters considered advanced a quarter-century ago—the regulations have favored established, end-of-the-pipe fixes over cheaper and more effective pollution prevention techniques, such as using nontoxic, citrus-based solvents. In addition, environmental laws in most countries are divided into fiefdoms—air, water, hazardous waste, and so on. Regulators dealing with one type of problem are often effectively required to ignore implications for other problems. Rules calling for sulfur scrubbers in smokestacks, say, produce solid waste problems in the form of toxic scrubber sludge.[17]

The patchwork texture of laws on the books worsens the situation. Many governments, for instance, heavily regulate water pollution from factories while nearly ignoring runoff of manure, fertilizer, and pesticides from farms. Other rules, such as zoning laws that limit the density of new neighborhoods, are too rarely even thought of as environmental policies, despite their major environmental effects. (See Chapter 8.) Worse, in rich and poor countries alike, many regulations are poorly enforced. In the United States, recent government audits found that state and federal officials had failed to issue or renew hundreds of pollution permits for factories and wastewater treatment plants that were still operating. Enforcement tends to be even weaker in poorer nations.[18]

Fortunately, these shortcomings have not escaped notice, and are leading to gradual reform. One response has been for governments to make regulations work more like taxes, in the sense of zeroing in on results rather than prescribing solutions. The Duales System Deutschland (DSD) offers a particularly far-reaching example of this approach. Established by the German government in 1991, the system makes manufacturers of products such as detergents and toys legally responsible for the plastic wrap, cardboard, bottles, and other packaging material in which they ship their products—even after the products are sold. (See Chapter 3.) Stores must accept the used cardboard boxes and shampoo bottles from customers; producers in turn must accept materials from stores.[19]

In principle, the German law forcibly closes the packaging materials loop in the economy but leaves businesses with flexibility in accommodating this new limit. Many companies, for instance, have found ways to reuse or recycle their materials, while others have opted for simpler packaging. Though not without problems, the system increased recycling of packaging materials to 4.8 million tons a year by 1994—a substantial 70 percent of all packaging materials—at a modest cost of some $20 a year per German resident. Austria, France, and Belgium have since adopted versions of the DSD system.[20]

The Netherlands has been a leader in rethinking not only the structure of regulations but the process through which they are formed. In 1989, it released a National Environmental Policy Plan after consulting with industry and public interest groups. Revised periodically, the plan has set national goals in eight problem areas, ranging from waste disposal to climate change. The government has then taken various steps toward these goals, including taxes, regulations, and quasi-voluntary covenants with industry. The covenants in particular need not be obeyed to the letter, but good-faith efforts are essentially required. Otherwise, more specific and more burdensome regulations may follow.[21]

The building industry in the Netherlands, for example, is well on its way to meeting its commitment to recycle 90 percent of its waste, mainly bricks and concrete from construction and demolition. Nationwide greenhouse gas emissions, on the other hand, have not fallen as hoped. But the country has phased out ozone-depleting chlorofluorocarbons (CFCs), as required by international treaty, and should come close to its goal of cutting pollutants that cause acid rain by 80 percent between 1980 and 2000.[22]

GLOBAL CHALLENGES, GLOBAL COOPERATION

The world's 200 nation-states have divided the Earth among themselves in ways that have little to do with geography, or with the anatomy of the global economy. So as natural resources, pollutants, trade, and investment increasingly course across arbitrary borders, the international dimensions of the environmental crisis steadily expand. The crisis therefore calls for an equally international response, and one with two main prongs. The treaties and institutions of international economic governance, such as the World Bank and the World Trade Organization (WTO), will need to take the environmental implications of their actions into fuller consideration. In addition, cooperation on the environment will be needed to protect oceans, seas, and many rivers, as well as biodiversity, natural habitat, and the atmosphere.

The need for international governance in solving international environmental problems has become well recognized in the latter half of the twentieth century, but in words far more than deeds. The World Bank in particular, with its historical roots in the rebuilding of Western Europe after World War II, has long been a major financier of giant public works projects such as coal plants and hydropower dams. In many developing countries, such projects have wrought grievous harm. In Singrauli, in the Indian state of Bihar, the Bank has lent billions to help build a giant complex of 12 open-pit mines and 11 coal plants. The huge projects have impoverished many peasants by poisoning the region's soils and forests; the plants have also become one of the world's largest sources of greenhouse gases.[23]

The World Bank's current president, James Wolfensohn, has apparently worked hard to reform the institution in order to incorporate environmental and other development concerns into its day-to-day operations. On balance, however, his efforts have so far deflected the course of the bureaucracy he commands only a few degrees. According to the Bank's own figures, it has lent six times as much for fossil fuel projects as for renewable energy and energy efficiency since 1992, the year its funders and clients signed the landmark treaty on global climate change at Rio. Moreover, the Bank still favors coal, the dirtiest fossil fuel, much more than private lenders do, at roughly 40 percent of its energy portfolio compared with 20 percent for private lenders.[24]

Consultants for the Bank have concluded that if the institution evaluated projects as if a modest $20-a-ton carbon tax were in place in client countries—in order to give some weight to environmental concerns—40 percent of the energy projects financed would fail a cost-benefit test. Of course, developing countries should be able to emit some carbon, especially while rich nations emit so much more and renewable energy technologies are maturing. Nevertheless, the Bank seems to be pushing developing countries along a development path bound to hit an environmental dead end.[25]

Through the World Bank and other Bretton Woods institutions—including the International Monetary Fund (IMF) and the World Trade Organization—nations have shown the willingness and ability to build international institutions strong enough to defend one principle many see as essential to long-term economic development, namely that trade and investment should flow easily across borders. In 1997 and 1998, for example, the IMF conditioned emergency loans to Asian nations in part on reforms that would, it hoped, draw private funds back into the countries by making life easier for international investors. And in 1998, the WTO ruled against a U.S. law prohibiting importation of shrimp caught with nets lacking devices that protect endangered sea turtles, calling the law an illegal restraint of trade. (See Chapter 5.)[26]

The power of these institutions makes them equally capable of becoming strong supporters of sustainable development. To do this, they would need to put into practice a more sophisticated conception of development, one that elevates environmental protection (along with education, health, and advancement of women) from the current status of a poor relation in the international economic policy arena. Institutions that absorbed that new view would be as eager to defend the environment as they now are to defend international capital.

There are hints that this view is gaining currency, and not just in the President's office at the World Bank. In late 1998, for example, the WTO partly reversed itself in the shrimp-turtle case, taking issue with the way the U.S. law was implemented rather than dismissing it outright.[27]

Similarly, nations that accepted this approach would provide adequate funds

for international environmental bodies such as the U.N. Environment Programme (UNEP), and would negotiate stronger environmental treaties.

Most international treaties and agreements have been inadequate to the problems at hand.

To date, governments have ratified more than 215 international environmental treaties, on everything from acid rain to desertification. Most are regional in scope. Agreements aimed at protecting 14 of the world's regional seas have been forged under the auspices of UNEP, for example, and have been signed by more than 140 nations. A few environmental treaties, however, are global, including the conventions on biodiversity and climate change signed at the U.N. Conference on Environment and Development, the Earth Summit, in Rio in 1992. Governments have also signed numerous action plans and communiqués that lack binding legal status.[28]

But most of the treaties and agreements have been inadequate to the problems at hand, either in design or in implementation and enforcement. The institutions they have created have typically been given ambitious mandates in principle, but minimal authority and funding.[29]

What can be said for these accords is that the international negotiating conferences that made them have helped pave the way for longer-term progress. For one, they have facilitated agreement on such questions as priorities for international development assistance. The International Conference on Population and Development in Cairo in 1994, for example, marked the widespread acceptance among governments and their aid agencies of the importance of improving the lot of poor women in order to slow population growth.[30]

The conferences have also made problems such as marine pollution and species extinction suddenly newsworthy. Attention from the press corps leads to attention from the public and can heighten support for action. Coverage of environmental issues, for example, reached new levels during the Rio conference. And by raising awareness, international conferences have helped catalyze organizations of nonprofit groups, legislators, and businesses within and across borders, creating stronger lobbies for action both domestically and internationally.

The Montreal Protocol is a template for effective treaties on much tougher international environmental problems.

Still, if nations are to exercise effective international environmental governance, such conferences will eventually need to produce more than beneficial side effects. They will need to forge strong treaties. Encouragingly, on a few issues they already have. In 1990, for example, the Convention on International Trade in Endangered Species of Wild Fauna and Flora banned cross-border trade in ivory. With markets dried up, elephant poaching in Africa plummeted and some herds began to recuperate (although some trade has been allowed again, and poaching is reportedly on the rise in some nations). In Western Europe, a series of international agreements during the last 20 years lie behind the steady decline in emissions of sulfur and nitrogen, the main causes of acid rain.[31]

Most spectacular has been the success of the 1987 Montreal Protocol on Depletion of the Ozone Layer. This treaty required industrial countries to halt CFC production and importation in 1996. Each nation used a different mix of taxes, regulations, and education programs to comply. The accord calls for a global phaseout by 2006, and for production of most other ozone-destroying chemicals to fall.[32]

In order to forge a strong treaty, signatories yielded sovereignty in several notable ways. To discourage individual nations from staying outside the treaty and becoming havens for CFC production, parties to the treaty accepted a rule that forbids them from trading with nonparties in CFCs or products containing them. (Whether this provision would survive a challenge under WTO rules is not clear.) They also set up a fund through which industrial nations can aid others in making the transition; some $750 million has been transferred so far. In addition, the Protocol requires consent from only two thirds of the signatories, including majorities of more and less industrial countries, to ratify accelerations of reductions. Tighter timetables were in fact approved unanimously in 1990 and 1993, but the threat of majority rule may have helped bring would-be stragglers into the fold of international consensus.[33]

In outline, the Montreal Protocol is a template for effective treaties on much tougher international environmental problems, including biodiversity loss and climate change. It recognizes that nations that are richer and have caused more of a problem need to take the lead in solving it. They may end up paying more (because they phase out CFCs faster and fund most of the research on substitutes), but precisely because they are wealthier, they are willing to spend more to prevent skin cancer deaths and crop damage. The result, ideally, is a treaty that serves each nation's interest, and at a price each can afford. And because of the way nations have yielded some sovereignty in this case, historians may cite the Montreal Protocol as an important, early instance of nations forging global governance in order to solve global problems.[34]

AN ECO-INDUSTRIAL REVOLUTION

Debate over environmental issues often centers on the whys and hows of government action. That emphasis is warranted, but it risks overshadowing the role that nongovernmental actors, including businesses, will need to play in fashioning a sustainable society. The creativity and entrepreneurship of businesses, after all, generated many of the economic and technological changes that shaped the twentieth century. Businesses will play no smaller a role in an eco-industrial revolution.

Of course, companies are not generally in the business of doing things out of moral duty. They exist primarily to make money. So the proper role of business in creating a sustainable society would necessarily be subtle. On the one hand, businesses would be the objects of change. They would be prodded along by strong environmental taxes and regulations, major international accords, and consumer pressure, and lured by the huge investment opportunities created by governments rewriting the ground rules of the $38-trillion-a-year global economy. On the other hand, they could be agents of change as they devised technologies that saved fuel or recycled water cheaply enough to trigger major shifts away from unsustainable technologies.[35]

In practice, however, the distinction between businesses as reactors and as actors is fuzzy. Ask CEO John Browne why British Petroleum (BP) is investing $1 billion in solar and wind energy R&D and he will probably give two overlapping answers: BP needs to prepare for a strong global climate treaty, which will dampen demand for oil. And BP wants to bring down the price of solar energy in order to lead the world, profitably, toward change. Gauging how large each consideration looms is as hard as predicting which will move faster—government policy or technology. Thus the holistic view that a shift toward sustainability would be systemic—driven by businesses, government, nonprofit groups, and consumers together—is perhaps most relevant. "Using uncertainty as an excuse for doing nothing," explains Browne, "only marginalizes us in an important and rapidly moving debate." Businesses have a role to play and an opportunity to exploit.[36]

The transition to sustainability would continue the economic dynamism that has characterized the two centuries after the Industrial Revolution. Corporate behemoths, such as BP, General Motors, and Dupont, that rose on the crest of the fossil fuel revolution could capture many of the new opportunities. Or they could be elbowed aside by the Microsofts of the new technological generation. (See Chapter 2.) For every declining coal industry, there would be a rising wind power industry. From businesses' point of view, government policy and consumer pressure would foreclose some profit opportunities, but open up others. Some jobs would regrettably be shed, but others would be created.

Regulations, a few environmental taxes, and consumer pressure are already giving a taste of what may come. Sales of organically grown food rose 19-fold in the United States between 1980 and 1996, from $180 million to $3.5 billion. The Montreal Protocol is shutting down markets for CFCs, but it has created billion-dollar demands for ozone-safe alternatives and for the refrigerators and air conditioners that use them. The international market for "environmental" goods and services that recycle, monitor and control pollution, and save energy reached roughly $450 billion in 1996.[37]

A full transition to sustainability would make these markets seem small. Fundamentally reconfiguring the global economy would cause demand for technologies that prevent pollution in the first place to mushroom. In fact, global wind power capacity additions quintupled between 1990 and 1997. Denmark, Germany, Spain, and India installed the most, thanks in part to strong subsidies. The wind industry now employs 20,000 in the European Union, up from practically zero in the 1970s. The latest global sales doubling for solar cells, which are made from silicon, took only four years, a growth rate worthy of silicon computer chips.[38]

Major investment opportunities would also materialize within existing industries. Indeed, most industries would see neither massive shrinkage nor massive growth on the way to a sustainable world. Many would, however, have to evolve in order to survive. A sustainable economy would need some paper, chemicals, and steel, for example, but makers of these products would have to overhaul how they operate in order to pollute much less and recycle much more.

It is during such times of turbulence that the industrial pecking order is most often rearranged. Those who anticipate change in the business environment—indeed, press it forward—will gain on their competitors. A growing list of corporations seem to be taking this message to heart with respect to sustainability.[39]

The key conceptual shift manufacturers need to make in becoming more sustainable is to see themselves as selling services rather than goods. As William McDonough, dean of the University of Virginia School of Architecture, points out, consumers do not buy televisions because they feel a powerful need to bring a box of circuit boards, toxic compounds, and metals purified at great environmental expense into their living rooms. They want information and entertainment. The challenge for business, then, is to maximize the provision of such services while minimizing the production of goods. Information and human intelligence then become the sources of most economic value—as they already are in software, movies, financial services, and other dynamic sectors.[40]

The techniques for generating more service with less environmental harm are many. (See Chapters 3 and 4.) Appliances, vehicles, even houses can be made both more efficient and more efficiently. Their usefulness can be stretched by making them more durable and easier to repair, upgrade, disassemble, and recycle. The Xerox Corporation, for instance, says that it sees itself as selling copies rather than copiers. When it provides a customer with a machine, it guarantees an agreed level of copier service for an agreed number of months. The company will replace or upgrade parts in its modularly designed units at no extra cost to the customer. And when a contract expires, Xerox takes its machine back in order to reuse it or scavenge it for parts. The company now recycles more than a million parts a year, saving some $100 million annually.[41]

As Xerox's experience suggests, devising these new ways of providing services will often cost much less than feared—so much so that frequently it will profit companies to press ahead of the environmental policy curve. One study of the costs of environmental laws for businesses found a dozen policies in the United States for which costs had been estimated both before and after entering into force. All but one policy turned out to cost half or less of what was originally projected, mainly because of unforeseen technological advances. And some saved money.[42]

As the CFC phaseout deadline approached in the early 1990s, for example, electronics giants such as AT&T, General Electric, and Texas Instruments worked together to find alternatives to

CFCs for cleaning new circuit boards. Eventually they settled on a more radical and efficient approach: soldering components together so neatly that they needed no cleaning in the first place. By 1992, they had refined the technique and halted CFC use. One company, Nortel, spent $1 million on the switchover, but saved $4 million in CFC purchase and disposal costs (and CFC taxes). The new process also raised efficiency and product quality.[43]

One reason "greener" can turn out cheaper is that the goal of environmental protection can energize employees, who are not just corporate cogs but human beings concerned about what they are doing to their communities and to their children's futures. People do better work when they care more about it. In addition, lack of time prevents companies from investigating all of the millions of process changes they could make. Thus practices that waste resources and money can persist for decades. Nortel, for example, for years stuck to money-wasting circuit board cleaning techniques simply because they had worked reasonably well in the past. The CFC phaseout, however, focused its corporate heart and mind. Engineers were put on the job of finding affordable alternatives, and in a matter of years they succeeded beyond expectation.[44]

Economies of scale also help companies cut the cost of environmentally benign technologies. The more widgets—or water purifiers, or solar cells—a company makes, the better it becomes at making them, which allows it to bring down prices, stoke demand, and make even more widgets. This virtuous circle can arise in any manufacturing business where change is afoot, which is why technologies often develop in unpredictable waves and pulses. Between 1975 and 1997, for instance, the price of a watt of solar cells dropped from $89 to $4.25 (in 1997 dollars)—or 30 percent for every doubling in cumulative sales. At this rate, another 10-fold increase in cumulative sales would bring prices to $1 per watt, often considered the threshold for competitiveness with coal and natural gas.[45]

Trends like that may explain why Toyota has begun selling an innovative electric-gasoline hybrid car, a sporty four-seater called the Prius, that gets twice the mileage of conventional models. Toyota is reportedly losing as much as $10,000 on every Prius that rolls out of the factory, but is evidently banking on the expectation that the more experience it develops with the new technologies, the more it can cut costs and sharpen its competitive edge in this strategic new market.[46]

Still, there is little reason to expect that businesses can bring about an eco-industrial revolution on their own. When two technologies compete, an overwhelming advantage usually goes to the one with the head start. Solar power, for instance, must compete with oil- and coal-burning technologies on an economic playing field that has been tilted in favor of fossil fuels for a century by subsidies and lax environmental laws. As a result, for every dollar that has been spent developing solar power, a hundred or a thousand have been spent refining its competitors. Thus governments will need to exercise substantial policy muscle to tip the market toward environmentally sound technologies. When that happens, the businesses that are best prepared will likely reap most of the profits for doing right by the environment.

CIVIL SOCIETY FOR A SUSTAINABLE SOCIETY

The disintegration of communism in the Eastern bloc unleashed a wave of environmental horror stories. From the "Black Triangle" at the nexus of East Germany, Czechoslovakia, and Poland to the eastern reaches of Siberia, there were reports of polluted forests where no birds chirped and no leaves sprouted from the trees, of whole nuclear reactors dumped into Arctic waters, of high cancer rates and mysterious clusters of children born without left forearms. Intriguingly, there were also reports, less publicized, that environmental groups, such as Ecoglasnost in Bulgaria, were a significant conduit for the groundswell of discontent that toppled communist regimes in 1989.[47]

The abysmal environmental record of the former Eastern bloc teaches an important lesson: a sustainable society almost certainly must be founded on a strong civil society, which is defined here as the realm in which people may work as individuals or in groups to shape their world on a nonprofit basis, without the sanction of violence that undergirds government action. Civil society includes voters, consumers, churches and mosques, political parties, unions, and a dizzying variety of other nongovernmental groups. In the West, where civil society comparatively thrived, pressure from voters and independent groups led governments and some businesses to take local environmental problems seriously. But Soviet dictatorship clamped down on civil society. As a result, local environmental problems had to become acute before there appeared a glimmer of response in those countries.

Still, Westerners should not take too much pride in the contrast. While rivers, seas, and forests are generally healthier in the West, lifestyles there are also grossly unsustainable. (See Chapter 3.) Democratic nations may have reduced local environmental problems, but by importing fish, timber, food, and minerals from the rest of the world and exporting pollutants such as carbon dioxide, they are doing more than their part to spoil the global commons. That points to the need for global environmental governance. But just as domestic civil society has had to press for domestic government action on the environment, a strong, global civil society, in which researchers, activists, policymakers, and citizens link up across borders, will be needed to press for international action.

In the final analysis, it is the power of individuals, channeled through civil society, that will drive governments, international institutions, and businesses toward sustainability.

Fortunately, recent trends here are positive. Polls show the global public becoming more worried about environmental problems every year. According to a 1998 survey by Environics International covering 30 nations as different as China and Italy, majorities in 28 feel that their governments need to do more to protect the environment. And during the 1990s, there has been a halting but global shift toward democracy and space for civil society. Increasingly, public concern about the inadequacy of governmental action on the environment is voiced, and is heard.[48]

The process is at work even in China, a country hardly known for brooking dissent. In Jiangsu province, a man whose 4,800-strong flock of ducks earned him the local name "King of Ducks"—and a good living from the eggs—awoke one morning in 1994 to find his piece of river pitch black. Within days, all of Lu Shihua's ducks were dead. In response, Lu and his neighbors launched a class action lawsuit against the polluters—state-owned distilleries and soymilk factories upstream. The villagers won, setting a important new precedent in China (though the case was under appeal as of early 1998). Given the strength of the central government in China, it is likely that this victory was a product of pressure from both below and above: of the plaintiffs' courage and persistence and of a greater openness in Beijing toward criticism of highly polluting state enterprises.[49]

As this example shows, getting things done in the civil sphere, as in business and government, usually takes organization. In the environmental realm, the groups that have so far made the most difference are of a type usually labeled, somewhat vaguely, as nongovernmental organizations, or NGOs.

The rise of nongovernmental groups has been one of the most striking and hopeful developments in societal structure in the last quarter-century. The gradually increasing space for civil society worldwide has given them room to grow. The seeming inability of governments to solve complex, modern problems such as poverty and environmental degradation has provoked them. And the spread of literacy and cheap electronic communication has nurtured them.[50]

In western democracies, environmental NGOs abound. On the Indian subcontinent, a huge number of small grassroots groups operate, drawing on a Gandhian tradition of self-help. In the Panchmahals district of India's Gujarat state, for instance, scores of villages have organized committees to protect and regenerate local forests in the last 10 years—forests that began declining after the government took them over from the departing British. In Latin America, a comparable number of Christian Base Communities, born out of the liberation theology movement of the 1980s, unite Catholicism with social action. Thousands more groups operate throughout the rest of Asia and sub-Saharan Africa. North Africa, on the other hand, has relatively few NGOs.[51]

The Internet has spurred many NGO efforts. In 1997, a ragtag coalition of groups ranging from the Third World Network in Malaysia to the Council of Canadians used the World Wide Web, electronic mail, and electronic conferences to quickly organize opposition to the Multilateral Agreement on Investments. The prospective treaty to liberalize international investment rules was being negotiated behind the closed doors of the Organisation for Economic Co-operation and Development (OECD). "If a negotiator says something to someone over a glass of wine," boasted Maude Barlow, chair of the Council of Canadians, "we'll have it on the Internet within an hour, all over the world." In April 1998, the OECD announced a six-month delay in negotiations, acknowledging that the NGOs had aroused enough opposition in many countries to derail the process. A similar network spearheaded the campaign to finalize a new treaty to ban land mines worldwide.[52]

Polls show the global public becoming more worried about environmental problems every year.

Increasingly, NGOs are linking up to test the limits of existing international law as well. In Nicaragua, the indigenous community of Awas Tingni is working with the U.S.-based Indian Law Resource Center (ILRC) in a bid to regain control of its homeland. With ILRC assistance, the community filed a petition in 1995 at the Inter-American Commission on Human Rights, arguing that the government had violated international as well as national law by unilaterally granting timber concessions to foreign loggers on Awas Tingni land. In 1998, the commission, an investigative body, found firmly in favor of the community and filed suit on residents' behalf in the Inter-American Court on Human Rights, which is part of the Organization of American States (OAS). The finding embarrassed the Nicaraguan government, but whether it will lead OAS members to raise the legal standing of indigenous land claims remains to be seen.[53]

Though policymakers may find the results unpleasant in the short run, it seems clear that fostering NGOs will serve society and government stability in the long run. Governments can support civil society in several ways. One essential step is to protect freedoms of press and assembly, something that often still runs against their nature. The Malaysian government, like many, has an uneasy relationship with NGOs. In 1997, it raided the offices of three of them in an apparent attempt to silence its critics.[54]

Another key step is for governments to make themselves more accountable to all the governed, since special interests often work to block progress. This calls for strengthening the more egalitarian avenues of influence over public policy formation, such as elections, while lessening those that favor the wealthy few, such as campaign donations.

Almost all governments maintain comfortable relationships with moneyed interests, which reduces the power of civil society as a whole. One of the most powerful men in Indonesia, for example, is Bob Hasan, a long-time friend and aide of former President Suharto. Under Suharto, the government sold Hasan huge logging concessions in the nation's rainforests at prices far below true worth, turning him into a billionaire even as it impoverished thousands of villagers dependent on the forests. Hasan almost certainly channeled some of his logging profits back to Suharto relatives and other key officials.[55]

One useful tack against corruption is for governments to make sure that officials who formulate and implement policy are paid well, in order to reduce the appeal of bribes. Also critical are adoption and enforcement of strong anti-corruption laws, periodic auditing of officials, and an independent judiciary; enforcement will never stamp out corruption, but it will increase the risks for potential bribe takers. Finally, reducing the discretion of bureaucratic decision-makers and making their actions public will further reduce the appeal of bribes. Sunlight is the best disinfectant.[56]

In industrial democracies, campaign donations create similar problems. In the 1995–96 U.S. election cycle, oil and gas companies gave $11.8 million to congressional candidates to protect tax breaks worth at least $3 billion over the period. Timber lobbies donated $3.6 million, mainly to members of committees that have set the U.S. Forest Service's timber sale quotas high enough to propel widespread clearcutting on public lands.[57]

Almost every industrial democracy has adopted its own mix of campaign finance reform measures during the last few decades, drawing from such ingredients as public financing, limits on contributions and spending, and bans on political television advertising. Some have worked better than others. In Canada, for instance, a 1974 package of reforms combined disclosure requirements, tax credits for private donations, strong spending caps for political parties, and direct public financing. These reforms limited campaign spending for the most recent federal elections to 80¢ per capita, compared with $9 in the United States. And the reforms appear to have facilitated the rise of new political parties.[58]

In addition to making sure the deck is less stacked against civil society groups, governments can give those groups additional cards to play. In particular, governments can release information about their own activities and those of businesses. The United States pioneered a potent system in this spirit, under a law whose passage owed much to support from environmental groups. In 1986, it began collating and publishing data on toxic chemical emissions from industrial plants. The database, known as the Toxics Release Inventory (TRI), for the first time gave citizens the right to know how much of various chemicals was being emitted by local industry.[59]

Especially now that it is available over the World Wide Web, the TRI has become an invaluable tool for local groups pressing factories to clean up, as well as for investors concerned about the associated costs. The negative publicity that independent groups generate from the data gives them clout with companies a hundred times as big. One study found that stock prices for firms on the TRI list dropped an average 0.2–0.3 percent ($4–6 million) the day the first results were released in 1989, with larger losses for heavier polluters. And the companies that lost the most value then cut their emissions the most, apparently in response. The TRI has inspired imitators in Australia, Canada, the Czech Republic, Egypt, Mexico, the Netherlands, South Africa, Switzerland, and the United Kingdom.[60]

In a potentially far-reaching step, the 55 nations of the U.N. Economic Commission for Europe, which covers North America and Europe, signed a convention in 1998 that obliges them to increase public access to information and broaden public participation in government decisionmaking related to the environment—in a word, to increase "transparency." The treaty also requires members to promote the same goals for international institutions they belong to, such as the World Trade Organization, which has been extremely secretive in its deliberations. The convention might result in the WTO court releasing transcripts of cases with environmental implications. Most likely, signatories will implement the convention in fits and starts—pushed forward by NGOs.[61]

THE POWER OF AN EDUCATED CITIZENRY

What is remarkable about nonprofit, nongovernmental organizations is that they wield power despite their seeming lack of it. They have no army or police force, no power to tax or regulate or ratify binding international accords. The for-profit sector dwarfs them financially. Their source of strength is far less tangible: it lies in education, broadly defined. Many NGOs are supported by foundations and individual donors motivated by understandings they have gained of major social problems. And many in turn work to educate the public and persuade policymakers about the need for action. This suggests that the fundamental challenge in building a sustainable society is one of education. What people think and feel about the world affects what they do as voters, consumers, and resource owners, and as government officials, international diplomats, and employees.

It is encouraging to note that mindsets can change quickly in response to education. In developing nations, education campaigns, along with increased availability of family planning services and contraception, are one major reason that fertility rates fell remarkably quickly between the early 1960s and the first half of the 1990s—from 6.0 births per woman to 3.3. (These figures exclude China, where particularly coercive polices reduced fertility even faster.) If this hopeful trend were to continue, fertility in the developing world would drop to the sustainable rate of slightly more than 2 children per woman by 2010–15. (Population growth would continue for some decades, however, because so many women will still have their childbearing years ahead of them.) The transition from high birth rates and high death rates to low birth rates and low death rates, which took 150 years in what are now the more industrial countries, would then have taken only 50 in developing countries.[62]

One striking reason fertility has fallen is that women are more educated not just about family planning, but generally. Many studies have found that a woman's education level is among the strongest, if not the strongest, predictor of how many children she will have. (See Figure 10–1.) Women who spend more time in school marry and have children later. They also work more in the formal economy and earn more. This gives them more to lose financially if they stay at home with young children, as well as less need for children to support them in old age. Educating girls also improves women's economic and social status, and thus is one of the best ways to make economic development both equitable and sustainable.[63]

A more specific role for educators lies in teaching children and adults about the environment—how it functions, how they depend on it, and how they affect it. Children in particular respond to these lessons. The seeds of understanding planted now will produce concerned citizens in a generation's time. One purpose of education is to give people the tools they need to become responsible citizens. Teaching students about the environment merely extends the understanding of "citizenship" to encompass their responsibilities as citizens of planet Earth.

Environmental education sounds straightforward, but doing it may well require major changes in how students are

taught. Education today teaches disconnection. Disciplines such as political science, economics, moral philosophy, anthropology, biology, psychology, chemistry, and thermodynamics are severed from each other even though each, in combination with the others, helps explain our environmental predicament. Moreover, points out David Orr, a professor at Oberlin College in Ohio, the very experience of classroom learning teaches disconnection, since it typically occurs in artificial indoor environments, which are maintained with environmentally costly flows of fossil fuels and water and which psychologically isolate students from the natural world. As a result, the structure of education itself trains students to ignore the ecological consequences of their actions.[64]

"Ecological literacy" is above all an ability to connect, to synthesize knowledge from the gamut of disciplines in order to see the big picture. To become ecologically literate, Orr argues, students need to experience education less as an exercise in taking dictation than as an ongoing dialogue, in which ideas are formulated, tested against everyday experience, and revised. This forces students to think about how the physics of solar cells and the chemistry of petroleum, say, shape the world economy and geopolitics.[65]

One of the most promising paths to such experience is for students to help manage their own campuses and neighborhoods. At the University of Jorge Tadeo Lozano in Bogatá, Colombia, for example, students and administrators have joined to launch a campus recycling program that aims to collect 17 tons a month of plastic, organic waste, and paper. In Ankara, Turkey, students and staff at the Middle East Technical University have spearheaded the reforestation of 1,500 hectares (3,750 acres) of wasteland into the largest green space in the city. In the United States, student pressure is perhaps the main reason 80 percent of campuses now recycle.[66]

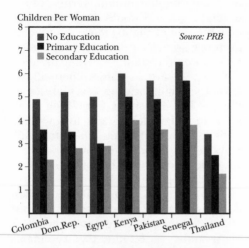

Figure 10–1. Fertility Rate by Education Level of the Mother, Selected Countries

The world's oldest institutions of education—though often not thought of as such—are arguably institutions of religion. Like universities and schools, they seek to help people understand the world. Like NGO leaders, religious leaders are primarily motivated by moral beliefs, and try to teach society how to translate those values into action. Some 3.5 billion people, more than half the planet's population, belong to organized religions. And the values of environmentalism—respect for the Creation, the importance of human health, and the right of the next generation to a secure future—are nearly universal, so it is not surprising that all major religions can be read as environmentalist. A Buddhist meditation, for example, runs, "Cut down the forest of your greed, before cutting real trees." Hinduism holds India's Ganges river to be sacred. And the Book of Genesis says, "The Lord God took the man and put him in the Garden of Eden to work it and take care of it."[67]

As moral educators, spiritual leaders can help people discover environmentalism within themselves and help them think about how to apply that ethic in their lives. In the United States, for example, the National Religious Partnership for the Environment, a coalition of groups from several faiths, lists more than 150 environmentally active congregations nationwide. These range from a Jewish youth group in San Diego that builds nature trails and does monthly cleanups in two parks to a Baptist congregation in Collinsville, Alabama, campaigning to unseat officials who approved a local landfill that parishioners say is polluting the groundwater. Meanwhile, in the Indian city of Varanasi, a hereditary Hindu priest and hydroelectric engineer named Veer Bhadra Mishra heads a foundation that is working on low-cost ways to clean up the Ganges, which is heavily polluted despite its sacredness.[68]

H.G. Wells foreshadowed much of the twentieth century when he wrote that "human history becomes more and more a race between education and catastrophe." The sort of education that will save us from catastrophe is not just a matter of disseminating information, for the planet is now awash in information. The education needed, rather, is the sharing of wisdom. Our knowledge of the natural world has raced far ahead of our wisdom in using it. As a result, we are razing our forests, grinding down our mountains, siphoning off our rivers, paving our plains, modifying our climate, polluting our air, and tainting our blood. We are producing, in other words, a world none of us wants.[69]

Environmental education may require major changes in how students are taught.

There is an alternative path. It cannot be described to the last detail, but it can be outlined convincingly. And there are hints that we are moving toward that path. Wind and solar power sales are skyrocketing. Water-conserving practices are spreading. Population growth is slowing. We can also draw hope from the rapidity of change during the century just ending. Technologies once hardly dreamed of became commonplace a generation later. Public attitudes, about smoking for example, also evolved rapidly in many countries.

The turning of the new millennium brings a historic moment of truth for global society. Will we rescue what is good in the modern economy while teaching it to cherish natural wealth and human health? Will we fashion an economy fit for the long haul?

Crossing over to a sustainable path will be a long and complex process. Governments need to play a large role, working within their borders and cooperating across them. Businesses will need to take many of the risks, generate many of the innovations, and create the new jobs. And pressing them all forward will be civil society in its many forms, grounded in an educated citizenry.

Like any economic revolution, this one will involve upheaval and even some sacrifice. In order to make way for new industries—and thus new jobs, investment opportunities, and products—others will be shed. But the benefits will be healthy air, safe drinking water, a secure food supply, and protection for the planet's diversity of species—in short, a planet we can be proud to leave for our children. The choice is ours to make.

Notes

Chapter 1. A New Economy for a New Century

1. Dave Walter, ed., *Today Then: America's Best Minds Look 100 Years Into the Future on the Occasion of the 1893 World's Columbian Exposition* (Helena, MT: American & World Geographic Publishing, 1992).

2. Ibid.

3. 1900 population estimates from Carl Haub, "How Many People Have Ever Lived on Earth," *Population Today*, February 1995; present population from United Nations, *World Population Prospects: The 1996 Revision* (New York: 1996); economic activities estimates from Worldwatch update of Angus Maddison, *Monitoring the World Economy 1820–1992* (Paris: Organisation for Economic Co-operation and Development (OECD), 1995); carbon dioxide concentrations from Timothy Whorf and C.D. Keeling, Scripps Institution of Oceanography, La Jolla, CA, letter to Seth Dunn, Worldwatch Institute, 2 February 1998.

4. Stephen Jay Gould, *Questioning the Millennium: A Rationalist's Guide to a Precisely Arbitrary Countdown* (New York: Harmony Books, 1997); Clive Ponting, *A Green History of the World: The Environment and the Collapse of Great Civilizations* (New York: Penguin Books, 1991); Jared Diamond, *Guns, Germs, and Steel: The Fates of Human Societies* (New York: W.W. Norton & Company, 1997).

5. Ponting, op. cit. note 4.

6. Ibid; Haub, op. cit. note 3.

7. Ponting, op. cit. note 4; Haub, op. cit. note 3; time to travel from New York to Boston is a Worldwatch estimate based on 55 kilometers per day in a stagecoach.

8. Ponting, op. cit. note 4.

9. Arnulf Grubler, Alan McDonald, and Nebojsa Nakicenovic, eds., *Global Energy Perspectives* (New York: Cambridge University Press, 1998); British Petroleum (BP), *BP Statistical Review of World Energy 1998* (London: Group Media & Publications, 1998); metals from *Metallgesellschaft AG and World Bureau of Metal Statistics, MetallStatistik/Metal Statistics 1985–1995* (Frankfurt and Ware, U.K.: 1996), and from Metallgesellschaft AG, Statistical Tables (Frankfurt: various years); paper from U.N. Food and Agriculture Organization (FAO), *FAOSTAT Statistics Database*, <http://apps.fao.org>; plastics from United Nations, *Industrial Commodity Statistics Yearbook* (New York: various years); dependence on naturally occurring elements from U.S. Congress, Office of Technology Assessment, *Green Products by Design: Choices for a Cleaner Environment* (Washington, DC: U.S Government Printing Office, September 1992).

10. James J. Flink, *The Automobile Age* (Cambridge, MA: The MIT Press, 1988); Worldwatch estimate based on American Automobile Manufacturers Association (AAMA), *World Motor Vehicle Facts & Figures 1997* (Detroit, MI: 1997), and on Standard & Poor's DRI, *World Car Industry Forecast Report* (London: February 1998); Wright brothers first flight from <http://www.nasm.edu>, viewed 6 November 1998; wingspan of Boeing

777 from <http://www.boeing.com>, viewed 6 November 1998.

11. *Popular Mechanics* from Wilson Dizard, Jr., *Meganet: How the Global Communications Network Will Connect Everyone on Earth* (Boulder, CO: Westview Press, 1997); Nicholas Denton, "Microsoft Capitalisation Exceeds $200bn," *Financial Times*, 26 February 1998.

12. Frances Cairncross, *The Death of Distance: How the Communications Revolution Will Change Our Lives* (Boston: Harvard Business School Press, 1997); telephone lines and cellular phones from International Telecommunication Union (ITU), *World Telecommunications Indicators on Diskette* (Geneva: 1996), with 1996 from ITU, *Challenges to the Network: Telecoms and the Internet* (Geneva: September 1997); satellite telephones from Iridium Corporation, "The World's First Global Satellite Telephone and Paging Starts Service Today," press release (Washington, DC: 1 November 1998); televisions from United Nations, *Statistical Yearbook* (New York: various years), and from "World TV Households: The Growth Continues," *Screen Digest,* March 1993; host computers connected to Internet from Network Wizards, "Internet Domain Surveys, 1981–1998," <http://www.nw.com>, viewed 6 February 1998.

13. World Health Organization (WHO), *The World Health Report 1998* (Geneva: 1998).

14. Tertius Chandler, *Four Thousand Years of Urban Growth: An Historical Census* (Lewiston, NY: Edwin Mellen Press, 1987); United Nations, *World Urbanization Prospects: The 1996 Revision* (New York: 1997).

15. Grain and water use increases are estimates of Lester Brown based on world population in 1900 and the assumption that grain consumption per person remained roughly the same between 1900 and 1950; grain increases since 1950 are from U.S. Department of Agriculture (USDA), *Production, Supply, and Distribution,* electronic database, Washington, DC, updated October

1998; water increases since 1950 from Sandra Postel, *Last Oasis,* rev. ed. (New York: W.W. Norton & Company, 1997).

16. World War I deaths from Eric Hobsbawm, *The Age of Extremes: A History of the World, 1914–1991* (New York: Vintage Books, 1994); World War II deaths from Ruth Leger Sivard, *World Military and Social Expenditures 1996* (Washington, DC: World Priorities, 1996); historical war casualties from William Eckhardt, "War-Related Deaths Since 3000 BC," *Bulletin of Peace Proposals,* December 1991.

17. Diamond, op. cit. note 4; trade figures from International Monetary Fund (IMF), *World Economic Outlook October 1997* (Washington, DC: 1997), from IMF, *Financial Statistics Yearbook,* November 1997, and from IMF, *International Financial Statistics,* January 1998.

18. Figure 1–1 and population estimates from Haub, op. cit. note 3, and from United Nations, op. cit. note 3.

19. United Nations, op. cit. note 3.

20. Ibid.; Population Reference Bureau, *World Population Data Sheet,* wallchart (Washington, DC: May 1998).

21. United Nations, op. cit. note 3.

22. Joint United Nations Programme on HIV/AIDS and WHO, *Report on the Global HIV/AIDS Epidemic* (Geneva: June 1998); historical plagues from Diamond, op. cit. note 4.

23. Figure 1–2 based on a Worldwatch update of Maddison, op. cit. note 3.

24. Ibid.; Herbert R. Block, *The Planetary Product in 1980: A Creative Pause?* (Washington, DC: U.S. Department of State, 1981).

25. United Nations, op. cit. note 3.

26. FAO, *The Sixth World Food Survey* (Rome: 1996); U.N. Development Programme (UNDP), *Human Development Report 1998* (New York: 1998).

27. Mark Landler, "Living for Rice, Begging for Rice," *New York Times*, 7 September 1998.

28. Ponting, op. cit. note 4.

29. Ibid.

30. Postel, op. cit. note 15.

31. Share of harvest from irrigated land in China from Working Group on Environmental Scientific Research, Technology Development and Training, "The Role of Sustainable Agriculture in China: Environmentally Sound Development," presented at the Fifth Conference of the China Council for International Cooperation on Environment and Development, Shanghai, 23–25 September 1996, and in India from Mark Lindeman, USDA, Foreign Agricultural Service, conversation with Brian Halweil, Worldwatch Institute, 14 December 1997; water table drops and grain share from north China Plain from Liu Yonggong and John B. Penson, Jr., "China's Sustainable Agriculture and Regional Implications," presented to the symposium on Agriculture, Trade and Sustainable Development in Pacific Asia: China and its Trading Partners, Texas A&M University, College Station, TX, 12–14 February 1998; Dennis Engi, China Infrastructure Initiative, Sandia National Laboratory, <http://mason.igaia.sandia.gov/igaia/china/water.html>, viewed 3 November 1998.

32. United Nations, op. cit. note 3; David Seckler, David Molden, and Randolph Barker, "Water Scarcity in the Twenty-First Century" (Colombo, Sri Lanka: International Water Management Institute, 27 July 1998).

33. I.A. Shiklomanov, "World Fresh Water Resources," in Peter H. Gleick, ed., *Water in Crisis: A Guide to the World's Fresh Water Resources* (New York: Oxford University Press, 1993); "Water Scarcity as a Key Factor Behind Global Food Insecurity: Round Table Discussion," *Ambio*, March 1998.

34. FAO, *State of the World's Forests 1997* (Oxford, U.K.: 1997).

35. Cindy Shiner, "Thousands of Fires Ravage Drought-Stricken Borneo," *Washington Post*, 24 April 1998; World Wide Fund for Nature, *The Year the World Caught on Fire*, WWF International Discussion Paper (Gland, Switzerland: December 1997).

36. Anthony Faiola, "Amazon Going Up in Flames," *Washington Post*, 27 April 1998; Molly Moore, "Fires Devastate Mexico," *Washington Post*, 12 April 1998; "The Sky Flashed," *The Economist*, 11 July 1998.

37. FAO, *Yearbook of Fishery Statistics: Catches and Landings* (Rome: various years), with 1990–96 data from FAO, Rome, letters to Worldwatch, 5 and 11 November 1997; 11 of 15 based on Maurizio Perotti, fishery statistician, Fishery Information, Data and Statistics Unit, Fisheries Department, FAO, Rome, e-mail to Worldwatch, 14 October 1997.

38. H. Dregne et al., "A New Assessment of the World Status of Desertification," *Desertification Control Bulletin*, no. 20 (1991).

39. Extinction rates from Chris Bright, *Life Out of Bounds* (New York: W.W. Norton & Company, 1998).

40. Kerry S. Walter and Harriet J. Gillett, eds., *1997 IUCN Red List of Threatened Plants* (Gland, Switzerland: World Conservation Union–IUCN, 1997).

41. Jonathan Baillie and Brian Groombridge, eds., *1996 IUCN Red List of Threatened Animals* (Gland, Switzerland: IUCN, 1996).

42. Bright, op. cit. note 39.

43. Theo Colborn, Dianne Dumanoski, and John Peterson Myers, *Our Stolen Future* (New York: Dutton Books, 1996).

44. J.T. Houghton et al., eds., *Climate Change 1995: The Science of Climate Change,*

Contribution of Working Group I to the Second Assessment Report of the Intergovernmental Panel on Climate Change (IPCC) (New York: Cambridge University Press, 1996); C.D. Keeling and T.P. Whorf, "Atmospheric CO_2 Concentrations (ppmv) Derived From In Situ Air Samples Collected at Mauna Loa Laboratory, Hawaii," Scripps Institution of Oceanography, La Jolla, CA, August 1998; Figure 1–3 from James Hansen et al., Goddard Institute for Space Studies, Surface Air Temperature Analyses, "Global Temperature Anomalies in .01 C, Meteorological Stations Only" and "Global Land-Ocean Temperature Index," <http://www.giss.nasa.gov/Data/GISTEMP>, viewed 25 September 1998, based on data for the first eight months of 1998.

45. Houghton et al., eds., op. cit. note 44; Robert T. Watson, Marufu C. Zinyowera, and Richard H. Moss, eds., *Climate Change 1995: Impacts, Adaptations, and Mitigation of Climate Change: Scientific-Technical Analyses*, Contribution of Working Group II to the Second Assessment Report of the IPCC (New York: Cambridge University Press, 1996); Hadley Centre from Paul Brown, "British Report Forecasts Runaway Global Warming," *Guardian* (London), 3 November 1998.

46. Mathew L. Wald, "Number of Cars is Growing Faster Than Human Population," *New York Times*, 21 September 1997; AAMA, op. cit. note 10; U.S. Department of Energy (DOE), Energy Information Administration (EIA), *Monthly Energy Review* (Washington, DC: September 1998).

47. USDA, op. cit. note 15.

48. BTM Consult ApS, *Ten Percent of the World's Electricity Consumption from Wind Energy!*, prepared for Forum for Energy & Development (Ringkobing, Denmark: October 1998); Esteban Morrás, Energía Hidroeléctrica de Navarra, Pamplona, Spain, discussion with Christopher Flavin, 23 October 1998; D.L. Elliott, L.L. Windell, and G.L. Gower, *An Assessment of the Available Windy Land Area and Wind Energy Potential in the Contiguous United States* (Richland, WA: Pacific Northwest Laboratory, 1991).

49. Christopher Flavin and Molly O'Meara, "Solar Power Markets Boom," *World Watch*, September/October 1998.

50. Table 1–2 based on the following: wind from Birger Madsen, BTM Consult, Ringkobing, Denmark, letter to Christopher Flavin, 10 January 1998, and from BTM Consult, *International Wind Energy Development: World Market Update 1996* (Ringkobing, Denmark: March 1997); solar photovoltaics data from Paul Maycock, "1997 World Cell/Module Shipments," *PV News*, February 1998, and from Paul Maycock, *PV News*, various issues; geothermal power data from Mary Dickson, International Institute for Geothermal Research, letter to Seth Dunn, Worldwatch Institute, 3 February 1997, and from Mary H. Dickson and Mario Fanelli, "Geothermal Energy Worldwide," *World Directory of Renewable Energy Suppliers and Services* (London: James & James Science Publishers, 1995); natural gas and oil use data from DOE, EIA, *International Energy Annual 1996* (Washington, DC: February 1998), and from BP, op. cit. note 9; hydropower and coal use data from United Nations, *Energy Statistics Yearbook 1995* (New York: 1997), and from BP, op. cit. note 9; nuclear power from Worldwatch Institute database. Wind potential in four countries from Madsen, op. cit. this note.

51. BP, "BP HSE Facts 1997: HSE," <http://www.bp.com>, viewed 24 August 1998; Jeroen van der Veer, Group Managing Director, Royal Dutch/Shell Group, "Shell International Renewables—Bringing Together the Group's Activities in Solar Power, Biomass, and Forestry," press conference, London, 6 October 1997; Colin J. Campbell and Jean H. Laherrere, "The End of Cheap Oil," *Scientific American*, March 1998.

52. Robert F. Service, "A Record in Converting Photons to Fuel," *Science*, 17 April 1998; "First World Hydrogen Conference

Opens in Latin America, Shell Is Briefed on Hydrogen," *Hydrogen & Fuel Cell Letter*, July 1998; Jacques Leslie, "Dawn of the Hydrogen Age," *Wired*, October 1997.

53. Bicycle production from "Focus on Foreign Markets," *1998 Interbike Directory* (Laguna Beach, CA: Miller-Freeman, 1998); AAMA, *World Motor Vehicle Data 1997* (Detroit, MI: 1997); AAMA, op. cit. note 10.

54. Elisabeth Rosenthal, "Tide of Traffic Turns Against the Sea of Bicycles," *New York Times*, 3 November 1998; Indonesia from "Living Dangerously," *Sustainable Transport*, summer 1996.

55. Patrick E. Tyler, "China Transport Gridlock: Cars vs. Mass Transit," *New York Times*, 4 May 1996.

56. OECD, "OECD Environment Ministers Shared Goals For Action," press release (Paris: 3 April 1998), <http://www.oecd.org/news_and_events/release/nw98-39a.htm>; Interface from Braden R. Allenby, *Industrial Ecology: Framework and Implementation* (Upper Saddle River, NJ: Prentice Hall, 1999).

57. Stephan Schmidheiny with the Business Council for Sustainable Development, *Changing Course* (Cambridge, MA: The MIT Press, 1992); William McDonough and Michael Braungart, "The Next Industrial Revolution," *Atlantic Monthly*, October 1998.

58. Greg Helten, "Canadian Timber Giant Renounces Clearcut Logging," *Environmental News Service*, 11 June 1998.

59. Ford cited in David Bjerklie et al., "Look Who's Trying to Turn Green," *Time*, 9 November 1998; Thomas R. Casten, *Turning Off the Heat: Why America Must Double Energy Efficiency to Save Money and Reduce Global Warming* (Amherst, NY: Prometheus Books, 1998).

60. Jose Maria Figueres, President of Costa Rica, address to Third Conference of the Parties of the UN Framework Convention on Climate Change, Kyoto, Japan, 8 December 1997; "Energy Market Report," *Financial Times Energy Economist*, October 1997; "Forestry Cuts Down on Logging," *China Daily*, 26 May 1998; Peter Norman, "SPD and Greens Agree German Energy Tax Rises," *Financial Times*, 19 October 1998.

61. "Special Double Issue on the 21st Century Economy," *Business Week*, 31 August 1998.

62. UNDP, op. cit. note 26.

63. Forbes estimates are described in ibid.

64. "Nigeria: A Catastrophe Bound to Happen," *The Economist*, 24 October 1998.

65. United Nations, op. cit. note 3.

66. United Nations, "United Nations Launches Fiftieth Anniversary of the Universal Declaration of Human Rights," press release, New York, 5 December 1997.

Chapter 2. Reinventing the Energy System

1. Dave Walter, ed., *Today Then: America's Best Minds Look 100 Years Into the Future on the Occasion of the 1893 World's Columbian Exposition* (Helena, MT: American & World Geographic Publishing, 1992); David E. Nye, *Electrifying America: Social Meanings of a New Technology, 1880–1940* (Cambridge, MA: The MIT Press, 1990); Sam H. Schurr and Bruce C. Netschert, *Energy in the American Economy, 1850–1975* (Baltimore, MD: Johns Hopkins University Press, 1960).

2. Edward Tenner, *Why Things Bite Back: Technology and the Revenge of Unintended Consequences* (New York: Vintage Books, 1996); Walter, op. cit. note 1.

3. Vaclav Smil, *Energy in World History* (Oxford, U.K.: Westview Press, 1994); Martha Hamilton, "Oil Prices Hit Lowest Level in 10 Years," *Washington Post*, 18 March 1998; Gary

McWilliams, "Living in a World of Cheap Oil," *Business Week*, 30 March 1998; Daniel Yergin, "Fueling Asia's Recovery," *Foreign Affairs*, March/April 1998; Ruth Daniloff, "Waiting for the Oil Boom," *Smithsonian*, January 1998; "Oil Drums Calling," *The Economist*, 7 February 1998; Ahmed Rashid and Trish Saywell, "Beijing Gusher," *Far Eastern Economic Review*, 26 February 1998.

4. Table 2–1 based on International Institute of Applied Systems Analysis (IIASA) data in Arnulf Grubler, Alan McDonald, and Nebojsa Nakicenovic, eds., *Global Energy Perspectives* (New York: Cambridge University Press, 1998), on John P. Holdren et al., *Federal Energy Research and Development for the Challenges of the Twenty-First Century*, Report of the Energy Research and Development Panel of the President's Committee of Advisors on Science and Technology (Washington, DC: November 1997), on United Nations, *Energy Statistics Yearbook 1995* (New York: 1997), and on British Petroleum (BP), *BP Statistical Review of World Energy 1998* (London: Group Media & Publications, June 1998); Martin V. Melosi, *Coping With Abundance: Energy and Environment in Industrial America* (New York: Newberry Award Records, Inc., 1985); Daniel Yergin, *The Prize: The Epic Quest for Oil, Money, and Power* (New York: Simon and Schuster, 1991).

5. Ernst von Weizsacker et al., *Factor Four: Doubling Wealth—Halving Resource Use* (London: Earthscan Publications, 1996); Thomas B. Johansson et al., eds., *Renewable Energy: Sources for Fuels and Electricity* (Washington, DC: Island Press, 1993); Peter Hoffmann, *The Forever Fuel: The Story of Hydrogen* (Boulder, CO: Westview Press, 1981).

6. Smil, op. cit. note 3; Vaclav Smil, *General Energetics: Energy in the Biosphere and Civilization* (New York: John Wiley & Sons, 1991).

7. Smil, op. cit. note 3; U.N. Development Programme (UNDP), *Energy After Rio* (New York: 1997).

8. Jean-Claude Debeir, *In the Servitude of Power: Energy and Civilization Through the Ages* (London: Zed Books, 1991); Martin V. Melosi, "Energy Transitions in the Nineteenth-Century Economy," in George H. Daniels and Mark H. Rose, eds., *Energy and Transport: Historical Perspectives on Policy Issues* (London: Sage Publications, 1982).

9. Holdren et al., op. cit. note 4; BP, op. cit. note 4; Smil, op. cit. note 3.

10. Colin J. Campbell and Jean H. Laherrere, "The End of Cheap Oil," *Scientific American*, March 1998.

11. Ibid.; Figure 2–1 based on U.S. Department of Defense, *Twentieth Century Petroleum Statistics* (Washington, DC: 1945), and on U.S. Department of Energy (DOE), Energy Information Administration (EIA), *International Energy Database*, <http://www.eia.doe.gov/emeu/international/contents.html>, viewed 21 August 1998.

12. Campbell and Laherrere, op. cit. note 10; Richard A. Kerr, "The Next Oil Crisis Looms Large—and Perhaps Close," *Science*, 21 August 1998; Scott Baldauf, "World's Oil May Soon Run Low," *Christian Science Monitor*, 23 September 1998; Worldwatch Institute estimate based on BP, op. cit. note 4.

13. Smil, op. cit. note 3; UNDP, op. cit. note 7; George Basalla, "Some Persistent Energy Myths," in Daniels and Rose, op. cit. note 8; Melosi, op. cit. note 4; World Health Organization, U.N. Environment Programme, and Earthwatch Global Environment Monitoring System, *Urban Air Pollution in Megacities of the World* (Cambridge: MA: Blackwell, 1992); World Bank, *Clear Water, Blue Skies: China in 2020* (Washington, DC: 1997); Elisabeth Rosenthal, "China Officially Lifts Filter on Staggering Pollution Data," *New York Times*, 14 June 1998.

14. Vaclav Smil, *Cycles of Life: Civilization and the Biosphere* (New York: Scientific American Library, 1997); Figure 2–2 and car-

bon dioxide data from Thomas A. Boden et al., *Trends '93: A Compendium of Data on Global Change* (Oak Ridge, TN: Oak Ridge National Laboratory, September 1994), from J.T. Houghton et al., eds., *Climate Change 1995: The Science of Climate Change*, Contribution of Working Group I to the Second Assessment Report of the Intergovernmental Panel on Climate Change (IPCC) (New York: Cambridge University Press, 1996), and from C.D. Keeling and T.P. Whorf, "Atmospheric CO_2 Concentrations (ppmv) Derived From In Situ Air Samples Collected at Mauna Loa Observatory, Hawaii," Scripps Institution of Oceanography, La Jolla, CA, August 1998; Robert T. Watson, Marufu C. Zinyowera, and Richard H. Moss, eds., *Climate Change 1995: Impacts, Adaptations, and Mitigation of Climate Change: Scientific-Technical Analyses*, Contribution of Working Group II to the Second Assessment Report of the IPCC (New York: Cambridge University Press, 1996); Michael E. Mann, Raymond S. Bradley, and Malcolm K. Hughes, "Global-Scale Temperature Patterns and Climate Forcing Over the Past Six Centuries," *Nature*, 23 April 1998.

15. Watson, Zinyowera, and Moss, op. cit. note 14; Molly O'Meara, "The Risks of Climate Change," *World Watch*, November/December 1997; James Hansen et al., Goddard Institute for Space Studies, Surface Air Temperature Analyses, "Global Land-Ocean Temperature Index," <http:// www.giss.nasa.gov/Data/ GISTEMP>, viewed 25 September 1998; J. Madeleine Nash, "The Fury of El Niño," *U.S. News & World Report*, 16 February 1998; Molly Moore, "Fires Devastate Mexico," *Washington Post*, 12 April 1998; Elisabeth Rosenthal, "Millions Wait for Flood Relief in North China," *New York Times*, 31 August 1998; Celia W. Dugger, "Monsoon Hangs On, Swamping Bangladesh," *New York Times*, 7 September 1998; William K. Stevens, "Warmer, Wetter, Sicker: Linking Climate to Health," *New York Times*, 10 August 1998; Sharon Begley, "Hell Niño," *Newsweek*, 9 March 1998; "The Season of El Niño," *The Economist*, 9 May 1998; Nigel Hawkes, "A Sunless Summer? It's the

Weather's Fault," *The Times* (London), 3 August 1998; Stevens, op. cit. this note; William K. Stevens, "If the Climate Changes, It May Do So Fast, New Data Show," *New York Times*, 27 January 1998; William B. Calvin, "The Great Climate Flip-flop," *Atlantic Monthly*, January 1998; Richard B. Alley and Peter B. deMenocal, "Abrupt Climate Changes Revisited: How Serious and How Likely?" U.S. Global Change Seminar Series, Washington, DC, 23 February 1998.

16. Nebojsa Nakicenovic, "Freeing Energy From Carbon," in Jesse H. Ausubel and H. Dale Langford, eds., *Technological Trajectories and the Human Environment* (Washington, DC: National Academy Press, 1997); Houghton et al., op. cit. note 14; Joby Warrick, "Reassessing Kyoto Agreement, Scientists See Little Environmental Advantage," *Washington Post*, 13 February 1998; Bert Bolin, "The Kyoto Negotiations on Climate Change: A Science Perspective," *Science*, 16 January 1998.

17. Melosi, op. cit. note 8; George Basalla, *The Evolution of Technology* (Cambridge, U.K.: Cambridge University Press, 1988).

18. Anne Goodman, "Bringing Down the Power Lines," *Tomorrow*, September/October 1998.

19. UNDP, op. cit. note 7; DOE, EIA, *International Energy Outlook 1998* (Washington, DC: April 1998); Arnold Pacey, *Technology in World Civilization: A Thousand-Year History* (Cambridge: The MIT Press, 1990); Melosi, op. cit. note 8.

20. Pacey, op. cit. note 19; Basalla, op. cit. note 17.

21. Holdren et al., op. cit. note 4; World Resources Institute (WRI), *Taking A Byte Out of Carbon* (Washington, DC: 1998); Barry Fox, "Stand By For Savings," *New Scientist*, 11 July 1998.

22. DOE, *Scenarios of U.S. Carbon Reductions: Potential Impacts of Energy Technologies by 2010*

and Beyond (Washington, DC: 1997); Holdren et al., op. cit. note 4.

23. DOE, op. cit. note 22; Nils Borg, "New Ballast May Start CFL Revolution," *International Association for Energy-Efficient Lighting Newsletter*, January 1998; Margaret Suozzo, *A Market Opportunity Assessment for LED Traffic Signals* (Washington, DC: American Council for an Energy-Efficient Economy, April 1998).

24. Pacey, op. cit. note 19; Smil, op. cit. note 3; Holdren et al., op. cit. note 4; DOE, op. cit. note 22; Electric Power Research Institute, *Renewable Energy Technology Characterizations* (Palo Alto, CA: December 1997); $2 billion (Worldwatch estimate) and Figure 2–3 based on Birger Madsen, BTM Consult, Ringkobing, Denmark, letter to Christopher Flavin, 10 January 1998, and on BTM Consult, *International Wind Energy Development: World Market Update 1996* (Ringkobing, Denmark: March 1997).

25. Christopher Flavin and Molly O'Meara, "Solar Power Markets Boom," *World Watch*, September/October 1998; Daniel McQuillen, "Harnessing the Sun," *Environmental Design and Construction*, July/August 1998; Figure 2–4 from Paul Maycock, "1997 World Cell/Module Shipments," *PV News*, February 1998, and from Paul Maycock, *PV News*, various issues; Flavin and O'Meara, op. cit. this note; Timothy J. Coutts and Mark C. Fitzgerald, "Thermophotovoltaics," *Scientific American*, September 1998.

26. Anthony DePalma, "The Great Green Hope," *New York Times*, 8 October 1997; Hoffmann, op. cit. note 5; Kenneth Gooding, "Fuel Cells More Than a Dream," *Financial Times*, 3 September 1998; Holdren et al., op. cit. note 4; Stuart F. Brown, "The Automakers' Big-Time Bet on Fuel Cells," *Fortune*, 30 March 1998.

27. James S. Cannon, *Harnessing Hydrogen: The Key to Sustainable Transportation* (New York: INFORM, Inc., 1995); Peter Hadfield and

Rebecca Warden, "Catalysts for Change," *New Scientist*, 28 February 1998; Robert F. Service, "A Record in Converting Photons to Fuel," *Science*, 17 April 1998; Oscar Khaselev and John A. Turner, "A Monolithic Photovoltaic-Photoelectrochemical Device for Hydrogen Production via Water Splitting," *Science*, 17 April 1998; Robert F. Service, "The Fast Way to a Better Fuel Cell," *Science*, 12 June 1998; Erik Reddington et al., "Combinatorial Electrochemistry: A Highly Parallel, Optical Screening Method for Discovery of Better Electrocatalysts," *Science*, 12 June 1998; Holdren et al., op. cit. note 4.

28. William J. Abernathy and Kenneth Wayne, "Limits of the Learning Curve," *Harvard Business Review*, September-October 1974.

29. Melosi, op. cit. note 4; Joseph A. Pratt, "The Ascent of Oil: The Transition from Coal to Oil in Early Twentieth-Century America," in Lewis J. Perelman et al., eds., *Energy Transitions: Long-Term Perspectives* (Boulder, CO: Westview Press, 1981); Flavin and O'Meara, op. cit. note 25; James S. Cannon, *Clean Hydrogen Transportation: A Market Opportunity for Renewable Energy*, Issue Brief No. 7 (Washington, DC: Renewable Energy Policy Project, April 1997); Gerard L. Cler and Michael Shepard, "Distributed Generation: Good Things Are Coming in Small Packages," *E Source Tech Update*, November 1996; Gerard Cler and Nicholas Lenssen, *Distributed Generation: Markets and Technologies in Transition* (Boulder, CO: E Source, December 1997); Shalom Zelingher, "Sewage and the Fuel Cell," *Public Power*, January-February 1998; Otis Port, "With These Gizmos, Your Cell Phone Can Run On Vodka," *Business Week*, 16 February 1998; Jonathan Beard, "Carry On Talking," *New Scientist*, 7 February 1998; Alden M. Hayashi, "Taking On the Energizer Bunny," *Scientific American*, April 1998; DePalma, op. cit. note 26.

30. Cler and Lenssen, op. cit. note 29; Richard F. Hirsch, *Technology and Trans-*

formation in the American Electric Utility Industry (New York: Cambridge University Press, 1989); DOE, op. cit. note 22.

31. DOE, op. cit. note 22; WRI, op. cit. note 21; Holdren et al., op. cit. note 4.

32. Ken Butti and John Perlin, A *Golden Thread: 2500 Years of Solar Architecture and Technology* (New York: Van Nostrand Reinhold, 1980); Nye, op. cit. note 1; William D. Siuru, Jr., "Backyard Power Production," *Public Power*, July-August 1998; Jacques Leslie, "Dawn of the Hydrogen Age," *Wired*, October 1997; DOE, op. cit. note 22; von Weizsacker et al., op. cit. note 5; Holdren et al., op. cit. note 4.

33. Michael Shnayerson, *The Car That Could: The Inside Story of GM's Revolutionary Electric Vehicle* (New York: Random House, 1996); Amory Lovins, "Halfway to Hypercars," *Rocky Mountain Institute Newsletter*, Spring 1998; Keith Naughton, "Detroit's Impossible Dream?" *Business Week*, 2 March 1998; William J. Cook, "Piston Engine, R.I.P.?" *U.S. News & World Report*, 11 May 1998; "Is Toyota's Hybrid for the U.S. Road?" (editorial), *New York Times*, 1 August 1998; "Toyota Plans Gas/Electric Hybrid for North America, Europe by 2000," *Wall Street Journal Interactive Edition*, 14 July 1998; "Space-age Cabs," *Economist*, 1 August 1998; Holdren et al., op. cit. note 4.

34. DOE, op. cit. note 22.

35. Holdren et al., op. cit. note 4; A.C. Dillon et al., "Storage of Hydrogen in Single-Walled Carbon Nanotubes," *Nature*, 27 March 1997; Cannon, op. cit. note 29; Robert Socolow, ed., *Fuels Decarbonization and Carbon Sequestration: Report of a Workshop*, Report No. 302 (Princeton, NJ: Princeton Center for Energy and Environmental Studies, September 1997); David Schneider, "Burying the Problem," *Scientific American*, January 1998.

36. Adam Serchuk and Robert Means, *Natural Gas: Bridge to a Renewable Energy Future*, Issue Brief No. 8 (Washington, DC: Renewable Energy Policy Project, May 1997); DOE, op.

cit. note 22; Leslie, op. cit. note 32; Michael Fitzpatrick, "Fuelled for the 21st Century," *Financial Times*, 5 October 1998; Pratt, op. cit. note 29.

37. Nye, op. cit. note 1; Schurr and Netschert, op. cit. note 1; Melosi, op. cit. note 4; Schurr and Netschert, op. cit. note 1; Nye, op. cit. note 1.

38. Ron Chernow, *Titan: The Life of John D. Rockefeller, Sr.* (New York: Random House, 1998).

39. Ibid.; Yergin, op. cit. note 4.

40. James J. Flink, *The Automobile Age* (Cambridge, MA: The MIT Press, 1988).

41. Melosi, op. cit. note 4; Hirsch, op. cit. note 30.

42. Chernow, op. cit. note 38.

43. Brad Knickerbocker, "Autos, 'Big Oil' Get Earth-Friendly," *Christian Science Monitor*, 6 October 1998; Kate Murphy, "Fighting Pollution—And Cleaning Up, Too," *Business Week*, 9 January 1998; "GE Power Systems, Plug Power Form New Worldwide Fuel Cell Joint Marketing Venture," *Hydrogen & Fuel Cell Letter*, October 1998; Cler and Lenssen, op. cit. note 29.

44. Daniel Yergin, *The Commanding Heights: The Battle Between Government and Marketplace That Is Remaking the Modern World* (New York: Simon & Schuster, 1998); Cler and Lenssen, op. cit. note 29; Thomas R. Casten, *Turning Off The Heat: Why America Must Double Energy Efficiency to Save Money and Reduce Global Warming* (Amherst, NY: Prometheus Books, 1998); Yergin, op. cit. this note.

45. "The Balance of Power," *The Economist*, 6 June 1998; UNDP, op. cit. note 7.

46. Shimon Awerbuch and Alistair Preston, eds., *The Virtual Utility: Accounting, Technology and Competitive Aspects of the Emerging Industry* (Boston: Kluwer Academic Publishers, 1997);

Karl R. Rábago, "Being Virtual: Beyond Restructuring and How We Get There," in ibid.

47. Lori M. Rodgers, "Green Electricity: It's In the Eye of the Beholder," *Public Utilities Fortnightly*, 15 February 1998; Ryan H. Wiser and Steven J. Pickle, *Selling Green Power in California: Product, Industry, and Market Trends* (Berkeley, CA: Lawrence Berkeley National Laboratory, May 1998); Ryan Wiser, Steven Pickle, and Charles Goldman, "Renewable Energy Policy and Electricity Restructuring: A California Case Study," *Energy Policy*, May 1998; Seth Dunn, "Green Power Spreads to California," *World Watch*, July/August 1998.

48. Pratt, op. cit. note 29.

49. UNDP, op. cit. note 7; David Mosvokitz et al., "What Consumers Need to Know if Competition is Going to Work," *The Electricity Journal*, June 1998.

50. Shnayerson, op. cit. note 33; Holdren et al., op. cit. note 4; CALSTART, *Electric Vehicles: An Industry Prospectus* (Burbank, CA: 1996); Cook, op. cit. note 33; Donald W. Nauss, "Car Mergers Propelled By Technology," *Los Angeles Times*, 18 May 1998.

51. David C. Moschella, *Waves of Power: Dynamics of Global Technology Leadership, 1964–2010* (New York: AMACOM, 1997); Chernow, op. cit. note 38.

52. Yergin, op. cit. note 4.

53. David S. Landes, *The Wealth and Poverty of Nations: Why Some Nations Are So Rich and Some So Poor* (New York: W.W. Norton & Company, 1998); Mortimer B. Zuckerman, "A Second American Century," *Foreign Affairs*, May/June 1998; Yergin, op. cit. note 4.

54. Holdren et al., op. cit. note 4; Martin I. Hoffert et al., "Energy Implications of Future Stabilization of Atmospheric CO_2 Content," *Nature*, 29 October 1998.

55. John Browne, "International Relations: The New Agenda for Business," The 1998 Elliott Lecture, St. Antony's College, Oxford University, 4 June 1998; Knickerbocker, op. cit. note 43; "Detroit Turns a Corner" (editorial), *New York Times*, 1 January 1998.

56. International Energy Agency (IEA), *Renewable Energy Policy in IEA Countries*, Vol. I (Paris: 1997); David Malin Roodman, *The Natural Wealth of Nations* (New York: W.W. Norton & Company, 1998).

57. John V. Mitchell, *The New Geopolitics of Energy* (London: Royal Institute of International Affairs, 1996); Peter Kassler and Matthew Paterson, *Energy Exporters and Climate Change* (London: Royal Institute of International Affairs, 1997); Martha Brill Olcott, "The Caspian's False Promise," *Foreign Policy*, summer 1998; Holdren et al., op. cit. note 4.

58. Mitchell, op. cit. note 57.

59. Holdren et al., op. cit. note 4; Soren Krohn, managing director, Danish Wind Turbine Manufacturing Association, discussion with Christopher Flavin, 7 November 1998.

60. UNDP, op. cit. note 7; Pacey, op. cit. note 19; Felipe Fernandez-Armesto, *Millennium: A History of the Last Thousand Years* (New York: Scribner, 1995); Jared Diamond, *Guns, Germs, and Steel: The Fates of Human Societies* (New York: W.W. Norton & Company, 1997).

61. Peter Hoffmann, "Iceland and Daimler-Benz/Ballard Start Plans for Hydrogen Economy," *Hydrogen & Fuel Cell Letter*, June 1998.

62. Debeir, op. cit. note 8.

63. Ibid.; Landes, op. cit. note 53; Langdon Winner, "Energy Regimes," in Daniels and Rose, op. cite note 8.

64. Chernow, op. cit. note 38; *Fortune Magazine*, "The Global 500 List," as viewed at

<http://www.pathfinder.com/fortune/global500/index.html>, viewed 26 August 1998; "Fortune 500 Largest Corporations," *Fortune*, 27 April 1998; World Bank, *1998 World Bank Atlas* (Washington, DC: 1998), with comparison between companies and countries based on exchange rate values, not purchasing power parity.

65. Ross Gelbspan, "A Good Climate For Investment," *Atlantic Monthly*, June 1998; John H. Cushman, Jr., "Industrial Group Plans to Battle Climate Treaty," *New York Times*, 26 April 1998; Shnayerson, op. cit. note 33; Sara Knight, "Bonn Brought to Standstill," *Windpower Monthly*, October 1997.

66. Martha M. Hamilton, "Shell Leaves Coalition That Opposes Global Warming Treaty," *Washington Post*, 22 April 1998; John H. Cushman, Jr., "New Policy Center Seeks to Steer the Debate on Climate Change," *New York Times*, 8 May 1998; Knight, op. cit. note 65; Carl Frankel, "Trends and Challenges," *Tomorrow*, January/February 1998.

67. Lewis J. Perelman, "Speculations on the Transition to Sustainable Energy," in Perelman et al., op. cit. note 29; Jan Bentzen, Valdemar Smith, and Mogens Dilling-Hansen, "Regional Income Effects and Renewable Fuels," *Energy Policy*, April 1998; Jesper Munksgaard and Anders Larsen, "Socio-Economic Assessment of Wind Power—Lessons from Denmark," *Energy Policy*, February 1998; UNDP, op. cit. note 7.

68. UNDP, op. cit. note 7; UNDP, *Human Development Report 1998* (New York: Oxford University Press, 1998).

69. Holdren et al., op. cit. note 4; Nye, op. cit. note 1; UNDP, op. cit. note 68; UNDP, op. cit. note 7; World Bank, *Rural Energy and Development: Improving Energy Supplies for Two Billion People* (Washington, DC: 1996); Douglas Barnes, Karl Jechowtek, and Andrew Young, "Financing Decentralized Renewable Energy: New Approaches?" *Energy Issues*, October 1998.

70. Smil, op. cit. note 3; IEA, *Indicators of Energy Use and Efficiency* (Paris: 1997); Allen R. Myerson, "U.S. Splurging on Energy After Falling Off Its Diet," *New York Times*, 22 October 1998.

71. David E. Nye, *Consuming Power: A Social History of American Energies* (Cambridge, MA: The MIT Press, 1998); Figure 2–5 based on IIASA, op. cit. note 4, and on BP, op. cit. note 4.

72. Howard T. Odum, *Environment, Power, and Society* (New York: John Wiley & Sons, 1971); Smil, op. cit. note 3; UNDP, op. cit. note 68.

73. Daniel Yergin, *Russia 2010—And What It Means for the World* (New York: Random House, 1993).

74. Earl Cook, *Man, Energy, Society* (New York: W.H. Freeman and Company, 1976); Holdren et al., op. cit. note 4; Smil, op. cit. note 6; Jack M. Hollander, ed., *The Energy-Environment Connection* (Washington, DC: Island Press, 1992); Clive Ponting, *A Green History of the World: The Environment and the Collapse of Great Civilizations* (New York: Penguin Books, 1991); Smil, op. cit. note 3.

75. Yergin, op. cit. note 4; Basalla, "Some Persistent Energy Myths," in Daniels and Rose, op. cit. note 8; Nye, op. cit. note 1; Edward Bellamy, *Looking Backward, 2000–1887* (New York: Penguin Books, reissue 1982).

Chapter 3. Forging a Sustainable Materials Economy

1. Based on data from World Resources Institute (WRI) et al., *Resource Flows: The Material Basis of Industrial Economies* (Washington, DC: WRI, 1997); revised data supplied by Eric Rodenburg, WRI, Washington, DC, e-mail to Payal Sampat, 10 October 1998. The 10 billion tons of materials used in the United States each year includes

both hidden and economically recorded flows. Hidden flows of materials include "overburden" earth that has to be moved to reach metal and mineral ores, as well as the unused portion of mined ore. Data throughout the chapter refer only to materials that enter the economy (roughly a third of all flows in the United States) except where otherwise stated. This includes all nonfuel and nonfood materials, namely minerals, metals, wood products, and fossil-fuel-based synthetic substances—such as plastics and asphalt—which are referred to throughout the chapter as synthetic materials. Although central to the discussion, global data for hidden flows are not available.

2.   U.S. consumption from United States Geological Survey (USGS), *Mineral Yearbook and Mineral Commodity Summaries* (Reston, VA: various years), and from data supplied by Grecia Matos, Minerals and Materials Analysis Section, USGS, Reston, VA, 27 July 1998.

3.   Periodic table from U.S. Congress, Office of Technology Assessment (OTA), *Green Products by Design: Choices for a Cleaner Environment* (Washington, DC: U.S Government Printing Office, September 1992); materials throughput from Robert U. Ayres, "Industrial Metabolism," in *Technology and Environment* (Washington, DC: National Academy Press, 1989).

4.   Mining contamination from Mineral Policy Center (MPC), *Golden Dreams, Poisoned Streams* (Washington, DC: 1997); synthetic chemicals from European Environment Agency (EEA), *Europe's Environment: The Second Assessment* (Luxembourg and Oxford, U.K.: Office for Official Publications of the European Communities and Elsevier Science Ltd., 1998).

5.   Peter N. Stearns, *The Industrial Revolution in World History* (Boulder, CO: Westview Press, 1993).

6.   Iron and steel technologies from David Landes, *The Unbound Prometheus: Technological*

Change and Industrial Development in Western Europe from 1750 to the Present (Cambridge, U.K.: Cambridge University Press, 1969), from Nathan Rosenberg, "Technology," in Glenn Porter, ed., *Encyclopedia of American Economic History: Studies of Principal Movements and Ideas*, vol. 1 (New York: Charles Scribner's Sons, 1980), and from Stephen L. Sass, *The Substance of Civilization: Materials and Human History from the Stone Age to the Age of Silicon* (New York: Arcade Publishing, 1998); historical production data from Metallgesellschaft AG and World Bureau of Metal Statistics, *MetallStatistik/Metal Statistics 1985–1995* (Frankfurt and Ware, U.K.: 1996), and from Metallgesellschaft AG, *Statistical Tables* (Frankfurt: various years); share of metals and materials from Great Britain Overseas Geological Survey, *Statistical Survey of the Mineral Industry: World Mineral Production, Imports and Exports* (London: various years), from USGS, op. cit. note 2, and from Matos, op. cit. note 2.

7.   Rosenberg, op. cit. note 6; Clive Ponting, *A Green History of the World: The Environment and the Collapse of Great Civilizations* (New York: Penguin Books, 1991); ore grades from Daniel Edelstein, Copper Commodity Specialist, USGS, discussions with Payal Sampat, 6 and 19 October 1998.

8.   Canada and Liberia from Stearns, op. cit. note 5; oil expansion from Joseph A. Pratt, "The Ascent of Oil: The Transition from Coal to Oil in Early Twentieth-Century America," in Lewis J. Perelman et al., eds., *Energy Transitions: Long-Term Perspectives* (Boulder, CO: Westview Press, 1981); declining energy prices from British Petroleum, *BP Statistical Review of World Energy* (London: June 1998); materials prices from data supplied by Betty Dow, World Bank, Washington, DC, e-mail to Payal Sampat, 8 October 1998.

9.   U.S. mining law from Charles Wilkinson, *Crossing the Next Meridian: Land, Water and the Future of the West* (Washington, DC: Island Press, 1992); Indonesia from

Charles Victor Barber, Nels C. Johnson, and Emmy Hafild, *Breaking the Logjam* (Washington, DC: WRI, 1994); Ghana from George J. Coakley, "The Mineral Industry of Ghana," *Minerals Information* (Reston, VA: USGS, 1996); Peru from Alfredo C. Gurmendi, "The Mineral Industry of Peru," *Minerals Information* (Reston, VA: USGS, 1996); logging roads from David Malin Roodman, *The Natural Wealth of Nations* (New York: W.W. Norton & Company, 1998).

10. Musket-making from Adam Markham, "The First Consumer Revolution," in *A Brief History of Pollution* (New York: St. Martin's Press, 1994); Ford from Thomas McCraw and Richard S. Tedlow, "Henry Ford, Alfred Sloan, and the Three Phases of Marketing," in Thomas McCraw, ed. *Creating Modern Capitalism* (Cambridge, MA: Harvard University Press, 1997), and from Vaclav Smil, *Energy in World History* (Boulder, CO: Westview Press, 1994).

11. Creation of consumer class from W.W. Rostow, "The Age of High Mass Consumption," in B. Hughel Wilkins and Charles B. Friday, eds., *The Economists of the New Frontier* (New York: Random House, 1963), and from Arthur M. Johnson, "Economy Since 1914," in Porter, op. cit. note 6; Ford wage increase from McCraw and Tedlow, op. cit. note 10; historian Witold Rybczynski quoted in Markham, op. cit. note 10; opposition of other employers from Juliet B. Schor, T*he Overworked American* (New York: Basic Books, 1991).

12. Department stores and catalogs from Markham, op. cit. note 10; consumer credit from Schor, op. cit. note 11; DuPont vice-president J.W. McCoy quoted in Jeffrey L. Meikle, *American Plastics: A Cultural History* (New Brunswick, NJ: Rutgers University Press, 1997); global advertising from U.N. Development Programme (UNDP), *Human Development Report 1998* (New York: Oxford University Press, 1998).

13. Aluminum use historically from Smil, op. cit. note 10, and from Ivan Amato, *Stuff: The Materials the World is Made Of* (New York: Basic Books, 1997); aluminum production from Metallgesellschaft AG and World Bureau of Metal Statistics, op. cit. note 6; plastics production from United Nations, *Industrial Commodity Statistics Yearbook* (New York: various years), and from data supplied by Matos, op. cit. note 2; plastics uses from Meikle, op. cit. note 12; chemical compounds from EEA, op. cit. note 4; synthetic chemicals production from Jennifer D. Mitchell, "Nowhere to Hide: The Global Spread of Synthetic, High-Risk Chemicals," *World Watch*, March/April 1997.

14. Military to consumer products switch from Robert Friedel, "Scarcity and Promise: Materials and American Domestic Culture During World War II," in Donald Albrecht, ed., *World War II and the American Dream: How Wartime Building Changed a Nation* (Washington, DC, and Cambridge, MA: National Building Museum and The MIT Press, 1995); Japanese consumer goods from Ponting, op. cit. note 7; car ownership from Seth Dunn, "Automobile Production Sets Record," in Lester Brown, Michael Renner, and Christopher Flavin, *Vital Signs 1998* (New York: W.W. Norton & Company, 1998); materials use in cars from Gregory A. Keoleian et al., *Industry Ecology of the Automobile: A Life Cycle Perspective* (Warrendale, PA: Society of Automotive Engineers, Inc., 1997).

15. Smil, op. cit. note 10; cement and asphalt from United Nations, op. cit. note 13; extensive development from Sierra Club, *The Costs and Consequences of Suburban Sprawl* (San Francisco: 1998); materials consequences from Scott Bernstein, Center for Neighborhood Technology, Chicago, discussion with Gary Gardner, 20 August 1998.

16. Paper and glass recycling from Organisation for Economic Co-operation and Development (OECD), *OECD Environmental Data Compendium 1997* (Paris: 1997); metals from Michael McKinley, Chief, Metals Section,

Minerals Information Team, USGS, discussion with Payal Sampat, 2 November 1998.

17. Table 3–1 and Figure 3–1 from Great Britain Overseas Geological Survey, op. cit. note 6, from USGS, op. cit. note 2, from Matos, op. cit. note 2, from United Nations, op. cit. note 13, and from U.N. Food and Agriculture Organization, *FAOSTAT Statistics Database*, <http://faostat.fao.org/>, viewed 15 June 1998.

18. Synthetic materials from United Nations, op. cit. note 13; historical metals data from Metallgesellschaft AG and World Bureau of Metal Statistics, op. cit. note 6.

19. U.S. historical data supplied by Matos, op. cit. note 2; world total from Great Britain Overseas Geological Survey, op. cit. note 6, from USGS, op. cit. note 2, and from Matos, op. cit. note 2; global model from Richard R. Wilk, "Emulation and Global Consumerism," in Paul C. Stern et al., eds., *Environmentally Significant Consumption* (Washington, DC: National Academy Press, 1997).

20. UNDP, op. cit. note 12.

21. Mathis Wackernagel and William Rees, *Our Ecological Footprint: Reducing Human Impact on the Earth* (Philadelphia, PA: New Society Publishers, 1996); WRI et al., op. cit. note 1; Rodenburg, op. cit. note 1.

22. Damage to virgin forests from Dirk Bryant, Daniel Nielsen and Laura Tangley, *The Last Frontier Forests* (Washington, DC: WRI, 1997); monocultures from Ashley T. Mattoon, "Paper Forests," *World Watch*, March/April 1998.

23. Services and habitat from Norman Myers, "The World's Forests and Their Ecosystem Services," in Gretchen C. Daily, ed., *Nature's Services: Societal Dependence on Natural Ecosystems* (Washington, DC: Island Press, 1997); China from Neelesh Misra, "Asia Floods Raise Questions About Man's Impact on Nature," *Associated Press*, 19 September 1998; mass extinction from Joby Warrick, "Mass

Extinction Underway, Majority of Biologists Say," *Washington Post*, 21 April 1998; role of forest products from Bryant, Nielsen, and Tangley, op. cit. note 22.

24. Copper ore excavated based on average grade from Donald Rogich and Staff, Division of Mineral Commodities, U.S. Bureau of Mines, "Material Use, Economic Growth and the Environment," presented at the International Recycling Congress and REC '93 Trade Fair, Geneva, Switzerland, January 1993; overburden numbers from Jean Moore, "Mining and Quarrying Trends," in USGS, *Minerals Yearbook* (Reston, VA: 1996), and from Jean Moore, USGS, discussion with Payal Sampat, 20 August 1998; Table 3–3 is based on metals production data from Metallgesellschaft AG and World Bureau of Metal Statistics, op. cit. note 6, on gold production from Gold Field Mineral Services, "World Gold Demand up 16 pct in 1997–GFMS," *Reuters*, 8 January 1998, and on average grade information from Rogich et al., op. cit. this note; Canada's wastes based on OECD, op. cit. note 16; gold waste based on Earle Amey, Gold Commodity Specialist, USGS, discussion with Payal Sampat, 13 August 1998 (waste does not include overburden moved to reach ores); mining and rivers from Frank Press and Raymond Siever, *Understanding Earth*, 2nd ed. (New York: W.H. Freeman and Co., 1998), and from John E. Young, *Mining the Earth*, Worldwatch Paper 109 (Washington, DC: Worldwatch Institute, July 1992).

25. MPC, op. cit note 4.

26. "Spanish Authorities Battle Tailings Disaster," *North American Mining*, April/May 1998; "Funding Pledges Coming in for Cleanup, Damages from Toxic Spill from Mine," *International Environment Reporter*, 27 May 1998; MPC, op. cit. note 4.

27. Jerome Nriagu, "Industrial Activity and Metals Emissions," in R. Socolow et al, eds., *Industrial Ecology and Global Change* (Cambridge, U.K.: Cambridge University Press, 1994); John A Meech et al., "Reactivity

of Mercury from Gold Mining Activities in Darkwater Ecosystems," *Ambio*, March 1998; Coakley, op. cit. note 9.

28. Energy consumed by materials processing from U.S. Department of Energy (DOE), Energy Information Administration, *Manufacturing Energy Consumption Survey*, <http://www.eia.doe.gov/emeu/consumption/>, viewed 17 August 1998; total U.S. energy consumption from DOE, *Annual Energy Review*, <http://tonto.eia.doe.gov/aer/>, viewed 5 October 1998, and from Mark Schipper, Energy Consumption Division, DOE, discussion with Payal Sampat, 6 October 1998; cement estimate is for 1995, based on Henrik G. van Oss, "Cement," in USGS, *Mineral Yearbook 1996* (Reston, VA: 1996), on Henrik van Oss, Cement Commodity Specialist, USGS, Reston, VA, discussion with Payal Sampat, 6 November 1998, and on Seth Dunn, "Carbon Emissions Resume Rise," in Brown, Renner, and Flavin, op. cit. note 14. If carbon emissions from fuel combustion and calcination are combined, cement production contributed some 300 million tons of carbon in 1995, approximately 5 percent of global emissions that year. This does not include electricity used by cement producers.

29. John Peterson Myers, "Our Untested Planet," *Defenders*, summer 1996.

30. Chlorofluorocarbons from Robert Ayres, "The Life-Cycle of Chlorine, Part I," *Journal of Industrial Ecology*, vol. 1, no. 1 (1997); Robert Repetto and Sanjay S. Baliga, *Pesticides and the Immune System: The Public Health Risks* (Washington, DC: WRI, March 1996).

31. Persistence and endocrine disruption from Theo Colburn, Dianne Dumanoski, and John Peterson Myers, *Our Stolen Future* (New York: Dutton Books, 1996); Susan Anderson, "Global Ecotoxicology: Management and Science," in Socolow et al., op. cit. note 27; Ayres, op. cit. note 30; National Academy of Sciences from Tim Jackson, *Material Concerns: Pollution, Profit, and Quality of Life* (London: Routledge, 1996).

32. Nitrogen increase from Robert U. Ayres, William H. Schlesinger, and Robert H. Socolow, "Human Impacts on the Carbon and Nitrogen Cycles," in Socolow et al., op. cit. note 27; biological consequences from William H. Schlesinger, "The Vulnerability of Biotic Diversity," in ibid.; major elements from Robert U. Ayres, "Integrated Assessment of the Grand Nutrient Cycles," *Environmental Modeling and Assessment*, vol. 2, pp. 107–28 (1997).

33. Waste survey from International Maritime Organization, *Global Waste Survey: Final Report* (London: 1995); V.I. Danilov-Danilyan, Minister of Environment and Natural Resources, "Environmental Issues in the Russian Federation," presented to the All-Russian Congress on Nature Protection, 3–5 June 1995; Superfund total sites from "The Facts Speak For Themselves," <http://www.epa.gov/superfund/accomp/index.htm>, viewed 27 October 1998; Superfund projected cost from Environmental Protection Agency, *1994 Superfund Annual Report to Congress* (Washington, DC: 1994).

34. Landfills and U.S. methane emissions from DOE, *Annual Energy Review*, op. cit. note 28.

35. "Mercury Deposition in United States is Global Problem," *International Environment Reporter*, 4 March 1998; dioxin from Ayres, op. cit. note 30.

36. Friends of the Earth Europe, *Towards Sustainable Europe* (Amsterdam: Friends of the Earth Netherlands, 1995); Friedrich Schmidt-Bleek, President, Factor 10 Institute, Carnoules, France, letters to Payal Sampat, 20 October and 2 November 1998; Friedrich Schmidt-Bleek and the Factor 10 Club, "MIPS and Factor 10 for a Sustainable and Profitable Economy," unpublished paper, Factor 10 Institute, Carnoules, France.

37. Austria from Schmidt-Bleek, op. cit. note 36; Netherlands from Lucas Reijnders, "The Factor X Debate: Setting Targets for Eco-

Efficiency," *Journal of Industrial Ecology*, vol. 2, no. 1 (1998); Germany from Federal Environmental Agency, Federal Republic of Germany, *Sustainable Development in Germany: Progress and Prospects* (Berlin: 1998); OECD, "OECD Environment Ministers Shared Goals For Action," press release (Paris: 3 April 1998), <http://www.oecd.org/news_and_events/release/nw98-39a.htm>.

38. Based on world materials consumption data from Matos, op. cit. note 2; global economic output data from International Monetary Fund, *World Economic Outlook* (Washington, DC: various years).

39. Oliviero Bernadini and Riccardo Galli, "Dematerialization: Long-term Trends in the Intensity of Use of Materials and Energy," *Futures*, May 1993; infrastructure completion from Donald Rogich, WRI, Washington, DC, letter to authors, 12 October 1998.

40. Table 3–4 from the following sources: plastics in cars from Keoleian et al., op. cit. note 14; aluminum from OTA, op. cit. note 3; container refilling from Frank Ackerman, *Why do We Recycle?* (Washington, DC: Island Press, 1997); lead batteries from Chris Hendrickson et al., "Green Design," presented at National Academy of Engineering, April 1994, and from OTA, op. cit. note 3; consumption increases from data supplied by Matos, op. cit. note 2; radial tires from Bernadini and Galli, op. cit. note 39; retreading difficulties from Center for Neighborhood Technology, *Beyond Recycling: Materials Reprocessing in Chicago's Economy* (Chicago: 1993); passenger car retreads of 33 million in 1977 from Harvey Brodsky, Tire Retread Information Bureau (TRIB), discussion with Gary Gardner, 30 September 1998; retread of 16 million in 1997 from TRIB Web site, <http://www.retread.org/>; mobile phones from Tim Jackson and Roland Clift, "Where's the Profit in Industrial Ecology?" *Journal of Industrial Ecology*, vol. 2, no. 1 (1998), and from Tim Jackson, e-mail to Gary Gardner, 2 October 1998; subscriptions from International Telecommunication Union, *World Telecommunication Indicators on Diskette* (Geneva: 1996).

41. OECD, *Eco-Efficiency* (Paris: 1998).

42. See, for example, Robert Ayres and Udo Simonis, eds., *Industrial Metabolism: Restructuring for Sustainable Development* (Tokyo: The United Nations University, 1994); William McDonough and Michael Braungart, "The Next Industrial Revolution," *Atlantic Monthly*, October 1998; Walter R. Stahel, "The Functional Economy: Cultural and Organizational Change," in *The Industrial Green Game* (Washington, DC: National Academy Press, 1997); and various articles by Friedrich Schmidt-Bleek.

43. Walter R. Stahel, "Selling Performance Instead of Goods: The Social and Organizational Change that Arises in the Move to a Service Economy," presented at Eco-efficiency: A Modern Feature of Environmental Technology, Dusseldorf, Germany 2–3 March 1998.

44. Braden R. Allenby, *Industrial Ecology: Framework and Implementation* (Upper Saddle River, NJ: Prentice Hall, 1999); remanufacture statistics from Xerox Web site, < http://www.xerox.com/ehs/1997/sustain.htm>, viewed 18 September 1998; future projections from Christa Carone, Xerox Corporation, Rochester, NY, discussion with Gary Gardner, 22 September 1998.

45. Laundry services from Walter R. Stahel, Director, Product-Life Institute, Geneva, letter to Payal Sampat, 12 October 1998, and from W.R. Stahel and T. Jackson, "Optimal Utilization and Durability—Towards a New Definition of the Service Economy," in Tim Jackson, ed., *Clean Production Strategies* (Boca Raton, FL: Lewis Publishers, 1993).

46. Robert Ayres, "Towards Zero Emissions: Is there a Feasible Path? Introduction to ZERI Phase II" (draft) (Fontainebleau, France: European Institute of Business Administration, May 1998).

47. Hendrickson et al., op. cit. note 40; Daniel C. Esty and Michael E. Porter, "Industrial Ecology and Competitiveness," *Journal of Industrial Ecology*, vol. 2, no. 1 (1998); John Carey, "'A Society That Reuses Almost Everything'," *Business Week*, 10 November 1996; World Business Council for Sustainable Development and U.N. Environment Programme (UNEP), *Eco-Efficiency and Cleaner Production: Charting the Course to Sustainability* (Geneva and Paris: 1996); Xerox from Carone, op. cit. note 44; recycling rate for durables from Franklin Associates, Ltd., *Solid Waste Management at the Crossroads* (Prairie Village, KS: December 1997).

48. German recycling from I.V. Edelgard Bially, Duales System Deutschland, letter and supporting documentation to Gary Gardner, 28 October and 3 November 1998; secondary packaging from Ackerman, op. cit. note 40.

49. John Ehrenfeld and Nicholas Gertler, "Industrial Ecology in Practice: The Evolution of Interdependence at Kalundborg," *Journal of Industrial Ecology*, vol. 1, no. 1 (1997); Hal Kane, "Eco-Farming in Fiji," *World Watch*, July/August 1997; Ayres, op. cit. note 46.

50. Walter Stahel, "The Service Economy: 'Wealth Without Resource Consumption'?" *Philosophical Transactions of the Royal Society of London*, vol. 355, pp. 1309–19 (1997); reusable containers from Ayres, op. cit. note 46; landfills from Franklin Associates, op. cit. note 47.

51. Repair versus landfills from Institute for Local Self-Reliance, "The Five Most Dangerous Myths About Recycling," factsheet (Washington, DC: September 1996).

52. Ackerman, op. cit. note 40; Stahel and Jackson, op. cit. note 45.

53. David Morris and Irshad Ahmed, *The Carbohydrate Economy: Making Chemicals and Industrial Materials from Plant Matter* (Washington, DC: Institute for Local Self-Reliance, 1992); OTA, *Biopolymers: Making Materials Nature's Way* (Washington, DC: U.S. Government Printing Office, September 1993).

54. Morris and Ahmed, op. cit. note 53.

55. OECD, op. cit. note 41; 6 million cars from Car Free Cities Network, <http://www.bremen.de/info/agenda21/carfree/>, viewed 20 October 1998.

56. Gloria Walker Johnson, City of Takoma Park Housing Department, Takoma Park, MD, discussion with Gary Gardner, 2 November 1998.

57. Wilkinson, op. cit. note 9.

58. Canberra from ACT government, <http://www.act.gov.au/nowaste/>, viewed 23 October 1998; Netherlands goal from <http://www.netherlands-embassy.org/env_nmp2.htm>, viewed 20 August 1998; Netherlands policy from Roodman, op. cit. note 9; Denmark from European Environment Agency, *Environmental Taxes: Implementation and Environmental Effectiveness* (Copenhagen: August 1996); U.S. projections from Thomas Kelly, USGS, "Crushed Cement Concrete Substitution for Construction Aggregates—A Materials Flow Analysis," 1998, <http://greenwood.cr.usgs.gov/pub/circulars/c1177/index.html>.

59. Institute for Local Self-Reliance, *Cutting the Waste Stream in Half: Community Record-Setters Show How* (draft) (Washington, DC: October 1998); Ackerman, op. cit. note 40.

60. Ackerman, op. cit. note 40.

61. Chlorofluorocarbons from Molly O'Meara, "CFC Production Continues to Plummet," in Brown, Renner, and Flavin, op. cit. note 14; UNEP, "Regional Workshops Highlight Need for Effective Action Against Hazardous Chemicals," press release (Geneva: 9 July 1998). The treaty is scheduled to be finalized by 2000.

62. Take-back laws from Michele Raymond,

"Will Europe's Producer Responsibility Systems Work?" *Resource Recycling*, May 1998; crates from Ayres, op. cit. note 46.

63. Friends of the Earth, U.K., "New Recycling Law Could Save Council Tax Payers Millions," press release (London: 17 September 1998); Duncan McLaren, Simon Bullock, and Nusrat Yousuf, *Tomorrow's World: Britain's Share in a Sustainable Future* (London: Earthscan Publications and Friends of the Earth, 1998).

64. Alexander Volokh, *How Government Building Codes and Construction Standards Discourage Recycling*, Reason Foundation Policy Study No. 202, <http://www-civeng. rutgers.edu/asce/recycle.html>, viewed 22 October 1998.

65. Canberra from ACT government, op. cit. note 58, and from Tony Webber, ACT government, discussion with Gary Gardner, 25 October 1998; Matamoros and Brownsville from <http://www.pbs.org/weta/planet/>, viewed 2 November 1998, based on a PBS three-part television series, "Planet Neighborhood," first broadcast 8 September 1997.

66. British consumers from Tim Jackson and Nic Marks, "Consumption, Sustainable Welfare, and Human Needs," *Ecological Economics* (forthcoming); Peter Travers and Sue Richardson, *Living Decently: Material Well-Being in Australia* (New York: Oxford University Press, 1993).

67. Global Action Plan for the Earth, <http://www.globalactionplan.org/ecoteam. htm>, viewed 15 October 1998; OECD, op. cit. note 41.

68. Bernstein, op. cit. note 15.

69. Roodman, op. cit. note 9.

70. "When it Breaks ... A Smart Guide to Getting Things Fixed," *Consumer Reports*, May 1998.

71. Schor, op. cit. note 11.

Chapter 4. Reorienting the Forest Products Economy

1. William Cronon, *Nature's Metropolis: Chicago and the Great West* (New York: W.W. Norton & Company, 1991).

2. John Perlin, *A Forest Journey: The Role of Wood in the Development of Civilization* (New York: W.W. Norton & Company, 1989); Dirk Bryant, Daniel Nielsen, and Laura Tangley, *The Last Frontier Forests* (Washington, DC: World Resources Institute (WRI), 1997).

3. Janet N. Abramovitz, *Taking a Stand: Cultivating a New Relationship with the World's Forests*, Worldwatch Paper 140 (Washington, DC: Worldwatch Institute, April 1998).

4. U.N. Food and Agriculture Organization (FAO), *State of the World's Forests 1997* (Oxford, U.K.: 1997).

5. Janet N. Abramovitz, "Valuing Nature's Services," in Lester Brown et al., *State of the World 1997* (New York: W.W. Norton & Company, 1997); Abramovitz, op. cit. note 3.

6. FAO, "Importance of NWFP," <http://www.fao.org/WAICENT/FAOINFO/FORESTRY/NWFP/NONWOOD.HTM>, viewed 11 February 1998.

7. India from "India flood toll pushes 1,800," *Agence France Presse* English Wire, 7 September 1998; Bangladesh from "Drowning," *The Economist*, 12 September 1998; Mexico from "Flooding Rampant Worldwide," *CNN Interactive* <http://www.cnn.com./WORLD>, viewed 10 September 1998; Yangtze watershed deforestation from Carmen Revenga et al., *Watersheds of the World* (Washington, DC: WRI, 1998); other China from Erik Eckholm, "China Admits Ecological Sins Played Role in Flood Disaster," *New York Times*, 26 August 1998, from Erik Eckholm, "Stunned by Floods, China Hastens Logging Curbs," *New York Times*, 27 September 1998, and from Vaclav Smil and Mao Yushi, *The Economic Costs of China's Environmental*

Degradation (Cambridge, MA: American Academy of Arts and Sciences, 1998).

8. Perlin, op. cit. note 2.

9. Ibid.; Michael Williams, "Industrial Impacts of the Forests of the United States, 1860–1920," *Journal of Forest History*, July 1997; current wood use for railroads from David B. McKeever, "Domestic Market Activity in Solid Wood Products (Preliminary Report)" (Madison, WI: U.S. Department of Agriculture (USDA), Forest Service, Forest Products Laboratory, 1998).

10. Increase in plantations from FAO, op. cit. note 4; Birger Solberg et al., "An Overview of Factors Affecting the Long-term Trends of Non-Industrial and Industrial Wood Supply and Demand," in Birger Solberg, ed., *Long-Term Trends and Prospects in World Supply and Demand for Wood and Implications for Sustainable Forest Management* (Joensuu, Finland: European Forestry Institute, 1996); 10 percent from Diana Propper de Callejon et al., "Sustainable Forestry within an Industry Context," in Sustainable Forestry Working Group, ed., *The Business of Sustainable Forestry: Case Studies* (Chicago: John D. and Catherine T. MacArthur Foundation, 1998).

11. FAO, op. cit. note 4.

12. Ibid.

13. International trade and volume from ibid.

14. Robin Broad, "The Political Economy of Natural Resources: Case Studies of the Indonesian and Philippine Forest Sectors," *The Journal of Developing Areas*, April 1995; production expansion of industrial round-wood and plywood from FAO, op. cit. note 4, and from FAO, *Forest Products Yearbook 1983–1994* (Rome: 1996); forest loss in Indonesia, Brazil, and Malaysia from WRI, *World Resources 1994–1995* (New York: Oxford University Press, 1994).

15. FAO, op. cit. note 4.

16. James L. Howard, "U.S. Timber Production, Trade, Consumption, and Price Statistics 1965–1994" (Madison, WI: USDA Forest Service, Forest Products Laboratory, June 1997); FAO, op. cit note 4; FAO, *Forest Products Prices 1963–1982* (Rome: 1983); FAO, *Forest Products Prices 1973–1992* (Rome: 1995).

17. Industrial efficiency from FAO, op. cit. note 4, and from Solberg, op. cit. note 10, based on *FAO Yearbooks*; Cronon, op. cit. note 1; Williams, op. cit. note 9.

18. U.S. Bureau of the Census, *Historical Statistics of the United States on CD-ROM, Colonial Times to 1970, Bicentennial Edition* (Cambridge, U.K.: Cambridge University Press, 1976); Howard, op. cit. note 16.

19. Processing efficiency from Propper de Callejon et al., op. cit. note 10; residue use and U.S. reduction of waste from Iddo K. Wernick, Paul E. Waggoner, and Jesse Ausubel, "Searching for Leverage to Conserve Forests," *Journal of Industrial Ecology*, summer 1997; Swedish Forest Industries Association, *The Swedish Forest Industry, Facts and Figures 1997* (Stockholm: 1998).

20. Growth in engineered wood products from "Engineered Wood Product Demand and Production Continue on Record-Setting Pace," press release (Washington, DC: APA-The Engineered Wood Association, 6 March 1998); oriented strand board market share from T.M. Maloney, "The Family of Wood Composite Materials," *Forest Products Journal*, February 1996.

21. Maloney, op. cit. note 20.

22. David B. McKeever, "Resource Potential of Solid Wood Waste in the United States," in Forest Products Society, *The Use of Recycled Wood and Paper in Building Applications* (Madison, WI: 1997); Propper de Callejon et al., op. cit. note 10; Kenneth E. Skog et al., "Wood Products Technology Trends: Changing the Face of Forestry," *Journal of Forestry*, December 1995; Maloney, op. cit.

note 20.

23. Catherine M. Mater, "Emerging Technologies for Sustainable Forestry," in Sustainable Forestry Working Group, op. cit. note 10.

24. Swedish Forest Industries Association, op. cit. note 19.

25. Ibid.; Solberg, op. cit. note 10; Elizabeth May, *At the Cutting Edge: The Crisis in Canada's Forests* (Toronto, ON, Canada: Key Porter, 1998); Michael M'Gonigle and Ben Parfitt, *Forestopia: A Practical Guide to the New Forest Economy* (Madeira Park, BC, Canada: Harbour Publishing, 1994).

26. Recycling rates from Ashley T. Mattoon, "Paper Recycling Climbs Higher," in Lester R. Brown, Michael Renner, and Christopher Flavin, *Vital Signs 1998* (New York: W.W. Norton & Company, 1998); solid waste from Peter J. Ince, "Recycling of Wood and Paper Products in the United States" (Madison, WI: USDA Forest Service, Forest Products Laboratory, January 1996), and from McKeever, op. cit. note 22.

27. FAO, op. cit. note 4; Construction Sponsorship Directorate, Department of the Environment, *Timber 2005: A Research and Innovation Strategy for Timber in Construction* (London: 1995).

28. Worldwatch calculations based on FAO data and on U.S. data in Richard W. Haynes et al., *The 1993 RPA Timber Assessment Update* (Fort Collins, CO: USDA Forest Service, Rocky Mountain Forest and Range Experiment Station, 1995), and on McKeever, op. cit. note 9.

29. Robert B. Phelps, "New Residential Construction in the United States by Structure Type and Size, 1920–1991," USDA Forest Service, unpublished manuscript, 1993; National Association of Home Builders, "Characteristics of New Single-Family Homes: 1975–1997," <http://www.nahb.com/sf. html>, viewed 29 May 1998; Bureau of Census, op. cit.

note 18; Howard, op. cit. note 16; Japan from Management and Coordination Agency of Japan, "Households and Household Members by Type of Household," <http://www.stat. go.jp/161106.htm>, viewed 9 July 1998.

30. Phelps, op. cit. note 29.

31. Perlin, op. cit. note 2.

32. Ann Edminster and Sami Yassa, *Efficient Wood Use in Residential Construction: A Practical Guide to Saving Wood, Money and Forests* (draft) (San Francisco: Natural Resources Defense Council, 1998); *Cost-Effective Home Building* (Washington, DC: National Association of Home Builders, 1994); Tracy Mumma et al., *Guide to Resource Efficient Building Elements* (Missoula, MT: Center for Resourceful Building Technology, 1997).

33. Edminster and Yassa, op. cit. note 32; Polly Sprenger, "SIPs Face the Skeptics," *Home Energy*, March/April 1998; "Structural Insulated Panels: An Efficient Way to Build," *Environmental Building News*, May 1998; U.K. estimate from Construction Sponsorship Directorate, op. cit. note 27.

34. Amount of construction waste from McKeever, op. cit. note 22; Edminster and Yassa, op. cit. note 32; "10 Building Projects Follow System to Reduce Waste," *Environmental Design and Construction*, January/February 1998.

35. Construction Sponsorship Directorate, op. cit. note 27; Duncan McLaren, Simon Bullock, and Nusrat Yousuf, *Tomorrow's World: Britain's Share in a Sustainable Future* (London: Earthscan Publications, 1998).

36. Robert H. Falk et al., "Recycled Lumber and Timber," in Masoud Sanayei, ed., *Restructuring: America and Beyond: Proceedings of Structural Congress 13*, 2–5 April 1995, Boston, MA, American Society of Civil Engineers; Lisa Geller, "High Value Markets for Deconstructed Wood," *Resource Recycling*, August 1998; David Eisenberg, Development Center for Appropriate Technology, e-mail to Janet

Abramovitz, 22 September 1998.

37. Ince, op. cit. note 26; R. Falk, "Housing Products from Recycled Wood Waste," *Proceedings of the Pacific Timber Engineering Conference,* Gold Coast Australia, 11–15 July 1994; McKeever, op. cit. note 22; Asia and Netherlands from Willem Hulscher, Chief Technical Advisor, Regional Wood Energy Development Programme in Asia (RWEDP), e-mail to authors, 23 September 1998; Sweden from "Forest Products Markets Strong in 1997 and 1998, Uncertainty Over the Short Term Outlook," UN/ECE Timber Committee Market Statement, 28 September–1 October 1998, <http://www.unece.org/trade/timber>, viewed 20 October 1998.

38. Certified area from Forest Stewardship Council, "Forests Certified by FSC-Accredited Certification Bodies," August 1998, <http://www.fscoax.org>, viewed 19 October 1998; buyers groups and resources from Certified Forest Products Council, <http://www.certifiedwood.org>, "Your Guide to Independently Certified Forest Products," <http://www.certifiedproducts.org>, 95 Plus Group, and <http://www.fsc-uk.demon.co.uk/95Plus Group.html>, all viewed 21 October 1998.

39. Certified Forest Products Council, "Construction Underway on Unique Habitat for Humanity Home Built with Certified Wood Products," press release (Beaverton OR: 19 May 1998); California buildings in Edminster and Yassa, op. cit. note 32.

40. Tsuen-Hsuin Tsien, *Written on Bamboo and Silk, The Beginnings of Chinese Books and Inscriptions* (Chicago: The University of Chicago Press, 1962); International Institute for Environment and Development (IIED), *Towards a Sustainable Paper Cycle* (London: 1996).

41. Figure 4–1 from FAO, *FAOSTAT Statistics Database,* <http://apps.fao.org/> (1995 data), with breakdown of major wood pulp sources from IIED, op. cit. note 40 (1993 data).

42. Figure for 1889 from Kurt J. Haunreiter, "200th Anniversary of the Paper Machine," *TAPPI Journal,* October 1997; figure for 1997 from FAO, op. cit. note 41; IIED, op. cit. note 40.

43. Figure for 1993, the last time such a calculation was made, from Wood Resources International Ltd., *Fiber Sourcing Analysis for the Global Pulp and Paper Industry* (London: IIED, September 1996); IIED, op. cit. note 40; Maureen Smith, *The U.S. Paper Industry and Sustainable Production* (Cambridge, MA: The MIT Press, 1997); Ronald J. Slinn, "The Impact of Industry Restructuring on Fiber Procurement," *Journal of Forestry,* February 1989; Swedish Forest Industries Association, op. cit. note 19; Forest Service, USDA, *Timber Trends in the United States* (Washington DC: 1965).

44. IIED, op. cit. note 40; Propper de Callejon et al., op. cit. note 10; Pulp and Paper International (PPI), *International Fact and Price Book 1997* (San Francisco, CA: Miller Freeman Inc., 1996); Charles W. Thurston, "Brazil Upgrading its Pulp Capacity," *Journal of Commerce,* 8 October 1997; Indonesia from World Wide Fund for Nature, *The Year the World Caught Fire* (Gland, Switzerland: December 1997).

45. Investments from Soile Kilpi, "New Opportunities in the South American Pulp and Paper Business," *TAPPI Journal,* June 1998; "Southern Hemisphere Plantations Turn Up Heat on Traditional Northern Wood Fiber Suppliers," *Pulp and Paper Week,* 20 December 1993; Stephanie Nall and William Armbruster, "U.S. Forest Products Companies Eye New Zealand," *Journal of Commerce,* 19 May 1997; Ricardo Carrere and Larry Lohmann, *Pulping the South* (London: Zed Books, 1996); Anita Kerski, "Pulp, Paper and Power—How an Industry Reshapes its Social Environment," *The Ecologist,* July/August 1995; predictability from Propper de Callejon et al., op. cit. note 10.

46. Increased trade from FAO, op. cit. note 4; U.S. share from PPI, op. cit. note 44: Japanese imports from FAO, *FAO Forest Products Yearbook 1983–1994* (Rome: 1996).

47. Figure for 1950 from IIED, op. cit. note 40; figure for 1996 from FAO, op. cit. note 41; projection from FAO, *Provisional Outlook for Global Forest Products Consumption, Production, and Trade to 2010* (Rome: 1997); share of different paper grades from IIED, op. cit. note 40.

48. FAO, op. cit. note 47; Southeast Asia from Gary Mead, "Tough Year Ahead for Pulp and Paper," *Financial Times*, 31 January 1998.

49. Figure 4–2 from FAO, op. cit. note 41, and from U.S. Bureau of the Census, *International Data Base*, <http://www.census.gov/cgi-bin/ipc>, viewed 18 December 1997; projections for 2010 from IIED, op. cit. note 40; United States from PPI, op. cit. note 44.

50. Three to four years from IIED, op. cit. note 40; PPI, *North American Fact Book 1997* (San Francisco, CA: Miller Freeman, Inc. 1996); Kirk J. Finchem, "Top Managers, Analysts Say Paper Industry Slow to Change," *Pulp and Paper*, December 1997.

51. Junk mail from Susan Headden, "The Junk Mail Deluge," *U.S. News and World Report*, 8 December 1997; mail order catalogs from Nels Johnson and Daryl Ditz, "Challenges to Sustainability in the U.S. Forest Sector," in Roger Dower et al., *Frontiers of Sustainability* (Washington, DC: Island Press, 1997); municipal solid waste from Franklin Associates, Ltd., "Characterization of Municipal Solid Waste in the United States: 1996 Update," report prepared for U.S. Environmental Protection Agency (EPA), Municipal and Industrial Solid Waste Division, Office of Solid Waste, June 1997.

52. Quote from Gunter Schneider, "Potential Threats Towards Publication and Catalogue Papers," *TAPPI Journal*, February 1996; electric paper from John B. Horrigan,

Frances H. Irwin, and Elizabeth Cook, *Taking a Byte Out of Carbon* (Washington DC: WRI, 1998); W. Wayt Gibbs, "The Reinvention of Paper," *Scientific American*, September 1998.

53. FAO, op. cit. note 41; FAO, op. cit. note 47.

54. FAO, op. cit. note 41; FAO, op. cit. note 47; *Journal of Industrial Ecology*, special issue on the industrial ecology of paper and wood, vol. 1, no. 3 (1998); five to six times from IIED, op. cit. note 40.

55. Smith, op. cit. note 43.

56. FAO, op. cit. note 47; China share of capacity from Joseph E. Atchison, "Twenty-five Years of Global Progress in Nonwood Plant Fiber Pulping," *TAPPI Journal*, October 1996.

57. Smith op. cit. note 43; David Morris and Irshad Ahmed, *The Carbohydrate Economy: Making Chemicals and Industrial Materials from Plant Matter* (Washington, DC: Institute for Local Self-Reliance, 1992); Institute for Local Self-Reliance, "The Fiber Revolution," *The Carbohydrate Economy* (newsletter), fall 1997; Atchison, op. cit. note 56; Meghan Clancey Hepburn, "Agricultural Residues: A Promising Alternative to Virgin Wood Fiber," in *Issues in Resource Conservation, Briefing Series No. 1* (Washington, DC: Resource Conservation Alliance, Center for Study of Responsive Law, 1998).

58. Relative role from Solberg et al., op. cit. note 10.

59. Estimate of 2 billion from FAO, op. cit. note 4; percentages from Solberg et al., op. cit. note 10; 40 of the world's poorest nations from U.N. Environment Programme, *Environmental Data Report 1993–94* (Oxford, U.K.: Blackwell Publishers 1993).

60. U.S. mill figures from Wernick, Waggoner, and Ausubel, op. cit. note 19; direct and indirect woodfuel consumption figures from Solberg et al., op. cit. note 10.

61. FAO, *European Timber Trends and Prospects Into the 21st Century* (New York: United Nations, 1996); U.S. figure from Ince, op. cit. note 26.

62. Gerald Leach and Robin Mearns, *Beyond the Woodfuel Crisis* (London: Earthscan Publications, 1988); Anil Agarwal, "False Predictions," *Down to Earth,* 31 May 1998; RWEDP, *Regional Study on Wood Energy Today and Tomorrow in Asia* (Bangkok: FAO, October 1997); Lars Kristoferson, "Seven Energy and Development Myths—Are They Still Alive?" *Renewable Energy for Development,* July 1997; Emmanuel N. Chidumayo, "Woodfuel and Deforestation in Southern Africa—A Misconceived Association," *Renewable Energy for Development,* July 1997; FAO, op. cit. note 4.

63. Leach and Mearns, op. cit. note 62; other sources from RWEDP, op. cit. note 62; B. K. Kaale, "Traditional Fuels," in Janos Pasztor and Lars A. Kristoferson, *Bienergy and Environment* (Boulder, CO: Westview Press, 1990).

64. Agarwal, op. cit. note 62; I. Natarajan, "Trends in Firewood Consumption in Rural India," *Margin* (National Council of Applied Economic Research, New Delhi), October–December 1995, as discussed in ibid.

65. D. Evan Mercer and John Soussan, "Fuelwood Problems and Solutions," in Narendra P. Sharma, ed., *Managing the World's Forests* (Dubuque, IA: Kendall/Hunt Publishing Company, 1992); Kaale, op. cit. note 63.

66. Mercer and Soussan, op. cit. note 65; P. Bradley and P. Dewees, "Indigenous Woodlands, Agricultural Production and Household Economy in the Communal Areas," in P.N. Bradley and K. McNamara, eds., *Living with Trees: Policies for Forestry Management in Zimbabwe* (Washington, DC: World Bank, 1993); Pasztor and Kristoferson, op. cit. note 63; Brazil tobacco from Beauty Lupiya, "All for Smoke," *Down to Earth,* 15 November 1997; Chidumayo, op. cit. note 62.

67. Chen Chunmei, "State to Plant Trees for Fuel," *China Daily,* 7 July 1997; FAO, op. cit. note 4; RWEDP, op. cit. note 62; sub-Saharan Africa from D.F. Barnes, *Population Growth, Wood Fuels, and Resource Problems in Sub-Saharan Africa* (Washington, DC: World Bank Industry and Energy Department, March 1990), cited in C.J. Jepma, *Tropical Deforestation,* (London, U.K.: Earthscan Publications, 1995).

68. Top-down approaches from Leach and Mearns, op. cit. note 62; Mercer and Soussan, op. cit. note 65; Kaale, op. cit. note 63; Daniel Kammen, "Cookstoves for the Developing World," *Scientific American,* July 1995.

69. David O. Hall et al., "Biomass for Energy: Supply Prospects," in Thomas B. Johansson et al., eds., *Renewable Energy: Sources for Fuels and Electricity* (Washington DC: Island Press, 1993); Sandra Brown et al., "Management of Forests for Mitigation of Greenhouse Gas Emissions," in Robert T. Watson et al., eds., *Climate Change 1995: Impacts, Adaptations and Mitigation of Climate Change: Scientific-Technical Analyses: Contribution of Working Group II to the Second Assessment Report of the Intergovernmental Panel on Climate Change* (New York: Cambridge University Press, 1996).

70. Solberg et al., op. cit. note 10; FAO, op. cit. note 4.

71. Worldwatch calculations based on FAO, op. cit. note 47; U.S. from Johnson and Ditz, op. cit. note 51.

72. Worldwatch estimates based on FAO data.

73. Ibid.

74. U.S. estimate from Wernick, Waggoner, and Ausubel, op. cit. note 19; U.K. estimate from McLaren, Bullock, and Yousuf, op. cit. note 35.

75. Christopher Uhl et al., "Natural Resources Management in the Brazilian

Amazon: An Integrated Research Approach," *Bioscience*, March 1997.

76. Worldwatch estimates based on FAO projections.

77. McKeever, op. cit. note 22.

78. Worldwatch estimates based on FAO, op. cit. note 47; 350 million tons from David Morris, Vice President, Institute for Local Self-Reliance, presentation at "Advancing the Demand Reduction Agenda," Minneapolis, MN, 26 June 1998; potential percentage breakdown from Smith, op. cit. note 43.

79. Co-op America, "WoodWise Consumer" (Washington, DC: 1998); McLaren, Bullock, and Yousuf, op. cit. note 35.

80. Insurance company from McLaren et al., op. cit. note 35; EPA from Horrigan, Irwin, and Cook, op. cit. note 52.

81. UN/ECE Timber Committee, *Forest Products Annual Market Review 1997–1998*, <http://www.unece.org/trade/timber/y-rev98.htm>, viewed 20 October 1998; David Ford, director, Certified Forest Products Council, discussion with Janet Abramovitz, 20 October 1998; Eric Hansen et al., "The German Publishing Industry: Managing Environmental Issues: A Teaching Case Study" (draft) (Corvallis, OR: Oregon State University, October 1998); BBC from speech by Nicholas Brett, BBC Worldwide Ltd., at Forests for Life Conference, San Francisco, 10 May 1997; Justin Stead, manager, WWF 1995 Plus Group, discussion with Janet Abramovitz, 22 October 1998.

82. David Eisenberg, Development Center for Appropriate Technology, e-mail to Janet Abramovitz, 22 September 1998; Edminster and Yassa, op. cit. note 32; Microsoft example from Preston Horne-Brine, "A Wood Recycling Enterprise: Clean Collection, Optimized Processing and Value-Added Manufacturing," *Resource Recycling*, June 1998; American Institute of Architects Committee on the Environment, <http://www.e-architect.com>.

83. Smith, op. cit. note 43; Nebraska from Duke Fuehrer, Chief Operating Officer, Heartland Fibers, discussion with Ashley Mattoon, 29 October 1998.

84. Swedish employment from Swedish Forest Industries Association, op. cit. note 19; Swedish and Canadian roundwood production from FAO, op. cit. note 41; Canadian employment numbers from Natural Resources Canada (NRC), "Statistics Canada, Labor Force Survey" (unpublished) (Ottawa, ON, Canada: 1998), received from David Luck, Canadian Forest Service, NRC, e-mail to Ashley Mattoon, 2 September 1998; Worldwatch calculations based on FAO and Canadian data.

85. U.S. Forest Service, *The Forest Service Program for Forest and Rangeland Resources: A Long-Term Strategic Plan, Draft 1995 RPA Program*, October 1995, cited in Sierra Club, "Ending Timber Sales on National Forests: The Facts," report summary, San Francisco, undated.

86. U.S. timber sale losses from Jim Jontz, "Forest Service Indictment: A Mountain of Evidence," in Sierra Club, *Stewardship or Stumps? National Forests at the Crossroads* (Washington, DC: June 1997); Randal O'Toole, "Reforming a Demoralized Agency: Saving National Forests," *Different Drummer*, vol. 3, no. 4 (1997); "National Forest Timber Sale Receipts and Costs in 1995," *Different Drummer*, vol. 3, no. 4 (1997); Paul Roberts, "The Federal Chain-saw Massacre," *Harper's Magazine*, June 1997; Indonesia from Charles Barber, Nels C. Johnson, and Emmy Hafild, *Breaking the Logjam: Obstacles to Forest Policy Reform in Indonesia and the United States* (Washington, DC: WRI, 1994).

87. British Columbia Ministry of Forests (BCMOF), "Timber Tenure System in British Columbia" (Victoria, BC, Canada: 1997); Barber, Johnson, and Hafild, op. cit. note 86; Owen J. Lynch and Kirk Talbott, *Balancing Acts: Community-Based Forest Management and National Law in Asia and the Pacific*

(Washington, DC: WRI, September 1995).

88. BCMOF, op. cit. note 87; Cheri Burda et al., *Forests in Trust: Reforming British Columbia's Forest Tenure System for Ecosystem and Community Health* (Victoria, BC, Canada: University of Victoria, Eco-Research Chair of Environmental Law and Policy, July 1997); BC Wild, "Overcut: British Columbia Forest Policy and the Liquidation of Old-Growth Forests" (Vancouver, BC, Canada: BC Wild, 1998).

89. Diana Jean Schemo, "To Fight Outlaws, Brazil Opens Rain Forest to Loggers," *New York Times*, 21 July 1997; Diana Jean Schemo, "Brazil, Its Forests Besieged, Adds Teeth to Environmental Laws" *New York Times*, 29 January 1998; William Schomberg, "Brazil Under Fire for Relaxing Environmental Law", *Reuters*, 14 August 1998; Sierra Legal Defense Fund (SLDF), "British Columbia Forestry Report Card 1997–98" (Vancouver, BC, Canada: 1998); SLDF, "Betraying Our Trust: A Citizen's Update on Environmental Rollbacks in British Columbia, 1996–1998" (Vancouver, BC, Canada: 1998); Ministry of Forests, Province of British Columbia, "Annual Report of Compliance and Enforcement Statistics for the Forest Practices Code: June 15, 1996–June 16, 1997," <http://www.for.gov.bc.ca.>, viewed 5 November 1997; Global Witness, "Just Deserts for Cambodia? Deforestation & the Co-Prime Ministers' Legacy to the Country," June 1997, <http://www.oneworld.org/global-witness>, viewed 23 September 1997; World Conservation Union–IUCN and World Wide Fund for Nature, "Illegal Logging in Russian Forests," *Arborvitae*, August 1997; Yangtze watershed deforestation from Revenga et al., op. cit. note 7; Eckholm, "Stunned by Floods," op. cit. note 7; "Forestry Cuts Down on Logging," *China Daily*, 26 May 1998.

90. Building codes from Eisenberg, op. cit. note 82; European Union directive from "Divided EU Agrees on Packaging Directive, Joint Ratification of Climate Change Treaty," *International Environment Reporter*, 12 January 1994; "Council Agrees on FCP Phase-out, Packaging Recycling, Hazardous Waste List," *International Environment Reporter*, 11 January 1995; "New Law Sets 60 Percent Recovered Paper Consumption Guideline in Japan," *Paper Recycler*, October 1996.

91. International Monetary Fund, "Statement by the Managing Director on the IMF Program with Indonesia," Washington, DC, 15 January 1998; Sander Thoenes, "Indonesian Wood Cartel Resists IMF Reforms," *Financial Times*, 13 February 1998.

Chapter 5. Charting a New Course For Oceans

1. Huxley cited in Tim D. Smith, *Scaling Fisheries: The Science of Measuring the Effects of Fishing, 1855–1955* (Cambridge, U.K.: Cambridge University Press, 1994).

2. Share of animal protein from fish from U.N. Food and Agriculture Organization (FAO), *Marine Fisheries and the Law of the Sea: A Decade of Change*, FAO Fisheries Circular No. 853 (Rome: 1993); oil and gas from Independent World Commission on Oceans (IWCO), *The Ocean...Our Future: The Report of the Independent World Commission on the Oceans* (New York: Cambridge University Press, 1998); world trade from Magnus Ngoile, "The Oceans: Diminishing Resources, Degraded Environment and Loss of Biodiversity," *Connect* (Paris: UNESCO) vol. 12, no. 3/4 (1997); Joel E. Cohen et al., "Estimates of Coastal Populations," *Science*, 14 November 1997.

3. Ocean industries value of $821 billion in 1995 dollars is Worldwatch Institute estimate based on late 1980s estimate of $750 billion from Michael L. Weber and Judith A. Gradwohl, *The Wealth of Oceans* (New York: W.W. Norton & Company, 1995), citing James Broadus, Woods Hole Oceanographic Institution, and from world commodity price index from International Monetary Fund, *International Financial Statistics Yearbook*

(Washington, DC: 1998); current fisheries value from Matteo Milazzo, *Subsidies in World Fisheries: A Reexamination*, World Bank Technical Paper No. 406, Fisheries Series (Washington, DC: World Bank, April 1998); ocean transport from United Nations Conference on Trade and Development (UNCTAD), *Review of Maritime Trade* (New York: 1997); oil and gas drilling from American Petroleum Institute (API), *Basic Petroleum Data Book* (Washington, DC: 1995); naval expenditures based on 0.3 percent of world military expenditures, according to James Broadus in Weber and Gradwohl, op. cit. this note; 1995 world military expenditures from Michael Renner, "Military Expenditures Continue to Decline," in Lester R. Brown, Michael Renner, and Christopher Flavin, *Vital Signs 1998* (New York: W.W. Norton & Company, 1998).

4.   Phyla from Elliott A. Norse, ed., *Global Marine Biological Diversity: A Strategy for Building Conservation into Decision Making* (Washington, DC: Island Press, 1993); goods and services from Robert Costanza et al., "The Value of the World's Ecosystem Services and Natural Capital," *Nature*, 15 May 1997; heat storage from "Ocean Research: Clarifying Ocean Role in Global Climate," <http://gk2.jamstec. go.jp/jamstec/ocean.html>, viewed on 21 July 1998; services from Melvin N.A. Peterson, ed., *Diversity of Oceanic Life: An Evaluative Review*, Significant Issues Series (Washington, DC: Center for Strategic and International Studies, 1992); value of coral reefs from World Resources Institute (WRI) et al. , *Reefs At Risk: A Map-Based Indicator of Threats to the World's Coral Reefs* (Washington, DC: 1998).

5.   FAO, *The State of World Fisheries and Aquaculture, 1996* (Rome: 1997); threatened coastlines from Don Hinrichsen, *Coastal Waters of the World: Trends, Threats and Strategies* (Washington, DC: Island Press, 1998); reefs from WRI et al., op. cit. note 4.

6.   Marine Conservation Biology Institute, "Troubled Waters: A Call to Action,"

(Redmond, WA: January 1998); quote from Dr. M. Patricia Morse, Biology Department, Northeastern University, Boston, MA, "Statement on Release of 'Troubled Waters: A Call to Action'," 8 January 1998, <http://www. mcbi.org>, viewed on 7 May 1998; Scott Sonner, "Scientists: Sorry State of World's Oceans Are a Warning to Humans," *Corvallis* (OR) *Gazette-Times*, 25 January 1998.

7.   Harold V. Thurman, ed., *Introductory Oceanography*, 5th ed. (Columbus, OH: Merrill Publishing Company, 1988); Thor Heyerdahl, "Ocean Highways," *Our Planet*, vol. 9, no. 5 (1998); "Homo Erectus May Have Been Seafarer," *Providence* (RI) *Journal-Bulletin*, 12 March 1998; John Noble Wilford, "In Peru, Evidence of an Early Human Maritime Culture," *New York Times*, 22 September 1998.

8.   Share of animal protein from FAO, op. cit. note 2; Meryl Williams, *The Transition in the Contribution of Living Aquatic Resources to Food Security*, Food, Agriculture, and the Environment Discussion Paper 13 (Washington, DC: International Food Policy Research Institute, April 1996).

9.   Heather Pringle, "Yemen's Stonehenge Suggests Bronze Age Red Sea Culture," *Science*, 6 March 1998; Egyptian stone tablets from Thurman, op. cit. note 7; Arabs from IWCO, op. cit. note 2.

10. John Greenwald, "Cruise Lines Go Overboard," *Time*, 11 May 1998.

11. Table 5–1 based on the following: fisheries data from FAO, op. cit. note 5, from Williams, op. cit. note 8, from Milazzo, op. cit. note 3, from Michael Strauss, "Fish Catch Hits a New High," in Brown, Renner, and Flavin, op. cit. note 3, and from FAO, *Fishery Statistics Yearbook: Commodities*, vol. 81 (Rome: 1997); trade data from UNCTAD, op. cit. note 3; cargo unloaded from "Making Waves," *South*, March 1997; naval expenditures from Broadus, op. cit. note 3, and from Renner, op. cit. note 3; oil and gas from API, op. cit. note 3. Future trade estimate from Office of the

Chief Scientist, National Oceanic and Atmospheric Administration (NOAA), *Year of the Ocean Discussion Papers*, prepared by U.S. Federal Agencies with Ocean-related Programs (Washington, DC: NOAA, March 1998).

12. Submersibles and acoustics from Sylvia A. Earle, *Sea Change* (New York: G.P. Putnam's Sons, 1995); William J. Broad, *The Universe Below: Discovering the Secrets of the Deep Sea* (New York: Simon & Schuster, 1997); K.O. Emery and J.M. Broadus, "Overview: Marine Mineral Reserves and Resources—1988," *Marine Mining*, vol. 8, no. 1 (1989).

13. Dick Russell, "Deep Blues: The Lowdown on Deep-Sea Mining," *Amicus Journal*, winter 1998; William J. Broad, "Undersea Treasure, and Its Odd Guardians," *New York Times*, 30 December 1997; United Nations General Assembly, *Report of the Secretary-General on His Consultations on Outstanding Issues Relating to the Deep Seabed Mining Provisions of the United Nations Convention on the Law of the Sea*, 9 June 1994; United Nations, Division for Ocean Affairs and the Law of the Sea, "International Seabed Authority Meets," *Go Between*, October/November 1997.

14. Stephanie Pain, "Mud, Glorious Mud," in Stephanie Pain, ed., *Unknown Oceans, New Scientist Supplement*, November 1996; Richard A. Kerr, "Life Goes to Extremes in the Deep Earth—and Elsewhere?" *Science*, 2 May 1997; Gregory Beck and Gail S. Habicht, "Immunity and Invertebrates," *Scientific American*, November 1996; Andy Coghlan, "Shark Chokes Human Cancers," *New Scientist*, 26 April 1997; Russell, op. cit. note 13.

15. Hjalmar Thiel, "Deep-Ocean Mining Needs Careful Study," *Forum for Applied Research and Public Policy*, Spring 1994; Wesley S. Scholz, "The Law of the Sea Convention and the Business Community: The Seabed Mining Regime and Beyond," *Georgetown International Environmental Law Review*, spring 1995; figure of 1.5 percent from Edward Carr, "The Deep Green Sea," *The Economist*, 23 May 1998.

16. Brad Matsen and Ray Troll, *Planet Ocean: Dancing to the Fossil Record* (Berkeley, CA: Ten Speed Press, 1994); 245 million years from Norse, op. cit. note 4.

17. Norse, op. cit. note 4; Boyce Thorne-Miller and John Catena, *The Living Ocean: Understanding and Protecting Marine Biodiversity*, The Oceanic Society of Friends of the Earth–U.S. (Washington, DC: Island Press, 1991).

18. Goods and services from Costanza et al., op. cit. note 4; rates of marine biological productivity from different areas of the ocean from D. Pauly and V. Christensen, "Primary Production Required to Sustain Global Fisheries," *Nature*, 16 March 1995; 80–90 percent of fish catch from John Cordell, "Introduction: Sea Tenure," in John Cordell, ed. *A Sea of Small Boats* (Cambridge, MA: Cultural Survival, Inc., 1989).

19. W. Jeffrey, M. Vesk, and R.F.C. Mantoura, "Phytoplankton Pigments: Windows into the Pastures of the Sea," *Nature & Resources*, vol. 33, no. 2 (1997); Gillian Malin, "Sulphur, Climate and the Microbial Maze," *Nature*, 26 June 1997; pump mechanism from Paul G. Falkowski et al., "Biogeochemical Controls and Feedbacks on Ocean Primary Productivity," *Nature*, 10 July 1998; global nutrient cycles from Peter M. Vitousek et al., "Human Domination of Earth's Ecosystems," *Science*, 25 July 1997.

20. Michael S. McCartney, "Oceans & Climate: The Ocean's Role in Climate and Climate Change," *Oceanus*, fall/winter 1996; sequestered rate from Falkowski et al., op. cit. note 19; current rate of uptake from David S. Schimel, "The Carbon Equation," *Nature*, 21 May 1998; future uptake from Jorge Sarmiento et al., "Simulated Response of the Ocean Carbon Cycle to Anthropogenic Climate Warming," *Nature*, 21 May 1998.

21. Lewis M. Rothstein and Dake Chen,

"The El Niño/Southern Oscillation Phenomenon," *Oceanus*, fall/winter 1996; "The Season of El Niño," *The Economist*, 9 May 1998; Gary Mead, "El Niño Wreaks Havoc on Fish Meal Industry," *Financial Times*, 28 May 1998.

22. John S. Gray, *Marine Biodiversity: Patterns, Threats and Conservation Needs*, Joint Group of Experts on the Scientific Aspects of Marine Environmental Protection (GESAMP) (London: International Maritime Organization, 1997).

23. Production data for 1984–96 from Maurizio Perotti, fishery statistician, Fishery Information, Data and Statistics Unit (FIDI), Fisheries Department, FAO, Rome, letter to author, 22 March 1998; 1950–84 world production from FAO, *Yearbook of Fishery Statistics: Catches and Landings* (Rome: 1967–91); figure of 11 out of 15 is a Worldwatch estimate based on data from Maurizio Perotti, FIDI, FAO, Rome, e-mail to author, 14 October 1997; 70 percent from FAO, op. cit. note 5.

24. Estimate for 1984 from FAO, *Aquaculture Production Statistics, 1984–1993*, FAO Fisheries Circular No. 815, Revision 7 (Rome: 1995); 1996 aquaculture estimate from Perotti, 22 March 1998; Carl Safina, *Song for the Blue Ocean: Encounters Along the World's Coasts and Beneath the Seas* (New York: Henry Holt and Company, Inc., 1997); Marjorie L. Mooney-Seus and Gregory S. Stone, *The Forgotten Giants: Giant Ocean Fishes of the Atlantic and Pacific* (Washington, DC: Ocean Wildlife Campaign, 1997); Lisa Speer et al., *Hook, Line and Sinking: The Crisis in Marine Fisheries* (New York: Natural Resources Defense Council, February 1997).

25. S. M. Garcia and C. Newton, "Current Situation, Trends, and Prospects in World Fisheries," in E.K. Pikitch, D.D. Huppert, and M.P. Sissenwine, eds., *Global Trends: Fisheries Management*, American Fisheries Society (AFS) Symposium 20 (Bethesda, MD: AFS, 1997); Daniel Pauly et al., "Fishing Down Marine Food Webs," *Science*, 6 February 1998.

26. Groundfish from Speer et al., op. cit. note 24; orange roughy from David Malakoff, "Extinction on the High Seas," *Science*, 25 July 1997.

27. Orange roughy from Malakoff, op. cit. note 26; Callum M. Roberts, "Effects of Fishing on the Ecosystem Structure of Coral Reefs," *Conservation Biology*, October 1995.

28. Williams, op. cit. note 8; figure of 83 percent is Worldwatch estimate based on FAO, op. cit. note 11.

29. Discards of 20 million tons from David Wilmot, Director, Ocean Wildlife Campaign, Washington, DC, e-mail to author, 12 February 1998, and from American Sportfishing Association and Ocean Wildlife Campaign, "Slaughter at Sea," press release (Washington, DC: 12 January 1998); bycatch and shrimps from Dayton L. Alverson et al., *A Global Assessment of Fisheries Bycatch and Discards*, FAO Fisheries Technical Paper 339 (Rome: FAO, 1994).

30. Charles Victor Barber and Vaughan R. Pratt, *Sullied Seas: Strategies for Combating Cyanide Fishing in Southeast Asia and Beyond* (Washington, DC: WRI and International Marinelife Alliance, August 1997).

31. Janet Raloff, "Fishing for Answers: Deep Trawls Leave Destruction in Their Wake—But for How Long?" *Science News*, 26 October 1996; Dick Russell, "Hitting Bottom," *Amicus Journal*, winter 1997; global estimate from Elliott A. Norse, "Bottom-Trawling: The Unseen Worldwide Plowing of the Seabed," *The NEB Transcript* (Beverly, MA: New England Biolabs, Inc.), January 1997.

32. Cohen et al., op. cit. note 2; China population data Hinrichsen, op. cit. note 5.

33. Seagrasses from IWCO, op. cit. note 2; mangrove data from Mark D. Spalding, "The Global Distribution and Status of Mangrove Ecosystems," *Intercoast Network*, March 1997, and from Elizabeth J. Farnsworth and Aaron M. Ellison, "The Global Conservation Status of

Mangroves," *Ambio*, September 1997.

34. GESAMP, *The State of the Marine Environment*, U.N. Environment Programme Regional Seas Reports and Studies No. 115 (Nairobi: 1990).

35. Tina Adler, "The Expiration of Respiration," *Science News*, 10 February 1996; Dick Russell, "Underwater Epidemic," *Amicus Journal*, spring 1998; David Malakoff, "Death by Suffocation in the Gulf of Mexico," *Science*, 10 July 1998.

36. General discussion and shellfish poisoning data from G.M. Hallegraeff, "A Review of Harmful Algal Blooms and Their Apparent Global Increase," *Phycologia*, vol. 32, no. 2, (1993); Christine Mlott, "The Rise in Toxic Tides: What's Behind the Ocean Blooms?" *Science News*, 27 September 1997; Ted Smayda, University of Rhode Island, Graduate School of Oceanography, "The Toxic Sea: The Global Epidemic of Harmful Red Tides," presented at Naval War College, Newport, RI, 11 August 1998; Theodore J. Smayda, "Novel and Nuisance Phytoplankton Blooms in the Sea: Evidence for a Global Epidemic," *Toxic Marine Phytoplankton: Proceedings of the Fourth International Conference on Toxic Marine Phytoplankton, Held June 26–30 in Lund, Sweden* (New York: Elsevier Science Publishers, 1990); toxic and nontoxic blooms from Donald M. Anderson, "Red Tides," *Scientific American*, August 1994; Jonas Gunnarsson et al., "Interactions Between Eutrophication and Contaminants: Towards a New Research Concept for the European Aquatic Environment," *Ambio*, September 1995. Table 5–4 based on the following: Smayda, "Novel and Nuisance Phytoplankton Blooms," op. cit. this note; Maine and New England from Linda Kanamine, "Scientists Sound Red Alert Over Harmful Algae," *USA Today International*, 15 November 1996; Puget Sound and Washington State from Donald F. Boesch et al., *Harmful Algal Blooms in Coastal Waters: Options for Prevention, Control and Mitigation*, NOAA Coastal Ocean Program, Decision

Analysis Series No. 10 (Silver Spring, MD: NOAA, February 1997); Texas from "Growing Red Tide Imperils Shellfishing Along Texas Gulf Coast," *New York Times*, 13 October 1996; John Ridding, "HK Fishermen Fear Drowning in 'Red Tide'," *Financial Times*, 15 April 1998.

37. Biblical reference from Hallegraeff, op. cit. note 36; tributyltin from "Chemicals in Ship Paints May Have Contributed to California Sea Otter Deaths," *Oceans Update* (Washington, DC: SeaWeb), April 1998; Ian M. Davies, Susan K. Bailey, and Melanie J.C. Harding, "Tributyltin Inputs to the North Sea from Shipping Activities, and Potential Risk of Biological Effects," *ICES Journal of Marine Sciences*, February 1998.

38. Janet Raloff, "Something's Fishy," *Science News*, 2 July 1994; Theo Colborn, Dianne Dumanoski, and John Peterson Myers, *Our Stolen Future* (New York: Penguin Group, 1996); Jennifer D. Mitchell, "Nowhere to Hide: The Global Spread of High-Risk Synthetic Chemicals," *World Watch*, March/ April 1997; spread to higher latitudes from Hal Bernton, "Russian Revelations Indicate Arctic Region Is Awash in Contaminants," *Washington Post*, 17 May 1993, and from Jerzy Falandysz et al., "Organochlorine Pesticides and Polychlorinated Biphenyls in Cod-liver Oils: North Atlantic, Norwegian Sea, North Sea and Baltic Sea," *Ambio*, July 1994.

39. Inuit from "Pollutants Threaten Arctic Wildlife, Inuit," *OceanUpdate*, September 1997, and from Mark Bourrie, "Global Warming Endangers Arctic," *InterPress Service*, 14 October 1998; health effects from "POPs and Human Health," *PSR Monitor* (Washington, DC: Physicians for Social Responsibility), February 1998.

40. Heavy metals from William C. Clark, "Managing Planet Earth," *Scientific American*, September 1989; Rolf O. Hallberg. "Environmental Implications of Metal Distribution in Baltic Sea Sediments," *Ambio*, November 1991; David Carpenter, "Great Lakes Contaminants: A Shift in Human Health Outcomes," *Health*

& Environment Digest, July 1996; John Tilden et al., "Health Advisories for Consumers of Great Lakes Sport Fish: Is the Message Being Received?" *Environmental Health Perspectives,* December 1997; Amy D. Kyle, *Contaminated Catch: The Public Health Threat from Toxics in Fish* (New York: Natural Resources Defense Council, 1998).

41. Broad ecological trends from Laurence D. Mee, "The Black Sea in Crisis: A Need for Concerted International Action," *Ambio,* June 1992; current status from "The Black Sea in Crisis," *Environmental Health Perspectives,* December 1997, and from Elliott Norse, President, Marine Conservation Biology Institute, Redmond, WA, e-mail to author, 22 April 1998.

42. James T. Carlton, "Bioinvaders in the Sea: Reducing the Flow of Ballast Water," *World Conservation,* April 1997-January 1998; global estimate from Lu Eldredge, "Transboundary: Shipping/Pollution," *Connect,* vol. 22, no. 3–4 (1997); 56 million tons from Peter Weber, *Abandoned Seas: Reversing the Decline of Oceans,* Worldwatch Paper 116 (Washington, DC: Worldwatch Institute, November 1993); San Francisco Bay and quote from Andrew N. Cohen and James T. Carlton, "Accelerating Invasion Rate in a Highly Invaded Estuary," *Science,* 23 January 1998.

43. "Fish Damage Linked to UV," *New York Times,* 18 March 1997; Donat-P. Häder et al., "Effects of Increased Solar Ultraviolet Radiation on Aquatic Ecosystems," *Ambio,* May 1995.

44. NOAA, "El Niño Causing Coral Bleaching in Panama," press release (Washington, DC: 14 April 1998); NOAA, "1998 Coral Reef Bleaching in Indian Ocean Unprecedented, NOAA Announces," press release (Washington, DC: 1 July 1998); International Society for Reef Studies, "ISRS Statement on Global Coral Bleaching in 1997–1998," posted on the Global Coral Reef Monitoring network <coral-list@coral.aoml.noaa.gov>, 13 October 1998.

45. Thermal expansion from David Schneider, "The Rising Seas," *Scientific American,* March 1997; William K. Stevens, "Storm Warning: Bigger Hurricanes and More of Them," *New York Times,* 3 June 1997.

46. Schneider, op. cit. note 45; risks and past rise from Molly O'Meara, "The Risks of Disrupting Climate," *World Watch,* November/December 1997; New York City from "Atlantic Sea Level Rise: Double the Average?" *Atlantic CoastWatch,* April 1998; estimate of $970 billion from David Pugh, "Sea Level Change: Meeting the Challenge," *Nature & Resources,* vol. 33, no. 3-4 (1997); Bangladesh from John Pernetta, "Rising Seas and Changing Currents," *People & the Planet,* vol. 7, no. 2 (1998); Colin Woodard, "Surf's Up—Way Up: Oceans Begin to Slosh Over World's Vulnerable Low-Lying Islands," *Christian Science Monitor,* 15 July 1998.

47. Michael Oppenheimer, "Global Warming and the Stability of the West Antarctic Ice Sheet," *Nature,* 28 May 1998; "Antarctic Ice Shelf Loses Large Piece," *Science News,* 9 May 1998; Judy Silber, "New Find May Provide Insight Into Rising Seas," *Christian Science Monitor,* 3 July 1998.

48. W. Jackson Davis, "Controlling Ocean Pollution: The Need for a New Global Ocean Governance System," in Jon M. Van Dyke, Durwood Zaelke, and Grant Hewison, eds., *Freedom for the Seas in the 21st Century: Ocean Governance and Environmental Harmony* (Washington, DC: Island Press, 1993).

49. Thucydides quote cited in David L. Giles, "Faster Ships for the Future," *Scientific American,* October 1997.

50. Thurman, op. cit. note 7; IWCO, op. cit. note 2.

51. Grotius quote and discussion from R.P. Anand, "Changing Concepts of Freedom of the Seas: A Historical Perspective," in Van Dyke, Zaelke, and Hewison, op. cit. note 48.

52. Moana Jackson, "Indigenous Law and the Sea," in Van Dyke, Zaelke, and Hewison,

op. cit. note 48; oceans not considered as wealth from Elisabeth Mann Borgese and David Krieger, "Introduction," in Elisabeth Mann Borgese and David Krieger, eds., *The Tides of Change: Peace, Pollution, and Potential of the Oceans* (New York: Mason/Charter, 1975).

53. Anand, op. cit. note 51.

54. Ibid.

55. Law of the Sea from Terry D. Garcia and Jessica A. Wasserman, "The U.N. Convention on the Law of the Sea: Protection and Preservation of the Marine Environment," *Renewable Resources Journal,* spring 1995; David M. Dzidzornu, "Coastal State Obligations and Powers Respecting EEZ Environmental Protection Under Part XII of the UNCLOS: A Descriptive Analysis," *Colorado Journal of International Environmental Law and Policy,* no. 2, 1997.

56. Sebastian Mathew, "Coastal Communities and Fishworkers: Factors in Fisheries Laws and Management," presentation at the Law of the Sea Institute, 30th Annual Conference, Al-Ain, United Arab Emirates, 20 May 1996, citing C. Sanger, *Ordering the Oceans: The Making of the Law of the Sea* (London: Zed Books, 1986); Garcia and Wasserman, op. cit. note 55; Dzidzornu, op. cit. note 55.

57. *Torrey Canyon* from Wesley Marx, *The Frail Ocean* (New York: Ballantine Books, 1967); Maria Gavouneli, *Pollution from Offshore Installations,* International Environmental Law and Policy Series (Norwell, MA: Kluwer Academic Publishers Group, 1995); Thomas Höfer, "Tankships in the Marine Environment," *Environmental Science and Pollution Research,* vol. 5., no. 2 (1998); Joanna Pegum, "Cleaning Up the Seas," *South,* March 1997; Janet Porter, "Tanker Oil Spill Figures Slip to a Record Low," *Journal of Commerce,* 12 July 1996; Hans Rømer et al., "Exploring Environmental Effects of Accidents During Marine Transport of Dangerous Goods by Use of Accident Descriptions," *Environmental Management,* vol.

20, no. 5 (1996).

58. Carlton, op. cit. note 42; International Maritime Organization Committee from John Waugh, "The Global Policy Outlook for Marine Biodiversity Conservation," *Global Biodiversity,* vol. 6, no. 1, 1995.

59. FAO, op. cit. note 2; FAO, *Report of the FAO Technical Working Group on the Management of Fishing Capacity, La Jolla, United States of America, 15–18 April 1998* (preliminary version) (Rome: 1998).

60. Land-based activities from Omar Vidal and Walter Rast, "Land and Sea," *Our Planet,* vol. 8, no. 3 (1998); Waugh, op. cit. note 58; "International Effort Would Phase Out 12 Toxins," *PSR Monitor* (Washington, DC: Physicians for Social Responsibility), February 1998; Janet Raloff, "Persistent Pollutants Face Global Ban," *Science News,* 4 July 1998.

61. David A. Balton, Director, Office of Marine Conservation, U.S. Department of State, Washington, DC, e-mail to author, 21 October 1998; Richard J. McLaughlin, "UNCLOS and the Demise of the United States' Use of Trade Sanctions to Protect Dolphins, Sea Turtles, Whales, and Other International Marine Living Resources," *Ecology Law Quarterly,* vol. 21, no. 1 (1994).

62. Suzanne Iudicello, "Protecting Global Marine Biodiversity," in William J. Snape III, ed., *Biodiversity and the Law* (Washington, DC: Island Press, 1996); Balton, op. cit. note 61; James Joseph, "The Tuna-Dolphin Controversy in the Eastern Pacific Ocean: Biologic, Economic and Political Impacts," *Ocean Development and International Law,* vol. 25, no. 1 (1994); Michael D. Scott, "The Tuna-Dolphin Controversy," *Whalewatcher,* 1996; Martin A. Hall, "An Ecological View of the Tuna-Dolphin Problem: Impacts and Trade-offs," *Reviews in Fish Biology and Fisheries,* vol. 8, 1998; signatories of the 1995 declaration that created the International Dolphin Conservation Program from Joshua R. Floum, "Defending Dolphins and Sea Turtles: On the Front Lines in an 'Us-

Them' Dialectic," *Georgetown International Environmental Law Review*, spring 1998.

63. Balton, op. cit. note 61; Anne Swardson, "Turtle-Protection Law Overturned by WTO," *Washington Post*, 13 October 1998.

64. World Trade Organization, Committee on Trade and Environment, *GATT/WTO Rules on Subsidies and Aids Granted in the Fishing Industry* (Geneva: 9 March 1998); Christopher D. Stone, "The Crisis in Global Fisheries: Can Trade Laws Provide a Cure?" *Environmental Conservation*, vol. 24, no. 2 (1997); Gareth Porter, "Natural Resource Subsidies and International Policy: A Role for APEC," *Journal of Environment & Development*, September 1997.

65. Elisabeth Mann Borgese, *Ocean Governance and the United Nations* (Halifax, NS, Canada: Dalhousie University, Center for Foreign Policy Studies, August 1996). Table 5–5 based on the following: Elisabeth Mann Borgese, "The Process of Creating an International Ocean Regime to Protect the Ocean's Resources," in Van Dyke, Zaelke, and Hewison, op. cit. note 48; Clif Curtis, Policy Advisor, Greenpeace, Washington, DC, "Abstract of Environmental/Conservation Community Statement in Support of U.S. Accession to the Law of the Sea Convention," 8 June 1995; United Nations, *The Law of the Sea: Official Text of the U.N. Convention on the Law of the Sea with Annexes and Index* (New York: U.N. Publications, 1983); James Carr and Matthew Gianni, "High Seas Fisheries, Large-Scale Drift Nets, and the Law of the Sea," in Van Dyke, Zaelke, and Hewison, op. cit. note 48; U.N. General Assembly, "Environment and Sustainable Development: Large-scale Pelagic Drift-net Fishing and Its Impacts on the Living Marine Resources of the World's Oceans and Seas," Forty-Ninth Session, Agenda Item 89, 5 October 1994; pockets of resistance and use of driftnets from David J. Doulman, "An Overview of World Fisheries: Challenges and Prospects for Achieving Sustainable Resource Use," presentation at the Law of the Sea

Institute, 30th Annual Conference, Al-Ain, United Arab Emirates, 20 May 1996; U.N. Conference on Environment and Development, "Protection of the Oceans, All Kinds of Seas, Including Semi-Enclosed Seas, and Coastal Areas and the Protection, Rational Use and Development of their Living Resources," *Agenda 21*, final advanced copy, adopted 14 June 1992; U.N. Department for Policy Coordination and Sustainable Development, "Programme for the Further Implementation of Agenda 21: Adopted by the Special Session of the General Assembly, 23–27 June 1997," advanced unedited text, 1 July 1997; "Special Session of U.N. Should Address Oceans' Sustainable Use, UNCED Official Says," *International Environment Reporter*, 30 April 1997; vessel compliance agreement from Balton, op. cit. note 61; FAO, *Code of Conduct for Responsible Fisheries* (Rome: 1995); Deborah Hargreaves, "Environmental Groups Attack Voluntary Fishing Code," *Financial Times*, 17 March 1995; no mention of subsidies in FAO code from Porter, op. cit. note 64; U.N. Non-Governmental Liaison Service, "UN Conference on Straddling and Highly Migratory Fish Stocks: Final Negotiating Session," *Environment and Development File* (New York: August 1995); Satya N. Nandan, "UN Takes a Big Step to Conserve Fish Stocks," *Environmental Conservation*, autumn 1995; Moritaka Hayashi, "Enforcement by Non-Flag States on the High Seas Under the 1995 Agreement on Straddling and Highly Migratory Fish Stocks," *Georgetown International Environmental Law Review*, fall 1996; vessel inspection and binding dispute from Giselle Vigneron, "Compliance and International Environmental Agreements: A Case Study of the 1995 United Nations Straddling Fish Stocks Agreement," *Georgetown International Environmental Law Review*, winter 1998; ratifications from Michael Sutton, "Top Fishing Nations Drag Feet on UN Fish Stocks Agreement," press release (Washington, DC: World Wildlife Fund, 25 November 1997); Jakarta Mandate from A. Charlotte de Fontaubert, David R. Downes, and Tundi Agardy, *Biodiversity in the Seas:*

Implementing the Convention on Biological Diversity in Marine and Coastal Habitats, IUCN Environmental Policy and Law Paper No. 32, Marine Conservation and Development Report, published jointly by the Center for International Environmental Law, World Conservation Union–IUCN, and World Wide Fund for Nature, 1996; Waugh, op. cit. note 58.

66. Kenneth Sherman, Director, Northeast Fisheries Science Center, National Marine Fisheries Service, NOAA, Washington, DC, letter to author, 13 October 1998; Global Environment Facility, *Operational Program #8: Water-Based Operational Program* (Washington, DC: 1996); Kenneth Sherman, *International Waters Assessments and Large Marine Ecosystems; A Global Perspective on Resource Development and Sustainability*, Narragansett Laboratory Report, March 1998; Global Environment Facility, *Valuing the Global Environment: Actions and Investments for a 21st Century* (Washington, DC: 1998); for general discussion, see Kenneth Sherman, Lewis M. Alexander, and Barry D. Gold, eds., *Large Marine Ecosystems: Patterns, Processes and Yields* (Washington, DC: American Association for the Advancement of Science, 1990).

67. Svein Jentoft and Bonnie McCay, "User Participation in Fisheries Management: Lessons Drawn from International Experiences," *Marine Policy*, no. 3, 1995; accountability from Evelyn Pinkerton and Martin Weinstein, *Fisheries That Work: Sustainability through Community-Based Management* (Vancouver, BC, Canada: David Suzuki Foundation, July 1995).

68. Robert S. Pomeroy et al., "Impact Evaluation of Community-Based Coastal Resource Management Projects in the Philippines" (Manila: Fisheries Co-management Project at International Center for Living Aquatic Resource Management (ICLARM) and North Sea Center, June 1996); for further discussion of Philippines, see Department of Environment and Natural Resources et al., *Legal and Jurisdictional Guidebook for Coastal Resource Management in the*

Philippines (Manila: Coastal Resource Management Program, 1997).

69. Waugh, op. cit. note 58.

70. Ibid.

71. J.W. McManus et al., *ReefBase Aquanaut Survey Manual* (Manila: ICLARM, 1997).

72. Michael Sutton, "The Marine Stewardship Council: New Hope for Marine Fisheries," *NAGA, The ICLARM Quarterly*, July 1996; Ehsan Masood, "Fish Industry Backs Seal of Approval," *Nature*, 29 February 1996.

73. Safina, op. cit. note 24.

Chapter 6. Appreciating the Benefits of Plant Biodiversity

1. Wild potato descriptions based on J.G. Hawkes, *The Potato: Evolution, Biodiversity and Genetic Resources* (Washington, DC: Smithsonian Institution Press, 1990); Irish potato famine from Cary Fowler and Pat Mooney, *Shattering: Food, Politics, and the Loss of Genetic Diversity* (Tucson, AZ: University of Arizona Press, 1990); resurgent potato blight information from Kurt Kleiner, "Save Our Spuds," *New Scientist*, 30 May 1998, from Pat Roy Mooney, "The Parts of Life: Agricultural Biodiversity, Indigenous Knowledge and the Third System," *Development Dialogue*, nos. 1–2, 1996, from "Potatoes Blighted," *New Scientist*, 21 March 1998, and from International Potato Center, "An Opportunity for Disease Control," <http://www.cgiar.org/cip/blight/lbcntrl. htm>, viewed 23 September 1998.

2. Plant species total from Vernon H. Heywood and Stephen D. Davis, "Introduction," in S.D. Davis et al., eds., *Centers of Plant Diversity: Volume 3, The Americas* (Oxford, U.K.: World Wide Fund for Nature, 1997).

3. Cultivated plant total from Robert and Christine Prescott-Allen, "How Many Plant Feed the World?" *Conservation Biology*,

December 1990; other agricultural information from Fowler and Mooney, op. cit. note 1;
medicinal information from Michael J. Balick
and Paul Alan Cox, *Plants, People and Culture:
The Science of Ethnobotany* (New York: Scientific
American Library, 1996).

4.   Global human population from U.N.
Population   Division,   *World   Population
Projections to 2150* (New York: United Nations,
1998); use of Earth's biological systems from
Peter M. Vitousek et al., "Human Domination
of Earth's Ecosystems," *Science*, 25 July 1997.

5.   Calculations of background extinction
rates from David M. Raup, "A Kill Curve for
Phanerozoic Marine Species," *Paleobiology*, vol.
17, no. 1 (1991). Raup's exact estimate is one
species extinct every four years, based on a
pool of 1 million species; the range here of
1–10 species per year is based on current estimates of total species worldwide. Estimates for
current rates of extinction are reviewed by
Nigel Stork, "Measuring Global Biodiversity
and Its Decline," in Marjorie L. Reaka-Kudla,
Don E. Wilson, and Edward O. Wilson, eds.,
*Biodiversity II: Understanding and Protecting Our
Biological Resources* (Washington, DC: Joseph
Henry Press, 1997), and by Stuart L. Pimm et
al., "The Future of Biodiversity," *Science*, 21 July
1995. Rates translated into whole numbers
based on an assumption of a total pool of 10
million species.

6.   Edward O. Wilson, *The Diversity of Life*
(New York: W.W. Norton & Company, 1992).

7.   Endangerment   information   from
Kerry S. Walter and Harriet J. Gillett, eds.,
1997 IUCN Red List of Threatened Plants (Gland,
Switzerland: World   Conservation   Union–
IUCN, 1997).

8.   Andean Colombia community endan-
germent from Andrew Henderson, Steven P.
Churchill, and James L. Luteyn, "Neotropical
Plant Diversity," *Nature*, 2 May 1991, from D.
Olson et al., eds., *Identifying Gaps in Botanical
Information for Biodiversity Conservation in Latin
America and the Caribbean* (Washington, DC:

World   Wildlife   Fund,   1997), and from J.
Orlando Rangel Ch., Petter D. Lowy C., and
Mauricio Aguilar P., *Colombia: Diversidad
Biotica II* (Santafé de Bogotá, Colombia:
Instituto de Ciencias Naturales, Universidad
Nacional   de   Colombia,   1997); western
Australia from Wilson, op. cit. note 6; New
Caledonia from J.M. Veillon, "Protection of
Floristic   Diversity   in   New   Caledonia,"
Biodiversity Letters, May/July 1993; Southeast
Florida habitats from Florida Natural Areas
Inventory, county summaries, <http://www.
fnai.org/dade-sum.htm> and <http://www.
fnai.org/natcom.htm>, viewed 3 September
1998, and from Lance Gunderson, "Vegetation
of   the   Everglades: Determinants   of
Community Composition," in Steven M. Davis
and John C. Ogden, eds., *Everglades: The
Ecosystem and Its Restoration* (Delray Beach, FL:
St. Lucie Press, 1994).

9.   H. Garrison Wilkes, "Conservation of
Maize Crop Relatives in Guatemala," in C.S.
Potter, J.I. Cohen, and D. Janczewski, eds.,
*Perspectives on Biodiversity: Case Studies of Genetic
Resource   Conservation   and   Development*
(Washington, DC: AAAS Press, 1993).

10.   Total   edible   plant   species   from
Timothy M. Swanson, David W. Pearce, and
Raffaello Cervigni, *The Appropriation of the
Benefits of Plant Genetic Resources for Agriculture:
An   Economic   Analysis   of   the   Alternative
Mechanisms for Biodiversity Conservation*, FAO
Commission on Plant Genetic Resources
(Rome: U.N. Food and Agriculture Organi-
zation (FAO), 1994); hunter-gatherer plant
use from Fowler and Mooney, op. cit. note 1;
wild grass harvesting from U.S. National
Research Council (NRC), *Lost Crops of Africa:
Volume I, Grains* (Washington, DC: National
Academy Press, 1996); Thailand information
from P. Somnasang, P. Rathakette, and S.
Rathanapanya, "The Role of Natural Foods in
Northeast Thailand," RRA Research Reports
(Khon   Khaen,   Thailand: Khon   Khaen
University—Ford Foundation Rural Systems
Research Project, 1988); Iquitos information
from Rodolfo Vasquez and Alwyn H. Gentry,

"Use and Misuse of Forest-Harvested Fruits in the Iquitos Area," *Conservation Biology*, January 1989, and from Alwyn Gentry, "New Nontimber Forest Products from Western South America," in Mark Plotkin and Lisa Famolare, eds., *Sustainable Harvest and Marketing of Rain Forest Products* (Washington, DC: Island Press, 1992).

11. Origins of agriculture from Fowler and Mooney, op. cit. note 1; centers of crop diversity from N.I. Vavilov, "The Origin, Variation, Immunity, and Breeding of Cultivated Plants," *Chronica Botanica*, vol. 13, no. I/6 (1949–50); potato species total from Karl S. Zimmerer, "The Ecogeography of Andean Potatoes," *Bioscience*, June 1998; Andean crops domesticated from Margery L. Oldfield, *The Value of Conserving Genetic Resources* (Washington, DC: U.S. Department of Interior, National Park Service, 1984), and from Mario E. Tapia and Alcides Rosa, "Seed Fairs in the Andes: A Strategy for Local Conservation of Plant Resources," in David Cooper, Renée Vellvé, and Henk Hobbelink, eds., *Growing Diversity: Genetic Resources and Local Food Security* (London: Intermediate Technology Publications, 1991).

12. Landrace utility from Michael Loevinsohn and Louise Sperling, "Joining Dynamic Conservation to Decentralized Genetic Enhancement: Prospects and Issues," in Michael Loevinsohn and Louise Sperling, eds., *Using Diversity: Enhancing and Maintaining Genetic Resources On-Farm* (New Delhi, India: International Development Research Centre, 1996); India landrace estimate from Swanson, Pearce, and Cervigni, op. cit. note 10.

13. Developing-country seed saving from Mark Wright et al., *The Retention and Care of Seeds by Small-scale Farmers* (Chatham, U.K.: Natural Resources Institute, 1994), and from V. Venkatesan, *Seed Systems in Sub-Saharan Africa: Issues and Options*, World Bank Discussion Paper 266 (Washington, DC: World Bank, 1994); hybrid seeds from Jack R. Kloppenburg, Jr., *First the Seed: The Political Economy of Plant Biotechnology, 1492–2000* (New York: Cambridge University Press, 1988), and from Fowler and Mooney, op. cit. note 1; illegality of seed saving from Tracy Clunies-Ross, "Creeping Enclosure: Seed Legislation, Plant Breeders' Rights and Scottish Potatoes," *The Ecologist*, May/June 1996, and from John Geadelmann, "Three Main Barriers: Weak Protection for Intellectual Property Rights, Unreasonable Phytosanitary Rules, and Compulsory Varietal Regulation," in David Gisselquist and Jitendra Srivastava, eds., *Easing Barriers to Movement of Plant Varieties for Agricultural Development*, World Bank Discussion Paper 367 (Washington, DC: World Bank, 1997).

14. FAO, *The State of the World's Plant Genetic Resources for Food and Agriculture* (Rome: 1996); Fowler and Mooney, op. cit. note 1.

15. FAO, op. cit. note 14; population estimate for rural poor supported by subsistence agriculture originally calculated in Edward C. Wolf, *Beyond the Green Revolution: New Approaches for Third World Agriculture*, Worldwatch Paper 73 (Washington, DC: Worldwatch Institute, 1986) and reverified by Worldwatch using 1997 data from FAO, *FAO-STAT Database*, <http://faostat.fao.org>; wheat landrace from Rural Advancement Foundation International (RAFI), *The Benefits of Biodiversity: 100+ Examples of the Contribution by Indigenous & Rural Communities in the South to Development in the North*, RAFI Occasional Paper Series (Winnipeg, MN, Canada: March 1994).

16. Oliver L. Phillips and Brien A. Meilleur, "Usefulness and Economic Potential of the Rare Plants of the United States: A Statistical Survey," *Economic Botany*, vol. 52, no. 1 (1998).

17. FAO, op. cit. note 14.

18. Senegal example from Tom Osborn, *Participatory Agricultural Extension: Experiences from West Africa*, Gatekeepers Series No. SA48 (London: International Institute for Environment and Development, 1995).

19. FAO, op. cit. note 14; Fowler and Mooney, op. cit. note 1; RAFI, "The Life Industry 1997," *RAFI Communiqué*, November/December 1997.

20. NRC, *Managing Global Genetic Resources: Agricultural Crop Issues and Policies* (Washington, DC: National Academy Press, 1993).

21. FAO, op. cit. note 14; NRC, op. cit. note 20; Netherlands study from Renée Vellvé, *Saving the Seed: Genetic Diversity and European Agriculture* (London: Earthscan Publications, 1992).

22. Donald L. Plucknett et al., *Gene Banks and the World's Food* (Princeton, NJ: Princeton University Press, 1987); NRC, op. cit. note 20.

23. FAO, op. cit. note 14; Brian D. Wright, *Crop Genetic Resource Policy: Toward A Research Agenda*, EPTD Discussion Paper 19 (Washington, DC: International Food Policy Research Institute, 1996); grassy stunt resistance from International Rice Research Institute, "Beyond Rice: Wide Crosses Broaden the Gene Pool," <http://www.cgiar.org/irri/Biodiversity/widecrosses.htm>, viewed 9 September 1998.

24. Balick and Cox, op. cit. note 3.

25. WHO figure cited in ibid.; Manjul Bajaj and J.T. Williams, *Healing Forests, Healing People: Report of a Workshop on Medicinal Plants held on 6–8 February, 1995, Calicut, India* (New Delhi: International Development Research Centre, 1995); over-the-counter drug value from Kenton R. Miller and Laura Tangley, *Trees of Life: Saving Tropical Forests and Their Biological Wealth* (Boston, MA: Beacon Press, 1991).

26. Balick and Cox, op. cit. note 3; China figures from Pei-Gen Xiao, "The Chinese Approach to Medicinal Plants," in O. Akerele. V. Heywood, and H. Synge, eds., *Conservation of Medicinal Plants* (Cambridge, U.K.: Cambridge University Press, 1991); Ayurvedic figures from Bajaj and Williams, op. cit. note

25, and from S.K. Jain and Robert A. DeFilipps, *Medicinal Plants of India, Vol. I* (Algonac, MI: Reference Publications, 1991); importance of traditional medicine for rural poor from John Lambert, Jitendra Srivastava, and Noel Vietmeyer, *Medicinal Plants: Rescuing a Global Heritage* (Washington, DC: World Bank, 1997), and from Gerard Bodeker and Margaret A. Hughes, "Wound Healing, Traditional Treatments and Research Policy," in H.D.V. Prendergast et al., eds., *Plants for Food and Medicine* (Kew, U.K.: Royal Botanic Gardens, 1998).

27. International medicinal trade details from M. Iqbal, *Trade Restrictions Affecting International Trade in Non-Wood Forest Products* (Rome: FAO, 1995); U.S. medicinal market from Jennie Wood Shelton, Michael J. Balick, and Sarah A. Laird, *Medicinal Plants: Can Utilization and Conservation Coexist?* (New York: New York Botanical Garden, 1997).

28. Lambert, Srivastava, and Vietmeyer, op. cit. note 26; A.B. Cunningham, *African Medicinal Plants: Setting Priorities at the Interface Between Conservation and Primary Health Care*, People and Plants Working Paper 1 (Paris: UNESCO, 1993); Panama information from author's fieldnotes, Darién province, Panama, 1998.

29. A.B. Cunningham and F. T. Mbenkum, *Sustainability of Harvesting* Prunus africana *Bark in Cameroon: A Medicinal Plant in International Trade*, People and Plants Working Paper 2 (Paris: UNESCO, 1993).

30. Number of plants assessed from Balick and Cox, op. cit. note 3; estimates of undiscovered drugs from Robert Mendelsohn and Michael J. Balick, "The Value of Undiscovered Pharmaceuticals in Tropical Forests," *Economic Botany*, April-June 1995.

31. Lack of healer apprentices from Balick and Cox, op. cit. note 3, and from Mark Plotkin, *Tales of a Shaman's Apprentice* (New York: Viking Press, 1994).

32. Percentage of material needs met by plants from the Crucible Group, *People, Plants, and Patents: The Impact of Intellectual Property on Trade, Plant Biodiversity and Rural Society* (Ottawa, Canada: International Development Research Centre, 1994); babassu uses from Peter H. May, "Babassu Palm Product Markets," in Plotkin and Famolare, op. cit. note 10; babassu economic importance from Anthony B. Anderson, Peter H. May, and Michael J. Balick, *The Subsidy from Nature: Palm Forests, Peasantry, and Development on an Amazon Frontier* (New York: Columbia University Press, 1991).

33. Palm cultures from Andrew Henderson, Gloria Galeano, and Rodrigo Bernal, *Field Guide to the Palms of the Americas* (Princeton, NJ: Princeton University Press, 1995).

34. Ecuador information from Anders S. Barfod and Lars Peter Kvist, "Comparative Ethnobotanical Studies of the Amerindian Groups in Coastal Ecuador," *Biologiske Skrifter*, vol. 46, 1996; Borneo information from Hanne Christensen, "Palms and People in the Bornean Rain Forest," Society for Economic Botany annual meetings, Aarhus, Denmark, July 1998; India information from Food and Nutrition Division, "Non-Wood Forest Products and Nutrition," in *Report of the International Expert Consultation on Non-Wood Forest Products* (Rome: FAO, 1995).

35. Timber tree total calculated from trade statistics of the International Tropical Timber Organization, <http://www.itto.or.jp/timber_situation/timber1997/appendix.html#app3>, viewed 7 September 1998; essential oil total from J.J.W. Coppen, *Flavours and Fragrances of Plant Origin* (Rome: FAO, 1995); gum and latex total from J.J.W. Coppen, *Gums, Resins and Latexes of Plant Origin* (Rome: FAO, 1995); dye total from C.L. Green, *Natural Colourants and Dyestuffs* (Rome: FAO, 1995).

36. Terry Sunderland, "The Rattan Palms of Central Africa and Their Economic Importance," Society for Economic Botany Annual Meetings, Aarhus, Denmark, July 1998; regional status of rattan resources from International Network for Bamboo and Rattan, "Bamboo/Rattan Worldwide," *INBAR Newsletter*, vol. 4 (no date) and vol. 5 (1997).

37. Biological dynamics of fragmented habitats from William S. Alverson, Walter Kuhlmann, and Donald M. Waller, *Wild Forests: Conservation Biology and Public Policy* (Washington, DC: Island Press, 1993); island and area effects were first synthesized by Robert H. MacArthur and Edward O. Wilson, *The Theory of Island Biogeography* (Princeton, NJ: Princeton University Press, 1967).

38. Río Palenque details from C.H. Dodson and A.H. Gentry, "Biological Extinction in Western Ecuador," *Annals of the Missouri Botanical Garden*, vol. 78, no. 2 (1991), and from Gentry, op. cit. note 10.

39. Richard B. Primack, *Essentials of Conservation Biology* (Sunderland, MA: Sinauer Associates, 1993).

40. Heywood and Davis, op. cit. note 2; Donald G. McNeil, Jr., "South Africa's New Environmentalism," *New York Times*, 15 June 1998.

41. Nitrogen overload effects from Anne Simon Moffatt, "Global Nitrogen Overload Problem Grows Critical," *Science*, 13 February 1998; climate change synergies from Chris Bright, "Tracking the Ecology of Climate Change," in Lester R. Brown et al., *State of the World 1997* (New York: W.W. Norton & Company, 1997).

42. Oliver L. Phillips and Alwyn H. Gentry, "Increasing Turnover Through Time in Tropical Forests," *Science*, 18 February 1994.

43. Conservation International study summarized in Lee Hannah et al., "A Preliminary Inventory of Human Disturbance of World Ecosystems," *Ambio*, July 1994, and from Lee Hannah, John L. Carr, and Ali Lankerani, "Human Disturbance and Natural Habitat: A Biome Level Analysis of a Global Data Set," *Biodiversity and Conservation*, vol. 4, 1995.

44. Walter and Gillett, op. cit. note 7; Zimmerer, op. cit. note 11.

45. Plucknett et al., op. cit. note 22.

46. Botanic Gardens Conservation International, "Introduction: Botanic Gardens & Conservation," <http://www.rbgkew.org.uk/BGCI/babrief.htm>, viewed 17 June 1998.

47. Plucknett et al., op. cit. note 22; Botanical Gardens Conservation International, op. cit. note 46.

48. Fowler and Mooney, op. cit. note 1; Plucknett et al., op. cit. note 22; Millennium Seed Bank information from R.D. Smith, S.H. Linington, and G.E. Wechsberg, "The Millennium Seed Bank, The Convention on Biological Diversity and the Dry Tropics," in H.D.V. Prendergast et al., eds., *Plants for Food and Medicine* (Kew, U.K.: Royal Botanical Gardens, 1998).

49. Plucknett et al., op. cit. note 22; Mooney, op. cit. note 1.

50. FAO, op. cit. note 14; Plucknett et al., op. cit. note 22; Wright, op. cit. note 23; landrace coverage in gene banks is questioned by Fowler and Mooney, op. cit. note 1, and by Pablo Eyzaguirre and Masa Iwanaga, "Farmer's Contribution to Maintaining Genetic Diversity in Crops, and Its Role Within the Total Genetic Resources System," in P. Eyzaguirre and M. Iwanaga, eds., *Participatory Plant Breeding: Proceedings of a Workshop on Participatory Plant Breeding, 26–29 July 1995, Wageningen, The Netherlands* (Rome: International Plant Genetic Resources Institute, 1996).

51. Total annual cost for accession maintenance calculated from figure of $50 per accession from Stephen B. Brush, "Valuing Crop Genetic Resources," *Journal of Environment & Development*, December 1996; Plucknett et al., op. cit. note 22; FAO, op. cit. note 14; Fowler and Mooney, op. cit. note 1.

52. FAO, op. cit. note 14; Plucknett et al., op. cit. note 22; Fowler and Mooney, op. cit.

note 1.

53. Louise Sperling, "Results, Methods, and Institutional Issues in Participatory Selection: The Case of Beans in Rwanda," in Eyzaguirre and Iwanaga, op. cit. note 50.

54. Gary P. Nabhan, *Enduring Seeds: Native American Agriculture and Wild Plant Conservation* (San Francisco, CA: North Point Press, 1989).

55. Global protected area total from IUCN, <http://www.iucn.org/info_and_news/index.html>, viewed 20 September 1998; Mt. Kinabalu from Heywood and Davis, op. cit. note 2; Manantlan from Hugh H. Iltis, "Serendipity in the Evolution of Biodiversity: What Good Are Weedy Tomatoes?" in Edward O. Wilson, ed., *Biodiversity* (Washington, DC: National Academy Press, 1988).

56. Carel van Schaik, John Terborgh, and Barbara L. Dugelby, "The Silent Crisis: The State of Rain Forest Nature Preserves," in Randall Kramer, Carel van Schaik, and Julie Johnson, eds., *Last Stand: Protected Areas and the Defense of Tropical Biodiversity* (New York: Oxford University Press, 1997).

57. P. Ramakrishnan, "Conserving the Sacred: From Species to Landscapes," *Nature & Resources*, vol. 32, no. 1 (1996); West Africa details from Aiah R. Lebbie and Raymond P. Guries, "Ethnobotanical Value and Conservation of Sacred Groves of the Kpaa Mende in Sierra Leone," *Economic Botany*, vol. 49, no. 3 (1995); Pacific Islander information from Balick and Cox, op. cit. note 3.

58. India information from Mark Poffenberger, Betsy McGean, and Arvind Khare, "Communities Sustaining India's Forests in the Twenty-first Century," in Mark Poffenberger and Betsy McGean, eds., *Village Voices, Forest Choices: Joint Forest Management in India* (New Delhi: Oxford University Press, 1996), and from Payal Sampat, "India's Choice," *World Watch*, July/August 1998; Belize information from Balick and Cox, op. cit. note

3, and from Rosita Arvigo, *Sastun: My Apprenticeship with a Maya Healer* (New York: Harper Collins, 1994).

59. Oliver Phillips, "Using and Conserving the Rainforest," *Conservation Biology*, March 1993; Jason W. Clay, *Generating Income and Conserving Resources: 20 Lessons from the Field* (Washington, DC: World Wildlife Fund, 1996); Plotkin and Famolare, op. cit. note 10; Charles M. Peters, *Sustainable Harvest of Non-timber Plant Resources in Tropical Moist Forest: An Ecological Primer* (Washington, DC: USAID Biodiversity Support Program, 1994).

60. A.P. Vovides and C.G. Iglesias, "An Integrated Conservation Strategy for the Cycad Dioon edule Lindl," *Biodiversity and Conservation*, vol. 3, 1994; Andrew P. Vovides, "Propagation of Mexican Cycads by Peasant Nurseries," *Species*, December 1997.

61. Vovides and Iglesias, op. cit. note 60; Vovides, op. cit. note 60; "CITES and the Royal Botanic Gardens Kew," <http://www.rbgkew.org.uk/ksheets/cites.html>, viewed 17 June 1998.

62. Karl S. Zimmerer, *Changing Fortunes: Biodiversity and Peasant Livelihood in the Peruvian Andes* (Berkeley, CA: University of California Press, 1996); Hopi example from Nabhan, op. cit. note 54; Mende example from NRC, op. cit. note 10.

63. Zimbabwe example from Seema van Oosterhout, "What Does In Situ Conservation Mean in the Life of a Small-Scale Farmer? Examples from Zimbabwe's Communal Areas," in Loevinsohn and Sperling, *Using Diversity*, op. cit. note 12; other information from Loevinsohn and Sperling, *Using Diversity*, op. cit. note 12, and from Eyzaguirre and Iwanaga, op. cit. note 50.

64. J.R. Whitcombe and A. Joshi, "The Impact of Farmer Participatory Research on Biodiversity of Crops," in Loevinsohn and Sperling, *Using Diversity*, op. cit. note 12; John Whitcombe and Arun Joshi, "Farmer Parti-cipatory Approaches for Varietal Breeding and Selection and Linkages to the Formal Seed Sector," in Eyzaguirre and Iwanaga, op. cit. note 47; K.W. Riley, "Decentralized Breeding and Selection: Tool to Link Diversity and Development," in Loevinsohn and Sperling, *Using Diversity*, op. cit. note 12.

65. Eyzaguirre and Iwanaga, op. cit. note 50; Swanson, Pearce, and Cervigni, op. cit. note 10; G.M. Listman et al., "Mexican and CIMMYT Researchers 'Transform Diversity' of Highland Maize to Benefit Farmers with High-Yielding Seed," *Diversity*, vol. 12, no. 2 (1996).

66. FAO, op. cit. note 14; RAFI, *The Leipzig Process: Food Security, Diversity, and Dignity in the Nineties*, RAFI Occasional Paper Series (Winnipeg, MN, Canada: June 1996); Swanson, Pearce, and Cervigni, op. cit. note 10.

67. Mooney, op. cit. note 1; Brush, op. cit. note 51.

68. Mooney, op. cit. note 1; Darrell A. Posey, *Traditional Resource Rights: International Instruments for Protection and Compensation for Indigenous Peoples and Local Communities* (Gland, Switzerland: IUCN, 1996); John Tuxill and Gary Paul Nabhan, *Plants and Protected Areas: A Guide to In Situ Management* (London: Stanley Thornes Publishers, 1998); Brush, op. cit. note 51.

69. InBio details from Michel P. Pimbert and Jules Pretty, *Parks, People and Professionals: Putting "Participation" Into Protected Area Management*, UNRISD Discussion Paper #57 (Geneva: United Nations Research Institute for Social Development, 1995), and from Anthony Artuso, "Capturing the Chemical Value of Biodiversity: Economic Perspectives and Policy Prescriptions," in Francesca Grifo and Joshua Rosenthal, *Biodiversity and Human Health* (Washington, DC: Island Press, 1997).

70. Drug development cost estimates from Shelton, Balick, and Laird, op. cit. note 27; bioprospecting details from Pimbert and Pretty, op. cit. note 69, and from RAFI,

"Biopiracy Update: The Inequitable Sharing of Benefits," *RAFI Communiqué*, September/October 1997; traditional resource rights from Posey, op. cit. note 68.

71. Crucible Group, op. cit. note 32; Swanson, Pearce, and Cervigni, op. cit. note 10; Bees Butler and Robin Pistorius, "How Farmers' Rights Can Be Used to Adapt Plant Breeders' Rights," *Biotechnology and Development Monitor*, September 1996; Henry L. Shands, "Access: Bartering and Brokering Genetic Resources," in June F. MacDonald, ed., *Genes for the Future: Discovery, Ownership, Access*, NABC Report #7 (Ithaca, NY: National Agricultural Biotechnology Council, 1995); RAFI, *Repeat the Term! Report on FAO's Gene Commission in Rome June 8–12, 1998*, RAFI Occasional Paper Series (Winnipeg, MN, Canada: July 1998).

72. Butler and Pistorius, op. cit. note 71; Crucible Group, op. cit. note 32; José Luis Solleiro, "Intellectual Property Rights: Key to Access or Entry Barrier for Developing Countries," in MacDonald, op. cit. note 71.

73. RAFI, "The Australian PBR Scandal," *RAFI Communiqué*, January/February 1998; "Foreign Invasion," *Down to Earth*, 28 February 1998.

74. RAFI, op. cit. note 71.

Chapter 7. Feeding Nine Billion

1. People fed per farmer from U.S. Department of Agriculture (USDA), <http://www.usda.gov/history2/text4.htm>; complete data set, 1900–90, from Eldon Ball, USDA, Washington, DC, discussion with Brian Halweil, Worldwatch Institute, 3 October 1998.

2. Estimated irrigation area in 1900 according to K.K. Framji and I.K. Mahajan, *Irrigation and Drainage in the World: A Global Review* (New Delhi, India: Cexton Press Private

Limited, 1969); share of grain harvest dependent on fertilizer is author's estimate based on national fertilizer use and grain production data.

3. Grain production in 1900 is author's estimate based on world population in 1900 and the assumption that grain consumption per person remained roughly the same between 1900 and 1950; current grain production from USDA, *Production, Supply, and Distribution*, electronic database, Washington, DC, updated October 1998.

4. Peter Tompkins and Christopher Bird, *Secrets of the Soil* (New York: Harper & Row, 1989).

5. Clive Ponting, *A Green History of the World* (New York: Penguin Books, 1991).

6. Jack Doyle, *Altered Harvest* (New York: Viking Penquin, 1985).

7. Ponting, op. cit. note 5; USDA, op. cit. note 3.

8. Ponting, op. cit. note 5.

9. U.N. Food and Agriculture Organization (FAO), *The Sixth World Food Survey* (Rome: 1996); U.S. Bureau of the Census, International Programs Center, "Historical Estimates of World Population," <http://www.census.gov/ipc/www/worldhis.html>, 1998.

10. Maurizio Perotti, fishery statistician, Fishery Information, Data and Statistics Unit, Fisheries Department, FAO, Rome, e-mail to Worldwatch, 11 November 1997; USDA, op. cit. note 3.

11. United Nations, *World Population Prospects: The 1996 Revision* (New York: 1996).

12. World Health Organization (WHO), *World Health Report 1998* (Geneva: 1998); Maggie Fox, "New Standards Mean Most Americans Overweight," *Reuters*, 4 June 1998; number of overweight people is Worldwatch estimate based on "Obesity: Preventing and

Managing the Global Epidemic," report of a WHO consultation on obesity, Geneva, 3–5 June 1997.

13. National Heart, Lung, and Blood Institute, "Clinical Guidelines for the Identification, Evaluation and Treatment of Overweight and Obesity in Adults" (Bethesda, MD: National Institutes of Health, June 1998).

14. "It's Official—Obesity Causes Heart Disease," *Reuters,* 2 June 1998.

15. FAO, op. cit. note 9.

16. WHO, "Child Malnutrition," Fact Sheet No. 119 (Geneva: November 1996).

17. FAO, op. cit. note 9; M. de Onis et al., "The Worldwide Magnitude of Protein-Energy Malnutrition: An Overview from the WHO Global Database on Child Growth," WHO, January 1998.

18. FAO, op. cit. note 9; Figure 7–1 from USDA, op. cit. note 3; population data from U.S. Bureau of the Census, *International Data Base,* electronic database, Suitland, MD, updated 15 June 1998.

19. De Onis et al., op. cit. note 17; USDA, op. cit. note 3; Population Reference Bureau (PRB), "1998 World Population Data Sheet," wall chart (Washington, DC: June 1998).

20. De Onis et al., op. cit. note 17; USDA, op. cit. note 3; PRB, op. cit. note 19; life expectancy from United Nations, op. cit. note 11.

21. USDA, op. cit. note 3; PRB, op. cit. note 19.

22. Worldwatch update of Angus Maddison, *The World Economy in the Twentieth Century* (Paris: Organisation for Economic Co-operation and Development, 1989).

23. World Bank, *Food Security for the World,* statement prepared for the World Food Summit by the World Bank, 12 November 1996.

24. USDA, op. cit. note 3.

25. Ibid.

26. Figure 7–2 from ibid., and from PRB, op. cit. note 19; United Nations, op. cit. note 11.

27. Population to be added from United Nations, op. cit. note 11.

28. Ibid.

29. USDA, op. cit. note 3; United Nations, op. cit. note 11.

30. Figure 7–3 from USDA, op. cit. note 3.

31. Idled land from USDA, Economic Research Service, "AREI Updates: Cropland Use in 1997," No. 5, Washington, DC, 1997.

32. Estimated irrigated area in 1900 from Framji and Mahajan, op. cit. note 2; FAO, *FAO-STAT Statistics Database,* <http://www.apps.fao.org>, Rome, viewed 4 October 1998.

33. Figure 7–4 from FAO, op. cit. note 32, and from Bureau of Census, op. cit. note 18.

34. FAO, op. cit. note 32.

35. David Seckler, David Molden, and Randolph Barker, "Water Scarcity in the Twenty-First Century" (Colombo, Sri Lanka: International Water Management Institute, 27 July 1998); Liu Yonggong and John B. Penson, Jr., "China's Sustainable Agriculture and Regional Implications," paper presented to the symposium on Agriculture, Trade and Sustainable Development in Pacific Asia: China and its Trading Partners, Texas A&M University, College Station, TX, 12–14 February 1998.

36. Seckler, Molden, and Barker, op. cit. note 35; PRB, op. cit. note 19.

37. Sandra Postel, *Last Oasis,* rev. ed. (New York: W.W. Norton & Company, 1997).

38. Wang Chengshan, "What Does the

Yellow River Tell?" *Openings,* No. 4, winter 1997; McVean Trading and Investments, Memphis, TN, discussion with author, 24 September 1998.

39. Postel, op. cit. note 37; United Nations, op. cit. note 11.

40. USDA, op. cit. note 3; figure of 1,000 tons of water for one ton of wheat from FAO, *Yield Response to Water* (Rome: 1979).

41. I.A. Shiklomanov, "World Fresh Water Resources," in Peter H. Gleick, ed., *Water in Crisis: A Guide to the World's Fresh Water Resources* (New York: Oxford University Press, 1993); "Water Scarcity as a Key Factor Behind Global Food Insecurity: Round Table Discussion," *Ambio,* March 1998.

42. Dennis Engi, China Infrastructure Initiative, Sandia National Laboratory, <http://mason.igaia.sandia.gov/igaia/china/water.html>, viewed 3 November 1998.

43. USDA, op. cit. note 3.

44. Ibid.

45. Thomas R. Sinclair, "Limits to Crop Yield?" in American Society of Agronomy, Crop Science Society of America, and Soil Science Society of America, *Physiology and Determination of Crop Yield* (Madison, WI: 1994).

46. L.T. Evans, *Crop Evolution, Adaptation and Yield* (Cambridge, U.K.: Cambridge University Press, 1993).

47. Prabhu Pingali et al., *Asian Rice Bowls: The Returning Crisis?* (New York: CAB International, 1997); P.L. Pingali and P.W. Heisey, "Cereal Crop Productivity in Developing Countries: Past Trends and Future Prospects," conference proceedings, *Global Agricultural Science Policy for the 21st Century,* Melbourne, Australia, 26–28 August 1996.

48. K.G. Soh and K.F. Isherwood, "Short Term Prospects for World Agriculture and Fertilizer Use," presentation at IFA Enlarged Council Meeting, International Fertilizer Industry Association, Monte Carlo, Monaco, 18–21 November 1997; FAO, *Fertilizer Yearbook* (Rome: various years); Mark W. Rosegrant and Claudia Ringler, "World Food Markets into the 21st Century: Environmental and Resource Constraints and Policies," revision of paper presented at the RIRDC-sponsored plenary session of the 41st Annual Conference of the Australian Agricultural and Resource Economics Society, Queensland, Australia, 22–25 January 1997.

49. USDA, op. cit. note 3.

50. MEDEA Group, *China Agriculture: Cultivated Land Area, Grain Projections, and Implications,* Summary report, prepared for the U.S. National Intelligence Council (Washington, DC: November 1997).

51. FAO, op. cit. note 9.

52. United Nations, op. cit. note 11.

53. Edward O. Wilson, *The Diversity of Life* (New York: W.W. Norton & Company, 1993).

54. "Broken Promises: U.S. Public Funding for International and Domestic Reproductive Health Care" (draft), prepared by the Mobilizing Resources Task Force, U.S. NGOs in Support of the Cairo Consensus, Washington, DC, 15 July 1998.

55. Nancy E. Riley, "Gender, Power, and Population Change," *Population Bulletin,* May 1997.

56. Grain-to-poultry ratio derived from Robert V. Bishop et al., *The World Poultry Market—Government Intervention and Multilateral Policy Reform* (Washington, DC: USDA, 1990); grain-to-pork ratio from Leland Southard, Livestock and Poultry Situation and Outlook Staff, Economic Research Service (ERS), USDA, Washington, DC, discussion with author, 27 April 1992; grain-to-beef ratio based on Allen Baker, Feed Situation and Outlook Staff, ERS, USDA, Washington, DC, discussion with author, 27 April 1992.

57. Postel, op. cit. note 37.

58. Figure 7–5 from USDA, op. cit. note 3; United Nations, op. cit. note 11.

59. USDA, op. cit. note 3.

Chapter 8. Exploring a New Vision for Cities

1. Charles Dickens, *Hard Times* (New York: Bantam Books, reissue ed., 1981); Peter Keating, "The Metropolis in Literature," in Anthony Sutcliffe, ed., *Metropolis 1890–1940* (Chicago: University of Chicago Press, 1984).

2. Tertius Chandler, *Four Thousand Years of Urban Growth: An Historical Census* (Lewiston, NY: Edwin Mellen Press, 1987).

3. Visions from Peter Hall, *Cities of Tomorrow*, updated ed. (Oxford, U.K.: Blackwell Publishers, 1996); engineers from David Perry, ed., *Building the Public City: The Politics, Governance, and Finance of Public Infrastructure*, Urban Affairs Annual Review 43 (Thousand Oaks, CA: Sage Publications, Inc, 1995); Ebenezer Howard, *Garden Cities of Tomorrow* (1902), cited in Robert Fishman, *Urban Utopias in the Twentieth Century* (New York: Basic Books, 1977); Le Corbusier, *The City of Tomorrow and its Planning*, translated from the 8th French Edition of *Urbanisme* (1924) by Frederick Etchells (Cambridge, MA: The MIT Press, 1971).

4. U.S. cities from James Howard Kunstler, *The Geography of Nowhere* (New York: Simon and Schuster, 1993); skyscrapers from David Malin Roodman and Nicholas Lenssen, *A Building Revolution: How Ecology and Health Concerns Are Transforming Construction*, Worldwatch Paper No. 124 (Washington, DC: Worldwatch Institute, March 1995).

5. World Commission on Environment and Development, *Our Common Future* (New York: Oxford University Press, 1987); Plato, *The Republic*, cited in James A. Clapp, *The City:*

A Dictionary of Quotable Thoughts on Cities and Urban Life (New Brunswick, NJ: Center for Urban Policy Research, Rutgers University, 1987); Jorge Hardoy, Sandy Cairncross, and David Satterthwaite, *The Poor Die Young: Housing and Health in Third World Cities* (London: Earthscan, 1990); World Resources Institute (WRI), United Nations Environment Programme (UNEP), and United Nations Development Programme (UNDP), World Bank, *World Resources 1996–97* (New York: Oxford University Press, 1996).

6. Mathias Wackernagel and William Rees, *Our Ecological Footprint: Reducing Human Impact on the Earth* (Philadelphia, PA: New Society Publishers, 1996); Herbert Girardet, "Cities and the Biosphere," UNDP Roundtable, The Next Millennium: Cities for People in a Globalizing World, Marmaris, Turkey, 19–21 April 1996; International Institute for Environment and Development (IIED) for the U.K. Department of Environment, *Citizen Action to Lighten Britain's Ecological Footprints* (London: IIED, 1995).

7. Clive Ponting, *A Green History of the World* (New York: Penguin Books, 1991); United Nations, *World Urbanization Prospects: The 1996 Revision* (New York: United Nations, 1998).

8. Norman Hammond, "Ancient Cities," *Scientific American*, Special Issue, vol. 5, no. 1 (1994); Robert M. Adams, "The Origin of Cities," *Scientific American*, September 1960 (reprinted in Special Issue, 1994); Lewis Mumford, *The City in History* (San Diego, CA: Harcourt Brace, 1961).

9. Josef Konvitz, *The Urban Millennium: The City-Building Process from the Early Middle Ages to the Present* (Carbondale, IL: Southern Illinois University Press, 1985); Joel Garreau, *Edge City: Life on the New Frontier* (New York: Doubleday, 1991); U.S. Department of Commerce, Bureau of the Census, *State and Metropolitan Area Data Book* (Washington, DC: U.S. Government Printing Office, 1997); Wendell Cox Consultancy, "US Urbanized

Area: 1950–1990 ó40 Data and Ranking Tables," at <http://www.publicpurpose.com>, viewed 10 November 1998.

10. Gregory Ingram, "Metropolitan Development: What Have We Learned?" *Urban Studies*, June 1998; United Nations Centre for Human Settlements (Habitat), *An Urbanizing World: Global Report on Human Settlements, 1996* (Oxford, U.K.: Oxford University Press, 1996); United Nations, op. cit. note 7.

11. Habitat, op. cit. note 10; Saskia Sassen, "Urban Impacts of Economic Globalization," Comparative Urban Studies Occasional Paper Series No. 5 (Washington, DC: Woodrow Wilson International Center for Scholars, undated); Robert Kaplan, "In the Lexicon of the New Cartography, All Roads Will Lead to City-States," *The World Paper*, July 1998.

12. Hall, op. cit. note 3; Chandler, op. cit. note 2; United Nations, op. cit. note 7; Pravin Visaria, *Urbanization in India: An Overview*, Working Paper No. 52 (Ahmedabad, India: Gujarat Institute of Development Research, September 1993).

13. United Nations, op. cit. note 7, and Chandler, op. cit. note 2; figure of 90 percent based on United Nations, op. cit. note 7.

14. United Nations, op. cit. note 7; John D. Karsada and Allan Parnell, *Third World Cities: Problems, Policies, and Prospects* (Newbury Park, CA: Sage Publications, 1993); "mega-villages" from Martin Brockerhoff and Ellen Brennan, "The Poverty of Cities in Developing Regions," *Population and Development Review*, March 1998.

15. Girardet, op. cit. note 6; Clark Wieman, "Downsizing Infrastructure," *Technology Review*, May/June 1996.

16. Mumford, op. cit. note 8.

17. Nineteenth-century engineers from Hans van Engen, Dietrich Kampe, and Sybrand Tjallingii, eds., *Hydropolis: The Role of Water in Urban Planning* (Leiden, the Netherlands: Backhuys Publishers, 1995); French cities from John Briscoe, "When the Cup's Half Full," *Environment*, May 1993.

18. Mark A. Ridgely, "Water, Sanitation and Resource Mobilization: Expanding the Range of Choices," in G. Shabbir Cheema, ed., *Urban Management: Policies and Innovations in Developing Countries* (Westport, CT: Praeger, 1993); World Health Organization (WHO), *Water Supply and Sanitation Sector Monitoring Report 1996* (Geneva: 1996); WHO, *The World Health Report 1998* (Geneva: 1998); WHO, *The Urban Health Crisis* (Geneva: 1996); WRI, UNEP, and UNDP, op. cit. note 5.

19. Vitruvius, *Ten Books on Architecture*, cited in van Engen, Kampe, and Tjallingii, op. cit. note 17; western United States from "Water in the West: Buying a Gulp of the Colorado," *The Economist*, 24 January 1998, and from William Booth, "Los Angeles Asked to Refill Dusty Lake It Drained in 1920s," *Washington Post*, 16 May 1997; China from "Official Says West Has Duty to Provide Grants, Loans, to Help Fight Water Shortage," *International Environment Reporter*, 29 April 1998, and from Wang Wenyuan, "High Time to Conserve Water Asset," *China Daily*, 20 April 1998; increase from I.A. Shiklomanov, "Global Water Resources," *Nature and Resources*, vol. 26, no. 3 (1990).

20. Chester Arnold and James Gibbons, "Impervious Surface Coverage: The Emergence of a Key Environmental Indicator," *Journal of the American Planning Association*, March 1996.

21. National Research Council, Academica de la Investigacion Cientifica, A.C., Academia Nacional de Ingenieria, A.C., *Mexico City's Water Supply* (Washington, DC: National Academy Press, 1995).

22. Sandra Postel, *Last Oasis*, rev. ed. (New York: W.W. Norton & Company, 1997); Peter Gleick, *The World's Water: 1998–1999: The Biennial Report on Freshwater Resources* (Washington, DC: Island Press, 1998).

23. Postel, op. cit. note 22; Rutherford Platt, "The 2020 Water Supply Study for Metropolitan Boston: The Demise of Diversion," *Journal of the American Planning Association*, March 1995; Jonathan Yeo, Massachusetts Water Resources Authority, Water Works Division, discussion with author, 27 October 1998.

24. Ismail Serageldin, *Water Supply, Sanitation, and Environmental Sustainability: The Financing Challenge*, Directions in Development (Washington, DC: World Bank, 1994).

25. Organisation for Economic Co-operation and Development (OECD), *Water Subsidies and the Environment* (Paris: 1997); Bogor from Ismail Serageldin, *Toward Sustainable Management of Water Resources*, Directions in Development (Washington, DC: World Bank, 1995).

26. Habitat, op. cit. note 10.

27. Tokyo Metropolitan Government, "Action Program for Creating an Eco-Society" (draft), Tokyo, February 1998.

28. Gleick, op. cit. note 22; "Sustainable Water Management Systems Must Be Developed Soon," *International Environment Reporter*, 18 March 1998.

29. Todd Wilkinson, "An Upstream Solution to River Pollution," *Christian Science Monitor*, 19 May 1997; Douglas Martin, "Water Projects Cost So Much That Even Environmentalists Worry," *New York Times*, 15 June 1998; Geoffrey Ryan, New York City Department of Environmental Protection, discussion with author, 28 October 1998.

30. Boston from Anne Whiston Spirn, *The Granite Garden: Urban Nature and Human Design* (New York: Basic Books, 1984); Mike Davis, *Ecology of Fear: Los Angeles and the Imagination of Disaster* (New York: Henry Holt, 1998).

31. Wetlands treatment in general from Robert Bastian and Jay Benforado, "Waste Treatment: Doing What Comes Naturally," *Technology Review*, February 1983; Arizona from David Rosenbaum, "Wetlands Bloom in the Desert," *Engineering News-Record*, 11 December 1995, and from David Schwartz, "Phoenix Uses Cleaning Power of Wetlands to Scrub Sewage," *Christian Science Monitor*, 16 January 1997.

32. Arif Hasan, "Replicating the Low-Cost Sanitation Programme Administered by the Orangi Pilot Project in Karachi, Pakistan," in Ismail Serageldin, Michael Cohen, and K.C. Sivaramakrishnan, eds. *The Human Face of the Urban Environment*, Proceedings of the Second Annual World Bank Conference on Environmentally Sustainable Development (Washington, DC: World Bank, 1995); Fred Pearce, "Squatters Take Control," *New Scientist*, 1 June 1996; Akhtar Badshah, *Our Urban Future* (London: Zed Books, 1996).

33. Funds needed for reliable water systems from Serageldin, op. cit. note 25; United Kingdom and France from David Suratgar, "World Water: Financing the Future," *The Journal of Project Finance*, summer 1998, and from Frederico Neto, "Water Privatization and Regulation in England and France: A Tale of Two Models," *Natural Resources Forum*, May 1998; percentage from private sources from Bradford Gentry and Lisa Fernandez, "Evolving Public-Private Partnerships: General Themes and Examples from the Urban Water Sector," *Globalisation and the Environment: Perspectives from OECD and Dynamic Non-Member Economies*, OECD Proceedings (Paris: OECD, 1998); privatization trend from Gisele Silva, Nicola Tynan, and Yesim Yilmaz, "Private Participation in the Water and Sewerage Sector—Recent Trends," *Private Sector*, September 1998; Buenos Aires from Emmanuel Ideolvitch and Klas Ringskog, *Private Sector Participation in Water Supply and Sanitation in Latin America*, Directions in Development (Washington, DC: World Bank, 1995).

34. Martin Melosi, *Garbage in the Cities* (College Station, TX: Texas A&M Press, 1981);

Mumford, op. cit. note 8; Dickens from Clapp, op. cit. note 5.

35. Mount Smoky from WRI, UNEP, and UNDP, op. cit. note 5, and from "Smoky Mountain Blues," *The Economist*, 9 September 1995.

36. Developing world from Habitat, op. cit. note 10; waste disposal methods from WHO, *Solid Waste and Health*, Local Authorities, Health and Environment Briefing Pamphlet Series No. 5 (Geneva: 1995).

37. Nutrient cycle from Gary Gardner, *Recycling Organic Waste: From Urban Pollutant to Farm Resource*, Worldwatch Paper 135 (Washington, DC: Worldwatch Institute, August 1997); New York from Toni Nelson, "Closing the Nutrient Loop," *World Watch*, November/December 1996, and from Vivian Toy, "Planning to Close Its Landfill, New York Will Export Trash," *New York Times*, 30 November 1996; nitrogen pollution from Peter Vitousek, *Human Alternation of the Global Nitrogen Cycle: Causes and Consequences* (Washington, DC: Ecological Society of America, 1997).

38. Waring cited in Spirn, op. cit. note 30; waste generation from Habitat, op. cit. note 10.

39. Organic waste from U.S. Environmental Protection Agency, *Organic Materials Management Strategies* (Washington, DC: 1998); industrial countries from OECD, *Environmental Data Compendium 1997* (Paris: 1997); European cities from Josef Barth and Holger Stöppler-Zimmer, "Compost Quality in Europe," *Biocycle*, August 1998.

40. UNDP, *Urban Agriculture: Food, Jobs and Sustainable Cities* (New York: 1996); Nelson, op. cit. note 37.

41. Waste-based industries from Jennifer Ray Beckman, "Recycling-Based Manufacturing Boosts Local Economies in U.S.," *Ecological Economics Bulletin*, Fourth Quarter

1997; recycling in U.S. cities from Institute for Local Self Reliance, *Cutting the Waste Stream in Half: Community Record-Setters Show How* (draft) (Washington, DC: October 1998).

42. Tokyo from "Tokyo Examines Fees For Collection of Garbage from Households by 1999," *International Environment Reporter*, 5 February 1997; Graz from *First Steps: Local Agenda 21 in Practice* (London: Her Majesty's Stationery Office, 1994); International Council for Local Environmental Initiatives (ICLEI), "Profiting from Pollution Prevention" (Toronto: 1994).

43. Susan Hall, "Lessons from a Semi-Private Enterprise in Bandung, Indonesia," in U.S. Agency for International Development, *Privatizing Solid Waste Management Services in Developing Countries*, Proceedings Paper (Washington, DC: International City/County Management Association, 1992); ICLEI, "Bandung, Indonesia: Solid Waste Management," Project Summary 67 (Toronto: 1991).

44. Kalundborg from Steven Peck and Chris Callaghan, "Gathering Steam: Eco-Industrial Parks Exchange Waste for Efficiency and Profit," *Alternatives Journal*, spring 1997; U.S. cities from Mark Dwortzan, "The Greening of Industrial Parks," *Technology Review*, 11 January 1998.

45. Glenn Yaro, *The Decline of Transit: Urban Transportation in German and U.S. Cities 1900–1970* (Cambridge, U.K.: Cambridge University Press, 1984).

46. United States from Steve Nadis and James J. MacKenzie, *Car Trouble* (Boston: Beacon Press, 1993); Bangkok from Malcolm Falkus, "Bangkok: From Primate City to Primate Megalopolis," in Theo Barker and Anthony Sutcliffe, eds., *Megalopolis: The Giant City in History* (London: St. Martin's Press, 1993), and from Peter Newman and Jeff Kenworthy, *Sustainability and Cities: Overcoming Automobile Dependence* (Washington, DC: Island Press, in press).

47. Le Corbusier, op. cit. note 3; WHO, *The World Health Report 1997* (Geneva: 1997).

48. WHO, *The World Health Report 1995* (Geneva: 1995); British Medical Association, *Road Transport and Health* (London: British Medical Association, 1997).

49. Jane Holtz Kay, *Asphalt Nation* (New York: Random House, 1997); Annalyn Lacombe and William Lyons, "The Transportation System's Role in Moving Welfare Recipients to Jobs," *Volpe Transportation Journal*, spring 1998; Michael Replogle and Walter Hook, "Improving Access for the Poor in Urban Areas," *Race, Poverty and the Environment*, fall 1995.

50. Michael Wals and Jitendra Shah, *Clean Fuels for Asia*, World Bank Technical Paper No. 377 (Washington, DC: World Bank, 1997); Jitendra Shah and Tanvi Nagpal, eds., *Urban Air Quality Management Strategy in Asia: Metro Manila Report*, World Bank Technical Paper No. 380 (Washington, DC: World Bank, 1997).

51. U.S. estimate is for 1982–92 and is from American Farmland Trust, *Farming on the Edge* (Washington, DC: March 1997); China estimate is for 1991–96 and is from Liu Yinglang, "Legislation to Protect Arable Land," *China Daily*, 15 September 1998; carbon calculation is based on population projections in United Nations, op. cit. note 7, and average carbon emissions per capita in 10 U.S. cities from Newman and Kenworthy, op. cit. note 46.

52. Newman and Kenworthy, op. cit. note 46; Gary Gardner, "When Cities Take Bicycles Seriously," *World Watch*, September/October 1998; Michael Bernick and Robert Cervero, *Transit Villages in the 21st Century* (New York: McGraw-Hill, 1997).

53. Jonas Rabinovitch and Josef Leitman, "Urban Planning in Curitiba," *Scientific American*, March 1996; Jonas Rabinovitch, "Innovative Land Use and Public Transport Policy," *Land Use Policy*, vol. 13, no. 1 (1996).

54. Mary Williams Walsh, "Instant Mobility, No Headaches," *The Sun*, 3 August 1998; European Academy of the Urban Environment, "Berlin: Stattauto-Germany Largest Car-Sharing Company," SURBAN-Good Practice in Urban Development (Berlin: June 1997). The SURBAN database is available on the Internet at <http://www.eaue.de/>.

55. Chris Bushell, ed. *Jane's Urban Transport Systems, 1995–96* (Surrey, U.K.: Jane's Information Group, 1995).

56. ICLEI, *Initiatives Newsletter*, November 1997; Gardner, op. cit. note 52.

57. Marcia Lowe, *Shaping Cities: The Environmental and Human Dimensions*, Worldwatch Paper 105 (Washington, DC: Worldwatch Institute, October 1991).

58. Jorge E. Hardoy and David Satterthwaite, *Squatter Citizen: Life in the Urban Third World* (London: Earthscan, 1989); Manal El-Batran and Christian Arandel, "A Shelter of Their Own: Informal Settlement Expansion in Greater Cairo and Government Responses," *Environment and Urbanization*, April 1998; Roush Wade, "Population: the View from Cairo," *Science*, 26 August 1994.

59. Streets from Jane Jacobs, *The Death and Life of Great American Cities* (New York: Random House, 1961), and from Peter Calthorpe, *The Next American Metropolis: Ecology, Community, and the American Dream* (New York: Princeton Architectural Press, 1993); parks from John F. Dwyer, Herbert Schroeder, and Paul Gobster, "The Deep Significance of Urban Trees and Forests," in Rutherford H. Platt, Rowan A. Rowntree, and Pamela C. Muick, eds., *The Ecological City* (Amherst, MA: University of Massachusetts Press, 1994), and from Michael Hough, *Cities and Natural Process* (London: Routledge, 1995); São Paulo from Raquel Rolnick, "Territorial Exclusion and Violence: The Case of São Paulo, Brazil," paper for the Woodrow Wilson International Center for Scholars' Comparative Urban Studies Project on Urbanization, Population, Security, and the

Environment, Washington, DC, 14–15 September 1998; Jacobs, op. cit. this note.

60. Transportation from Newman and Kenworthy, op. cit. note 46; buildings' materials and energy use from Roodman and Lenssen, op. cit. note 4.

61. Rutgers University Center for Urban Policy Research, *Impact Assessment of New Jersey, Interim State Development and Redevelopment Plan* (New Brunswick, NJ: 1992); Maryland Office of Planning, *Land Use and Development Patterns in Maryland* (Baltimore, MD: 1994); Chicago from E. Gregory McPherson, David J. Nowak, and Rowan A. Rowntree, *Chicago's Urban Forest Ecosystem: Results of the Chicago Urban Forest Climate Project* (Radnor, PA: Northeastern Forest Experiment Station, Forest Service, U.S. Department of Agriculture, June 1994).

62. Richard Moe and Carter Wilkie, *Changing Places: Rebuilding Community in the Age of Sprawl* (New York: Henry Holt, 1997); Alan Thein Durning, *The Car and the City* (Seattle, WA: Northwest Environment Watch, 1996); Mike Burton, Portland Metro Chief, Portland, OR, discussion with author, 18 June 1998.

63. Philip Langdon and Corby Kummer, "How Portland Does It: A City That Protects its Thriving Civil Core," *The Atlantic,* November 1992; Newman and Kenworthy, op. cit. note 46.

64. Anne Spackman, "The Pressure is on for a Brown Future," *Financial Times,* 13–14 June 1998; Thomas K. Wright and Ann Davlin, "Overcoming Obstacles to Brownfield and Vacant Land Redevelopment," *Land Lines,* Newsletter of the Lincoln Institute of Land Policy, Cambridge, MA, September 1998; Wes Sanders, "Environmental Justice, Urban Revitalization, and Brownfields," *Orion Afield,* spring 1998; "EPA Awards Grants to 17 More Brownfields Projects in Midwest," *PR Newswire,* 15 July 1998.

65. Hardoy and Satterthwaite, op. cit. note 58; Curitiba from Bill McKibben, *Hope: Human*

and Wild (Boston: Little, Brown and Company, 1995).

66. Roodman and Lenssen, op. cit. note 4; Nina Munkstrup and Jakob Lindberg, *Urban Ecology Guide—Greater Copenhagen* (Copenhagen: Danish Town Planning Institute, 1996).

67. John Spears, "Rebuilding Lives Through Sustainable Solar Community Development," presented at the American Solar Energy Society Conference, June 1998; Will Zachman, "'Whole Building' Approach to Sustainable Design," *Environmental Design and Construction,* July/August 1998; Peter Wilkinson, "Housing Policy in South Africa," *Habitat International,* September 1998.

68. Spirn, op. cit. note 30.

69. Abel Wolman, "The Metabolism of Cities," *Scientific American,* March 1965; Herbert Girardet, *Cities: New Directions for Sustainable Urban Living* (London: Gaia Books, 1992); John Eberhard, "A Third Generation of Urban Systems Innovations," *Cities: The International Journal of Urban Policy and Planning,* February 1990.

70. Eric Carlson, "The Legacy of Habitat II," *The Urban Age,* August 1996; United Nations, *Report of the United Nations Conference on Human Settlements (Habitat II),* Istanbul, 3–14 June 1996 (New York: 1996).

71. Jay Moor, Global Urban Observatory, e-mail to author, 16 October 1998; Christine Auclir, "Researchers Needed for Global Urban Database," *Urban Age,* spring 1998.

72. ICLEI from Richard Gilbert et al., *Making Cities Work: The Role of Local Authorities in the Urban Environment* (London: Earthscan, 1996); Local Agenda 21s from ICLEI, discussion with author, 17 August 1998; United Nations, op. cit. note 70; Habitat, "Urban Problems Mushrooming—First Ever Database of Urban Solutions Created," press release (Nairobi: 20 November 1995); Habitat,

"Database of Human Settlements Best Practices Released," press release (Nairobi: 5 October 1998). The database is available at <http://www.bestpractices.org/>.

73. Mega-Cities Project Inc, *Environmental Innovations for Sustainable Mega-Cities: Sharing Approaches that Work* (New York: 1996); Janice Perlman, "Mega-Cities: Global Urbanization and Innovation," in Cheema, op. cit. note 18; European Commission, *European Sustainable Cities* (Brussels: 1996); Ayse Kudat, "Urban Environmental Audits: Networking and Participation in Six Mediterranean Cities," in Serageldin, Cohen, and Sivaramakrishnan, op. cit. note 32.

74. Paul Lewis, *Shaping Suburbia: How Political Institutions Organize Urban Development* (Pittsburgh, PA: University of Pittsburgh Press, 1996); David Rusk, *Cities Without Suburbs* (Washington, DC: Woodrow Wilson Center Press, 1993); Myron Orfield, *Metropolitics: A Regional Agenda for Community and Stability* (Washington, DC: Brookings Institution Press, 1997); Penelope Lemov, "Building it Smarter, Managing it Better," *Governing Magazine*, October 1996.

75. Portland from Durning, op. cit. note 62; Denmark and the Netherlands from European Commission, op. cit. note 73; ICLEI, in cooperation with the United Nations Department for Policy Coordination and Sustainable Development, *Local Agenda 21 Survey* (New York: March 1997).

76. Habitat, op. cit. note 10.

77. Ismail Serageldin, Richard Barrett, and Joan Martin-Brown, eds., *The Business of Sustainable Cities: Public-Private Partnerships for Creative Technical and Institutional Solutions*, Environmentally Sustainable Development Proceedings Series No. 7 (Washington, DC: World Bank, 1995); nineteenth century from World Bank, *World Development Report 1994* (New York: Oxford University Press, 1994); UNDP from "Public-Private Partnerships for the Urban Environment," <http://www.undp.org/>, viewed 26 October 1998.

78. David Malin Roodman, *The Natural Wealth of Nations* (New York: W.W. Norton & Company, 1998).

79. UNDP from Jonas Rabinovitch, presentation at Woodrow Wilson International Center for Scholars' Comparative Urban Studies Project on Urbanization, Population, Security, and the Environment, Washington, DC, 14–15 September 1998; microcredit from Gary Stix, "Small (Lending) is Beautiful," *Scientific American*, April 1997; World Bank from Ismail Serageldin, "Helping Out with Tiny Loans," *Journal of Commerce*, 2 April 1997.

80. Dinesh Mehta, "Participatory Urban Environmental Management: A Case of Ahmedabad, India," paper for the Woodrow Wilson International Center for Scholars' Comparative Urban Studies Project on Urbanization, Population, Security, and the Environment, Washington, DC, 14–15 September 1998; Jonathan Karp, "Muni Bonds Become Novel Way of Funding City Projects in India," *Wall Street Journal*, 26 November 1997; Patralekha Chatterjee, "India ULBs Give Lenders More than IOUs," *Urban Age*, vol. 5, no. 2 (1997); Priscilla Phelps, ed., *Municipal Bond Market Development in Developing Countries: The Experience of the U.S. Agency for International Development* (Washington, DC: U.S. AID Finance Working Paper, November 1997).

Chapter 9. Ending Violent Conflict

1. Muravyov quoted in Hague Appeal for Peace, <http://www.haguepeace.org/>, viewed 24 July 1998.

2. Czar quote from Charles Chatfield and Ruzanna Ilukhina, eds., *Peace/Mir: An Anthology of Historic Alternatives to War* (Syracuse, NY: Syracuse University Press, 1994); Brigitte Hamann, *Bertha von Suttner: A Life for Peace* (Syracuse, NY: Syracuse University Press, 1996); "1899–1928: The

Hague Convention," <http://www.lib.byu.edu/~rdh/wwi/hague.html>, viewed 20 July 1998.

3. Eric Hobsbawm, *The Age of Extremes: A History of the World, 1914–1991* (New York: Vintage Books, 1994); 1880–1914 increase in military spending from Eric Hobsbawm, *The Age of Empire: 1875–1914* (New York: Vintage Books, 1989); army and navy growth calculated from Paul Kennedy, *The Rise and Fall of the Great Powers* (New York: Vintage Books, 1987).

4. Nobel from Hamann, op. cit. note 2; Bliokh from Hobsbawm, *The Age of Empire*, op. cit. note 3; John Keegan, *The Second World War* (New York: Penguin Books, 1989).

5. Hamann, op. cit. note 2; Nobel Web site <http://www.nobel.se>, viewed 20 July 1998.

6. Hamann, op. cit. note 2.

7. Hague Appeal for Peace, op. cit. note 1.

8. Preambles from Louise Doswald-Beck and Sylvain Vité, "International Humanitarian Law and Human Rights Law," *International Review of the Red Cross*, No. 293, pp. 94–119 (1993); "Declaration Renouncing the Use, in Time of War, of Certain Explosive Projectiles. St. Petersburg, 29 November/11 December 1868," <http://www.lib.byu.edu/~rdh/wwi/1914m/gene68.html>, viewed 20 July 1998.

9. Loss of military-age men from Hobsbawm, *The Age of Extremes*, op. cit. note 3; 20 million wounded from James Trager, *The People's Chronology: A Year-by-Year Record of Human Events from Prehistory to the Present* (New York: Henry Holt and Co., 1994); civilian share of victims calculated from Ruth Leger Sivard, *World Military and Social Expenditures 1996* (Washington, DC: World Priorities, 1996); civilian conditions from Richard M. Garfield and Alfred I. Neugut, "The Human Consequences of War," in Barry S. Levy and Victor W. Sidel, eds., *War and Public Health* (New York: Oxford University Press, 1997).

10. Keegan, op. cit. note 4; Hobsbawm, *The Age of Empire*, op. cit. note 3; 65 million figure from Kennedy, op. cit. note 3; percentages of population from Professor Arthur Rubinoff, lecture on International Relations, University of Toronto, 16 June 1998, and calculated from ibid.

11. Soldiers from John Elting, U.S. Military Academy, "Costs, Casualties, and Other Data," Grolier Online World War II Commemoration, <http://www.grolier.com/wwii/wwii_16.html>, viewed 22 July 1998; 45 million figure is a Worldwatch estimate; share of labor force from Alan L. Gropman, *Mobilizing U.S. Industry in World War II*, McNair Paper 50 (Washington, DC: Institute for National Strategic Studies, August 1996).

12. Economic mobilization for war from Gropman, op. cit. note 11; Soviet loss of human life from Sivard, op. cit. note 9; capital assets lost from Hobsbawm, *The Age of Extremes*, op. cit. note 3.

13. Tank and aircraft production calculated from Gropman, op. cit. note 11, and from "A World of Tanks," <http://www.geocities.com/Pentagon/Quarters/1975/>; including Japan and Italy, aircraft production rose to 837,000 in 1939–45, calculated from Kennedy, op. cit. note 3; munitions production from Gropman, op. cit. note 11, who reports $250 billion in 1944 prices; U.S. share of arms production from Keegan, op. cit. note 4.

14. Figure of 52 million calculated from Sivard, op. cit. note 9; percent of population dead from Hobsbawm, *The Age of Extremes*, op. cit. note 3; refugees from ibid., and from Keegan, op. cit. note 4.

15. Stephen Schwartz, ed., *Atomic Audit: The Costs and Consequences of U.S. Nuclear Weapons Since 1940* (Washington, DC: Brookings Institution Press, 1998); Sivard, op. cit. note 9.

16. "Known Nuclear Tests Worldwide," NRDC Nuclear Program, Natural Resources

Defense Council, <http://www.nrdc.org/nrdc pro/nudb/datainx.html>, viewed 31 July 1998; Figure 9–1 based on "Global Nuclear Stockpiles, 1945–1996," ibid., viewed 4 August 1998; explosive force from Sivard, op. cit. note 9.

17. Growing weapons sophistication from Ruth Leger Sivard, *World Military and Social Expenditures 1987–88* (Washington, DC: World Priorities, 1987). Between 1946 and 1997, the United States spent a total of $1,382 billion (in 1996 dollars) on military R&D programs. The global figure is based on the assumption that the United States accounted for perhaps 40 percent of global expenditures. Worldwatch Institute calculation, based on Office of the Undersecretary of Defense (Comptroller), *National Defense Budget Estimates for FY 1996* (Springfield, VA: National Technical Information Service, March 1995).

18. World War I expenditures, expressed in 1913 dollars, came to $82.4 billion. Calculated from Kennedy, op. cit. note 3. Although there is no price deflator series that could accurately translate this into modern-day dollars, a rough calculation using U.S. consumer price index data yields an approximate figure of $1.4 trillion in 1996 dollars. World War II spending is a Worldwatch estimate based on Elting, op. cit. note 11. (Elting provides U.S. expenditure data; the assumption here is that the United States may have accounted for as much as 40 percent of all powers' military spending.) Cold war military expenditures from U.S. Arms Control and Disarmament Agency (ACDA), *World Military Expenditures and Arms Transfers 1996* (Washington, DC: U.S. Government Printing Office, July 1997).

19. Cumulative arms trade value is a Worldwatch estimate, based on various editions of ACDA, *World Military Expenditures and Arms Transfers* (Washington, DC: U.S. Government Printing Office), and on Sivard, op. cit. note 9; number of arms transferred calculated from ACDA, op. cit. note 18.

20. War trends from Michael Renner, "Armed Conflicts Diminish," in Lester R. Brown, Michael Renner, and Christopher Flavin, *Vital Signs 1998* (New York: W.W. Norton & Company, 1998); Korea and Viet Nam population losses from Garfield and Neugut, op. cit. note 9.

21. United Nations, Department of Public Information, *Charter of the United Nations and Statute of the International Court of Justice* (New York: April 1994).

22. The provisions and full texts of many relevant agreements, treaties, and conventions can be found on a variety of sites on the World Wide Web, most of which are maintained by university departments. See, for example, "1899–1928 The Hague Convention," <http://www.lib.byu.edu/~rdh/wwi/hague.ht ml>, and "Multilaterals Project Chronological Index," <http://tufts.edu/fletcher/multi/ chrono.html>. The latter site, maintained by the Fletcher School of Law and Diplomacy, also contains a page with links to other relevant treaty collections. Many international treaties are deposited with the United Nations Secretary-General, and the United Nations maintains a Treaty Collection that now can be accessed and searched online: <http://www. un.org/Depts/Treaty/overview.htm>. See also Dieter Fleck, ed., *The Handbook of Humanitarian Law in Armed Conflicts* (New York: Oxford University Press, 1995), and Doswald-Beck and Vité, op. cit. note 8.

23. "Convention on the Prohibition of Military or Any Other Hostile Use of Environmental Modification Techniques," <http://www.tufts.edu/fletcher/multi/texts/ BH700.txt>, viewed 17 August 1998; Doswald-Beck and Vité, op. cit. note 8.

24. Teheran conference quoted in Doswald-Beck and Vité, op. cit. note 8; United Nations Treaty Collection Web page, op. cit. note 22; Ian Browline, ed., *Basic Documents on Human Rights* (Oxford, U.K.: Clarendon Press, 1992); Fleck, p. cit. note 22; "Multilaterals

Project Chronological Index," op. cit. note 22.

25. Growth of intergovernmental organizations from Allen Sens and Peter Stoett, *Global Politics* (New York: ITP Nelson, 1998); number of treaties from Steven R. Ratner, "International Law: The Trials of Global Norms," *Foreign Policy*, spring 1998.

26. United Nations, op. cit. note 21; Security Council activity from Michael Renner, "U.N. Peacekeeping Contracts Further," in Brown, Renner, and Flavin, op. cit. note 20.

27. Renner, op. cit. note 26.

28. UNESCO Charter quoted in <http://www.unesco.org>, viewed 28 June 1998; Nobel Peace prizes awarded to U.N. agencies and officials from "Major Achievements of the United Nations," <http://www.un.org/Overview/achieve. html>, viewed 10 August 1998.

29. Web site of the International Court of Justice, <http://www.icj-cij.org/>, viewed 1 August 1998; Sens and Stoett, op. cit. note 25; World Court not called upon to interpret environmental agreements from Monique Chemillier-Gendreau, "The International Court of Justice between Politics and Law," *Le Monde Diplomatique*, November 1996, with English version available at <http://www. globalpolicy.org/wldcourt/icj.htm>.

30. Benjamin B. Ferencz, *From Nuremberg to Rome: Towards an International Criminal Court*, Policy Paper 8 (Bonn, Germany: Development and Peace Foundation, May 1998); "Basic Principles For an Independent and Effective International Criminal Court (ICC)," Lawyers Committee for Human Rights, <http://www. lchr.org/icc/paplist.htm>, viewed 20 July 1998; Iain Guest, "Beyond Rome—What are the Prospects for the International Criminal Court?" *On the Record*, 27 July 1998; "A Court Is Born," *On the Record*, 17 July 1998; Alessandra Stanley, "U.S. Dissents, but Accord is Reached on War-Crime Court," *New York Times*, 18 July 1998.

31. ACDA, op. cit. note 18; Bonn International Center for Conversion, *Conversion Survey*, various editions (New York: Oxford University Press); "Global Nuclear Stockpiles, 1945–1996," op. cit. note 16; Sivard, op. cit. note 9; *The Arms Control Reporter* (Institute for Defense and Disarmament Studies (IDDS), Cambridge, MA) various editions.

32. "A Brief History of Chemical Disarmament," <http://www.opcw.nl/basic>, viewed 7 August 1998.

33. Chatfield and Ilukhina, op. cit. note 2; Ervin Laszlo and Jong Youl Yoo, exec. eds., *World Encyclopedia of Peace*, Vol. 3 (New York: Pergamon Press, 1986).

34. Laszlo and Yoo, op. cit. note 33.

35. Miriam Elman, ed., *Paths to Peace: Is Democracy the Answer?* (Cambridge, MA: The MIT Press, 1997); Hobsbawm, *The Age of Extremes*, op. cit. note 3; "Democracies and War: The Politics of Peace," *The Economist*, 1 April 1995.

36. William Greider, "The Global Crisis Deepens: Now What?" and John Gray, "Not for the First Time, World Sours on Free Markets," both in *The Nation*, 19 October 1998.

37. Dimensions of the downside to global economic integration are explored by David C. Korten, *When Corporations Rule the World* (West Hartford, CT: Kumarian Press, 1995), by Jerry Mander and Edward Goldsmith, eds., *The Case Against the Global Economy and for a Turn Toward the Local* (San Francisco: Sierra Club Books, 1996), and by Benjamin R. Barber, *Jihad vs. McWorld* (New York: Ballantine Books, 1995).

38. Sherle Schwenninger, "The Case Against NATO Enlargement," *The Nation*, 20 October 1997.

39. Stephen F. Cohen, "Why Call it Reform?" *The Nation*, 7/14 September 1998; Daniel Singer, "Twilight of the Czar," and

James S. Henry and Marshall Pomer, "Can Russia Save Russia?" both in *The Nation*, 21 September 1998; Clifford G. Gaddy and Barry W. Ickes, "Russia's Virtual Economy," *Foreign Affairs*, September/October 1998; Judith Matloff, "Moscow Losing Grip on Regions," *Christian Science Monitor*, 9 September 1998.

40. List of current "dangerous interstate situations" in Carnegie Commission on Preventing Deadly Conflict, *Preventing Deadly Conflict: Final Report* (Washington, DC: December 1997); "Will Today's Asia-Pacific End Up Like Europe in 1914?" Conference on Alternative Security Systems in the Asia-Pacific announcement, <http://www.focusweb.org/focus/pd/sec/sec.conference.html>, viewed 28 September 1998.

41. Michael T. Klare, "The Era of Multiplying Schisms: World Security in the Twenty-First Century," in Michael T. Klare and Yogesh Chandrani, eds., *World Security: Challenges for a New Century* (New York: St. Martin's Press, 1998); Michael Renner, *Fighting for Survival* (New York: W.W. Norton & Company, 1996).

42. Renner, op. cit. note 41; Klare, op. cit. note 41.

43. See Robert C. Johansen, "Building World Security: The Need for Strengthened International Institutions," in Klare and Chandrani, op. cit. note 41; Renner, op. cit. note 41.

44. A voluntary code of conduct was adopted by the European Union in June 1998, but it has a number of shortcomings. The code is reprinted in Joseph Di Chiaro III, *Reasonable Measures: Addressing the Excessive Accumulation and Unlawful Use of Small Arms*, Brief 11 (Bonn, Germany: Bonn International Center for Conversion, August 1998). For a critical analysis, see Saferworld, "The EU Code of Conduct on the Arms Trade. Final Analysis," <http://www.gn.apc.org/SWORLD/ARMSTRADE/code.html>, viewed 5 October 1998.

45. Costa Rica, Haiti, and Panama from Joaquin Tacsan, "Reports on Projects and Activities of the Center for Peace and Reconciliation," in Arias Foundation, *Arias Foundation for Peace and Human Progress Performance Report 1988–1996* (San José, Costa Rica: 1996); Liechtenstein from Bart Horeman, Marc Stolwijk, and Anton Luccioni, *Refusing to Bear Arms: A World Survey of Conscription and Conscientious Objection to Military Service, Part 1: Europe* (London: War Resisters' International, November 1997); Jonathan Dean, Randall Forsberg, and Saul Mendlovitz, "Global Action to Prevent War: A Program for Government and Grassroots Efforts to Stop War, Genocide, and Other Forms of Deadly Conflict," Union of Concerned Scientists, IDDS, and World Order Models Project, 15 May 1998.

46. Brian Hall, "Overkill Is Not Dead," *New York Times Magazine*, 15 March 1998; Jonathan Schell, "The Gift of Time," *The Nation*, 2/9 February 1998; on the principle of universality, see Johansen, op. cit. note 43.

47. "1899–1928. The Hague Convention," op. cit. note 22; sidestepping the "dum dum" ban from Michael Klare, discussion with author, 13 October 1998; Chemical Weapons Convention, the convention banning anti-personnel landmines, and the blinding-laser prohibition from IDDS, *Arms Control Reporter 1997* (Cambridge, MA: 1997).

48. Phyllis Bennis, *Calling the Shots: How Washington Dominates Today's UN* (New York: Olive Branch Press, 1996). For documents and further discussion of reform efforts, see the Global Policy Forum Web site, <http://www.globalpolicy/reform/index.htm>.

49. The suggestion to establish criteria for permanent membership was made, for example, by Jeffrey Laurenti, *The Common Defense: Peace and Security in a Changing World* (New York: United Nations Association of the United States, 1992).

50. For a more detailed discussion of

peacekeeping reform, see Michael Renner, *Critical Juncture: The Future of Peacekeeping*, Worldwatch Paper 114 (Washington, DC: Worldwatch Institute, May 1993). In 1997, the U.N. Trust Fund received just $4.5 million, from the Netherlands and Norway; Trevor Findlay, "Armed Conflict Prevention, Management and Resolution," in Stockholm International Peace Research Institute, *SIPRI Yearbook 1998: Armaments, Disarmament and International Security* (New York: Oxford University Press, 1998). For a detailed discussion of conflict prevention needs and opportunities, see Carnegie Commission, op. cit. note 40.

51. Johansen, op. cit. note 43; Commission on Global Governance, *Our Global Neighborhood* (New York: Oxford University Press, 1995).

52. James N. Rosenau, "The Dynamism of a Turbulent World," in Klare and Chandrani, op. cit. note 41.

53. Ibid.; Barber, op. cit. note 37.

Chapter 10. Building a Sustainable Society

1. Payal Sampat, "What Does India Want?" *World Watch*, July/August 1998; Sam Dillon, "Capital's Downfall Caused by Drinking... of Water," *New York Times*, 29 January 1998; Jillian Lloyd, "In Colorado, Beekeepers Are Stung by Nation's Honeybee Losses," *Christian Science Monitor*, 10 March 1998; William Souder, "A Possible Leap Forward on Amphibian Abnormalities," *Washington Post*, 16 March 1998; Andrew Schaeffer, "1995 Canada-Spain Fishing Dispute (The Turbot War)," *Georgetown International Environmental Law Review*, spring 1996.

2. Jared Diamond, *Guns, Germs, and Steel: The Fates of Human Societies* (New York: W.W. Norton & Company, 1997).

3. Emissions of more than 2 billion tons a year leading to atmospheric carbon dioxide concentrations above 400 parts per million from John T. Houghton et al., eds., *Stabilization of Atmospheric Greenhouse Gases: Physical, Biological and Socioeconomic Implications*, IPCC Technical Paper 3 (Geneva: Intergovernmental Panel on Climate Change, 1997); figure of 10 billion is the U.N. medium projection, from United Nations, *World Population Projections to 2150* (New York: 1998); distance estimate based on U.S. Department of Energy, *Model Year 1998 Fuel Economy Guide* (Washington, DC: 1997), and on Gregg Marland, "Carbon Dioxide Emission Rates for Conventional and Synthetic Fuels," *Energy*, vol. 8, no. 12 (1983), and assumes 90-percent efficiency in converting petroleum to gasoline; current emissions from T.A. Boden, G. Marland, and R.J. Andres, *Estimates of Global, Regional and National Annual CO_2 Emissions from Fossil Fuel Burning, Hydraulic Cement Production, and Gas Flaring: 1950–92* (Oak Ridge, TN: Oak Ridge National Laboratory, Carbon Dioxide Information Analysis Center, 1995).

4. Christopher Flavin and Nicholas Lenssen, *Power Surge* (New York: W.W. Norton & Company, 1994).

5. Arthur Cecil Pigou, *The Economics of Welfare*, 4th ed. (London: Macmillan, 1932; first published 1920), cited in Mikael Skou Andersen, *Governance by Green Taxes: Making Pollution Prevention Pay* (Manchester, U.K.: Manchester University Press, 1994).

6. Figure of $650 billion is a Worldwatch estimate, detailed in David Malin Roodman, *The Natural Wealth of Nations* (New York: W.W. Norton & Company, 1998); U.S. Congress, Committee on Natural Resources, Subcommittee on Oversight and Investigations, *Taking from the Taxpayer: Public Subsidies for Natural Resource Development, Majority Staff Report* (Washington, DC: 1994); Sitka price from Kathie Durbin, "Sawdust Memories," *The Amicus Journal*, fall 1997.

7. Bela Bhatia, *Lush Fields and Parched Throats: The Political Economy of Groundwater in Gujarat* (Helsinki: World Institute for Development Economics Research, 1992); subsidy total from Organisation for Economic Co-operation and Development (OECD), *Agricultural Policies, Markets and Trade in OECD Countries* (Paris: 1997); U.S. distribution from U.S. Department of Agriculture, Economic Research Service, "Number of Farms and Net Cash Income by Size Class, 1996," <http://www.econ.ag.gov/briefing/fbe>, viewed 5 December 1997.

8. Brazil from Lester R. Brown, Christopher Flavin, and Sandra Postel, *Saving the Planet* (New York: W.W. Norton & Company, 1991); Susan Brackett, Communications Director, Mineral Policy Center, Washington, DC, discussion with author, 19 October 1998.

9. OECD, International Energy Agency, *Energy Policies of IEA Countries* (Paris: various years). Figures in Table 10–1 are Worldwatch estimates, converted to dollars using market exchange rates, using data for the former Soviet Union from Andrew Sunil Rajkumar, *Energy Subsidies*, Environment Department working paper (Washington, DC: World Bank, 1996), and data for other countries from World Bank, Environment Department, *Expanding the Measure of Wealth: Indicators of Environmentally Sustainable Development* (Washington, DC: 1997). The regional estimates allocate the $10 billion that the Rajkumar study estimates for countries not systematically analyzed based on their carbon emissions.

10. Figure of 8 percent is based on $7.5 trillion a year in global tax revenues, a Worldwatch estimate, based on gross domestic product (GDP) and tax revenue figures for western industrial countries from OECD, *Revenue Statistics of OECD Member Countries 1965–1997* (Paris: 1998), on GDP figures for other countries from World Bank, *World Development Report 1996* (New York: Oxford University Press, 1996), and on central government tax revenue as a share of GDP for other countries from World Bank, *World Development Indicators* (Washington, DC: 1997). Note that some of the subsidy cut would take the form of reduction in the effective taxes that arise from policies that raise food prices. Per capita figures based on OECD, op. cit. this note.

11. Table 10–2 is based on the following sources: Germany and Norway from European Environment Agency, *Environmental Taxes: Implementation and Environmental Effectiveness* (Copenhagen: 1996); Netherlands from Hans Th. A. Bressers and Jeannette Schuddeboom, "A Survey of Effluent Charges and Other Economic Instruments in Dutch Environmental Policy," in OECD, *Applying Economic Instruments to Environmental Policies in OECD and Dynamic Non-member Economies* (Paris: 1994), and from Kees Baas, Central Bureau of Statistics, The Hague, e-mail to author, 24 September 1997; Sweden from Swedish Environmental Protection Agency (SEPA), *Environmental Taxes in Sweden: Economic Instruments of Environmental Policy* (Stockholm: 1997); U.S. tax from J. Andrew Hoerner, "Tax Tools for Protecting the Atmosphere: The U.S. Ozone-depleting Chemicals Tax," in Robert Gale and Stephan Barg, eds., *Green Budget Reform: An International Casebook of Leading Practices* (London: Earthscan, 1995).

12. History from Andersen, op. cit. note 5; statistical analysis of relationship between charges and pollution from Bressers and Schuddeboom, op. cit. note 11; emissions from Baas, op. cit. note 11.

13. Technology development from Jan Paul van Soest, Centre for Energy Conservation and Environmental Technology, Delft, Netherlands, letter to author, 11 October 1995.

14. Revenue figures are Worldwatch estimates, based on GDP and tax revenue figures for western industrial countries from OECD,

op. cit. note 10, on GDP figures for other countries from World Bank, *World Development Report*, op. cit. note 10, and on central government tax revenue as a share of GDP for other countries from idem, *World Development Indicators*, op. cit. note 10. "Taxes on work and investment" excludes land taxes, which are liberally estimated at half of total property taxes in OECD countries, and excludes energy and environmental taxes, using figures for the European Union (EU) from Commission of the European Communities, Statistical Office of the European Communities, *Structures of the Taxation Systems in the European Union* (Luxembourg: Office for Official Publications of the European Communities, 1996), and for non-EU OECD countries from OECD, *Environmental Taxes in OECD Countries* (Paris: 1995). For non-OECD countries, land, energy, and environmental taxes are assumed to generate at most 15 percent of tax revenues, a figure that appears liberal based on International Monetary Fund (IMF), *Government Finance Statistics Yearbook 1994* (Washington, DC: 1994). All figures are for 1994, converted to dollars using market exchange rates.

15. Table 10–3 sources are as follows: Sweden description from P. Bohm, "Environment and Taxation: The Case of Sweden," in OECD, *Environment and Taxation: The Cases of the Netherlands, Sweden and the United States* (Paris: 1994); Sweden quantity from Nordic Council of Ministers, *The Use of Economic Instruments in Nordic Environmental Policy* (Copenhagen: TemaNord, 1996); Denmark 1994 from Mikael Skou Andersen, "The Green Tax Reform in Denmark: Shifting the Focus of Tax Liability," *Journal of Environmental Liability*, vol. 2, no. 2 (1994); Spain description from Thomas Schröder, "Spain: Improve Competitiveness through an ETR," *Wuppertal Bulletin on Ecological Tax Reform* (Wuppertal, Germany: Wuppertal Institute for Climate, Environment, and Energy), summer 1995; Spain quantity from Juan-José Escobar, Ministry of Economy and Finance, Madrid, letter to author, 29 January 1997; Denmark 1996 from Ministry of Finance, *Energy Tax on*

Industry (Copenhagen: 1995); Netherlands description from Ministry of Housing, *Spatial Planning, and Environment, The Netherlands' Regulatory Tax on Energy: Questions and Answers* (The Hague: 1996); Netherlands quantity from Koos van der Vaart, Ministry of Finance, The Hague, discussion with author, 18 December 1995; United Kingdom from "Landfill Tax Regime Takes Shape," *ENDS Report* (Environmental Data Services, London), November 1995; Finland from OECD, *Environmental Taxes and Green Tax Reform* (Paris: 1997); Germany from Peter Norman, "SPD and Greens Agree German Energy Tax Rises," *Financial Times*, 19 October 1998; total tax revenues for all countries from OECD, op. cit. note 10.

16. Economic modeling results from John P. Weyant, Stanford University, Energy Modeling Forum, Stanford, CA, draft manuscript, June 1995, and from John P. Weyant, letter to author, 10 October 1995; carbon content of fuels from Marland, op. cit. note 3, and assumes a 90-percent efficiency in converting petroleum to gasoline; concentration stabilization based on T.M.L. Wigley, R. Richels, and J.A. Edmonds, "Economic and Environmental Choices in the Stabilization of Atmospheric CO_2 Concentrations," *Nature*, 18 January 1996; current concentration from Seth Dunn, "Carbon Emissions Resume Rise," in Lester R. Brown, Michael Renner, and Christopher Flavin, *Vital Signs 1998* (New York: W.W. Norton & Company, 1998).

17. George R. Heaton, Jr., and R. Darryl Banks, "Toward A New Generation of Environmental Technology: The Need for Legislative Reform," *Journal of Industrial Ecology*, vol. 1, no. 2 (1997); Marian R. Chertow and Daniel C. Esty, "Environmental Policy: The Next Generation," *Issues in Science and Technology*, fall 1997; John Atcheson, "Can We Trust Verification?" *The Environmental Forum*, July/August 1996.

18. Heaton and Banks, op. cit. note 17; John H. Cushman, Jr., "E.P.A. and States

Found to Be Lax on Pollution Law," *New York Times*, 7 June 1998; developing nations from Michel Potier, "China Charges for Pollution," *The OECD Observer*, February/March 1995, and from Sergio Margulis, "The Use of Economic Instruments in Environmental Policies: The Experiences of Brazil, Mexico, Chile and Argentina," in OECD, op. cit. note 11.

19. Frank Ackerman, *Why Do We Recycle? Markets, Values, and Public Policy* (Washington, DC: Island Press, 1997).

20. Ibid.

21. Brad Crabtree, "A Viable Framework for Steward Ship," *Perspectives* (World Business Academy, San Francisco), vol. 9, no. 3 (1995).

22. Ibid.; Royal Netherlands Embassy, "Measuring Environmental Progress," <http://www.netherlands-embassy.org>, viewed 30 July 1998.

23. Christopher Flavin, "Banking against Warming," *World Watch*, November/December 1997.

24. Ibid.

25. Ibid.

26. "WTO Shrimp-Turtle Appellate Body Decision," *Bridges Weekly Trade News Digest* (International Centre for Trade and Sustainable Development, Geneva), 12 October 1998.

27. Ibid.

28. U.N. Environment Programme (UNEP), *1996 Register of International Treaties and Other Agreements in the Field of the Environment* (Nairobi: 1996); Hilary F. French, *After the Earth Summit: The Future of Environmental Governance*, Worldwatch Paper 107 (Washington, DC: Worldwatch Institute, March 1992); Halifa O. Drammeh, Senior Programme Officer, UNEP, Water Branch, Nairobi, letter to Lisa Mastny, Worldwatch Institute, 30 October 1998; Hilary F. French,

Partnership for the Planet: An Environmental Agenda for the United Nations, Worldwatch Paper 126 (Washington, DC: Worldwatch Institute, July 1995).

29. French, *Partnership for the Planet*, op. cit. note 28.

30. Lori S. Ashford, "New Perspectives on Population: Lessons from Cairo," *Population Bulletin*, March 1995.

31. M. Lynne Corn and Susan R. Fletcher, *African Elephant Issues: CITES and CAMPFIRE* (Washington, DC: Congressional Research Service, 1997); Marc A. Levy, "European Acid Rain: The Power of Tote-Board Diplomacy," in Peter M. Haas, Robert O. Keohane, and Marc A. Levy, eds., *Institutions for the Earth: Sources of Effective International Environmental Protection* (Cambridge, MA: The MIT Press, 1993).

32. Hilary F. French, "Learning from the Ozone Experience," in Lester R. Brown et al., *State of the World 1997* (New York: W.W. Norton & Company, 1997).

33. Ibid.; figure of $750 million from Secretariat for the Multilateral Fund for the Implementation of the Montreal Protocol, "General Information," <http://www.unmfs.org>, viewed 24 October 1998; Hilary French, "Making Environmental Treaties Work," *Scientific American*, December 1994.

34. Graciela Chichilnisky, Geoffrey Heal, and David Starrett, *International Markets with Emissions Rights: Equity and Efficiency* (Stanford, CA: Stanford University, Center for Economic Policy Research, 1993); French, op. cit. note 32.

35. Figure of $38 trillion uses purchasing power parities and is a Worldwatch estimate, based on Angus Maddison, *Monitoring the World Economy, 1820–1992* (Paris: OECD, 1995), on idem, *Chinese Economic Performance in the Long Run* (Paris: OECD, 1998), and on IMF, *World Economic Outlook, October 1998* (Washington, DC: 1998).

36. British Petroleum, "BP HSE Facts 1997: HSE," <http://www.bp.com>, viewed 24 August 1998; quote from John Browne, "A New Partnership to Make a Difference," *Our Planet,* vol. 9, no. 3 (1997).

37. Figure of $180 million from Gary Gardner, "Organic Farming Up Sharply," in Lester R. Brown, Christopher Flavin, and Hal Kane, *Vital Signs 1996* (New York: W.W. Norton & Company, 1996); figure of $3.5 billion from Carole Sugarman, "Organic? Industry Is Way Ahead of Government," *Washington Post,* 31 December 1997; on CFCs, see generally Elizabeth Cook, ed., *Ozone Protection in the United States: Elements of Success* (Washington, DC: World Resources Institute, 1996); market size from David R. Berg and Grant Ferrier, *Meeting the Challenge: U.S. Industry Faces the 21st Century* (Washington, DC: U.S. Department of Commerce, Office of Technology Policy, 1998).

38. Christopher Flavin, "Wind Power Sets Records," in Brown, Renner, and Flavin, op. cit. note 16; Marlise Simons, "In the New Europe, a Tilt to Using Wind's Power," *New York Times,* 7 December 1997; Molly O'Meara, "Solar Cell Shipments Hit New High," in Brown, Renner, and Flavin, op. cit. note 16.

39. "When Green Begets Green," *Business Week,* 10 November 1997.

40. McDonough from Joan Magretta, "Growth through Global Sustainability: An Interview with Monsanto's CEO, Robert B. Shapiro," *Harvard Business Review,* January-February 1997.

41. Joseph J. Romm, *Lean and Clean Management: How to Boost Profits and Productivity by Reducing Pollution* (New York: Kodansha International, 1994).

42. Hart Hodges, *Falling Prices: Cost of Complying with Environmental Regulations Almost Always Less than Advertised,* Briefing Paper (Washington, DC: Economic Policy Institute, 1997).

43. Pamela Wexler, "Saying Yes to 'No Clean'," in Cook, op. cit. note 37.

44. On employee motivation, see Magretta, op. cit. note 40; Herbert Simon, *The Sciences of the Artificial,* 3rd ed. (Cambridge, MA: The MIT Press, 1996); Stephen J. DeCanio, "Barriers within Firms to Energy-Efficient Investments," *Energy Policy,* September 1993; Alan H. Sanstad, "'Normal' Markets, Market Imperfections and Energy Efficiency," *Energy Policy,* October 1994; Wexler, op. cit. note 43; Michael E. Porter and Claas van der Linde, "Toward a New Conception of the Environment-Competitiveness Relationship," *Journal of Economic Perspectives,* fall 1995.

45. W. Brian Arthur, *Increasing Returns and Path Dependence in the Economy* (Ann Arbor, MI: University of Michigan Press, 1994); Kenneth Arrow, "The Economic Implications of Learning by Doing," *Review of Economic Studies,* June 1962; figure of 30 percent is a Worldwatch estimate, based on price and cumulative sales data, from *PV News,* various issues.

46. Sandra Sugawara, "Toyota Steps on the Gas," *Washington Post,* 14 December 1997.

47. Hilary F. French, *Green Revolutions: Environmental Reconstruction in Eastern Europe and the Soviet Union,* Worldwatch Paper 99 (Washington, DC: Worldwatch Institute, November 1990); Mike Edwards, "Lethal Legacy," *National Geographic,* August 1994.

48. Civicus, *Citizens: Strengthening Global Civil Society* (Washington, DC: 1994); Environics International, "Citizens Worldwide Want Teeth Added to Environmental Laws," press release (Toronto, ON, Canada: 4 June 1998).

49. Bay Fang, "New Class Struggle," *Far Eastern Economic Review,* 19 March 1998.

50. Lester M. Salamon, "The Rise of the Nonprofit Sector," *Foreign Affairs,* July/August 1994.

51. Alan B. Durning, *Action at the Grassroots: Fighting Poverty and Environmental Decline*, Worldwatch Paper 88 (Washington, DC: Worldwatch Institute, January 1989); Gujarat from Sudeep Mukhia, "The Roots of Prosperity," *Down to Earth*, 15 December 1994.

52. Guy de Jonquieres, "Network Guerrillas," *Financial Times*, 30 April 1998; quote from Madelaine Drohan, "How the Net Killed the MAI," (Toronto) *Globe and Mail*, 29 April 1998; P.J. Simmons, "Learning to Live with NGOs," *Foreign Policy*, fall 1998.

53. Julia Preston, "It's Indians vs. Loggers in Nicaragua," *New York Times*, 23 June 1996; James Anaya, University of Iowa, College of Law, Iowa City, IA, and Indian Law Resource Center, Albuquerque, NM, discussion with author, 4 August 1998.

54. S. Jayasankaran, "Watch It: NGOs Fear Government Crackdown," *Far Eastern Economic Review*, 30 January 1997.

55. Robin Broad, "The Political Economy of Natural Resources: Case Studies of the Indonesian and Philippine Forest Sectors," *Journal of Developing Areas*, April 1995; John McBeth and Jay Solomon, "First Friend," *Far Eastern Economic Review*, 20 February 1997.

56. Susan Rose-Ackerman, *Redesigning the State to Fight Corruption: Transparency, Competition, and Privatization*, Viewpoint Note No. 75 (Washington, DC: World Bank, 1996); Honduras from Ved P. Gandhi, Dale Gray, and Ronald McMorran, "A Comprehensive Approach to Domestic Resource Mobilization for Sustainable Development," in U.N. Department for Policy Coordination and Sustainable Development, *Finance for Sustainable Development: The Road Ahead*, Proceedings of the Fourth Group Meeting on Financial Issues of Agenda 21, Santiago, Chile, 1997 (New York: 1997).

57. Value of oil and gas tax breaks is based on low estimate for oil tax breaks only, from Douglas Koplow and Aaron Martin, *Federal Subsidies to Oil in the United States* (Washington, DC: Greenpeace USA, 1998); contributions exclude "party" and "soft" money, and are from Center for Responsive Politics (CRP), *The Big Picture: Where the Money Came from in the 1996 Elections* (Washington, DC: 1997); history of subsidizing legislation from Charles F. Wilkinson, *Crossing the Next Meridian: Land, Water, and the Future of the West* (Washington, DC: Island Press, 1992).

58. F. Leslie Seidle, "Regulating Canadian Political Finance: Established Rules in a Dynamic Political System," prepared for the Round Table on Political Reform in the Mature Democracies, Tokyo, 25–27 August 1996; figure of $9 based on $2.4 billion total spending figure from CRP, op. cit. note 57.

59. John E. Young, "Using Computers for the Environment," in Lester R. Brown et al., *State of the World 1994* (New York: W.W. Norton & Company, 1994).

60. Ibid.; responses to TRI from David Austin, "The Green and the Gold: How a Firm's Clean Quotient Affects Its Value," *Resources* (Resources for the Future, Washington, DC), summer 1997; list of countries from Instituto Nacional de Ecología, "Registro de Emisiones y Transferencia de Contaminantes," <http://www.ine.gob.mx/retc/prtring.html>, viewed 11 August 1998.

61. Claudia Saladin and Brennan Van Dyke, "The New ECE Public Participation Convention: A Boost for Access to WTO-Related Environmental Information," *Bridges* (International Centre for Trade and Sustainable Development, Geneva), July-August 1998.

62. United Nations, *World Population Prospects: The 1996 Revision* (New York: 1996); Ashford, op. cit. note 30.

63. Ashford, op. cit. note 30.

64. David W. Orr, *Ecological Literacy: Education and the Transition to a Postmodern*

World (Albany, NY: State University of New York Press, 1992); see also Herman E. Daly and John B. Cobb, Jr., *For the Common Good: Redirecting the Economy Toward Community, the Environment, and a Sustainable Future* (Boston: Beacon Press, 1989).

65. Orr, op. cit. note 64.

66. William H. Mansfield, "Taking the University to Task," *World Watch*, May/June 1998.

67. Figure of 3.5 billion from Microsoft Corporation, *Encarta 98 Encyclopedia* (Redmond, WA: 1998); views of nature from Mary Evelyn Tucker and John Grim, "Series Forward," in Mary Evelyn Tucker and Duncan Williams, eds., *Buddhism and Ecology: The Interconnection of Dharma and Deeds* (Cambridge, MA: Harvard Center for the Study of World Religions and Harvard University Press, 1997); meditation from Herman E. Daly, *Beyond Growth: The Economics of Sustainable Development* (Boston: Beacon Press, 1996); Genesis 2:15, *New International Version*, anthologized in *The Comparative Study Bible: A Parallel Bible* (Grand Rapids, MI: Zondervan Publishing House, 1984).

68. National Religious Partnership for the Environment, <http://www.nrpe.org>, viewed 14 October 1998; Mishra from Ann Gold, Professor of Religion, Syracuse University, Syracuse, NY, e-mail to author, 19 October 1998.

69. *The Columbia Dictionary of Quotations* (New York: Columbia University Press, 1995).

Index

Crom & xix~

Count your fingers -- one through 10, right?

Then follow through 1 to 100 First Century

2d c. begins where 1st co -- or perhaps 101?

follow through ·· the 1st millennium

+ therefore ENDS at 1,000, NOT 99

Follow through - the year 2000

ENDS 2d C. (!!)

Now you can import all the tables and graphs from *State of the World 1999* and all other Worldwatch publications into your spreadsheet program, presentation software, and word processor with the ...

1999 Worldwatch Database Disk

The Worldwatch Database Disk Subscription gives you current data from all Worldwatch publications, including the *State of the World* and *Vital Signs* annual book series, *World Watch* magazine, Worldwatch Papers, and other Worldwatch books.

The disk covers trends from mid-century onward . . . much not readily available from other sources. All data are sourced, and are accurate, comprehensive, and up-to-date. Researchers, students, professors, reporters, and policy analysts use the disk to—

- ◆ *Design graphs to illustrate newspaper stories and policy reports*
- ◆ *Prepare overhead projections on trends for policy briefings, board meetings, and corporate presentations*
- ◆ *Create specific "what if?" scenarios for energy, population, or grain supply*
- ◆ *Overlay one trend onto another, to see how they relate*
- ◆ *Track long-term trends and discern new ones*

Order the 1999 Worldwatch Database Disk for just $89 plus $4 shipping and handling. To order by credit card (Mastercard, Visa or American Express), call (800) 555-2028 or fax to (202) 296-7365. Our e-mail address is wwpub@worldwatch.org. You can also order from our Web site at www.worldwatch.org, or by sending your check or credit card information to:

Worldwatch Institute
1776 Massachusetts Ave., NW
Washington, DC 20036
www.worldwatch.org